THE BUTLERS
OF IBERVILLE PARISH, LOUISIANA

LOADING SUGAR ON THE MISSISSIPPI RIVER.

THE BUTLERS
OF IBERVILLE PARISH, LOUISIANA

Dunboyne Plantation in the 1800s

David D. Plater

Louisiana State University Press • Baton Rouge

Published by Louisiana State University Press

Manufactured in the United States of America
First printing

Designer: Michelle A. Neustrom
Typeface: Whitman, text; Livory, display
Printer and binder: Maple Press

Frontispiece: "Loading Sugar on the Mississippi." Engraving by Kilburn. The Historic New Orleans Collection. Gift of Mr. Harold Shilke and Mr. Boyd Cruise, acc. number 1959.159.17

Library of Congress Cataloging-in-Publication Data

Plater, David D. (David Dunboyne), 1936– author.
The Butlers of Iberville Parish, Louisiana : Dunboyne Plantation in the 1800s / David D. Plater.
pages cm
Includes bibliographical references and index.
ISBN 978-0-8071-6128-9 (cloth : alk. paper) — ISBN 978-0-8071-6129-6 (pdf : alk. paper) — ISBN 978-0-8071-6130-2 (epub : alk. paper) — ISBN 978-0-8071-6131-9 (mobi : alk. paper) 1. Butler, Edward George Washington, 1800–1888. 2. Butler, Frances Parke, 1797– 1875. 3. Plantation owners—Louisiana—Iberville Parish—Biography. 4. Iberville Parish (La.)—Biography. 5. Dunboyne Plantation (La.) 6. Butler family. I. Title.
F377.I2P55 2015
976.3'44050922—dc23
[B]
2015008666

The paper in this book meets the guidelines for permanence and durability of the Committee on Production Guidelines for Book Longevity of the Council on Library Resources. ♾

CONTENTS

ACKNOWLEDGMENTS

Numerous people rendered patient and professional assistance in this undertaking. It began well before 2005, in the Butler Family Papers at the Historic New Orleans Collection. Since then, the research has taken me to the Tennessee State Library and Archives; Robertson County, Tennessee Archives; Andrew Jackson's Hermitage, Tennessee; the Special Collections at the Tracy W. McGregor Library, University of Virginia Library of the University of Virginia; the Mount Vernon Ladies' Association Library (renamed the Fred W. Smith National Library for the Study of George Washington); the Woodlawn Plantation of the National Trust for Historic Preservation; the Duke University Rare Book, Manuscript, and Special Collections Library; the Special Collections at Hill Memorial Library of Louisiana State University; the Special Collections at Howard-Tilton Memorial Library of Tulane University; the Archives at Ellender Memorial Library of Nicholls State University; the New York State Library in Albany; the Dolph Briscoe Center for American History at the University of Texas, Austin; the New Orleans Public Library; the Virginia Historical Society in Richmond; the National Archives; the Library of Congress; and the Offices of Clerks of Court of Iberville and West Feliciana Parishes, Louisiana, and of Clarke and Frederick Counties, Virginia. I could not ask for more than the aid I received at these great institutions, which preserve the record of America's past.

A number of individuals gave me invaluable help in the research. They include Yolanda Reid of the Robertson County, Tennessee, Archives; the indefatigable DeeDee DiBenedetto of St. Amant, Louisiana; E. W. McDonald of Dry Prong, Louisiana; Jessie Heitzmann of Pass Christian, Mississippi; Jimmy Jean Bowman and Dilys Wilson (both now deceased) of Shreveport, Louisiana; Fletch Coke of Nashville; Joanne Ryan and Thurston Hahn of Coastal Environments, Inc., Baton Rouge; Jean Meaney Wheatley of Lawton, Oklahoma; Colette Endrizzi of Tucson, Arizona; Madeleine Joyce of Little River, South Carolina; my genealogist brother, Ormonde Plater, of New Orleans; and Ann Weller of West Feliciana Parish, Louisiana.

Then there were those who valiantly read drafts of the work. My wife, Sheela, happily joined me on travels to far-off research centers and demonstrated a keen eye and ear reading or listening to my readings of chapters. Thomas Becnel ploughed through all of the chapters, some of them twice, providing me with incisive comments and suggestions. William Dudley, my former college mate, supplied comments from someone unfamiliar with the topic but versed in the writing of history. And R. Plater Robinson demonstrated an unfailing expertise in his detailed reviews of portions of the work.

I save for last my appreciation to the people who inspired me to this endeavor. There was, first, my father, Richard C. Plater Jr. He faithfully collected, preserved, and gave family documents to archives. In relating enthusiastically the tales he heard about his ancestors, he perpetuated their memory among his kin and friends. And he more than proved his devotion to American history by saving General Daniel Morgan's Revolution-era grain mill from certain destruction. Three excellent teachers, now deceased, must be acknowledged: Robert G. L. Waite showed me the significance of ideas in history and stimulated me to their study; Frederick R. Rudolph challenged my conceptions of the southern past and regularly asked about my progress with the book; and just when I needed it, Hugh F. Rankin provided professional training in historical research and writing. At this time, another friend and former professor, Syd Eisen, awaits the results of his continuing encouragement. I hope that the faith of all of these mentors has not been in vain.

THE BUTLERS
OF IBERVILLE PARISH, LOUISIANA

Introduction

In 1830, Lieutenant Edward George Washington Butler was an aide to Major General Edmund P. Gaines, who commanded one of the army's two divisions. Unhappy with his duties, the junior officer yearned to find some place to settle permanently. Drawn by family connections and military assignments to Louisiana during the 1820s, Butler imagined his family's future in the state's booming sugar cane economy. After several years of searching, he located two modest-sized tracts along the Mississippi River in Iberville Parish and slaves to work the land. Upon completing the purchases, Butler wrote to his wife, Frances, who was visiting her parents in Fairfax County, Virginia. He informed her of his successful efforts and conveyed the great anticipation of his New Orleans–based cousins, who "rejoiced that you are coming to live near them." Frances nervously awaited her husband's return and their trip to a new, distant home.[1]

This book explores several themes, chief among them the lives of a man and woman who were joined to the families of George and Martha Washington, Lawrence and Eleanor Parke Lewis of Virginia, and Andrew and Rachel Jackson of Tennessee. Birth-heirs to the American Revolution and to the early Republic, they descended from and succeeded revolutionary patriots and the nation's founders. How did those of the "next generations" view their obligations to their country and ancestry, and how faithful were they to their heritage? Written accounts of the inheritors of the trust are few, and this study aims to fill some of the void.

The book is set primarily in the American South, in Louisiana; the time frame is the nineteenth century. Curiosity endures about southerners in the 1800s—especially of slaveowners and their bonded servants: how men and women lived, what their attitudes were, how they treated each other and coexisted, and how they survived and adapted to the vast changes precipitated by the Civil War and Reconstruction. Edward G. W. Butler and Frances Parke Butler came from, were molded by, and existed on a slave-supported plantation system. The institution's effects on Americans have been long-lasting.

The Butlers joined the Great Migration, a phenomenon that began with early European travelers to the western hemisphere. They were clearly driven by a desire for wealth and status—goals that continue to motivate. Along with countless other Americans who left their homes after the War of 1812 and sought a new existence, the couple moved to the "Old Southwest." They settled on and cultivated the richly endowed land alongside the lower Mississippi River. Buying and working slaves, they strove to acquire and then keep their social status and wealth. Theirs was a time of American optimism, and successes were many. The Butlers' attempts to gain entrance to the elite sugar cane planter class exacted emotional, physical, and financial tolls. Having once attained a degree of prosperity, maintaining it during and after America's great civil conflict was elusive. Exploring these topics is a goal of the book.

Another theme that is explored throughout this work is Edward G. W. Butler's role in the American military establishment. During his participation in the U.S. Army, the nation concentrated on defense from invasion, on the subjugation and resettlement of American Indians, and on national expansion. Butler's education at West Point and his army service in the 1820s afforded him outstanding training and self-discipline. His thirst for glory to match the distinction bestowed upon Revolution-era ancestors remaining unappeased, Butler returned to fight in America's war with Mexico, 1846–48. He served in northern Mexico as commander of the army's newly formed 3rd Dragoon Regiment. A relatively small number of writings exist about the warriors who pursued elusive fame in the hinterlands of that war. Even fewer works treat the wives like Frances Butler, who remained at home—often alone—to manage plantation affairs, oversee slaves, and care for children.

The protagonists of *The Butlers of Iberville Parish, Louisiana,* corresponded fully and ardently. Many diligently retained the letters they received. With foresight and care, their descendants preserved the missives, photographs, military reports, and business records. What we know about the people who embellish this American epic must come from such manuscripts. That sense of how significant were the treasures in the attic trunks and armoires pervades the story of the Butlers.

1

Edward G. W. Butler

The New Soldier, 1816–1822

The father of Edward George Washington Butler was Edward Butler. Born in 1762 and having served in the American Revolution, by the late 1790s he was a captain in the U.S. Army stationed in Tennessee. Captain Butler led a modest number of troops who manned Tellico Block House, a fortified frontier "factory," or trading seat, in East Tennessee. Tellico was designated by President Washington as one of many such posts to serve as places where inexpensive goods could be exchanged for furs and other items originating with nearby Indians. Captain Butler, his wife, Isabella, and their two daughters celebrated the birth of a son on February 22, 1800. At the time, the post commander was conducting a review of troops on the small parade ground. In order to commemorate George Washington's birthday following the former president's death the previous December, such formalities were required by Commander in Chief General Alexander Hamilton at all military outposts. When he arrived home after the ceremony to find a newborn son, Captain Butler named him George Washington in honor of the revered hero. The infant's mother, however, insisted on the first name Edward. Thus did the child receive his full name, Edward George Washington Butler.[1]

Captain Butler was the youngest of five sons born to the Irish immigrant Thomas Butler, who became a prominent gunsmith in Carlisle, Pennsylvania, during the mid-eighteenth century. All sons of Thomas Butler received commissions in the Continental Army, Edward Butler joining in 1777 or 1778 at the age of sixteen. He rose from the rank of ensign to lieutenant while serving under his eldest brother, Colonel Richard Butler, in the 9th, 5th, and 3rd Pennsylvania Regiments. On July 14, 1788, Edward Butler married Isabella Fowler, a daughter of British Grenadier Captain George Fowler, who had fought against American colonists at Bunker Hill. Their union produced Caroline Swanwick Butler (b. 1789) and Eliza Eleanor Butler (b. 1790). When war with the Indians in the

Northwest Territory broke out in 1790, young Butler returned to army duty. He won distinction and served as adjutant general to General Anthony Wayne. Butler was part of a force of the army's 4th Regiment sent to Tennessee from Fort Washington at Cincinnati under the command of Lieutenant Colonel Thomas Butler Jr., another brother. Headquartered at Fort Southwest Point near present-day Kingston and the Tellico Block House, Thomas Butler Jr. protected the Cherokee Indians from encroachment by white settlers. He accompanied commissioners officially charged with establishing the boundary between the Cherokees and the State of Tennessee. Numerous settlers already were trespassing on Indian land, and the army commenced their removal following the boundary survey. Strong public opposition in Tennessee to the military enforcement of the boundary, however, led to the Tellico Treaty of 1798, which returned many homesteads to the former settlers. The newly established boundary separated the Indians' territory from that of the state. Appointed by his brother Thomas to be a U.S. commissioner, Captain Butler assisted in marking the new treaty boundary.[2]

Because its need to police the Indian boundary with Tennessee was minimized by the Tellico Treaty of 1798, Captain Butler's 4th Regiment was discharged in 1802, and he was transferred to the 2nd Infantry Regiment. He now was weary of military life and of the frustrations of having to protect Indians whose boundaries whites continued to disregard. Captain Butler bought land located on the south side of Sulphur Fork of the Red River in Robertson County, Tennessee. He moved his family, which included a second son born in 1802 and named Anthony Wayne Butler, after Captain Butler's former commanding general. The new home, christened Bellville, was constructed near Springfield, the Robertson County seat of government, just north of Nashville.

Among the friends of both Captain Edward Butler and Colonel Thomas Butler Jr. was Andrew Jackson. While a U.S. senator, Jackson criticized what he initially considered the overly zealous efforts of the army (and Colonel Butler) to safeguard the interests of the Cherokees, but he had become a family friend by the time Edward Butler moved to Tennessee. Soon after Butler received permission to establish a grist mill, he died on May 6, 1803. Left with four children and no nearby relatives to assist, his widow, Isabella, turned for help to Andrew Jackson, pleading for him to become the guardian of her two daughters and two sons. Jackson consented, promptly deposited a bond of $8,000, and received appointment as "Guardian for the Orphan children of Captn Edward Butler Decd."[3]

For most of the remainder of his youth, Edward G. W. Butler spent his out-of-school time at the home of Rachel and Andrew Jackson. A visitor in 1815 described it as "a roomy log-house," in front of which "was a grove of fine forest trees," with Jackson's "cotton and grain fields" to the rear. For the rest of their lives, the Jacksons remained devoted to all four Butler children, often advising and sheltering them. Rachel Jackson's Donelson family was joined in marriage to Butler's sister Eliza and to other Butler cousins. Their love for and commitment to Captain Butler's family commenced a role of guardianship or adoption of many children of relatives or friends, including children of Captain Butler's brother Thomas. Jefferson Davis, who visited the Hermitage as a child, later observed that the couple proved affectionate and generous to those in their charge, as well as to visitors. Jackson also became a dominant influence upon young Edward G. W. Butler.[4]

Isabella Butler remarried within a few years to William B. Vinson, a Marylander who invested in Robertson County land, but Jackson continued as guardian of her Butler children. The new stepfather took little interest in the Butler children and was not well accepted by them. By 1813, Jackson was arranging for the schooling and boarding of young Edward and then of both Edward and his brother, Anthony. Their school was Cumberland College in Nashville, which was guided by a prominent scholar, James Priestly. Its trustees included Jackson, Priestly's sponsor and friend. Among the Butler boys' schoolmates were Rachel Jackson's nephew, Andrew Jackson Donelson, who would be a candidate for the vice presidency; the later Whig congressman and Louisiana governor Edward Douglas White; and William Selby Harney, destined to earn fame in the U.S. Army as an Indian fighter and negotiator and also as commander of a regiment of dragoons in the war with Mexico. The school's curriculum contained courses on mathematics, moral philosophy, rhetoric, logic, and natural philosophy. Priestly's resignation in 1816 coincided with Jackson's decision to remove Edward Butler and to send him away for a higher education. With considerable help from President Monroe, the U.S. Military Academy at West Point by then had become a desirable place for influential citizens to seek appointments for their sons. Jackson strongly supported a professional cadre of army officers, and he sponsored the sixteen-year-old Butler as a candidate for West Point in 1816. At that time, the general believed no school was better.[5]

Butler's orders of July 8, 1816, from Secretary of War William Crawford commanded him to report "on the month of September next" to West Point, where, if he passed an exam, he would receive permission to enter. The criteria for admission were stated in the notice: "Each Cadet . . . must be able to read distinctly and pronounce correctly; to write correctly; to write a fair, legible hand; and to perform with facility and accuracy, the various operations of the ground rules of arithmetic, both simple and compound; of the rules of reduction; of single and compound proportion; and also, of vulgar and decimal fractions."

In March 1816, the War Department established rules for the cadets requiring them to pursue a four-year course of study and to take examinations twice yearly. After the four years and completion of their work, an "Academy Board" ranked cadets by order of general merit and made assignments based upon their ranked positions.[6]

The documented record of Butler's schooling at the Academy is sketchy. Jackson diligently wrote Butler, but Cadet Butler "destroyed all the letters . . . received up to 1821," including "a detailed account of [Jackson's] operations before New Orleans leading up to and during the great Battle with the British, 1814–1815." Even so, a fairly accurate picture can be reproduced. Butler's military education took place during times of change in the Academy policy and personnel. His beginning was less momentous than that of his classmate George D. Ramsay: Ramsay arrived in 1814 at the cadet staging ground and awakened his first morning of army service to witness the execution of a soldier who was a court-martialed deserter. Ramsay was twelve years old. Although Butler recorded no such excitement in August 1816, his trip from Tennessee was arduous and lengthy. It began by stage to the East Coast, continued by several steamboats to New York City, and ended only after a slow steamboat or sloop voyage up the Hudson River. Three months later, in November 1816, Butler reported to Jackson that he was managing his studies, working on French and algebra, and was involved with "various duties belonging to a Soldier." Cadets from the South, noted Butler, were becoming concerned about the onset of winter, for which they were unprepared, while "Yankee" students, fond of skating and other winter sports, were excited. "I never before experienced such blasts of wind as blow continually from the North."

In his later years, Ramsay wrote a memoir of his experiences as a cadet, and those recollections list duties in the austere, if not primitive, environment of the school. They included making fires in the open fireplaces that yielded the only source of heat in the dorms, sweeping rooms, shoveling snow, and hauling water in deep snow from the hillside springs nearby. Although served on bare tables with benches for seats and scarcely edible, the food was welcome. In the words of another contemporary, John H. B. Latrobe, those in attendance ate "with our knives and two-pronged forks, on plain boards, and . . . the reply to the carver standing up at the head of the table when he asked a cadet what part of the roast or boiled beef he preferred, was 'a big bit anywhere.'" Insufficient government funding forced the Academy to close in winter. The students took a "vacation" from December to late March. Like Ramsay, Butler probably remained at West Point in those months, using the time to study, to take artillery practice across the icy Hudson River, and to skate on ponds and the river, which provided the only bathing other than a washbasin.

The superintendent whom Butler first encountered, Captain Alden Partridge, instituted a modicum of reform in what was described as lax discipline and disorganized curriculum. While liked by cadets, Partridge was widely disliked by the faculty. A frugal and ascetic individual who had few associates that were "not connected with his official duties," Partridge involved himself in all details of life at the Academy. But he neglected the "more enlarged sphere of duty." Although the first-year cadets—called plebes—were required to be over fourteen years old, those rules were not enforced by officials in Washington. The ages of Butler's 1820 classmates ranged at admission from twelve to nineteen. In addition, because new cadets were allowed to enter at any time, group instruction was almost impossible. Students commonly complained to their sponsors or parents about any incident whereby they experienced an "infraction on their rights."[7]

The confused situation at West Point changed in 1817 when a new superintendent, Major Sylvanus Thayer, was appointed. In an interview near the end of his life, Butler described Thayer as a "gallant soldier of the War of 1812," who, nonetheless, "knew nothing of tactics," and who in 1819–1820 allowed first classman Butler "practical control of the drill of the Cadet Corps." Despite gaps in his knowledge, Thayer proved to be the sort of leader that the Academy needed. Upon arrival, Thayer promptly consulted with his faculty to hear their ideas on courses and with their support was able to construct a better four-year course of instruction and training. The aims of the Academy under Thayer were not only to produce engineers, but to have graduates who were disciplined, were proficient in military tactics, and who conducted themselves honorably. Math and French were fundamental to the curriculum, the latter in order to allow for the use of the much-respected French military texts. Plebes also studied algebra, geometry—taught for the first time using blackboards—and trigonometry and "mensuration" (a term used to describe training in measurements). Second-year students undertook additional courses in drawing, analytical geometry, and fluxions, or calculus. By the third year, a cadet learned physics, chemistry, and topographical drawing, including battlefield drawing and extensive field work in surveying. Finally, in his last year, the cadet's courses were in engineering, mineralogy, rhetoric, and moral and political science.

Besides initiating changes in the courses, Thayer tightened discipline and instilled a greater sense of unity and respect for the institution. When he arrived, for instance, Thayer found that the cadets were away on their "extended vacation," a situation he corrected by ordering their immediate return. Thayer promptly dismissed forty-three of the cadets, termed "bad bargains." Cadets thereafter were restricted to West Point and not allowed leave without permission. Summer vacations, except for one granted to members of the Third Class, were replaced with summer training marches, encampments, and living in tents. Prior to Thayer's time, money was often sent indiscriminately to cadets by their sponsors or parents, fueling temptations and allowing many cadets advantages over their classmates. With some exceptions, Thayer restricted cadets' income to what they received from the government. In order to solve a problem of lack of commitment to national service, Thayer made cadets pledge to serve at least one year in the U.S. Army after graduation. When the Board of Visitors arrived in 1819, its members were impressed with the changes. They reported to Congress and the secretary of war that "the Police and Administration of the Academy, and the moral and orderly conduct of the Cadets is scarcely susceptible of improvement" and praised Thayer for allowing his charges "no time . . . for dissipation or for contracting bad habits."

Such well-meant goals were hard to achieve: the Board also noted the embarrassing existence of an ordinary nearby that the cadets frequented and recommended a "purchase of Mr. North's land adjoining the West Point Tract. . . . The Tavern kept on this land within 100 Yards of the Cadet Barracks, & over which the Regulations of the Academy do not extend, has been productive of the very worst consequences to some of the Cadets, tho' the vigilant Superintendence of the Commanding Officer has . . . diminished the evil . . . it still exists to too great an extent to render the Cost of removing it, an object of serious consideration." According to historian Stephen Ambrose, even faced with such hurdles, Thayer brought to the Academy a personal aura that allowed him to institute needed reforms. His dedication made the "Cadets feel the strength of his intelligence, his character, and his discipline."[8]

Not until Butler's class endured examinations in June 1818 was any record of class standings published. His group numbered forty-two cadets, of which there were two sections. Butler stood tenth in his section of twenty-three. His grades placed him in the middle of the entire class. In 1817, meanwhile, Butler welcomed to West Point his fellow ward and schoolmate at Cumberland College, Andrew Jackson Donelson. At the end of his first year in 1818, Donelson was first in the Class of 1821. He then was advanced to the Class of 1820, and at the end the school year in 1819 Donelson stood fifth and Butler seventeenth out of twenty-eight cadets. At the time of their graduation in July 1820, Butler ranked ninth out of thirty cadets, and Donelson, second. Donelson ultimately became Jackson's secretary, political advisor, and campaign organizer. Edward Butler always gave thanks for his good fortune in having attended West Point, and the Jacksons had reason to be proud of their protégés.[9]

As wards of Andrew Jackson, Butler and Donelson remained dependent upon the general for expense money. Unlike Donelson, Butler did not have familial access to the Jacksons' funds. Butler's guardian expected Butler family properties in Robertson County, Tennessee, and elsewhere to supply reimbursement for advances for both sons of Captain Edward Butler. However, the extensive land holdings that had been left to the Butler children were either unrewarding or depleted. As Anthony Wayne Butler completed Yale College in 1822, he sought funds from Jackson for education in the law. The family farmland in Tennessee generated little income, wrote Jackson, and "at present could not be sold for near its value." Jackson managed to arrange for Anthony's college education with Richard Butler, a cousin of the Butler boys who lived upriver from New Orleans at Ormond Plantation in St. Charles Parish. Anthony's efforts at economizing frequently fell short, and Jackson informed the youth that he could not rely upon the general for legal training after college. Cadet Butler, too, felt the financial pinch. He received from Jackson a sum of $298 in September 1817 (reimbursement for $203 in travel expenses to West Point the prior year and for $95 during his first year there). Thereafter, Butler only was allowed an amount to take care of his living costs. It was too little, and during Butler's last few months at West Point he and Jackson corresponded about the problem. Butler's complaint was not the first on the subject. In April 1820, Donelson received $500 from Jackson, of which $400 was for his own use, and $50 each for Edward and Anthony. Even with a government stipend, Butler complained about his impoverishment:

> I am almost ashamed to address you on the subject, but as I am about to leave this Institution, and after the strictest economy for three years being now

> nearly three hundred dollars in debt, I deem it necessary to apply to you for four hundred dollars, as I shall have to purchase a uniform and some other articles previous to commencing my new course. You will no doubt consider my application somewhat exorbitant, but when you reflect that my pay is but one hundred and ninety-two dollars a year and that we have to pay the most exorbitant price for all articles which we purchase, I trust that you will acquit me of the best pretentions to prodigality.

Ignorant both of his family's financial situation and of the monetary resources over which Jackson had custody, Butler was reminded that any advances came out of the guardian's own pockets, which—following the Panic of 1819—were also relatively empty. Butler was faced with creditors who expected payment and with the expense of acquiring "clothing necessary to enter the army." He persisted in his pleas to Jackson and promised that he would visit the general personally "for the purpose of adjusting all matters," if the secretary of war would grant him a few weeks' leave. He soon found himself sharing with his sisters the obligations for unpaid expenses for rent, board, washing, and other necessaries incurred by their mother, who died in August 1821.[10]

We do not know how young Butler resolved his finances before he put on his new uniform and reported for duty, but somehow he managed. In April 1820, at the same time that he asked Jackson for money, Butler requested that he be posted to the Southern Division of the army and for his guardian to apply for him "to any station that you think proper." Jackson did intervene with Secretary of War John C. Calhoun on behalf of Butler and Donelson. Although Calhoun could not be definite, pending final "standing on the roll of merit," he stated that Butler's likely assignment would be to the artillery. If Butler was attached to the Northern Division of the army, Calhoun believed he could easily obtain an exchange to the Southern Division and be closer to Jackson. Before his June examinations, Butler wrote to Jackson that the secretary of war would be at the Academy on July 1. Butler expected soon after graduation to participate in a march of the Corps of Cadets from New York across New Jersey to Philadelphia. He received his commission as a second lieutenant from the War Department on July 6. His class held no graduation ceremony whatsoever, the commission was subject to the confirmation of the Senate, and his assignment was to report to the 3rd Battalion, Corps of Artillery, Southern District, in New Orleans.[11]

Before his departure from West Point, however, Butler joined the entire Corps of Cadets on a lengthy march. A "tramp" was becoming an annual affair for U.S.

Military Academy students, and in 1820 the destination was the metropolis of Philadelphia. Probably under Butler's leadership, the Corps hoofed it across New Jersey, cheered by citizens and by Princeton students along the way. The young soldiers were forced to halt before reaching Philadelphia, as the city was under the cloud of a yellow fever epidemic. Butler's classmate Ramsay remembered that, nevertheless, "Phila. with all its beauty most obligingly came to the camp and on the banks of the beautiful Schuylkill many happy hours were enjoyed." On its return route north, the Corps visited New York City, drilled in the park at City Hall, and had dinner with the local authorities before embarking on the boat trip upriver to West Point. According to Ramsay, the cadets felt "refreshed and invigorated and with lively recollections of the girls we left behind us."[12]

In late August, while still at West Point, Butler received orders to proceed to Boston instead of a posting to New Orleans. His reimbursement for travel and other moving expenses was $209. His superior was Major James Kearney, of the Army Topographical Engineers, and he was beginning a series of assignments that lasted well into 1824. Butler and fellow Academy graduates William Turnbull and Henry A. "Hal" Thompson of Maryland often would serve together, performing topographic duty and undertaking surveys and soundings of bays, rivers, and shorelines. Butler seldom remained in one spot for long. In March 1821, Kearney ordered Butler, then in New York, to Beaufort, North Carolina, where he was to report to Thompson, who "will indicate the duties to which your attention will be directed." By May, he again was on the move, this time to New Orleans to perform "ordnance duties." Now assigned to the 4th Regiment of Artillery, in the fall of 1821 and for several months thereafter Butler resided in Baton Rouge. He was to help construct a large, three-story arsenal and related structures, the "ordnance storage point for the forces assigned to the defense of the Gulf Coast." In an interview late in his life, Butler explained that Congress failed to appropriate construction funds for the arsenal, which Butler was "detailed to superintend," so that he remained "there with nothing to do for many months." Butler shared his time of idleness with his former school friend Lieutenant William S. Harney, an infantry officer. They were fortunate to avoid the sickness and death that overtook many soldiers during the building of the arsenal, parade, magazine, workshops, and barracks. The two friends instead enjoyed exploring the vicinity of Baton Rouge. The town, described by the traveler Estwick Evans in 1818, was "a very considerable place" to which ships of five hundred tons "would ascend the river . . . and receive from the plantations, cargoes of sugar and cotton." Nearby, "towards evening, the porticos of the dwelling houses are filled with ladies" who could look out over the moonlit river and listen to "celestial music" coming from many boats. The two friends admired the opulent plantations that lined the river's banks, beginning upstream at Pointe Coupée, and which resembled "a continuous village as far as the City of New Orleans."[13]

During his Baton Rouge duty, Butler frequently visited his sister Caroline and brother-in-law Robert Bell. They lived on a St. James Parish plantation down-river from Baton Rouge, struggling but ever hopeful to achieve the good life in Louisiana. The Bells began to solicit Butler's help in scouting for slaves and land, and Caroline asked Butler to contribute money to pay off their deceased mother's debts. Although the Bells hinted at the possibility of Butler joining them in the sugar business, he resisted their enticements. In the spring of 1822 he was ordered by General Edmund Pendleton Gaines, commanding the Eastern District of the U.S. Army, to assist Major Kearney in the survey of Pensacola Bay. Kearney was already employing Turnbull and Thompson in topographic duty there. In late July, Butler received orders to proceed from Pensacola to New York, where Kearney and his party all were reassigned, thus ending his time of duty along the Gulf Coast.[14]

After the War of 1812 the U.S. Army had become a small military force, and it was reduced further by Congress in 1821. Charged mainly with the construction and the maintenance of coastal and frontier fortifications and roads, the army began the gradual and disagreeable task of uprooting the Cherokee, Creek, and other Indian tribes in the East. The Indians were moved to places where there would be minimal interaction with white settlers, whose thirst for land and disdain for treaty provisions were seemingly boundless. Army officers like Butler were well schooled and disciplined but underpaid and lacked opportunity for promotion. According to an historian of the U.S. Army in the nineteenth century, "half of the ten regimental commanders in 1823 would stay in command of their regiments for more than twenty years." Inter-regimental promotions seldom occurred. Postings frequently carried officers far from relatives, and their duties subjected them to criticism from the civilian sector. Resignations averaged about 20 percent each year during the 1820s. Other opportunities, especially for West Point–trained engineers, opened up as the nation built and improved canals and railroads. Butler became discouraged with his prospects not long into his career. In late 1821, he wrote General Jackson proposing to resign and to join the Russian military. Jackson's aide, who also was Butler's cousin, Robert Butler, responded for the general (who was ill), urging patience. Lieutenant Butler affirmed that he had served dutifully, with a "love of Country," but he believed that the military profession was held in "utter contempt" by the nation. Nevertheless, agreeing to "content myself," he relied upon the advice of his guardian and other friends "that necessity will, ere long, render our Army respectable."[15] Butler eventually found satisfaction in his military life—and a distinguished wife as well.

2

Edward and Frances

"But . . . What about Julia?"

Butler departed from the Florida coast for New York in July 1822. He and his fellow surveyors were unaware that Pensacola soon would be ravaged by yellow fever. Its causes poorly understood and its treatment almost nonexistent, the fever repeatedly scourged nineteenth-century coastal America from New York on south. His friend and future brother-in-law, Robert Carter "Cary" Nicholas, had recently retired from the army and served as Pensacola's postmaster. Nicholas informed Butler in August that several army friends and other acquaintances were dead and "a good many of your frds. very much scared." Major Nicholas himself became sick but managed to flee. Butler believed that he had escaped just in time, but the disease spread quickly across the Gulf South. Butler contracted it, possibly aboard the steamboat carrying him up the Mississippi River on his way to the Hermitage for a visit with the Jacksons and his sister Eliza. Beloved by them, Eliza Butler often visited the Hermitage and went with the Jackson entourage to New Orleans following the American victory in January 1815. A future wife of John Donelson IV (1787–1840), a nephew of Mrs. Jackson, Eliza evinced talents for nursing during her New Orleans stay. After caring for American soldiers, she received the sobriquet "The Daughter of the Regiment." Her gifts served her brother well: he suffered a "severe indisposition" at the Hermitage, during which "Dear Eliza sat by my bed each night & day." Traveling with his old friend Lieutenant William S. Harney, Butler left the Jacksons' home before he was recovered. Eliza accompanied them the first thirty miles to be sure that Butler could withstand the journey, but by the time he reached the village of Wythe, Virginia, Butler was "unable to sit upon the stage half the time." He arrived at Washington City too sick to continue. Nursed back to a semblance of health by Harney, Butler nonetheless was incapable of performing field duty for Major Kearney. He suffered a relapse en route to New York and was kept under a physician's care for six days in Philadelphia before he could proceed by steamboat. His condition greatly worried his superiors and his friends, who along with his doctors urged him to rest and cure in the New York area. Even after a long and tedious convalescence, Butler was unable to rejoin his regiment. Kearney in early 1823 sent him to Washington "to finish the drawings etc. of the Survey of Pensacola Bay & harbor." He missed additional assignments in Pensacola and in the Chesapeake Bay and rivers of lower St. Mary's County, Maryland. There, Major Kearney and Butler's friends Turnbull and Thompson spent much of 1823. All three assured Butler in letters that the hard work of surveying in the Chesapeake, as well as the lack of good medical care, made Butler's absence from the field a wise and fortunate choice. Quartered in a farmer's house, the survey party lived in undesirable conditions. "Here we are," wrote Kearney, "up to our eyes in mud water, living sumptuously on creeky boards, corn bread, rusty bacon and mint juleps." Butler should be thankful at "having so many kind and attentive friends about you—and they are better than all the medicine in the doctor's shop." Further, advised Kearney, "I have no doubt that with prudence on your part and the pure air of Duchess [County, New York] they will soon get you on your feet again."[1]

What finally lifted Butler back onto his feet was the care of the extended family of General Morgan Lewis. A veteran of the American Revolution and War of 1812 and a former governor of New York, Lewis lived at Staatsburg on the Hudson River, north of New York City. General Lewis and his wife, Gertrude Livingston Lewis, and several other relatives all assisted Butler. The long-lasting connection of Edward Butler with the Lewis and Livingston families dated from his West Point years, when Butler matriculated with Morgan Lewis Livingston (Class of 1819). He was the eldest son of Mathurin and Margaret Lewis Livingston and a grandson of General and Mrs. Lewis. Morgan Livingston introduced Butler to his sister Julia at some social occasion. For young army officers who were off duty, the life in cities like New York, Washington, and New Orleans was socially active, with frequent parties. Described by Morgan Livingston as "soirees" with numerous "fair damsels," and a grand ball "the most splendid that has been given this winter," they attracted Butler and his friends. He led the pack of revelers. Writing to his brother Anthony from New York in December 1822, Butler fretted that "I dislike the idea of leaving New York this winter. Mrs. Gibbs's party has commenced the gaiety of the season, and I expect they will scarcely give a fellow time to rest for the remainder of the season." His experiences were commonplace. In New Orleans, after duty in Pensacola, Hal

Thompson wrote to Butler that he "had passed a very pleasant time . . . 'avec les damoiselles' . . . balls were few yet I went my regular rounds every day and theatre every night." Even the hard work involved with surveying waterways and shorelines in the Chesapeake occasionally gave way to recreation. Writing in detail, William Turnbull described one occasion for Butler:

> A day or two ago I was at a fish feast in the other side of the River—where I saw all the belles and beaux of the neighborhood assembled, and was a very handsome dinner (of fish) after which, we retired to a gentlemans house close by, and danced untill midnight (rather warm). There was a large collection of Ladies, some very pretty ones . . . there was some *flatbacks* among them with all heads long corke screw curls, broad blue ribbons (say six inches) round their waists (very low in front and cocked up behind so as to give them the appearance of *Coached backs*, yellow Morocco shoes, and could dance a jig equal to any body—I was quite astonished to see the familiarity between the gentlemen and ladies particularly the genteeler part—taking them by the hand etc.—& though it might be the custom of the country and did not like to appear singular so I siddled up to a very pretty little girl and made a dead set at her—before the evening closed we were extremely intimate and when we parted she gave me a pressing invitation to call and see her at Mulberry Grove—[2]

Such conviviality unsurprisingly led to romances. Quite soon after meeting the New Yorker, Julia Livingston, Butler was smitten. After the Eastern Division army headquarters moved between New York City, Staatsburg, and West Point, it settled at Fort Columbus. Still in existence and known by its original name, Fort Jay, the post is located on Governor's Island off the southern tip of Manhattan, at the entrance to the East River. Butler was welcomed as if he were one of their own by the Lewis and the Livingston families, who maintained residences in both the city and in Dutchess County. Julia's presence made easy the choice of a place of convalescence. Soon, Butler's brother Anthony, at Yale, and his friends were speculating on a match. Butler wrote admiringly of Julia in late December 1822, promising that when Anthony became acquainted with her, "you will find her a modest but at the same time the best informed woman of her age in America. Two qualities which seldom go together." In a frank exchange of letters in early 1823, Anthony advised his elder brother to marry Julia, in order that he not incur "dishonor" or "inflict misery" upon her. Lieutenant Butler hesitated. On the one hand, he informed Anthony, he was interested in marriage, but he also wanted to meet people of good standing.

When sent by Major Kearney to Washington that winter, Butler and his friends discovered the socially close-knit city to be festive. They received the "marked attention of . . . the great folks," including President Monroe, Secretary of War Calhoun, and Chief of Engineers General Alexander Macomb, all of whom were "condescending and polite." As Butler quipped, satisfyingly, "One trip to Washington is worth a dozen campaigns."

At one of the social events he met Frances Parke Lewis, a friend of Julia. Julia had recommended Frances Lewis to Butler, in fact. "Julia is much pleased that you have not found her description of Miss Lewis exaggerated," Morgan Livingston wrote Butler. But Julia's beau was making a quick course change. The instantly enamored lieutenant confessed to his brother of having left Julia without "a perfect understanding." But he planned to advise her that he could not marry, as he had "another object which I trust in god may be equally as worthy of" his affections. "I found her friend Miss Lewis a remarkably genteel, elegant and accomplished woman. She invited me very particularly to accompany her to Woodlawn on the Mount Vernon estate, and [she] expressed much regret at not being able to introduce me into society, as she is mourning for a relation." Inner struggle and indecision followed. Butler reluctantly told friends that his choice of occupation and his life in the military would not allow him to deprive Julia "of the advantages of the good society" and the life to which she was accustomed.[3] It was an obvious excuse, but his vacillation with Julia and his preference for Julia's friend Frances Parke Lewis soon placed Butler in difficulty.

Butler received a promotion to first lieutenant effective November 6, 1823, and a posting with Major General Edmund P. Gaines as one of two aides-de-camp. General Gaines was a native Virginian who in 1801 served under Lieutenant Colonel Thomas Butler Jr. in the 4th Army Regiment in East Tennessee. After distinguishing himself in the War of 1812, Gaines assisted Andrew Jackson in confronting the Creek and Seminole Indians. Rising quickly in rank, Gaines alternated with General Winfield Scott in command of the Eastern and Western Departments into which the War Department divided army functions. The headquarters for the Western Department was initially at Louisville, Kentucky, and reestablished at Cincinnati, Ohio, in 1826. As noted before, the Eastern Department eventually was situated at Fort Columbus in New York Harbor. Gaines's earlier service with Butler's kin, not to mention mutual connections with Jackson, allowed for the lieutenant's favorable reception with his new commander. Lieutenant Butler handled a variety of business for Gaines during the commander's absence on trips and eventually became Gaines's acting adjutant general.[4]

Although Butler's promotion brought him much responsibility, he fortunately shared duties with another comrade from the Class of 1820 at West Point, Rawlins Lowndes, a South Carolinian of distinguished parentage. Lowndes took charge when Butler accompanied Gaines or was sent on special assignment. The two developed a good working relationship, and their friendship lasted beyond their retirements from active duty in the early 1830s. Butler requested that he remain in New York for most of 1824 and that Lowndes travel. His official duties, which were relieved by "those to the ladies—balls every night," included answering correspondence for Gaines, transmitting the general's orders to officers regarding postings, and arranging for courts-martial. In October, Butler received high praise from Gaines: Butler excelled in "the discharge of the duties of the office from which you have afforded so many interesting testimonials of the accuracy and vigilance of a soldier." The general believed that Butler promised "by his conduct not to halt or change his course until he shall have reached the head of his profession." Aide-de-camp Butler evidently was no longer inclined to abandon a military career.[5]

In the spring of 1825, Gaines called upon Butler to accompany him on a southern tour. While they were still in Washington to receive instructions, Butler narrowly escaped a career-ending censure. As he and Gaines awaited a visit with the newly elected President John Quincy Adams, Butler refused to shake hands with Secretary of State Henry Clay. Ever defensive of Andrew Jackson's honor, the young lieutenant thought—along with many others—that a "corrupt" Clay received a promise of high office in order to help Adams gain the presidency over Jackson. Clay's reaction to Butler's rudeness at first was to think nothing of the matter, but he apparently did not forget the slight and wrote Gaines. Noting that when Butler did not offer an immediate apology, Clay determined that "he [Butler] really meditated offering me an insu[lt]." Clay admonished Gaines concerning "the utility of the observance of urbanity, as a necessary part of that discipline, for which the American Army is so eminently distinguished." The secretary of state in addition complained to President Adams, who then inquired about the issue through Major General Jacob Brown. In spite of requests for an explanation from both his superiors, Brown and President Adams, Gaines ignored them. No doubt because of Gaines, Butler managed to avoid formal punishment, but the effect of this small incident was that Gaines failed to receive a promotion during Adams's term. Jackson's political victory in 1828 almost certainly saved the military careers of both Gaines and Butler.[6]

Soon after, the two soldiers headed to Florida and Georgia, where they encountered numerous adventures. A steamboat carrying Gaines's party along a deserted stretch of the flooded Savannah River, between Augusta and Savannah, hit a tree on one bank. When it caromed off and across the river, it collided with another tree, injuring two of the crew members. The crew and nervous passengers, including women, hailed a boat that happened to be heading downstream. Butler and Gaines were forced to sit atop cotton bales and suffer exposure to inclement weather for thirty hours. During a gun salute to General Gaines at the Savannah garrison, a misfire severely crippled two soldiers.[7]

Undoubtedly the most memorable military experience that year, if not of Butler's army career, was his participation in negotiations between the United States, the Creek Indian nation, and the government of Georgia. Gaines was ordered to calm an explosive situation that featured dissatisfaction by the Creeks with a treaty determining Creek and Georgia boundaries. After the Augusta River and Savannah experiences, Gaines, as a special agent, and Butler rode horseback into the Georgia wilderness to the Lower Creek Indian village of Broken Arrow, on the Chattahoochee River. The Creeks already were beaten down and deprived of ancient lands in Alabama and Georgia during and after the War of 1812. They believed that much of their territory from the Flint River west to the Chattahoochee River would be taken by Georgia with little or no compensation. The Creeks split ranks over the Treaty of Indian Springs of 1821 and were threatened with expulsion by Georgian whites. Gaines found a tense and suspicion-laden atmosphere, due primarily to the activities of Georgia politicians, led by Governor George M. Troup. During the summer and fall of 1825, Butler was secretary to the U.S. mission charged with resolving the disputes. He busily kept notes of the proceedings with the Creeks and Georgia representatives, "reducing them to form" in a journal. Having to assure Frances Parke Lewis in Virginia that "I am in no danger of losing my hair," Butler in concert with Gaines became convinced that "the only enemies we shall have to contend with will be the Crazy governor and his corrupt and designing politicians." Rather than encountering dishonest and dangerous savages, Butler reported that the Creeks presented "themselves superior to Americans in virtue and magnanimity." A year later, Butler wrote his former guardian Jackson that he considered the Creek nation to be "a brave, patient and injured people." In his opinion, Gaines "gained the confidence and gratitude of these poor Indians, and merits the thanks of the civilized world." Gaines succeeded temporarily in blocking a Georgia survey of the lands ceded under the Treaty of Indian Springs, but its terms ultimately took effect. The Creeks began a forced removal to Alabama from their Georgia homeland.[8]

Between Butler's elevation to the position of aide-de-camp to General Gaines and his return north to New York in late 1825, two other major events occurred: Butler's brother Anthony died at sea in September 1824, and Butler became engaged to Frances Parke Lewis.

Born in 1802, Anthony Wayne Butler shared many friends with his brother during the years when both were in the Northeast. A promising youth about to complete his undergraduate studies at Yale, Anthony traveled to Louisiana in late 1823. He needed money to pay for study under Judge James Gould, at the renowned Litchfield School of Law in Connecticut. Anthony met first with the heirs and administrators of the succession of his cousin Richard Butler, who financed his Yale education and who resided at Ormond Plantation in St. Charles Parish. After a visit to his sister Caroline Bell, he proceeded to St. Francisville to remain with another cousin, Judge Thomas Butler Jr. Judge Butler provided him with financial aid and oversaw his legal study. On August 25, 1824, however, Anthony wrote his brother that he hoped to find passage aboard the "first northbound vessel."

Anthony's urgency to return apparently was sharpened by what Judge Butler termed "an attraction of an object of tender attachment," one Sarah Butler (no relation), of New Haven. The judge cautioned his cousin not to take passage aboard a vessel on which anyone was ailing. On or about September 20, Anthony departed for New York, intending to reunite with his brother. Within a few days Anthony became ill. At first he appeared only to have seasickness, but his condition worsened on September 24 and, despite the close attendance of several other passengers, he died. He was buried at sea on October 3. The ship's captain, William Connell, later reported to Edward Butler that the chief officer died three days following Anthony; and Thomas Butler wrote, "I am informed that the mate was brought on board sick after the vessel had weighed anchor." The obvious conclusion was that both victims died of yellow fever.

A distressed brother sought solace with the family of Morgan Livingston in

Staatsburg. "Here," offered Livingston, "you will feel more at home than in the City & may pass your time either in total solitude or only interrupted by the society of friends who knowing the value of what you have lost will know how to sympathise in your feelings." The loss of Anthony was felt not only by Butler and his family but by the brothers' wide circle of friends in New York and Washington. In one positive turn, Anthony Butler's fiancée, Sarah, married Anthony's Yale college mate, Alexander Duncan Jr. Duncan, who also had become a devoted friend of Edward Butler, would provide him and his family with essential financial assistance during their struggles after the Civil War.[9]

Sometime before he learned of Anthony's death, Butler offered his love to Frances Parke Lewis. Born in 1799, Frances Lewis was the oldest child of Major Lawrence Lewis and Eleanor Parke Custis Lewis. Virginia aristocrats, they were counted among the most socially prominent couples in the young Republic. Major Lewis was a son of Colonel Fielding Lewis and George Washington's sister Betty Washington Lewis of Fredericksburg on the Rappahannock River. He served in 1797–99 as a personal secretary to his uncle, George Washington. Washington chose him as one of the executors of his will. Among the members of the Mount Vernon household were a granddaughter of Martha Washington, Eleanor Parke Custis, nicknamed Nelly, and her brother George Washington Parke Custis. George and Martha Washington adopted them both before General Washington's death in December 1799. Aided by proximity, Lawrence Lewis eventually won Nelly's heart, and their marriage took place at Mount Vernon on February 22, 1799, General Washington's birthday. Frances Parke, called Parke by her mother and Frances by others, was born on November 27, 1799, a few weeks before George Washington died. Lewis planned to move with Nelly to Frederick County, where he owned a large farm. Hoping to keep them in the vicinity, the Washingtons presented the Lewises with Dogue Run Farm. It adjoined Mount Vernon and included a prosperous double-stone grain mill and distillery (both now restored and operating). By 1801, Nelly and Lawrence Lewis's Georgian-style mansion, designed by William Thornton, was being constructed. The house was named Woodlawn.[10]

Butler was taken with Frances Lewis upon their meeting in Washington City in early 1823. The courtship between the socially prominent young lady and the soldier blossomed gradually the following December, either in Washington or at Woodlawn. Nelly entrusted Butler to carry an article intended for her son, Lorenzo, in Philadelphia, where he was in school, and to deliver it to her childhood friend Elizabeth Bordley Gibson. No doubt Nelly was angling for an opinion from Gibson: "I am happy to find you much pleased with G. W. Butler," wrote Nelly in reply to a letter from Gibson, allowing herself to comment on Butler's "guileless heart and temper" and on his worldly experiences. "Although," she continued, "it was reported & believed in NY that he was engaged to Julia Livingston . . . there is no truth in it. All the family prize him very highly, he is much with them but no love in the case." Butler's old guardian, once again a U.S. senator, kept an eye on his former ward and wrote Butler in April 1824 that he was about to "visit Mrs. Lewis; to whom & her amiable daughter I shall take the liberty to present your respects." Butler called at Woodlawn in May and afterward from New York reported to Anthony that "we have just returned from a visit to my kind friends . . . (whom I am anxiously expecting here) and was delighted with them." In the company of Butler, Frances, her sister Angela, brother Lorenzo, and Nelly traveled later in the summer of 1824 to visit the Lewis and Livingston families in Staatsburg. Nelly wrote Gibson: "Your favorite Lt Butler came with us & will go away on Thursday. He is amiable as ever, but his mind is not *first* rate, he has had very *moderate* improvement I think. . . . He is not fond of reading. I wonder often that he is not tired to death of doing nothing." Nelly's faultfinding may have been due in part to Butler's discomfort in the presence of both Julia Livingston and Frances Parke Lewis. He probably had not ended his romance with Julia in a tidy manner. Or was Butler simply at a loss, while at Staatsburg, to articulate how he felt?[11]

During Butler's struggle between keeping and abandoning a love relationship with Julia Livingston, he met with some resistance from friends. In the prior winter of 1824, for example, Butler consulted William Turnbull on his opinion of Frances Lewis versus Julia Livingston. Turnbull wrote from Washington City:

> I have become acquainted with your friend Miss Lewis who has been in the City for some time. Likewise with Miss Livingston but I am not sufficiently intimate with them to make the comparison you desired. I admire Miss Lewis very much. She is certainly a very elegant woman and one of very superior mind, but there is an air of stiffness and sedateness about her and also of superiority which I do not like. Now on the contrary there is an air of sprightliness and grace about Miss Livingston, which I admire and withal is not less dignified, but she is more of a woman of the world (as it is termed) than Miss Lewis. I take it, Miss Lewis is not very fond of gaiety.

Nevertheless, Butler received help in his growing preference for Frances from General Gaines, who was well aware of his aide-de-camp's activities and thoughts. Gaines regretted having to recall Butler from his stay in Staatsburg, "a place where you cannot be otherwise than happy." Butler was to replace Rawlins Lowndes in New York City, so that Lowndes could join General Gaines. The general wished Butler "to say all the kind things for me that you can say, to Mrs. Lewis, her amiable daughter and nieces—and to Mrs. Lewis of Virginia and her daughter." Frances had "made an impression to which it would be difficult for me to give utterance, without going back, about 20 years, and selecting the best that poets have said, or lovers dreamed. She is indeed 'rich in all woman's loveliness.'"[12]

Before he could achieve an engagement with Frances Lewis, Butler was presented with two challenges: the first was to obtain the permission of Nelly Lewis to court Frances. Because it needed to be accomplished quickly, Butler wrote Nelly on September 25, 1824, after the visit to Staatsburg and his parting with the Lewises. He had been led to "reflect anxiously on the state of my feelings" and sought "a perfect understanding" between him and Frances. "On the eve of your departure from Elizabethtown I requested Miss Parke to correspond with me: she expressed a willingness . . . but remarked that you would not consent to it. I hope I am justified . . . in believing, as also from her general deportment toward me, that my feelings are reciprocated." Understandably, Butler had trouble getting to the point: "As I know that you appreciate, and would not, intentionally, wound the feelings of a young soldier, who has, perhaps unfortunately, inherited no small show of pride from his ancestors,—I feel authorized in addressing you thus, and avowing a sincere and disinterested attachment for your daughter, which if reciprocated by her, and finally approved of by yourself and all others who are responsible for her happiness,—it shall be my pride to cherish." Butler succeeded: Nelly gave Frances her permission to communicate with the lieutenant.

A second test faced Butler: he must resolve Frances's doubts about Julia. The issue was raised by Frances, who could not accommodate Butler's proffer of love with her understanding of the facts. She mailed Butler a letter—now lost—in early October 1824, addressed from the Olmstead boarding house in Philadelphia; the Lewis entourage, en route home to Woodlawn, was there resting and visiting with the Gibsons. Butler replied, repeating her query: "You ask me if I can be certain that the sentiments I now possess are calculated to stand the test of time and absence." He thought that they already had resolved the issue, wrote an uncomfortable Butler. In addition, he promised, "all that man could be to a woman (so far as a disposition and corresponding efforts for her happiness could contribute) I would be to you." But, Frances asked about Julia Livingston: had Butler never been her "lover" and "never gave her reason to suppose so?" His response demanded caution. "The occasion requires" frankness, wrote Butler:

> Shortly after I completed my studies at West Point, my duty called me to this city, where I was introduced to Genl. Lewis' family and received in the kindest and most friendly manner. I, consequently, became intimate with all the family, and particularly pleased with Miss Julia. Sometime afterwards I became sick in New York, and was induced, at the instance of Dr. Horack, to accept an invitation to . . . Staatsburgh. I finally conceived an attachment for Miss Julia which, although disapproved of by myself (knowing that our feelings and sentiments were totally different!) I was impelled to declare to her by a sense of honor and a combination of circumstances which, through respect to her, I shall not mention. This was, however, induced, from mistaken or mercenary motives to quibble, or rather to trifle with feelings that could never brook insult, and she must bear the consequences.—You will, perhaps, brand me with inconstancy, and doubt the sincerity of my declarations to you, but my conscience acquits me. Before we were personally known to each other, I admired your character. . . . Our acquaintance confirmed that admiration, and for the last year you have occupied my thoughts, exceedingly.[13]

Sent without any salutation, the young officer's letter may have helped but did not succeed entirely. Some mistrust or at least continuing uncertainty on the part of both remained. In February 1825, while visiting relatives in Georgetown, Frances admonished Butler for being neglectful. He expressed surprise, adding that "there is a coldness and indifference in your manner of addressing me, that I regret to say, savour but little of love, and are calculated to depress and discountenance it. The effect of this you do not appear to have discovered, and the sentiments I am wont to cherish for you have been chilled by it, and can only be restored to their pristine warmth by the kind reciprocation of a confiding heart." His language gave Frances additional pause. Butler wrote soon again, expressing impatience that Frances did not reply to his letter: "It would be happiness to me to know that your silence and apparent coldness towards me were the result of anything but indifference." Yet, Butler continued, "I cannot alter my opinion of you unless you compel me to it." At least Butler rejoiced to know of her strong approval of Andrew Jackson, who represented "his country's beacon, that will ever guide her safely." He at the same time expressed disdain for the newly elected president, John Quincy Adams, as no "man of honor, or as a friend to the Republic." Somehow the winter's chill dissipated, warmth returned, and by April 1825 they were formally engaged. "He is the choice of my Child," Nelly reported to Gibson. "After mature deliberation she says. . . . She is willing to be a Soldiers wife, to follow his fortunes. . . . She is convinced that this roving life . . . will make her more healthy & happy." In a presage of storm clouds, Nelly proceeded, "His income is only $1400. . . . I have told you how unexceptional his character & disposition are. He is honorable, correct, dignified—with a most amiable & affecte disposition, but he is not such a *mind* as I thought Parke would have selected. . . . I tremble at the thought of the difficulties, the privations she will endure." Monetary assistance was impossible, but Nelly intended to provide the couple, for a nominal $1, with "600 acres of Kenahwa Land—not of much value at this time, if ever." The property located on the Kanawha River in present-day West Virginia had been given her from the estate of George Washington.[14]

The courtship progressed, although not without a pall from rumors that circulated about Butler and his old flame Julia. He addressed them with Frances:

> The report . . . does not astonish me in the least! It is such a report as is daily encountered in large cities and without which the fashionable world could not exist; and although it implies a want of feeling and delicacy in both of us, were I . . . inclined, I would rather cherish than repress it. I will, however, write to Mrs. Golden, lest, in the plenitude of your pride, you should reject me. But, I am very much afraid it will give rise to reports of a contrary nature, and I would not wound Julia's feelings, or those of her family, for the world; for I am convinced they never countenanced such a report.

Nelly Lewis's continued misgivings denote an understandable misreading of the personality and strength of her eldest daughter. Frances received an education at home by her mother and, from 1814, at Madame Deborah Grelaud's French School in Philadelphia. The school was attended by daughters of numerous early American elites, including Catherine Carter Tayloe and Frances's cousins Eliza Law, Columbia and America Peter, and Caroline Calvert. She was taught to play the piano and the harpsichord, to draw, and to dance. Students at the school were trained in "elegance of carriage," and, despite strict rules against such practices, they attended parties and mixed with the high society of Philadelphia and, soon, Washington City. If there was a question regarding the extent to which Frances attained what her mother and others considered the model of educational upbringing for a young lady, in some ways she received more-than-ample training. Less stylish in her dress and less inclined to be the "belle" that some thought appropriate, she made her own strong impressions. By 1825 a woman in her mid-twenties who was comfortable amid the societies of Washington, Philadelphia, and New York, Frances Lewis was unafraid to stand her ground. Butler's friend Rawlins Lowndes observed her at a function in the White House soon after the presidential election. Frances shared Butler's feelings about Adams and his victory over Jackson and made no bones about them. "I saw Mrs. and Miss Lewis last evening at the presidents," Lowndes reported to Butler, "and paid my respects to them. The young Lady looked very charming and was very warm at the results of the election, expressed her opinions with great freedom, and with little regard as to who heard her." Nelly's doubts about the match between Lieutenant Butler and Frances were tempered during the summer of 1825. Butler impressed the Lewises with his letters describing his and General Gaines's travels along the Florida and Georgia coastlines and in the Georgia backcountry. Frances's father, Major Lewis, approved of Butler, "except on the score of property." Butler had attempted to allay those fears the previous March:

> . . . I frankly acknowledge that my situation in life is more or less influenced by the vicissitudes incident to the Profession of Arms, and that my income ($1400) will not enable me support your daughter in the style she is accustomed to, or that I would wish, [but] I cannot but believe that in following my destinies her health would be improved, and that a slight addition to my [pay], with a retrenchment in some of the necessities of life, would enable us to live comfortably, respectably, and happy. I do not wish for fortune, neither do I wish you to incommode yourself by giving her the portion mentioned by her Mother, all that I ask is that you and Mrs. Lewis will permit us to love each other, and when circumstances authorize it, in your judgment, that we may be united. I hope to see you in a few days, when I do not despair of obviating all objections.

Matters resolved formally, Nelly wrote Elizabeth Gibson in early October 1825 of having given "my son in law . . . my entire approbation." Despite wishing that "his *pecuniary* recommendations were greater," Nelly contented herself: "I could not ask for a more noble heart & disposition, & they are the most important."[15]

Because Butler was to be stationed in Cincinnati, with Gaines, much nervousness remained at the prospect of Frances heading into what Nelly and Frances Lewis and their contemporaries believed to be an American wilderness. "I dread her going to the West," wrote Nelly in December 1825, after Butler returned to Woodlawn unwell and looking poorly from the rigors of his southern trip. It was a common worry of women who watched kinfolk head across the Alleghenies. "The distance, the difficulties in traveling, her delicate & indulged habits, poor B's limited resources," moaned Nelly, "all make me dread her going so far out of my sphere of action." If Frances became pregnant and had difficulties, that would be the worst of situations. By Nelly's count, Frances was "naturally nervous & low spirited & that situation is peculiarly calculated to excite depression." Was the critical and anxious Nelly Lewis simply failing to comprehend that her well-educated daughter was becoming a mature person with her own inquiring mind? Was she afraid of losing control? Or was she understandably concerned with dangers that might be the lot of a soldier's wife? A sanguine view of the prospective move came from Butler's former host and friend General Morgan Lewis. He did not blame Lieutenant Butler for choosing Frances Parke Lewis instead of his granddaughter Julia Livingston. Cincinnati, General Lewis observed, "might be more pleasant to the Lady of your choice, than she, or her friends apprehend." Additional support came from General Gaines, who recognized firm character and beauty in Frances and advised Butler to "appreciate her worth." He was confident of Frances's suitability for the adventure awaiting her. After all, the lieutenant's marriage to Frances represented an "alliance with a fair representative of him who was 'first in war, first in peace, first in the hearts of his countrymen.'" Gaines enthusiastically invited the young couple to reside with him and Mrs. Gaines in Cincinnati until they found other quarters. He recommended their own hotel run by Colonel Mack; or the newlyweds might reside in a suite of rooms at the "boarding house kept by Mrs. Bainbridge, a daughter of Commodore Truxton, a very amiable and respectable woman." Her "house appears to be fine and airy" and cost only $3 a week. Sensitive to the concerns of the family, Gaines asked Butler to assure Major and Mrs. Lewis that he and Mrs. Gaines "will contribute to lessen as far as practicable the privations which long absence from them of their daughter in a strange land is calculated to produce."[16]

Frances Parke Lewis and Edward G. W. Butler wed at Woodlawn on April 4, 1826. Dr. William H. Wilmer officiated a "merry wedding" at which Frances was, by her mother's account, "so much nervous & so much agitated that we exerted ourselves to make her gay." The groomsmen were Lorenzo Lewis, brother of the bride, her cousin George Washington Peter, Dr. John Knox of Philadelphia, and two of Butler's fellows in the artillery, William Turnbull and Robert Livingston Armstrong. For her maids, Frances chose her cousins Rosalie Stuart, Mary Custis—later wife of Robert E. Lee, America Peter, and Hettie Lewis, as well as her sister Angela. Other guests were the family friend and neighbor William Foote, the Lewis physician and friend Dr. Henry Daingerfield, and Butler's friend and the future secretary of war in Jackson's Cabinet, John H. Eaton. Additional cousins, an aunt of Frances, and several others came. Only a few of the Lewis family were invited: "Our house would not accommodate more," according to Nelly. Before the Butlers departed, the transfer of land was arranged, for 1,207 acres (not 600, as Nelly had written Elizabeth Gibson) on the "west side of Kanawa River," near Point Pleasant in Mason County. The tract was part of 10,549 acres of land "surveyed for the heirs of George Washington" by George McKee in 1804. The newlyweds spent several days of festivities at Woodlawn. They then headed to Arlington, where Nelly's brother "Wash" (George Washington Custis) lived, and on to Georgetown to see other relatives, the Peter family, at Tudor Hall. Edward and Frances soon were happily on their way by stagecoach across the spring-clad mountains to Wheeling and then by steamboat on the Ohio River to Cincinnati. Having resigned his Senate seat after the election of President Adams, Andrew and Rachel Jackson could not attend the wedding. Butler described it to his former guardian, and in his reply Jackson expressed his love for the child of his old friend Captain Edward Butler and, by extension, for Butler's new bride. Jackson likely recollected his own dedication to Rachel Donelson, when they united years before.

> Mrs. J. unites with me in a tender to you of our heartfelt congratulations on this joyous occasion—May you be as happy as we wish you, and if thus blessed, it must meet with the measure of your earthly desires—This union, if formed on the basis of pure affection, its results must be happiness to you both—may you long live to enjoy that happiness wise providence bestows upon you in his happy union. . . . We hope to have the pleasure of seeing you both, ere long.[17]

3

From Soldier to Planter

The Allure of Louisiana

The marriage and the move to Ohio *were* felicitous. Cincinnati belied back-home fears of "Western wilds," and the assignment suited Edward and Frances Butler. Frances enthusiastically reported in mid-May to Elizabeth Gibson in Philadelphia. The city, "which 20 years ago since had no existence— . . . contains . . . fine brick houses, admirably paved streets, beautiful gardens, Green Houses, abounding in the most rare exotics, and a society more polished, interested, and refined, than I had supposed it possible to meet with west of the Allegheny." The couple took up rooms at the Cincinnati Hotel, owned by the entrepreneur and local politician Andrew Mack. General Gaines and his wife, Barbara Blount, were in residence at the hotel, and Butler rented a convenient office part of the time. He received some additional compensation for his quarters and office. Although the hotel was costly, the $8 weekly bill for "board" included meals.[1]

Settled in 1789 and defended until 1808 by a spacious, well-built fort named for George Washington, Cincinnati in 1826 was a major center of commerce. It contained an estimated sixteen hundred people. Frances Butler's description did not refer to its glass, woolen, and cotton factories, paper mills, iron foundries, and powder works. Located within an easy walk of the Butlers' hotel, the town market was available most days of the week. There, one found "several hundred wagons, tilted white canvas . . . backed against the pavement, or footway," their tailboards let down to create virtual shops, each offering varied produce, such as good meat, pork, fish, Indian corn, flour, and vegetables. During the Butlers' stay, the English traveler William Bullock visited Colonel Mack's hotel. He considered it to be "an establishment of order, regularity, and comfort that would do credit to any city of Europe." Bullock found its guests to be "notable." At a reception and elegant dinner held by Colonel and Mrs. Mack upon his arrival on Easter Sunday of 1827, Bullock met them all, no doubt including the Butlers. He counted seventy ladies and gentlemen at the dinner, and the Englishman thought the food good. His sole complaint was "the want of warm plates, and a little more time to have enjoyed the repast, twenty minutes only being allowed by the industrious habits of this part of America, for their principal meal." The Butlers relished their time in Ohio, and each sought to allay any fears at Woodlawn that they were anything but safe and well. "The health of Cincinnati continues," Butler commented to his father-in-law in July 1826, "and the weather now is very cool and delightful. Frances looks better than you ever saw her, and with the exception of a slight indisposition, occasioned by my sedentary duties, I have enjoyed good health." The couple received a visit in June from their common friend Julia Livingston. Her companionship, Butler's sister Caroline thought, provided more fun for Frances than the society of the much older wife of General Gaines.[2]

The Northwest Ordinance prohibited slavery north of the Ohio River, but Frances disregarded the words of caution from General Gaines and brought along her personal slave, Lucinda. She was a young girl of perhaps fourteen, descended from one of Martha Washington's slaves. Attending the Butler family through her life, Lucinda was to become "in charge of everything" in the household, as Butler put it shortly after her death in 1853. Using domestic slaves was common for army officers and their families stationed in the West. The Butlers paid an additional $2 a week for housing their "servant." Occasional charges for Lucinda such as "Cotton & Shoes" appear on Frances Butler's lists of expenses in 1827–28.

The Butlers added a "furnished parlour" to their rooms by late summer 1826, at an extra charge of $3 a week, and bought candles to illuminate the rooms. Once cold weather set in, they paid $1.50 each for fires to heat their quarters and the office. Another necessity included hiring a washerwoman, Eliza Parsell, who charged slightly more than 4 cents per "piece." Frances took advantage of the opportunities offered by Cincinnati to acquire reading material, a desk and writing paper, an expensive clock, clothes, and sewing items. The hotel invoices show that the Butlers entertained "at home." Charges appear on their bill, for example, for "Friends meals" in September 1826. Occasional payments were for brandy, whiskey, and cigars. A separate expense with McAlister & Co. was for a sizeable amount of Madeira wine, brandy, and "Brown Stout," and the jugs in which to keep the spirits. General Gaines and his wife immediately took Frances under their wings, and the Lewises maintained communications. By mid-summer, for instance, Frances's harp was on its way from far-off Woodlawn—first on a sailing ship to New Orleans, and then on a Mississippi River steamboat. Probably reflecting Major Lewis's contribution, a barrel of salted herrings accompanied the harp. The fish were much preferred to western river fish, which, although "sufficient in abundance, are coarse and tasteless." Concerned about Frances's health, Nelly shipped some Seidlitz powders. They were a mixture of elements to make effervescent salts used as a purge and headache relief when combined with water. The remedy was one of Nelly Lewis's favorites.[3]

Butler's myriad duties required him to keep orderly records and correspond with the adjutant general in Washington, the War Department, commandants of army posts, and many others. Because Lowndes had been relieved of duty for an extended period, Butler's job became all-consuming, and Frances felt lonely. Writing her cousin Mary Custis about his absence, she noted her husband's preoccupation with his work. Butler had "scarcely a moment to himself, and there are few days in a month, in which I enjoy his society even for a few moments—only at night and after candle light, or to take a short walk late in the evening." Although physically confining, Butler's duties engendered habits that proved invaluable through the rest of his life.

Later in the year, he continued a conversation with Major Lewis that began much earlier when the two discussed politics and the fate of Andrew Jackson's run for president in 1824. Nelly Lewis had come to share Butler's enthusiasm for Jackson. Together with her brother George Washington Parke Custis, they gave Washington family relics to the Jacksons. But there may have been some hesitation on the part of Major Lewis about Old Hickory. The chat between Lewis and Butler could only have been interesting: Butler a devotee of Jacksonian Democracy, and Lewis an heir to the standard of Washingtonian Federalism. Butler admired Ohio for practicing the "liberty and equality" principles of the Republic as interpreted by Andrew Jackson. They were in contrast with standards in other areas of the country that represented "monied aristocracy." Butler thought that the idea might offend Major Lewis, but he believed that Virginia's aristocracy was different. It owed more to "British origins and institutions," which carried democratic features that ultimately were embodied in the Constitution. The major expressed his worry about the increasing loss of power of freeholders in the Virginia legislature. Butler argued, in response, that the more people who could vote, the less likely there would be political corruption. He sought to calm his federalist-leaning father-in-law.[4]

Butler did not mention that Frances became pregnant soon after their wedding and was due to give birth early in 1827. Upon learning of the upcoming event, Nelly Lewis boasted to her friend Gibson that Frances "has never had an hours sickness, is stronger & fatter than she ever was in her life, is very active, in fine spirits, takes more exercise than she ever did & is comfortable & surrounded by very kind friends." Nelly at first planned a trip to Cincinnati in late November, but an illness prevented her from leaving Virginia. She nevertheless felt reassured by Frances's good health and happiness and by the invitation of Barbara Gaines to move to her quarters. There, Frances would have "the best physician and best nurses." The new boy, named after his father, arrived at least a month early, on December 4, 1826. Butler reported on December 13 to Major Lewis that both mother and son were in good health. Besides Lucinda, another nurse was employed to stay with Frances and the baby. Possibly a recent immigrant from Europe, and following her custom, she "placed the youngster in a bucket of water the last two mornings, in order to strengthen him, and she says he bears it like a little hero." Butler proudly noted that Frances, who "can scarcely be said to have been sick," also "has been sitting by the fire nearly all day." He urged Lewis to write them more frequently, about crops or politics or whatever else interested him.[5]

The presence of a first grandchild in far-off Cincinnati was too great a magnet for Nelly Lewis. In 1827, she and Frances's younger sister Angela made a summertime trip west to see the Butlers, but while they were there, on September 19, the baby died. Butler had secured a furlough before he and General Gaines began a scheduled move back to the Eastern Department headquarters. He had determined to bring Frances and their son to the Hermitage on their way to the home of his sister and brother-in-law Caroline and Robert Bell in Louisiana. Relieved to have a chance to assuage their grief and to see old friends, they kept to their travel plans and departed in early November after Angela and Nelly Lewis, accompanied by General Gaines, began the trip back to Woodlawn. The Butlers boarded a steamboat for Port William [now Carrollton], Kentucky. There, they visited a Butler cousin, William Orlando Butler, the future general in command of U.S. forces in Mexico in 1848, then went on by carriage via Shelby County to see another cousin, Pierce Butler. Upon arrival at the Hermitage, they took pleasure in viewing a new portrait of General Jackson. The sitting had been arranged by Butler the previous spring with the Nashville resident artist Ralph E. W. Earl. Initially the work was to be a portrait of Butler's father, Captain Edward Butler, costing a fee of $50. However, soon after Jackson reported seeing "Mr. Earl, on the subject of your father's portrait," Butler also instructed the artist to paint "my dear old General in his uniform." It would remind the "political demogogues" that Jackson, "like Washington, won" his patriotism "in his country's greatest need." Butler relished the idea of the Old Warrior becoming president, and on the next anniversary of the Battle of New Orleans he dedicated a poem, praising his hero:

> Firmly stood! And nobly shielded
> From disgrace his Country's name! . . .
> Is there one who vainly toiling
> Fain would lessen Jackson's name?
> On his coward head recoiling
> Heavy fall contempt and shame!
> . . .
> Then let his praise be sounded
> By a grateful nation's voice
> He the hero of our heads,
> The ruler of our choice.—[6]

By now, the Butlers wanted a change, and former residents of Tennessee who moved to Louisiana would shape their destinies. Principal among those who exercised influence on the Butlers' future were Caroline and Robert Bell, Butler's sister and brother-in-law. In early 1812, Robert Bell's older brother, George Bell, was the first of the Bell family to arrive in Louisiana. He acquired from the succession of Joseph Mollex thirteen and one-half arpents of land on the right descending bank of the Mississippi River in Iberville Parish. George Bell more than likely was attracted to Louisiana by his close friend and fellow Tennessean Joseph Erwin. Erwin already was a major landowner in the state and became the second influence on the Butlers' move south. Erwin agreed to be a surety for George Bell and soon after to provide security on notes totaling $12,014 for a purchase by Bell of twenty-one slaves. By September of the following year, Robert Bell was "now resident" of Iberville and had given George Bell his power of attorney to sell property back in Tennessee.[7]

Little is known of the Bell brothers before they surfaced in Louisiana in 1812–13. They appear to have been related to the wife of Judge John McNairy, a native of North Carolinia. McNairy was an early associate of Andrew Jackson and a Nashville notable, who became the state's first federal judge. The McNairys helped raise Robert Bell, and the two families continued to enjoy close ties. In

1799, George Bell was in Springfield, Robertson County, Tennessee, north of Nashville, where he operated a store and bought other property. By 1806 he resided in Davidson County, of which Nashville was the county seat. Andrew Jackson's early biographer, James Parton, depicted George Bell as a second in a March 1806 pistol duel near Nashville. The affair occurred between John McNairy's brother Nathaniel, an associate of Charles Dickinson, and John Coffee, a Jackson friend and business associate who later became one of Jackson's generals at the Battle of New Orleans. Although he invested and spent much time in the state, George Bell never officially settled in Louisiana.

Perhaps as early as 1805, Robert Bell married a sixteen-year-old Tennessee woman. She was Caroline Swanwick Butler, the eldest child of U.S. Army captain Edward Butler and Isabella Fowler Butler. Bell shared in the management of his brother's store in Tennessee and raced and traded horses in the neighborhood of Nashville. He, too, was acquainted with both Jackson and Erwin. Following the birth of two sons, Robert and William, the Bells migrated to Louisiana. In the fifteen years after their arrival, Robert and George Bell often partnered, and Robert acquired, sold, and rented numerous properties on which he grew and milled sugar cane. His investments spread across several parishes, including Iberville.[8]

The Iberville Parish portion of the "Mississippi River Coast" of Louisiana featured elevated land consisting of cultivable and relatively well-drained alluvial soils. Enriched by sediment during annual floods, they were similar to the lands on each side of the river extending up from present-day Plaquemines Parish through the area of Pointe Coupée Parish, and beyond the entrance of the Red River into the Mississippi. Populated initially by American Indians, the river edges were settled by Europeans and early arriving Anglo-Americans for many years prior to the arrival of the Erwins and Bells. Iberville developed modest-sized farms with small numbers of slaves, if any. James Pitot, a prominent New Orleans businessman at the turn of the nineteenth century, affirmed that in 1801 most sugar plantations along the river worked no more than forty or fifty slaves, some holdings as few as a dozen. A total of ten thousand to twelve thousand slaves were located that year extending south of Baton Rouge. Pitot calculated that only four thousand of them labored on about sixty plantations that manufactured sugar. By the end of the decade, a U.S. Army officer, Amos Stoddard, observed that about forty thousand slaves were in Louisiana, but he also concluded that "sugar cane is not raised above the island of Orleans. . . . No sugar estates are found more than one hundred miles above the city, but cotton is cultivated in all parts of the country."[9]

After the War of 1812, the entire region as far north as Concordia Parish in central Louisiana experienced a surge of economic and social change. Migrants from other states obtained credit, bought and leased land, and strove to make their fortunes. Like most places in the Lower Mississippi River Valley, southern Louisiana transformed into a slave-based and large-scale system of agriculture. In this case, the recast increasingly was to sugar cane cultivation and its milling and the exportation of sugar to the North and in the foreign trade. As sugar cane gradually replaced cotton and indigo in larger operations, the smaller, self-sufficient farms were bought and consolidated into plantations. Some statistics from the late 1820s were assembled by Louisiana planters and agricultural groups at the request of Congress, then deliberating on the issue of tariff charges on imported sugar. They help to illustrate the tremendous growth of the industry. In 1827–28 an estimated 3 steam engines and sugar mills, 27 animal-powered sugar mills, and 115 kettles were acquired by sugar planters in Louisiana. The following year, the purchases of steam engines and mills, animal-powered sugar mills, and kettles numbered 15, 56, and 460, respectively. The acquisitions increased in 1829–30 to 37 steam engines and sugar mills, 133 animal-powered mills, and 723 kettles. Sugar planters purchased 24,000 slaves in those three years, at an approximate cost of $12 million, vastly increasing the number of slaves working sugar operations in Louisiana, to an estimated 35,000. The sugar plantation system came to dominate life in the Mississippi River parishes south from Louisiana's boundary with the state of Mississippi and west principally into the Attakapas region of Bayou Teche and along Bayous Lafourche and Terrebonne.[10]

The second agent of change for the Butlers, the Bells' friend Joseph Erwin, became a major player in the conversion from cotton to sugar cane and its manufacture in south Louisiana after the War of 1812. In 1807, Joseph and Lavinia Erwin migrated from Tennessee and established their home on the right bank of the Mississippi River, below the village of Plaquemine, in Iberville Parish. From Nicholas Rousseau, Erwin acquired rich alluvial land about five and one-half arpents wide fronting on the river downstream from its junction with Bayou Plaquemine. Natives of North Carolina who had moved to Nashville in the 1790s, the Erwins had successfully raised cotton at Peach Blossom Plantation near the Tennessee settlement. Although the records are few, Erwin and Andrew Jackson appear to have been friends, if not also associates in business. In addition, the men were avid racers of horses, in common with many in that era. Jackson, who was both a judge and the general of the Western Tennessee militia, also operated a store from which he supplied the countryside.

Joseph and Lavinia Erwin made a precipitate decision to leave Tennessee. In late 1805, their son-in-law Charles Dickinson had arranged a race between one of Erwin's horses, Ploughboy, and a steed of Jackson's named Truxton. A sizeable wager was involved, and when Erwin cancelled the race, his withdrawal triggered a forfeit. In discussions held at the store owned by the Bells, a minor disagreement occurred over the notes used to pay the forfeit penalty. The disagreement became personal, reached local newspapers, and escalated. Jackson and Dickinson exchanged emotionally charged letters. In the resulting pistol duel, held across the state border in Kentucky in May 1806, Jackson received a severe wound but killed Dickinson. Stories differed, yet the Nashville community generally believed that Jackson acted unfairly, if not dishonorably, because he recocked and fired his weapon after an initial misfire. No doubt Erwin already had been investigating economic opportunities in Louisiana. He had become familiar with the area when he shipped his crops to New Orleans in Dickinson's care. But the duel culminating in the death of their daughter Jane's husband pushed the Erwins into a move. Then in their late forties, they left behind their family, most of whom were married and settled in Tennessee, and made the long and difficult trip south by flatboat. Their riverfront plantation in the new U.S. Territory of Orleans was Erwin's first land purchase of many in Iberville and neighboring parishes. Named "Home Place," the plantation initially grew cotton.[11]

Erwin's land empire was well established by the end of the War of 1812. The new cotton-growing areas already were markets for slaves sold from states of the Upper South. There, tobacco farming was in decline precisely at the time that slave birth rates were on the rise. The end of the international slave trade in 1808 cut off new sources of supply for slave labor, but Louisiana had few laws until 1831 to prevent interstate slave trafficking. Erwin soon was involved in acquiring slaves, especially from Maryland and Virginia, sometimes acting as a slave trader and offering them for resale. Among his good friends and associates in Louisiana were the newcomers Robert and George Bell. One of their business arrangements was a partnership in 1822 to acquire land on which first to grow cotton, and then sugar cane. Their land, which Robert and Caroline Bell pronounced the finest they had ever seen, was located on Bayou Grosse Tête, in Pointe Coupée Parish just north of its boundary with Iberville Parish. Erwin and the Bell brothers were only beginning their push into sugar cane, and the prospects for success in the Grosse Tête region were promising. In order to work the land, slaves were needed. Erwin located a large group of slaves belonging to Warner Washington II, of Virginia, one of George Washington's cousins. The slaves lived on Audley Farm, in the Shenandoah Valley in Frederick County near Battletown (now Berryville, Clarke County).[12]

The ninety-three slaves Joseph Erwin acquired from Warner Washington in June of 1822 for $34,000 were paid for partly in cash, partly through debt. They evidently shipped out of Baltimore on a sailing vessel, bound for New Orleans. Many families comprised the group. It included eighteen men of age eighteen and over, seventeen boys ages ten to seventeen, sixteen women age fifteen and over, ten boys between ages three and nine, seven girls age three to twelve, and twelve children under age three. George Bell assisted in the purchase, the uprooting of the slaves from their old homes, and their transport. They were to be used specifically on the newly acquired property on Bayou Grosse Tête, which, Caroline Bell somehow reasoned, the slaves liked better than living on land fronting the Mississippi River. It gratified her, she wrote Butler, "as their comfort and happiness, poor creatures—ought to be a consideration with every feeling heart." Like slaveowners everywhere, the Bells' pity for the hard lives that slaves led did not mean that they opposed the slave trade, which tore slave communities apart. As noted by historian Bruce Levine, southern attitudes toward their slaves reflected "a fascinating quality of the human mind," which is "its ability to hold firmly and simultaneously to contradictory ideas."

In purchasing the slaves from Virginia, Erwin incurred debt of $28,000. As security, he gave Washington a first mortgage on his "Iberville Farm of over 3,000 acres." The mortgaged debt was to be paid off in three equal installments in the form of notes due June 3 of 1828, 1829, and 1830, at 6 percent interest per year, until all the debt was paid. Significantly, at the end of the purchase deed, almost appearing as an afterthought, Warner Washington *assigned the mortgage notes* (also called bonds) to none other than Lawrence Lewis of Fairfax County, Virginia, the future father-in-law of Edward G. W. Butler. They were "in consideration of his agreement to give me credit for the amount of same when received." The slaves had been acquired in hopes of the fortunes to be made on the rich land the Bells and Erwins planned to farm on Bayou Grosse Tête, but the venture eventually ended disastrously after the property was flooded, destroying new buildings and crops. According to Caroline Bell, an "unfeeling overseer" caused the drowning of one of "the Washington sett of Negroes." Numbers of other slaves died of illness, which, Caroline Bell wrote Butler, was "owing to its being their first year in the climate." The partnership was dissolved in June 1824, Bell losing $1,500 and Erwin absorbing the financial loss from the slave deaths.[13]

The explanation for the assignment to Lewis of the bonds of indebtedness from Warner Washington II is that Lewis was a creditor of Washington. In 1818, Lewis sold to Washington his one thousand-acre property named Llewellyn, located not far from Washington's home in Frederick County, for $101,075. Washington needed a way to meet his obligations under that transaction. The assignment of the Erwin notes from Washington to Lewis was a good arrangement for Major Lewis, who now owned a first mortgage on Erwin's valuable Home Place Plantation. It represented a profitable and safe obligation that not only paid interest income but could be used to secure other business arrangements that Lewis might want to enter into. Still apparently unable fully to repay his debts to Lewis, in 1825 the aging Warner Washington II conveyed his ownership in the twelve hundred-acre Audley Farm to Lewis for $56,000. It became the home of Lawrence and Nelly Lewis's son, Lorenzo, and eventually the final residence of Nelly before her death on July 15, 1852.[14]

The new creditor-debtor relationship between Major Lewis and Joseph Erwin proved significant to the Butlers. Within a year after their marriage, Major Lewis made a donation to his daughter Frances of the Erwin note that was due in 1828. The gift constituted separately owned property of Frances Butler, a matter of much consequence later in her life, but Edward Butler as husband managed and controlled the debt. It, like many other assets of Frances, would be used for acquiring the land and slaves or financing other needs on the plantation they ultimately acquired. With that gift, the Butlers became entwined with the fate of Joseph Erwin by reason of their joining Major Lewis in the role of favored creditors holding a first mortgage. The mortgage primed any other creditors. In case Erwin failed to pay the bond interest and principal in a timely manner, they could seize and sell the Erwins' Home Place Plantation. Lawrence and Nelly Lewis in fact were motivated by the hope that the Butlers would establish their residence at Audley Farm. It would place them within visiting distance of the Lewises at Woodlawn in Fairfax County. The Butlers then could use their gift to purchase slaves to work Audley.[15]

The scheme of Major Lewis to entice the Butlers to live in Virginia did not succeed. Instead, Caroline and Robert Bell increasingly influenced the Butlers to look south for their future. Caroline's letters to her brother during the 1820s and early 1830s, all of which he preserved, are a treasure, revealing an intelligent, articulate, and well-schooled woman. As a girl, she studied in Bethlehem, Pennsylvania, at the Moravian Seminary for Young Women. She is listed in the school in 1800, along with Colonel Thomas Butler's daughter, her first cousin Lydia Butler. Lydia Butler later married Stockley Donelson Hays, a nephew of Rachel Jackson. After the death of Isabella Butler Vinson in 1821, Caroline Bell became to Edward Butler a mother surrogate. She doted upon her family, all regrettably far away. Urgings to her brother to join the Bells in Louisiana began even before the Butlers married, when Butler was stationed in Baton Rouge in 1821–22. When she was in Florence, Alabama, visiting her sister Eliza Donelson in 1825, Caroline repeated the oath that she had made to her father to "love, cherish, and take good care of you as long as I should live." She assumed the role of Butler's mentor in the lore of their parents, grandparents, and other family members of whom her brothers knew little. Caroline made sure that Butler respected the family's military traditions. She gave him a prized British Grenadier cap that had been awarded his grandfather, Captain George Fowler, by Fowler's commander, Sir Robert Paget, following the Battle of Bunker Hill. And she agonized over the family bereavement due to the death of Anthony, in 1824. It added to the sorrow over losing her mother and to her anguish over their geographic separation. Although the Bells experienced occasional good fortune, Caroline often bemoaned her situation, which imprisoned her. When Robert Bell was off on business trips, she felt isolated and insecure, poorly provisioned, even impoverished. She "might as well be in the deserts of Arabia," Caroline once complained. Her sentiments were echoed by Robert Bell, who had undergone many economic difficulties. In Bell's estimation, "Poverty is said to be no crime, [but] it is a very disagreeable companion which has ever stuck close to me as a leach." He considered Edward Butler the sole person in his and Caroline's family "that possess[es] an independent spirit in monied matters, & that have a correct estimate of their value."[16]

The suasive ways and love that the couple bore for Edward Butler easily transferred to Frances following their marriage. After the Butlers visited Louisiana from 1827 into the next year, Caroline described her husband's warm reaction to Frances and his delight "with the interest she seemed to take in the *plantation* affairs. . . . She knows now, more of the process of sugar than half the people in this country." Butler, too, happily noted that Frances "is charmed with the [Mississippi River] coast," and in August 1827, even before her visit, Frances advised her father that she wished to move to Louisiana. There, she wrote, Butler would be relieved of "confinement to his desk," and the family could prosper and afford to give their young son the best education. In Louisiana, Frances also would show Major Lewis "what an industrious person I intend to be."[17] She had little desire to move back to Virginia and live under close parental watch.

Nelly Lewis viewed her daughter Frances's talents and fortitude with skepticism. She considered the refined upbringing that she had given Frances to be inadequate preparation for life on a slave-operated sugar plantation. But Frances Butler anticipated—even insisted on—choosing her future home and making other family decisions. Their late-1827 visit to Louisiana occurred during a season when southern Louisiana's climate is often mild, in contrast with harsh northern winters. She and Butler no doubt were inclined to overlook faults with the climate of "the coast." The couple disregarded the widespread and already severe epidemics in the Gulf South. They both praised the region's merits to her father, who suffered from gout, eye trouble, and other ailments in Virginia's cold winters. And they encouraged him also to move to Louisiana, where Colonel Lewis surely would "prolong his life." Frances liked the landscape and demonstrated a high intelligence and a degree of observation that helped her quickly develop an understanding of the local economy. Given the responsibilities that she would share with Butler in the management of the plantation, a grasp of the sugar cane industry would be useful.

The Butlers' search for land in Louisiana was under way even before mid-1827, when Butler received advice from Bell about acquiring land "near us," in St. John the Baptist Parish. His decision to enter agriculture was common for military men in the 1820s. They included future president Zachary Taylor, who combined occupations and sought improvement in his social position. A partnership with Robert Bell did not materialize at that time, but the Butlers increasingly committed to the prospect of it. Early in 1828, Butler wrote Major Lewis from Louisiana that he anticipated being "a rich man" as a sugar planter within five years after leaving the service of his country. He then could acquire the sort of status that his mentor Andrew Jackson attained and that increasingly defined southerners. His marriage and fatherhood were steps taken; now he must own slaves, achieve wealth, and become one with the planter class. On this same visit to the Bells, Frances Butler discovered that she was pregnant again. Only three months along and after the Butlers missed their scheduled steamboat for the northbound voyage to Cincinnati, Frances miscarried, giving birth to stillborn twin girls. She received the care of Butler and his sister and "most kind & excellent nurses." Nelly Lewis relayed word from Frances that by the fifth day her daughter "was then sitting up at work, & was doing uncommonly well. . . . My child is adored by all around her."[18]

While convinced that a good life awaited them in Louisiana, the Butlers remained for the time committed to the army. The relocation of General Gaines to the Eastern Department took Butler to Washington City during much of 1828 and 1829. He labored with topographical matters and provided sketches of harbors and forts to General Gaines. Correspondence to him frequently was addressed to Woodlawn Plantation, near Alexandria, where Frances was happily staying. Except for July 1829, when he visited Canada, Butler worked nearby. They called upon her Custis kin at Arlington, across the Potomac from Washington City; Butler may have observed Jackson's first swearing-in ceremony (Jackson fled the raucous celebration following his inauguration); and life was tempered by furloughs that allowed the Butlers to attend family excursions to the Lewis farm in the Shenandoah Valley. A new son, also named for his father, arrived on June 4, 1829, while the Butlers resided at Woodlawn. The child soon became a Lewis household darling.[19]

In late 1829, Gaines was transferred west and set up headquarters in Nashville. By mid-January 1830, Butler was on his way there by coach, via Danville, Virginia, unaccompanied. Although his family planned to meet him in Tennessee, Butler remained in Nashville only until mid-summer, when he requested and received from the War Department another furlough. By then Butler had made known to his superiors his intentions to quit the army. Adjutant General Roger Jones attempted to dissuade Butler, hoping that he "may find stronger inducement to continue in the Army." Butler was back at Woodlawn, reunited with Frances and their son, in early July.[20]

Affording the cost of a change of occupation presented a major hindrance. The Butlers first had to collect on the Erwin note that was due in 1828, and that task proved difficult. It is illustrative of how complicated and chance-ridden financial affairs were in America. As early as 1825, the Bells found Joseph Erwin, who was well into his sixties, to be mentally imbalanced, drinking heavily, and in financial distress. Writing in November 1825 to her brother, Caroline Bell referred to Erwin as their "unfortunate friend." Soon after the Butlers moved to Cincinnati in 1826, Major Lewis grew concerned about Erwin's finances and through Butler sought information about Erwin from the Bells. Repeated and disastrous floods engulfed his properties. Home Place Plantation and the adjoining Evergreen, where his daughter Eliza (Mrs. Nicholas) Wilson lived, remained inundated from three levee crevasses as of July 2, 1828. Erwin eventually was forced to sell Home Place to Durham Tudor Hall of St. Bernard Parish. Hall paid $55,000 cash, assumed mortgages totaling $106,000, and became obligated to Erwin for the remaining $59,000 of the total $220,000 purchase price. The Butlers' trip to Louisiana in 1827–28 had been prompted partly so that Butler might receive payment of the bond interest that was owed him, Frances, and Major Lewis. When the collection proved impracticable, Bell on behalf of Butler and Lewis sought payment on the bonds, advised Butler on ways to enforce the obligation, and reported on Erwin's financial status. Exasperated by the chronic delay in payment on his debts, Bell concluded that Erwin was "a great shuffler." But as a close friend of the Erwins as well as someone concerned over the financial interests of Lewis and Butler, Bell accepted the Erwin family's request to become an executor of Joseph Erwin's estate.[21]

Joseph Erwin's financial situation seemed too serious to allow him to become additionally obligated to anyone. While he was undergoing bouts of "melancholy," however, another transaction transpired that would have future significance for the Butlers: Robert Bell gained Erwin's assistance in acquiring some valuable property in March of 1826, in Iberville Parish, at what was thought to be the low price of $30,000. The sale involved land that belonged to Philip Thomas and his wife of New York, and according to Caroline Bell it was "a beautiful plantation with forty negroes." Having a frontage on the Mississippi of six arpents, with a depth of forty arpents, it provided a healthy location. The plantation was not adjacent to marshes or deep swamp, as was the case with the downriver St. John the Baptist property on which the Bells had been living. It was situated on the right bank of the river only about seven or eight miles below Erwin's home. The sale consideration took the form of six notes signed by Robert Bell of equal $5,000 amounts, which were assigned to the vendors. The notes were payable at the New Orleans Branch of the Bank of the United States to Joseph Erwin and by him to a factor known as John Hagan and Co. Probably because Erwin owed Bell for losses Bell incurred in the earlier Grosse Tête partnership, all of the notes were endorsed by Erwin and secured the sale of the plantation. The first note was paid promptly, in June of 1827, but the others were not paid until 1832, when a full release was given.[22] The Bells' acquisition became their long-sought permanent home; it, too, was the magnet that attracted the Butlers.

Robert Bell bought his land both for himself and for his brother, George, who continued their business association in Louisiana and in Nashville. In the late summer of 1827, however, George Bell contracted yellow fever and became sick while on a trip to Natchez to sell a plantation on behalf of Joseph Erwin. Returning in a state of debilitation to the Erwin residence in Plaquemine, the ailing Bell died there on September 11. He had no written will and no heirs other than his brother. When George Bell's succession was probated in late 1829, Robert Bell acquired his brother's half-interest in the Thomas tract and twenty-six of the slaves for $7,646, thus becoming sole owner.[23]

The Butlers must have wondered whether they ever would achieve their plans. By January 1829, Erwin was living with his daughter Eliza Wilson, who described him "now once more completely deranged his sufferings . . . beyond description." Caroline Bell saw him in early April, after which she wrote Butler that Erwin, confined to his bedroom, appeared emaciated and miserable, and was deranged on "some subjects." By mid-month, Joseph Erwin was dead; he had committed suicide. He had lost the Home Place residence the previous year, and it and the three thousand-acre plantation were occupied by the new owner, Durham Hall. Somehow, before Erwin's death in the spring of 1829, Lewis and Butler, helped by Robert Bell, persuaded Erwin to pay part of the interest owed on the three bonds. On October 28, 1828, Major Lewis and Butler collected $1,120 and $560, respectively. The principal amount of the unpaid bonds fortunately still constituted a first mortgage on the land and slaves on the former Erwin estate. No doubt the Butlers and Major Lewis thought that Hall would be more reliable in paying the debts represented by their notes.[24]

In early 1829, even before the death of Erwin, the Bells moved to their new property in Iberville Parish. Their holdings included seventy-six slaves and were by far the most impressive in the immediate neighborhood. Caroline Bell commenced establishing order in the house, tending the sick workers, and planting orange, myrtle, live oak, and magnolia trees, as well as flowers and shrubs. Her plans included raising the house (evidently an older cottage, on short piers) and adding on to it. The Butlers thought that they would be able finally to form their partnership with the Bells and acquire their land and slaves. In order to establish their line of credit, the Butlers assigned Frances's note in pledge to the merchant banker Hagan and Co. and its partner Thomas Barrett of New Orleans in late February 1829. Several attempts to complete the business arrangements failed, however, partly due to miscommunications between the Bells, Butlers, and Lewises; they found that the great distance and delays in communication were insuperable. Entreaties again were made by Robert Bell to the Butlers to join the Bells, and Bell wrote Butler that "I feel the want of a friend, to whom I could confide & tell all things freely. I know in you I should find that person." Robert Bell had lacked any such confidant since the loss of his brother, George. Bell once more pointed out to Butler how the Butlers' own interests would be served by their coming to Louisiana. Bell depended as well upon the Erwin debt repayment for his own financial needs. Furthermore, Major Lewis agreed to sell twenty-five slaves to Bell from Woodlawn. Although that arrangement fell through, it was evidence of the participation of Lewis in the Butler plans for Louisiana. He intended to make a profit and to relieve the growing strain of maintaining Woodlawn Plantation.[25]

Wishing to address financial needs of all the parties, Bell and Hall made a trip to New Orleans in early 1830 to visit bankers and redeem the Erwin bonds. But Bell lacked physical possession of the note certificates as well as the power of attorney from both Butler and Lewis. Without them and evidence of payment of the interest, Bell was unable to have the banks honor a request to redeem the notes or to use them as collateral for a loan. In addition, Bell remained tied down with the finances and operation of his leased plantation in St. John the Baptist Parish. He missed a chance to acquire more land adjoining his Iberville place and experienced financial hardships due to the previous season's poor sugar cane crop. After a second trip to the city in March proved equally unsatisfactory, Bell advised Butler, then in Nashville, to wait until the autumn of 1830, when he should visit in person. Filing a lawsuit to execute on the bonds was determined to be too expensive, and collection had to be delayed. Caroline Bell reminded Butler that he should be assured of the notes' security by reason of the high value placed on the former Erwin plantation and its slaves.[26]

Drawn by loyalty to and regard for his sister and her husband, Butler was attracted to the neighborhood of the Bells because of an additional family responsibility. As a half-brother of the much younger Susan Vinson, Butler partly assumed the burden of her education. Their mother, Isabella, had died in August 1821 while Isabella and Susan visited the Bells in St. James Parish, Louisiana. After Isabella was buried "on the [Bayou] Lafourche," Susan lived in the Bell household as Caroline's charge. Caring for her own children and managing a household, ministering to ill slaves, and overseeing the plantation during Robert Bell's absence, Caroline found herself unable to raise Susan. She called on Butler to help financially. In her pleas for him to visit, she stressed Susan's personal appeals to her adored relative. Unable to find in the area appropriate schooling for her, Caroline placed Susan in a boarding school in Nashville. It was under the oversight of "Mrs. and Dr. Berry from Salem, Massachusetts, formerly the first teachers in the female academy." Butler paid a portion of the cost of the school, which was expensive. While in Nashville en route to Louisiana in November 1827, for example, he provided Berry with $200 as part payment of Susan's board and tuition between October 1824 and June 1826. In the spring of 1830, nineteen-year-old Susan was joined in Louisiana by a friend, Margaret Gordon. Writing on April 28 to Butler, who then was in Nashville, Caroline informed him that the two young ladies were en route back to Tennessee. Caroline thought he would find Susan much improved in appearance and urged him to be considerate to the girl and encourage her to greater study. Caroline wished, as well, that Susan Vinson was "well married to some clever fellow."[27] Soon thereafter, probably in June, Caroline was on her way to be with Susan. Until the following December 1830, she stayed with her and other relatives in and near Nashville and visited her oft-ailing sister Eliza Eleanor (Mrs. John) Donelson in Florence, Alabama. Bell, unable to join Caroline and Susan because of plantation business, found their absence difficult. He complained that he had been "too long in this climate."[28]

It is certain that the Bells' protégé, Butler, did not appreciate how complex and hard life would be on a sugar plantation. But the end to the Butlers' task of finding land in Louisiana was not far off. After Caroline's long absence, during which Robert Bell represented Butler and himself, Butler arrived at the Bells on New Year's Eve, 1830. He wrote Frances of his and Bell's continued uncertainty over whether the notes would be honored. A new complication was the recent destruction by fire of the Home Place sugar mill. Collection appeared hopeless, as Hall's ability to pay off the bonds had been damaged. There now was some land available near his sister and brother-in-law, and a means of paying for the land—other than using the cash or credit from the Erwin notes—would have to be found. In mid-February 1831, Butler at last was able to finance his project partly using two notes totaling $1,800 representing obligations to Bell. With his endorsement, the notes were assigned to the vendors. Additionally, an $8,000 mortgage was given, which both Butler and Bell were jointly obligated to pay off in three equal installments by March 3, 1834. The long-desired and -planned land acquisition occurred on February 19, 1831.[29]

Butler's new plantation consisted of two modest-sized tracts in Iberville Parish adjoining the Bells and fronting the Mississippi River. The land was planted in forty acres of ratoon cane and sufficient "seed" cane to plant another twenty acres. The upriver parcel sold to Butler by Joseph Henry (or Henri) measured three arpents in width fronting on the river and extended back from the river forty arpents. Its side lines opened two and one-half degrees. The second tract, located not far downstream but separated from Henry's land by property of another landowner, was acquired from Victorian Allain. One and one-half arpents wide, it also extended back forty arpents, with a one-degree opening of the side lines. The property description in the Henry sale included a new, wooden "sugar house and works for other sugar making," which, with "mill and fixings," cost Butler $3,200. The mill "opens to about ten acres . . . on the back land." Henry and Allain, evidently partners, wanted to replace the mill machinery they sold to Butler. Therefore, Butler paid a cash consideration of $9,800 and additionally was to "furnish a sugar mill . . . on any plantation of the vendors in this parish that they may designate." Estimated by Butler to be worth $500, the mill parts were specified in such a manner that the dimensions of the new mill would be similar to the one that he acquired. Butler had until August to comply, or else to forfeit the existing sugar mill. By March 27, 1833, all financial obligations were met and the mortgagees were released.[30]

In order to cultivate his plantation, Butler estimated that he required twenty-five "Negro men." He obtained slaves almost simultaneously with the land acquisition through a purchase of thirty-eight slave adults and children. The seller was Anne Marie Barnes, a widow of Colonel Richard Povall of nearby Ascension Parish, and she received $14,000. According to an 1830 estimate by the Agricultural Society of Baton Rouge, the normal investment then for a slave was $600. If the figure is fairly accurate for 1831, Butler's average cost of $368 per slave represented a bargain. Of the thirty-eight slaves, seventeen adults and one infant were mortgaged to Major Lawrence Lewis for $4,666. His father-in-law's loan assisted Butler in the slave purchase. The $9,334 remainder of the purchase seems to have been financed with funds that had been preserved in the first Erwin note owned by the Butlers. The note was the property of Frances, assigned in pledge to Thomas Barrett in 1828. Butler's intent was to acquire another one hundred acres of public land to the rear of the existing property. Butler was concerned about an imbalance in his partnership. He believed that after the additional land purchase, and when he obtained laborers, "I shall then be somewhat on a footing with Mr. Bell, and I shall feel less reluctant in becoming his partner, upon terms of equality."[31]

The still-unresolved problem of the repayment of the principal on the all-important notes was soon to be determined, with assistance from Lavinia Erwin, Joseph's widow. The difficulties suffered by Durham Hall at Home Place opened some doors for Lavinia, who was one of Joseph Erwin's heirs. With Hall in financial straits due to the loss of his sugar mill and his inability to produce sugar, the Erwin family had a chance at regaining their old home. Having signaled her intention to acquire the family property, Lavinia experienced difficulty in obtaining credit. The bankers who held the mortgage on Home Place did not want to risk financing any sale to her. After all, they would be secured only by a second mortgage, because the longstanding Joseph Erwin notes acquired by Lawrence Lewis primed all other debts secured by the land and slaves. In the meantime, Bell and Butler, increasingly impatient about the unpaid notes, threatened to sue. As of April 10, 1831, the matter still hung over all parties. Colonel Andrew Hynes of Nashville was Lavinia Erwin's representative and son-in-law, married to Ann Erwin. Hynes wrote to the Bank of Louisiana acknowledging the patience of Colonel Lewis and appealing for a loan to Mrs. Erwin of sufficient sums to pay off the debt as well as to acquire Home Place and settle obligations regarding slaves.[32]

Within days, the long-held Erwin notes were sold to one Nathaniel Rime of New York City. His agent in New Orleans, Archibald Gracie, then paid to Thomas Barrett, as assignee of the Butler-owned note, and Lawrence Lewis the principal due of $28,000 plus interest. Rime immediately assumed the role of creditor against the Hall (formerly Erwin) property. Of significance in the act of assignment was the intervention of Colonel Hynes, on behalf of Lavinia Erwin. He recited that "after having read the above assignment declared that the said Mrs Erwin being actually or intending shortly to become the proprietor of said plantation, & slaves, now in the name of Durham Tudor Hall, . . . and considering herself as being therein directly interested, hold herself through her said agent duly notified of the present act of assignment."[33]

By June 11, 1831, Home Place again belonged to the Erwins. They also persuaded the Tennessean John Craighead, married to Lavinia's daughter Jane Erwin (the widow of Charles Dickinson by her first marriage), to manage the various plantations. Lavinia reacquired another property, named Irion, sold a few years earlier by her husband to Robert Anderson Irion. She had been able to obtain financing from the Bank of Louisiana to buy Home Place. The sale included 236 named slaves and was paid for with $87,000 in cash; the Erwin children and survivors of deceased children assumed numerous other mortgages that totaled over $200,000. Lavinia Erwin had attempted earlier to reward her son-in-law Andrew Hynes for his assistance by offering him a one-fourth interest in return "for his services . . . rendered in managing and settlement of said estate." But ultimately, all family members participated in the ownership and assumed the estate's debts.[34]

One other thing remained before Butler and his family could head south: a formal resignation from the U.S. Army. By practice and rule, he made arrangements for leaves of absence with his commander, General Gaines, who charitably allowed his aide time to travel and to visit family. Once, when Gaines himself was away, Butler sought permission for furlough from General in Chief Alexander Macomb; and in 1830, Butler looked to Adjutant General Roger Jones for his leave. Both times, he traveled to Louisiana to negotiate for land and slaves and to make the final efforts at collecting on the bonds. The arrangements with Jones were to last as long as General Gaines was absent, and Butler needed to extend the time of his leave. Gaines informally agreed and eventually made official his permission for Butler's absence. He wrote on April 2, 1831, that "I will now redeem my promise by you without the usual forms (or) orders, desiring to consider yourself on furlough until the 31 of May, next month." Butler resigned from the army on May 28, 1831, after fifteen years of service that included four years at the U.S. Military Academy. General Gaines would miss his trusted aide: "I should not do justice to your merits & past services, were I to withhold from you, or from the President of the United States, when a fit decision offers, the assurance that your qualifications and industry are equal to any duties of the highest branch of the General Staff in peace or war."[35]

Having accomplished his business in Louisiana, Butler joined his family at Audley Farm, where they were visiting Lorenzo Lewis. While in Virginia, the Butlers and Nelly Lewis associated a young artist living in Alexandria, John Gadsby Chapman, who began work on a portrait of Edward Butler Jr. Nelly was determined to have something by which to remember him; she was distressed to see her daughter and grandson leave. Writing on July 10, Caroline Bell advised Frances Butler on what to bring to Louisiana. She also cautioned Frances not to expect comforts of the sort that she enjoyed at Woodlawn, or at Audley.

Caroline hoped to remodel her house, which the Butlers would share until they constructed a residence. Also expressing her optimism, she wished especially that she and Robert Bell might be able finally to spend summers away, so that Mr. Bell could restore his health. Reminiscent of some of Nelly Lewis's concerns, Caroline wondered if Frances understood the difficulties typically experienced by a Louisiana plantation mistress in running the house, particularly in the kitchen and laundry. She directed Frances to have Butler purchase a new "cooking machine," which she herself hoped to acquire from France. Caroline stressed that Butler should buy a male cook, because "it is a terrible thing for a poor woman to stand over a fire from morning till night in this climate."[36]

It is helpful to summarize how Frances and Edward Butler came to forsake military lives and come to far-off Louisiana. Following his exciting trip with General Gaines to Georgia in 1825, Butler saw military duty mainly from behind a desk. He was restless and tired of administrative work. His old army friends were elsewhere. In 1826, Rawlins Lowndes, Butler's associate aide-de-camp, married Julia Livingston's sister, Gertrude Laura Livingston; he alone remained of Butler's West Point comrades. "Age and intercourse with the world," Lowndes wrote Butler, made old friends into mere acquaintances. Having resigned from the army in 1830, Lowndes was newly occupied as a rice planter in South Carolina.[37]

Family pressure on both sides played a role in persuading the Butlers to remake their lives. Nelly and Lawrence Lewis, concerned about Butler's financial wherewithal, touched a sensitive chord in Butler. With little in the way of family inheritance and an uncertain future in the military, he lacked status and security. Louisiana held almost certain prospects for earning a good living and for proving his worthiness. The Butlers' decision to settle near the Bells in 1831 answered the prayers of Robert and, particularly, Caroline Bell, who longed for family to be nearby. For Edward Butler, it filled a need to rejoin a long-separated sister. Without the constant love, commitment, and encouragement of the Bells, the Butlers probably would not have given Louisiana much consideration.

The choice to migrate to Louisiana resulted from several years of thought, discussion, investigation, and constructing a financial groundwork. Decisive help came from Butler's in-laws, and especially from Major Lewis, whose generosity allowed the young couple to make the investment in land and to equip it with slave workers. The death of George Bell created a vacuum in the Bell plantation partnerships and a strong need by Robert Bell for someone to assist in the business. The personal and financial collapse of Joseph Erwin at first delayed but, ironically, ultimately aided the Butlers in their move. And General Gaines, whom Butler served faithfully for many years, encouraged Butler and accommodated him with leaves of absence to attend to family affairs.

Most important, Edward G. W. and Frances Parke Butler both demonstrated resilience and independence. When he could visit Louisiana during intervals between army assignments, Butler acquired useful business contacts and knowledge about the Iberville neighborhood. Frances proved steadfast in her will to bring her new family to a land far from her origins. Awaiting her were physical and social environs and roles that were very different from those of her Virginia past. The couple was to need these attributes, and more, in the coming years.

4

A Sugar Plantation Family of Iberville Parish

The Butlers, 1831–1840

Notwithstanding his military heritage and his association with Andrew Jackson, Butler remained dissatisfied. His resources and social station contrasted with those of his in-laws, Lawrence and Nelly Lewis. Jackson and General Gaines allowed Butler entrée into the highest levels of the American military and political establishments, but he and Frances were receptive to the call of a new occupation and to the allures of Louisiana.[1] As he informed his father-in-law in late October 1827, the demand for sugar "must increase with the population of the world," and the regions for growing it were limited. The cotton market would fluctuate, thought Butler, but not that of sugar. Like so many moving from the North, Butler was convinced that the Deep South, and the fertile valley of the Mississippi River in Louisiana, in particular, offered the good life and wealth to support it. Frances Butler, too, held few qualms about living distant from family and old friends. She wanted "to give our boy the advantage of a good education" and to promote change for her industrious husband, who "suffers from confinement to his desk."[2] How they could attain such goals, and whether their grasp matched their reach, are primary topics in the next few chapters.

The two modest-sized tracts acquired in 1831 received the name Dunboyne Plantation, after Butler's ancestral lands in Ireland. The properties faced the right descending bank of the Mississippi River in Iberville Parish, downstream from Baton Rouge. Because none of the existing dwellings was adequate, the Butlers either had to construct a new home or renovate some existing house. They planned to reside at first with the Bells on their larger adjoining property; for a while, sharing a house was more than satisfactory.

During the late autumn of 1831, the Butlers and their two-year-old son were en route from their Lewis kin in Virginia, first overland and then by steamboat.

From Louisville the boat trip on the Ohio and Mississippi took a long nine days, plagued by low water and foggy nights. The Butlers suffered a severe loss when the riding mare and fillies that they were bringing with them died after taking ill with symptoms Butler referred to as the "mad staggers." He attributed their condition to the "cold taken on board the steamboat, which produced inflammation on the brain." Having invested in and kept horses at Audley Farm with Lorenzo Lewis, Butler was heartbroken. "Their loss to me has been that of friends," he wrote to Major Lewis.

At this time of year, traffic on those major rivers was lessening, but the family was treated to a grand adventure. Along the Ohio River, deep, dense forests were interspersed with small farms and villages. The autumn leaves were mostly gone, and the air was crisp. The waters of the Ohio as described by the contemporary traveler Timothy Flint were "calm and placid and except when full . . . limpid to a degree." The Ohio contrasted starkly with the more dangerous Mississippi River: "Its [the Mississippi's] face . . . is always turbid; the current every where sweeping and rapid; and it is full of singular boils, where the water, for a quarter of an acre, rises with a strong circular motion, and a kind of hissing noise, forming a convex mass of waters above the common level, which roll down and are incessantly renewed. The river seems always in wrath, tearing away the banks on one hand with gigantic fury, with all their woods to deposit the spoils in another place." Although the Butlers had experienced the trip in 1827, the excitement of their voyage south was high. As they proceeded, they saw vast river bottoms, lakes, and "gloomy" cypress swamps that were flooded each spring, giving way to different, thicker vegetation. Finally, large plantations began to appear, and the river showed great sandbars on inner sides of bends, and loess bluffs on the left descending bank. Suddenly, the violent, crude views of under-the-hill Natchez came into sight, followed later by Baton Rouge with her prominently situated five-structure, two-story U.S. Army barracks.

The steamboat carrying the Butler family presented a "prodigious establishment, with all its fittings of deck common, and ladies' cabin apartments." Their needs were attended to by a servant similar to what the writer-tourist Washington Irving depicted on his own voyage: an "old negro steward—very black, with bright madras handkerchief on head—large feet, gold earrings—shirt collar up to his ears—white jacket and trousers, chequered apron to his armpits." One of hundreds navigating the rivers, the steamboat passed many flatboats of different sizes, manned by colorful crews [which that year included Abraham Lincoln on his second float to New Orleans]. The boats hauled autumn harvest produce, livestock, poultry, lumber, whiskey, and tobacco. Trading and selling goods along the way, flatboats and steamboats both normally moored nightly along the banks, or at landings from which were springing small trade centers. Frances and Edward Butler heard the sounds of livestock, the laughter of boat crews and their fiddle playing, the chants and chorusing of Negro boat men. They saw the washerwomen hanging out clothes, the smoke of cooking fires, the river's undulations made by boats. The couple experienced the sharp light of stars and moon and the "silent, primeval forest sleeping" along each side of the river: in Irving's words, "still forest—forest—forest." The Mississippi long had offered the "cheapest, easiest, fastest, and climatologically congenial way to get Western shipments to market." It symbolized, too, the restless emigrant looking for better land—but also to satisfy a desire for a "new country, and in new views and combinations of things, something that we crave but have not."

When they arrived at the Bells in December, Butler found the 1831 crop to have been harvested. Because Butler's delayed trip south prevented him from participating, Bell surely planted, cultivated, and brought in and processed the crop on land that Butler acquired from Henry and Allain the prior winter. The Bells' "rolling time" proved better than most in the neighborhood, partly a result of their new "sugar house," as any mill was called. It was handy and modern, powered by steam, featuring innovations that were unavailable to smaller planters. Bell planned to undertake ditching and to make bricks for a mill "purgery"—a place in which sugar placed in hogsheads was drained of molasses—and for slave dwellings.[3]

As the year 1832 passed and Butler enthusiastically began his career in agriculture, the happy tone was set by the birth on February 7 of Eleanor Isabella Butler. Named for Butler's mother and grandmother and called Sissy, she soon became a favorite of her father. In March he described her to Major Lewis, who was recovering from influenza and gout, saying she was "my very *sweet* and *beautiful* daughter." And again, when Butler reported to the Lewises in August, Sissy was "your incomparable grandaughter in beauty and intelligence. . . . Her uncle Bell and herself are great friends."[4]

In Cincinnati, a place of "fine houses, lovely gardens, polished society, much commerce" amid a country in which "you are so entirely alive," Frances Butler had found friendship with Barbara Gaines. The Gaines and the Butlers were convivial, and Caroline Bell described Barbara as "the warmest companion of . . .

[my] childhood." But having visited the Bells in late 1827 and early 1828, Frances became enraptured by the South Louisiana countryside and climate and fascinated by its sugar economy. Now there permanently, she quickly came to love her new Iberville Parish surroundings. When in May 1832 she commiserated with her father on his "continued indisposition," Frances counseled him to spend the winters in Louisiana, so as to "prolong your life many, many years." While the Bells were prepared to do all they could to make a visit by the Lewises a comfortable one, Frances set her sights on soon building their own "nice pretty house, large enough to contain you all in comfort." Her parents would relish "this place, old soil, these trees—the beautiful country and culture and manufacture of the Cane."[5] The Butlers were enjoying their first year along the Mississippi River coast of Louisiana.

Butler set about learning the complexities of his new occupation. Despite a longtime interest in politics originating in his associations with Jackson's family and friends, little thought was given to the Old General's campaign and reelection or even to local politics. By early March 1832, the planting of sugar cane (in those days a late winter/early spring task) was almost complete, and Bell negotiated to sell the sugar and molasses from 1831. A flatboat cargo of lime for use in field preparation and soil fertility, or in the milling process, was bought at $1.12½ per barrel in exchange for molasses valued above the market, at 24 cents a gallon. Major Lewis, a creditor of both Butler and Bell, wanted details of the farming and sugar manufacturing operation; Butler provided them.[6]

Along with the creation of state and local banks, available credit distinguished Louisiana's business climate in the 1830s. Beginning a series of dizzying financial arrangements, Butler looked into buying stock in the newly formed Union Bank of Louisiana, his purchase to be secured by his land and slaves. State banking institutions exerted a weighty influence on local and regional economies by providing essential credit. In time and with better communications, eastern and Deep South banks more closely integrated and coordinated operations. The Union Bank and the Citizens Bank, with which Butler associated early on, were established to assist sugar planters suffering from several bad crops and from lower protective tariffs. Planters like Butler who subscribed to the initial bank stocks typically paid for their shares through mortgages on their property, which each bank then used as collateral to acquire state bonds. They in turn were used in Europe to raise money for beginning their banking operations. Branches were set up in local areas, helping planters whose access to the private credit market often was restricted by New Orleans merchants and factors.

Once his assets were valued, Butler reviewed his financial situation for Major Lewis: "My land, for which I gave $10,200, was valued . . . at about $17,000, and the worst half of my negroes, which are worth about two-thirds as much as those mortgaged to you, were valued at $9,300. . . . You may recollect that I gave but $14,000 for the whole of them." Butler counted on producing outstanding crops. He estimated that he would harvest four hundred hogsheads of corn and forty-five hundred bushels of peas and pumpkins for animal and human consumption. The land appeared to be a cornucopia, and horses and wild cattle were "passing daily from Mex and Tex to NO." No doubt they were driven on the two eighteenth-century "roads" into Iberville from the Atchafalaya River and further west. The roads terminated near the villages of Bayou Goula and Plaquemine. In a reference to Rezin Bowie, an Iberville resident and elder brother of the soon-notorious James Bowie, Butler reported that "Mr Bowie, who has been much in Texas, assures me that any number of horses can be procured there for one dollar a head."[7]

The Lewises awaited news and sent counsel and guidance. They were unfamiliar with Louisiana and uncertain if not distrustful of the environs of Dunboyne. Writing Frances in the spring of 1832, her nervous mother passed on advice of the family physician and friend, Dr. Henry Daingerfield: she and Butler should not build their own home until "you have well tried the climate, he much fears it is too bilious for your constitution." Frances was not to send her parents any expensive gifts, having "much to pay yet before you are perfectly independent." Nelly, interested in medicinal plants, wanted only "specimens of digital" and "rare and beautiful wild flowers," which Frances must ship "wrapped in brown paper." Under no circumstances was she to allow "Sonny [E.G.W. Butler Jr.] or any one go for them liable to be injured by snakes."[8]

Despite Nelly's cautions, the Butlers began renovating a house during the winter of 1832–33. Butler wrote Major Lewis in January 1833 to express his gratitude "for the trouble you both have taken to aid me" and to extend the Lewises an invitation to visit, "provided I stop the *leaks in our old house.*" The renovations at first may have been modest, because the structure was the very same in which Robert and Caroline Bell had been living and which they shared with the Butlers. The Bells were in the process of relocating their holdings downriver to St. James Parish. Recent archaeological investigations have placed the Butlers' residence within the property which Robert and George Bell bought in 1826. It was the house in which Philip Thomas lived during the 1810–26 time frame. Some 100 to 150 yards away from the Butlers, on the downriver side facing the river, was a sizeable slave quarter. Until the Bells' departure, the cabins were shared by Bell's slaves and those purchased by Butler from the Povall estate.[9]

Among Butler's activities was moving another house—perhaps the Henry residence—from the front of their property back to the sugar house. It may have been intended for the chief worker in the mill, known as the sugar maker. Butler was acquiring seed cane (also called "plant cane") from another plantation upriver and arranging its transport to Dunboyne by a "keelboat" out of the town of Plaquemine, the seat of government of Iberville Parish. The brig *Malaga* picked up the plantation's sugar and molasses to be shipped to and sold in Philadelphia, which became a frequent market for Butler's produce. He was not to forget his relatives: the *Malaga* carried a box of much-desired pecans for Nelly Lewis. Butler declined the subscription of stock of the Union Bank and decided to obtain a loan and to work free of all debt in a few years. He determined to acquire more field hands, as well as a cooper and "a *seamstress* & *washerwoman* for Frances." The Butlers rarely referred to domestic needs in correspondence, but they may have taken Caroline Bell's advice to obtain a male cook. Perhaps Lucinda, who accompanied the Butlers to Louisiana, added those duties to child care. Frances obtained at least a portion of her domestic supplies locally. Sales receipts from May 1832 show acquisitions of cotton clothing and cambric, thread, and small "muggs" from B. F. Owen in Plaquemine, some eight miles upriver.[10]

The need for field hands was caused by the Bells' decision to sell out to the Butlers and locate elsewhere. The Bells had implored the Butlers to move to Louisiana and to associate in business, but Robert Bell evinced an ever-restless quality, looking for better places and arrangements. He prepared to resettle his slaves to another plantation downriver from Iberville, in St. James Parish. About a half-day carriage ride from Dunboyne, it originally was called Pope Plantation. Giving it a new name, "White Hall," Bell went into business with an old associate, sugar commission merchant Thomas Barrett. He already had undertaken improvements and begun a search for an overseer. Because the families' separation failed to revive Caroline's correspondence with her brother, who religiously preserved all documents, there is little evidence of what exactly prompted Bell to forsake his partnership with the Butlers. No longer would Caroline be near her relations, whom she adored and helped convince to come to Louisiana. Bells and Butlers living in the tight quarters of one house may have been an irritation, but there existed no apparent hard feelings or any serious disagreement; and the families exchanged visits over the decade. Perhaps Bell wished to assist the Butlers in expanding their holdings, because he willingly negotiated with Butler to buy out his property. Their arrangement more than tripled the Butlers' acreage.

Little wonder, then, that Butler, who shared the workforce with Bell on Dunboyne, felt pressured to find additional field hands, as well as the money to acquire them. In February 1833, Butler requested that his father-in-law locate and buy for him thirty slaves in Virginia. Lewis was instructed to purchase them even if he paid a premium and had to sell Frances Butler's Kanawha River land, which Nelly and Lawrence Lewis had given to Frances when she was married. In order to finance their purchase, Butler also awaited the loan from the Union Bank and obtained another loan from the Bank of Donaldsonville, at the parish seat of Ascension Parish, where Bayou Lafourche diverged from the Mississippi River. He expected to depart for Virginia soon in order to complete the acquisition of slaves.[11]

Butler initially hoped to go to New York and then to Virginia, but he was forced to delay his trip north. Writing to Major Lewis that he wanted to pay off the last two installments of the plantation mortgage, which Lewis held, Butler recorded that he would "take with me $8,000; which will enable me to buy negroes enough." He also contemplated exchanging the Kanawah property for at least a dozen slaves to be paid for partially on credit, partially with cash.[12]

The final decision to leave was not made until May 1833, when Butler determined to try first to seek slaves in Kentucky. If unsuccessful there, he would head across to Virginia via Frankfort, Lexington, and Maysville. Because Louisiana law prohibited the use of a formal agency arrangement in an out-of-state purchase, as a subterfuge Butler asked Lewis to deliver the slaves as a "present." Butler's search for more laborers was pressing. He had completed arrangements to buy the adjoining property, with its main residence, improved sugar mill, and cabins. The purchase price was $35,000, financed in part by the Bank of Louisiana. His deal with the Union Bank apparently fell through, but he borrowed $10,000 from the Bank of Donaldsonville, payable in eight years at 8 percent interest. Butler determined to use that amount to make an installment due of $2,666⅔ on the "property which I originally purchased" and still have $7,334 to use for the slaves. He would have to borrow another $3,000 from the same commission merchant, Thomas Barrett, with whom Bell was entering into a new partnership. He intended to acquire stock in the newly formed Citizens Bank to use as collateral to borrow enough to pay off all prior debts. In addition, Bell, the seller, owed Major Lewis $12,000 on his Iberville plantation, and Lewis made a donation to Frances of the promissory note of Bell. Because Lewis's note followed Butler's acquisition of the Bell land, Butler now was in debt to Frances, adding another to his growing list of obligations to her.[13]

On May 6, 1833, Butler carried with him $10,000 aboard the steamboat *Amulet* en route to Virginia. He had found a potential buyer, one Chamberlain of Maine, for the Kanawah land, for an expected price of $6,000. Butler asked Lewis to advertise for thirty hands of both sexes "with or without their usual encumbrances,—and children, old men & old women," who probably could be found in Richmond. Butler gaily reported to Lewis the developments at home: "I left Frances busily engaged tearing *up* floors and *down* chimneys, for the comfort and convenience of our visitors, *next winter.*" He no doubt received advice on slave trading from his relatives Robert Bell and Lawrence Lewis, as well as from Andrew Jackson and Joseph Erwin; all knew well the traffic in humans. And he was familiar with the slave markets of New Orleans and Washington City, where he visited or lived. Butler's decision to buy slaves in the Upper South and to ship them to Louisiana reflected common practice. Slaves were less expensive in Virginia than if obtained locally, and the coastal routes for bringing slaves south, especially from Norfolk and Baltimore, were long-established. Remaining in Virginia through most of June, Butler succeeded well. No sooner had he secured his purchase of the "finest lot of negroes ever shipped from Richmond . . . I am offered ($100) advances upon one man by a citizen of this place." Richmond bankers offered to lend him money. Butler asked Major Lewis to send on to him from Woodlawn a trunk of his personal items via the ship *Potomac*. They could be transferred at Norfolk aboard the same ship, the brig *Ajax*, on which Butler arranged for the slaves to be sent to Louisiana.[14]

Having acquired and arranged to ship his slaves, Butler left by stagecoach on June 21 from Richmond, traveled west to White Sulfur Springs, and then across the Alleghenies to the Ohio River at Guyandotte. He boarded a steamboat, the *Transport*, to Louisville, where, to remedy deficiencies in the stores at Dunboyne, he purchased supplies to be carried home with him. They included tow linen (a cloth made of short or broken fiber), a barrel of flour, two hogsheads of bacon, and five barrels of potatoes. After changing vessels, Butler endured a river trip south that was slowed by the steamboat having to pull "four large flatboats . . . —one loaded with lumber, two with corn, & the remaining one with sheep and beeves." Such tows, common practice on western rivers, were equivalent to freight as opposed to passenger trains and much impeded travel. Ever mindful of the great need for food for his labor force, which like most relied upon corn as a staple of its diet, Butler bought one of the flatboats of corn. It carried 1,000 bushels, and the $175 cost included the tow to the Dunboyne Plantation landing. On July 23, the *Ajax* and her cargo of laborers arrived in New Orleans—a place to which Major Lewis had cautioned him not to bring them due to cholera—after thirty days' journey from Norfolk. The slaves were on the plantation by 7:00 A.M. on July 25, ten days following Butler's own homecoming. All of them were in good health save one young girl, who had whooping cough. Butler wrote to Major Lewis of having paid over $13,000 for the twenty-eight slaves, two thirds of whom were young males, and he planned to add another two men (to bring the total expense up to $14,000).

Most of the costs for the slaves and their shipment were recorded in an account book kept by Lancaster, Denby and Company of Richmond, a receipt for which was retained by Butler. It provides insight into the economics of a slave acquisition from afar. The thirty slaves (a different, no doubt more accurate figure from what Butler reported to Lewis) came from several sellers, some of the slaves apparently originating at "Nottoway Plantation" in Virginia. An agent, or slave seller, named Smithers received a 1 percent commission as well as some cash for assisting the transport of slaves to Richmond and on to Norfolk, for which the steamboat fare was $45. Insurance for the value of the cargo, estimated at $15,000, cost Butler $187.50. Butler needed clothing, shoes, and food for his human cargo, as well as blankets and eating utensils. For his own return trip, Butler withdrew $145.42, and he bought port wine and whiskey to place aboard the *Ajax*. Not including the charges for the *Ajax* or for Butler's own stage and boat expenses, the total expenditure was $18,014.95, an average investment per slave of over $600.[15]

Despite the time and effort involved in traveling all the way to Virginia and back, Edward Butler showed business astuteness and saved money. In 1833, traders in New Orleans received about $800 apiece for male field hands brought from the Upper South. This price represented an increase from around $579 in 1830. For slaves shipped from Norfolk, the costs of transport and maintaining the slaves were about 15 percent of the price received. Butler's cost figures are not broken down by gender, making true comparisons difficult. By purchasing directly, Butler averaged a cost per slave in 1833 that was still less expensive than if he had shopped the New Orleans slave market.[16]

During Butler's absence, not only was Frances in charge of remodeling the house that was to be their home, but she alone managed the entire plantation. The task challenged her. Already relocated, the Bells also were away on a visit to

Nashville until early August. There being no one in the family to whom Frances could turn for assistance, she found her situation even more difficult after Butler let go of an overseer without securing another for the time he was absent. Frances thus had the responsibility of directing the labor force, which tended both food and market crops. Although the area suffered from cold weather the prior winter and excessive rains in May, the sugar cane in the newly ditched and cleaned fields appeared in June to show promise. It no longer required much cultivation and was partially "laid by" within the normal time of mid-June; the cane stalks were growing, and their leaves covered three-foot-wide "avenues." Only one more plowing was required on the rest of the crop, after which "earth to be drawn to it with the hoes." Land was being cleared, and oak, elm, and sweet gum wood was prepared for use as fuel in the sugar mill and for heating houses. Butler proudly wrote Major Lewis in mid-June that the crop's "extraordinary promise must be attributed to the superior management of my most sensible, rational and industrious wife." He probably was unaware of the presence of cholera in the neighborhood, a yearly threat to all residents of the lower Mississippi Valley, notably in 1833. The loss from cholera to the humanity and economy of a particular plantation could be devastating. In 1835, for instance, an outbreak on the Erwin plantation not far upstream from Dunboyne killed twenty-eight slaves in addition to the overseer. Upon his return, Butler found that "the neighborhood" was much in admiration of Frances for her administration of the plantation affairs. She especially deserved praise for protecting the slave force from the cholera that felled so many in Louisiana that summer.[17]

While the record of the particulars in the Butler household is minimal, Nelly Lewis became concerned as her daughter's responsibilities multiplied. Among those slaves upon whom Frances relied, Lucinda became the "mammy" of Edward G. W. Butler Jr., and of Isabel, devotedly caring for them and mending their clothes. When Lucinda died in 1853, Sonny lamented the loss of his nurse and friend, who had been a "precious gift" to his mother. "Good-bye, dear 'Mammy!'" the grieving youth wrote to his father from school in Massachusetts, "Your sufferings are at an *end*—and, *you* have received the reward of the *faithful*!!" The Butlers' precarious economic situation in the 1830s may have prevented their affording many house servants, causing Frances to undertake more on her own. Even so, there is little to show that she resented her domestic and plantation mistress tasks. The couple's correspondence remains relatively sanguine throughout the mid-1830s. Contrary to Nelly's observations, Frances's life at Dunboyne did not appear to be unbearable, nor that uncommon, even within her family circle. An example is the wife of her uncle George Calvert, Rosalie Stier Calvert, a close friend of Nelly Lewis. Calvert performed similar duties at her husband's Maryland plantation, named Riversdale. She recorded them: "The wines, the provisions, the servants' work, horses, carriages, garden, dairy—I am in charge of all that." In addition, "I have to supervise every thing, often cutting and fitting [clothing] myself," as well as educate children and create remedies for ill servants. Frances Butler had not been educated specifically for her new roles, but those roles were ordinary.[18]

Following her experience in supervising affairs on Dunboyne, Frances was prompted to express pride in her contributions. Writing Major Lewis in August 1833, she wished her parents to be there when the very first crop of Butler's *and* her own doing was harvested: "The cane crop is more promising than it has been for many years, I never look out at the fields without wishing for you—the cane is so rich and green, the earth is so closely covered with it—and there is such an air of strength,—I might almost say of grandeur about it—." Such delight with and hope for the crop, she further said, was shared by Edward. He was busy in the mill "setting his boilers" and placing additional kettles, or "pots." These were the iron receptacles of varying size and arranged in a row, which contained the cane juice for boiling and reduction to a thickness adequate for granulation. Frances observed that he intended to harvest and grind every stalk of cane.[19]

As of the end of 1833, the Butlers owned land fronting on the Mississippi River twelve and one-half arpents wide. The plantation included the original 1831 acquisition, the larger portion of which measured three arpents front on the Mississippi River by forty arpents in depth. It was separated from another, smaller tract on the downstream side by property that belonged to Francis Evan Bush, whose land was forty arpents deep and one and one-half arpents wide. Just below the Bush family tract was the lower Butler piece, also one and one-half by forty arpents. In addition, now the Butlers owned the adjacent upstream, eight-arpent-wide Bell plantation, which held their residence and the all-important sugar mill. In the rear of the plantation a "backlands" portion of sixty arpents in area that Bell acquired by patent from the United States made up the remainder. The Butlers owed considerable money—with Frances as spouse joining *in solido* in the mortgage process—for their lands and slaves. The recorded transactions in Iberville Parish show frequent juggling and refinancing of the debt throughout the time between 1831 and 1846. Influenced by Andrew Jackson,

Butler perceived debt as a condition to be dreaded, and he once expressed to his father-in-law an abhorrence of its "ill effects," which entailed "sacrifices of feeling, of honor, of happiness." But indebtedness was a reality common to most planters in the South Louisiana sugar region. In spite of planters' discomfort, an economic historian of the time has pointed out that the "debt often is incurred for productive purposes, to finance capital formation in an expanding economy. . . . Borrowing at 6 per cent in the expectation of earning 10 per cent is a burden that countless businessmen and farmers have happily assumed." With some irony, Major Lewis was involved with the Butlers and the Bells by reason of the mortgages he held on their plantations. He, too, relied upon the success of the sugar economy and in particular on the Butlers' operation.[20]

The Butlers and Lewises planned to reunite, but illness of Major Lewis and the delay in readying the Dunboyne residence prevented Frances from hosting her parents. Frustrated, Nelly Lewis complained that her husband would not leave home unless their family friend and physician Dr. Henry Daingerfield pushed him to it. In Nelly's opinion, living so distantly apart ordained her and Frances for unhappiness; she pined "to spend the winter with my poor child, & her precious babes."[21] The much-awaited first visit of several began in the late autumn of 1833 soon after Nelly grumbled to her Philadelphia friend Elizabeth Gibson that Frances endured the absence of Butler for three months "surrounded with cholera & alone among strangers." If Nelly Lewis was coming all the way to Louisiana to see her darlings, she was determined to stay the entire winter.[22]

Traveling by coach across the Alleghenies and by steamboat down the Ohio and Mississippi from Woodlawn Plantation to Iberville Parish took a long and tiring three weeks. Major Lewis, Nelly, and Angela arrived safely in early December 1833, and Nelly reported soon thereafter, and again in February 1834, to Gibson. Notable for its insight and detail, her letter is about a Louisiana that evoked both wonder and doubt in a skeptical Nelly Lewis:

> December 1833:
>
> She [Frances] likes this climate, and has been hitherto well, but . . . she is buried alive here. Her fine mind, her attainments are all thrown away. Hers is a life of domestic toil far from everyone of congenial tastes & habits. . . . I shall always hope & pray that my Darling Parke . . . remove to a home more congenial to her taste, more favorable to the improvement of her children.

> There are no schools, no churches here for many miles. Sunday among the French & Creoles indeed among the Americans too is like any other day. Pedlars go about, cake sellers, & they really appear to have no idea beyond this world & its enjoyments. . . . There are numbers of Indians living a few miles off. . . . Parke has been very kind to them & they often come, the women with baskets to sell & always present some to her & the children. . . . The men sometimes come & bring venison. They are almost naked & appear to be almost insensible to the cold.
>
> The Mississippi is more winding & noble river [than the Ohio], but it is as muddy as possible, the banks continually falling in . . . canes, trees &c slipping in the banks. . . .
>
> There are some splendid live oaks on this place. It spreads very far and produces a most delightful shade.

And in February 1834:

> The Planters are burning off the cane tops & we have all along the coast on both sides the most brilliant & beautiful fires at night. The Houses are so near each other on the river that it looks like a village on each side. . . . Innumerable steamboats, most of them very large & splendid, *ships* & *brigs* lached to small steamboats ply up & down between Natchez & New Orleans. . . . flat boats, sloops, *acres* of driftwood ever vary the scene. The public road passes by the Gate, just beyond is the Levee. . . . It is very pleasant to walk on the Levee & see the waves dashing along. . . . the grass is very green, hyacinths, jonquils & narcissus have been in bloom since Decr. & wild violets. The yard is full of mocking birds, red birds, & others. . . . The gentlemen say that no thing can be more delightful than riding by moonlight here. The nights are so very bright and in summer so very pleasant. . . . They have delightful Spanish saddles in this country which I think must be better than ours.[23]

Nelly described the Butlers' residence as "a small house, indeed quite a cottage," but "she has made it as neat as a band box, & we have quite comfortable rooms."

Nelly Lewis limited any enthusiasm for the Louisiana adventure on which Frances and her family were embarked. The promise of wealth and social comfort, but never achieving them; the idea that Frances was "wasting" talents and was "lost" to a foreign, uncongenial, foggy and damp, even deadly, place; Nelly's personal deprivation in being too far from her children—these are omnipresent in the letters to Gibson. Some of her pessimism, if not criticism, found expression within the Butler household on this and other visits. It became unwelcome particularly to Edward, whose keen sensibilities about his social standing and his responsibility to provide well for his family were intertwined with personal honor. Unrecognized at the time, Nelly Lewis set a course that would lead to a collision between her and Butler. Major Lewis, in contrast, and notwithstanding initial reluctance to make the trip, found Louisiana to his liking. Almost free from his bothersome gout and enjoying walks and horseback rides along the levee, her husband, Nelly wrote Gibson, "is delighted with the country."[24]

The Butlers established deep roots and fully believed in their future. A look at their Iberville Parish plantation business as well as their personal lives helps to show just how they managed. From the time that Butler acquired the Bells' plantation until 1846, he accounted for "nett proceeds" of his crops. The profits fluctuated considerably (although the record is not always clear or complete), and proceeds are recorded by "crop year" rather than by calendar. Sales of the harvest of 1833, for example, were from the fall of 1833 and winter of 1833–34, and Butler made only $5,185.08 from the 1833 crop. His figures were echoed by the dismal observation of Nelly Lewis in her December 1833 missive to Gibson that "they have had several frosts in Novr. which injured the cane very much & the uncommon long drought too has been a great disadvantage." Sugar cane, a grass crop, is hardy, but a deep and extended "killing frost," especially one following drought conditions and succeeded by warm, damp days, is feared. Such weather can cause a breakdown and acidification of the sucrose in the cane stalk juice and damage the roots. Probably due to these factors, the 1833 harvest failed to achieve the Butlers' hopes.[25]

The Lewises' visit in Louisiana extended to the late spring of 1834. As of May 23, a New Orleans friend, William F. Krumbhaar (1804–71), whose wife, Jane, descended from Butler's uncle William, prepared to leave by sailing vessel or steamboat from the increasingly hot and uncomfortable city of New Orleans. He promised Major Lewis "to make arrangements with the Capt. to call for you and . . . select the most comfortable stateroom."[26]

Frances's parents departed from Louisiana knowing about the prospective birth of her second daughter, which occurred on August 20, 1834. Writing on August 23, Butler announced the arrival of Caroline Swanwick Butler (1834–76), named for his older sister and nicknamed "Caro." The proud father noted that

Frances had undergone an unusually easy delivery and was sitting up and sewing. But the occasion was an anxious one, at least for him: Caroline Bell "(who dislikes traveling in Steam Boat at this season . . . and was prevented coming by land by the Frequent rains) sent Clarissa up in the 'Bayou Sara' . . . ; her [the infant's] arrival was most unfortunate, as [she] was born before the arrival of the midwife, Madam Lambremone" [the wife of Pierre Michel Lambremont, newly resettled nearby from a few miles downstream]. Nevertheless, Frances "rallied her frightened troops, and prevented any accident . . . by that uncommon firmness which she exhibits on such occasions." The younger Lewis daughter Angela had become engaged to Charles Magill Conrad, a prominent New Orleans lawyer, and possibly the Lewises were too enmeshed with Angela's wedding plans to remain for Caro's birth. Major Lewis complained that his wife was determined to accompany the Conrads to New Orleans from Virginia after their marriage in the coming autumn. "It was . . . very painful for many considerations that she should leave me, & encumber the young people with the expense of maintaining her." Occupied with business at home, Lewis wanted Nelly to use her money to help Angela, instead of spending it on what he thought was a needless trip. Angela's marriage did not occur until the following year, but the ill-defined family disagreement about the wedding plans remained a sore point.[27]

The Butlers' renewed confidence in their soon-to-be-harvested third cane crop had been aided by rains. Butler secured most of the wood that the plantation needed to fuel the "rolling time," as harvest and grinding season were termed, saved most of the livestock fodder, and had sufficient corn for the next year. He expected to obtain a loan of at least $25,000. Unpleasant discussions about finances prompted the Butlers' child Sonny, then five years old, to express concern about his father succeeding with the fall harvest sufficiently "that you may pay your debts." In November, the mill required repair of "cracked batteries," a reference to end kettles under which the furnace was located. They received much heat. The plantation was using new horse carts to haul harvested cane, and by November 8 only the plant cane placed in the ground the prior winter remained to be cut. Butler hoped to produce 250 hogsheads of sugar, barring a freeze. He was so preoccupied overseeing work at the mill that he sent Frances and the three children to visit the Bells at White Hall for a few weeks. The final count of 230 hogsheads of sugar was twenty hogsheads less than the earlier estimate, and thirteen thousand gallons of molasses were manufactured. Part of the product, one hundred hogsheads, was sold and shipped to Richmond, Virginia.

The Bells visited Dunboyne for the 1834 Christmas holiday, and Butler reported that Robert Bell was still cutting cane but was out of wood for his mill. Despite the success of the harvest, Nelly Lewis fretted about the Butlers' "precarious business" and wrote Gibson of the need for another harvest at least as good: "What a bar to comfort & independence and happiness is a narrow income."[28]

The crop thankfully marked an improvement over 1833 for the Butlers, producing $16,336.39, more than threefold earlier proceeds. These results were not accomplished without Butler's act of business caution in obtaining insurance on a shipment. When it was lost in a storm off Cape Fear, North Carolina, the insurance payment recouped $70 per hogshead of sugar and 22 cents a gallon for molasses. "I shall not cry if the other shares the same fate," Butler reported, referring to plans for a second planned sale in Richmond. Unfortunately, the Lewises only slowly learned of Butler's insurance payment: "Poor Ed must be trying to make both ends meet by planting cotton with the cane that is not quite dead [after a winter freeze]. This year he made the only tolerable crop he has made since he went there, & part of that was lost on the way to Richmond." Their good harvest and ensuing sugar sales impelled the Butlers to look for additional property specifically for the use of Major Lewis, whom the Butlers wanted living near them. Soon, too, both of the Lewis daughters resided in Louisiana.[29]

During these years, Butler maintained close supervision and established business customs that persisted through the 1840s. Like so many planters, much of his sugar was sold in New Orleans. Probably because of contacts in Virginia and northern markets, Dunboyne sugar was delivered to numerous other destinations: in 1835 and 1841, for example, Butler shipped sugar to Richmond; in 1840, to Cincinnati; in 1841, to Philadelphia and Baltimore; in 1842, to Nashville, Louisville, and again to Philadelphia; and in 1843 and 1845, once again to Louisville. Sugar was sent north as far as New York in 1843. Neighbors benefited from close availability of high-quality, Dunboyne-manufactured sugar for home use, and sugar and molasses often were exchanged for provisions brought by flatboat and steamboat. The goods in exchange included pork, oats and corn, potatoes, flour, bacon, apples, and sundries such as tubs, floor mats, soap, and linen. One might conclude that the plantation was not completely self-sufficient. It is true that, on occasion, food production simply fell short. Sometimes, purchasing corn and other food for humans, hogs, cattle, and draft animals made some economic sense, based upon the profitability of the sugar crop. For most dwellers along the Mississippi, however, the trade off of flatboats and steamboats provided an almost constant supermarket of northern goods, livestock, and produce and other items of all kinds. The Butlers took full advantage of the river-borne merchants. By 1839, coal became a source of energy for households (mills still used wood fuel at this time) and was delivered almost door-to-door. Sugar and molasses were exchanged for lumber and shingles, lime for the fields and sugar purification, and barrel staves, and on occasion for horses and sheep. In January 1843, Butler acquired "one English Bull" costing $100 off of a flatboat. It probably was intended for breeding stock. An entry on April 10 that year showed Butler buying forty gallons of whiskey at 21 cents a gallon. Because the Butlers' liquor tastes emphasized wines, the whiskey may have been intended for the overseer and carpenter, and even for slaves on special occasions. Most such deliveries came by flatboat, as opposed to steamboat. Unless Butler exchanged his milled products for goods on flatboats, the heavy barrels of sugar and molasses were loaded on steamboats to New Orleans (except for an occasional sailing ship towed upstream). Steam-driven boats provided the main way to send his product upriver. In March 1837, Butler paid $165.15 to send off on a steamboat 45.3 hogsheads of sugar, a high rate of about $3.65 per hogshead. On December 1 of the next year, 75 hogsheads were shipped at a charge of $131.71, or $1.76 each. The varying shipping costs always affected profit. Butler kept account of any molasses and sugar that his family, overseers, and laborers used.

Dunboyne sugar and molasses were packed in hogsheads (large barrels in which bacon and other goods were stored and shipped), with sugar normally weighed and paid for by the pound, molasses by the gallon. Sugar prices varied from year to year and during the crop year, from about 4½ cents to 7 cents per pound. Molasses prices ranged from 20 cents to as high as 50 cents a gallon. Frequently, vessel cargoes included "cistern sugar," which was the residue sugar at the bottom of drained molasses cisterns, and which sometimes fetched higher prices than normal sugar. As high as the costs of sending products to New Orleans by steamboat were, those for out-of-state destinations were substantially higher. But prices received for the latter shipments were better. In March 1841, for example, Butler sent 50 hogsheads (49,815 pounds) of sugar to Philadelphia, receiving $3,599.43, but paying $512.78½ to ship. The net of $3,086.54½ was 6.2 cents per pound. An accounting of the true profit of his operation is difficult, because Butler's records show few other expenses, such as carrying costs on the mortgage loans on land and slaves.[30]

Trading with flatboat and steamboat merchants stopping at his plantation had its perils. Experience dictated care in conducting business with strangers. Local newspapers reported an 1841 incident involving a passenger named Wilson aboard the steamer *Maid of Kentucky.* Wilson took the opportunity to visit Butler while the boat was gathering firewood near Dunboyne. Wilson said that he was an Illinois merchant and had aboard the boat valuable produce destined for New Orleans. He wanted to see Butler's sugar. Butler was about to depart "for the Donaldsonville races" but ordered his overseer to show Wilson the sugar and gave Wilson a letter of introduction to his New Orleans agent. Wilson proceeded to purchase ten barrels of potatoes at a neighboring plantation, for which he paid with an altered note on the Bank of Illinois. When the seller "found out he had been duped . . . Wilson protested his innocence and invited the owner to return with him to Maj. Butler's. Whilst passing through the yard the rascal escaped amidst the shrubbery." Other incidents involving the shady man came to light, and the newspaper cautioned others that "there is no doubt that Wilson belongs to one of those gangs of counterfeiters and negro stealers which infest the swamps of the Mississippi. He . . . also has the signature of Maj. Butler, and the police should keep a strict lookout for him."[31]

Although Dunboyne featured commerce in sugar and molasses, in January 1836 and in March 1838 Butler sold bales of cotton. Once the Iberville staple, cotton was raised following years of low sugar cane yields. Butler's sugar crop of 1838, however, was outstanding, and the records from then until 1846 reveal no further effort at raising anything for commercial purposes other than sugar cane.[32]

The successes of 1834 did not extricate Dunboyne from debt. From New Orleans in late February 1835, where he was seeking a loan from the Union Bank of Louisiana, Butler complained of "temporary arrangements to meet . . . payments to the Louisiana & Canal Bank, which become due next month." He suggested to Major Lewis that together they raise sugar cane and cotton (as Butler was about to undertake). Lewis should acquire the smaller, downriver tract of one and one-half arpents width that Butler bought in 1831 and then "send out your hands next fall." Major Lewis had in mind a more profitable use of his slave labor than he could foresee for them in Virginia, and "in the case of my not succeeding in the cultivation of cotton" on the Mississippi River coast, he would sell them "to advantage." In partnership with Butler, who owned "a first rate gin house," their combined operations would make sugar and cotton crops. No doubt for the benefit of Frances's mother, as a further inducement Butler added that New Orleans "is improved beyond belief since you were here, and the buildings are magnificent."[33]

Perhaps anticipating a move to Louisiana, Major Lewis made gifts of a number of slaves to the Butlers in the 1830s. Among them was a laundress named

Dolcy, a daughter of Nelly Lewis's laundress, and the aunt of Frances's personal servant, Lucinda. (Years earlier, the mother of Nelly's laundress performed those duties for Martha Washington). Lewis wanted to promote the success of the Butler enterprise. Besides being motivated as a father to the beloved Frances, Lewis remained a creditor of the Butlers. In May 1836, he owned two mortgages. One, for $7,713.47, was on the property originally owned by the Bells and now belonging to the Butlers. Butler still owed Lewis $4,666.56 on the slaves that had been part of the contingent of workers on the properties that Butler acquired in 1831. Obligations to Major Lewis had been larger but were reduced by an 1833 gift to Frances of a part of the debt. Butler subscribed to stock in Citizens Bank of Louisiana and wanted to make a loan from the bank in order to extinguish the debt to Major Lewis. But Lewis was asked, and willingly agreed, to postpone "his own mortgage to any that the bank might make to" Butler.[34]

During 1835–36, Nelly remained dubious about the Butlers' prospects. Writing Gibson, she worried that "my darling Parke has been in delicate health all the summer, weak and nervous . . . very much depressed." Frances faced "many trials and evils," and Nelly wished her to come home to visit the "Springs" (probably White Sulfur Springs). "Seeing her kind friends would do her more good than anything—but Ed is not prosperous as I could wish, & it is not in our power to make him so." From Nelly's view, the Butlers' neighborhood lacked what she would describe as "proper society," despite signs of some upswing as more "new American settlers from Miss." came to live. Louisiana was represented mainly by "lazy Creoles . . . indolent and dirty; & places which will produce with scarcely any trouble, flower & every thing beautiful are really disgusting under their management." If her son-in-law made a good crop in 1836, it would relieve "my child from anxiety" and allow Frances to visit Angela Conrad in New Orleans and to mix with a more acceptable group of people. While on a difficult and sickness-ridden summertime visit to Louisiana in 1836, Nelly wrote her oft-repeated concerns to Elizabeth Gibson: "Here she is literally buried alive, her health her spirits destroy'd by over exertion, no congenial mind or pursuits to compensate for domestic drudgery. I have often lamented that Ed left the Army. He has never yet made a good crop & Parke has endured fatigue & privations which I never anticipated for her."[35]

Just how was Frances faring and handling her life in 1835–36, and to what degree did her mother's attitudes reflect her own? Many women who migrated from eastern seaboard states in the 1820s considered their resettlement as "loss" and, like Nelly Lewis, compared the experience to death. The common Upper South view of the Old Southwest was of a violent and unhealthy, lonely and depressing place. Women seldom had a choice about their moves. But as noted earlier, Frances Butler arrived in Louisiana with full and eager acquiescence, reported activities in the neighborhood and on the plantation, and wrote little of misery and loneliness. Many of the neighbors were culturally different, yet the Butlers were received with kindness. Others who lived close by, such as the families of J. R. Thompson of New Jersey, Henry McCall of Philadelphia, Henry Doyle of Mississippi, and later Alvarez Fisk of Boston and Natchez came from similar backgrounds. Physical location was no detriment at Dunboyne: it faced a busy river, shared a thickly populated, socially active settlement along both its banks, and featured easy access to New Orleans and elsewhere.[36] Was Nelly overstating the problems?

The crop production at Dunboyne in 1835 did amount only to a net of $7,195, including $1,704 from twenty-five cotton bales sold in February 1836. The Butlers' fortunes were like many, suffering ups and downs. Perhaps because of the promise of a better harvest in the fall of 1836, Butler was able to add land nearby to his plantation. On November 1, a sale from Ribert Hebert detailed land one and three-fourths arpents wide by forty arpents deep. The full price was only $750, payable the following March. In addition, Butler picked up another tract one and three-fourths arpents wide by twenty-five arpents deep, below and adjacent to Ribert Hebert's tract but beginning back at the thirty-five-arpent line from the river. It was in a place normally understood to have inferior soil quality near the "back swamp." Its location close to Dunboyne, however, gave the land value. The mortgages on both of the new tracts were cancelled in the spring of 1837, perhaps using $6,000 from the sale of Frances's Kanawha River land. Acknowledging a need for additional labor, in November 1836 Butler had Lewis buy for him nine additional slaves from W. Absalom Remington. That May, Butler borrowed $30,000 and through his brother-in-law Charles Conrad arranged to mortgage a large portion of his property to the Union Bank of Louisiana. The instrument, recorded on May 3, 1837, described the mortgaged land as eleven arpents front by fifty deep, or six hundred superficial arpents, bounded above by lands of Louis Baugnon and below by those of the widow of Francis Evan Bush. The sale listed seventy-six slaves by name, and the existing mortgages were noted: an original loan from the Bank of Louisiana for $24,000 on the upper eight arpents (acquired from Bell), now reduced to $14,000; and one to New Orleans

Canal and Banking Company for $10,000, reduced now to $7,500, on his original (Henry) three arpents as well as on the small (Allain) tract below of one and one-half arpents by forty. All of the mortgages finally were canceled in 1851.[37]

Butler's reliance upon and involvement with banks is noteworthy. His former guardian Andrew Jackson consistently opposed the banking system—especially the Bank of the United States—as well as large corporations and centralized and strong state and federal governments. Louisianans in general expressed their "republican" thinking in such terms. From the time of his arrival in Iberville, however, Butler encumbered his property to banks, frequently mortgaging separate portions of it to different institutions. He toyed with buying shares in new banks and finally acquired shares of the Citizens Bank of Louisiana. His dependence on these institutions contrasted with his expressed opinions. When loans were called and specie payments suspended in Louisiana in 1837 and thereafter during the nationwide economic depression, Butler vented anger to his first cousin Judge Thomas Butler Jr. of St. Francisville. Banks were "rascally . . . corporations," not competent to "meet their obligations and take up their paper." Unable to predict what the banks and factors would do in the current situation, "I have ever been opposed to Banks, National & State, upon constitutional grounds, and now I am more than ever opposed to them on the grounds of expediency." Butler remained a lifelong devotee of Jackson, but like many of both Democrat and Whig affiliations in the 1830s, his actions and attitudes blurred: he became president of an Iberville bank in the 1840s.[38]

The most distressed member of the extended family in the time of the Panic of 1837 was Major Lewis. His hopes to recoup family fortunes in Louisiana remained unfulfilled. At first tempted to buy land there, Lewis was dissuaded both by conflicting stories about profit to be made and by tales of migrants. They spoke of the South's "vile disease" which "would destroy . . . happiness" and "over balance any prospect" of achieving the sort of fortune that kept families provided. Like so many landowners in nineteenth-century Virginia, Frances's father produced insufficient income to maintain his plantation slaves. In 1836, he unhappily rented them out to Dr. Henry G. Doyle, a native of Mississippi residing on a plantation near Dunboyne. Doyle's "overseer is a perfect Savage, & my people in danger of being knocked in the head for a trifle," moaned Lewis. He begged Butler to take them after Doyle's rental term was done—"to aid in securing your crops, it will gratify me to know they will be of service." Lewis wanted Butler to sell them for $10,000, much more than they could fetch in

Virginia. He somehow found cash to afford a visit to New Orleans in late 1837 and early 1838: the Lewises wished to see the children, and Major Lewis remained financially involved in the area. He requested that Butler send him some interest from the Bank of Plaquemine that was due. But it was with reluctance: "My wife says that she wants the money and cannot do without." His elaborate home in Virginia was a burden, and his son, Lorenzo, could not meet expenses at the Audley Farm. "My income is nothing," Lewis admitted, and "Woodlawn is worse than nothing." He was financially stretched. The longtime practices of Nelly, who maintained and entertained at Woodlawn in luxury, were ruinous. Major Lewis was critical of the "imprudent" course that "my wife was running. . . . Alas, the habit has become a disease without a cure." Lewis reiterated his resolve to sell his slaves to a "good master" in Louisiana and give the proceeds (or notes representing the debt from the sale) to Angela or to her husband, Charles. Major Lewis would reserve to himself part of the interest on the notes from the sale and ultimately divide up the rest of the debt owed to him in order to help the Butlers. In compliance, Butler found a buyer not far upstream, Valery Hebert, who on December 31, 1836, bought twenty-four of the slaves. Hebert paid $19,000 for them, at 8 percent interest over five years in installments of $3,800. After the mortgage was paid off, the proceeds were sent to Charles Conrad, to whom Lewis willed the notes upon Angela Conrad's death in 1839.[39]

In 1837, Frances Butler gave birth to another son, described by his parents as a "blackeyed boy." Days before, Frances promised her father she would name the baby Lawrence Lewis. Nelly may have been present for the March 16 event but more likely attended to Angela Conrad, whose one-year-old namesake, Angela Lewis Conrad, died in early 1837. More bad news that year was the passing of Butler's much-loved and respected half-brother, William Vinson. On the verge of becoming a physician in New Orleans, Vinson died from a tooth infection and its treatment. Butler himself suffered during most of the summer from a "bilious fever," a reference probably to the mysterious and widespread disease malaria. Major Lewis, afflicted with eye trouble, worried about his son-in-law, whose plantation expenses "are so great, & this with interest at 10 pr cent makes so large a deduction in the crop that little is left after tis paid." Additionally, their cane crop endured a severe drought. Nelly powered through her increasing infirmities, complaining especially of deafness in one ear and stiffness in her limbs. She tested her eyes trying to finish "so many pieces of work for my darlings."[40]

When the Lewises visited Louisiana again, in the fall of 1837, Nelly may have given Frances Butler her treasured *Housekeeping Book*; still preserved, the album and scrapbook had been in progress at least since the Butlers moved south. Especially appropriate for Virginia, it is filled with instructions for operation of a household, including food recipes, medical and herbal treatments, and clothing and its care. Some of the recipes and housekeeping directions derived from Lewis slaves. The Lewises split their time between daughters and relished New Orleans. Late in March 1838, Frances wrote her father that she remained on the lookout for him on the steamboat *Brilliant.* An enthusiast of fine horseflesh, he delayed his trip to Dunboyne until "after the races" (there being three racetracks in the area of New Orleans around 1845). Meanwhile, Butler and the older children had driven by carriage for a week's stay with the Bells, leaving Frances at home with Caro and Lawrence.[41]

Dunboyne Plantation's fortunes improved from the sugar cane crops of 1838, 1839, and 1840, during the troubled economic times following the Panic of 1837. With prices for sugar at 7 cents a pound and molasses at 30 cents a gallon in the late fall of 1838 through May of 1839, the 1838 crop brought better than $21,400, well over that of 1837. Sales of sugar and molasses began in late 1839 and continued through most of 1840, yielding $22,000, despite lower prices during 1840 (as low as 4 cents for sugar). The crop year of 1840–41 saw slightly improved prices, and Butler sold sugar in Philadelphia and Richmond, where his cargo received 7⅛ cents to 8 cents per pound, less shipping costs. Despite the good fortune for the Butlers in 1838 while others suffered, Nelly Lewis stated her feelings in writing to Gibson about nine-year-old Sonny having broken a thigh: "Most sincerely do I wish their lot had been Phila. or Virginia instead of *La.*"[42]

The Butlers customarily shared their largess with the Lewises, and they sent a much-appreciated shipment of sugar and molasses to Woodlawn in April 1839. Indulging in a pleasure that became a long-lasting hobby, Butler ordered wine later that year from Phineas Jones, a merchant in Alexandria, Virginia. At Woodlawn, Major Lewis's activities included the preservation of "some shad" and "some herrings," which were "treated in the old way using Saltpeter etc. for since I have adopted the new method my fish have never been as good." Still concerned about Butler's health, Major Lewis proposed that his son, Lorenzo, the family physician Henry Daingerfield, and he meet the Butlers at White Sulfur Springs. But Frances was expecting once again. Her letters were "filled with the charms & intelligence of her little flock, particularly the youngest Lawrence." Even so, demurred Nelly: "She has an arduous task in having to teach her eldest Latin, French, & English, & her two little girls their lessons, besides making the greater part of their clothing & all her own." The schooling of Edward Butler

Jr. *was* a concern. By 1837, his father communicated with Judge Thomas Butler about possibly sending Sonny, then seven years old, to be educated in the vicinity of St. Francisville, a plan to which Frances would not yet agree. For a while, Sonny received instruction from a "Dr. Granet," but Granet's departure for New Orleans in 1838 "leaves Edward idle." The Butlers remained anxious to find a way to maintain the boy's improved habits of learning and to relieve his mother of that formidable task.[43]

Late 1839 brought misery in spite of a satisfactory sugar crop. Angela Lewis Conrad died on September 21, followed by Major Lawrence Lewis on November 20—severe blows to everyone in the family. The Butlers' new son, born on October 24 and named Ormonde Butler, lived only until January 2, 1840. Shortly afterward, Andrew Jackson visited Louisiana to celebrate the twenty-fifth anniversary of the Battle of New Orleans and stayed with Caroline Bell. From White Hall on January 17, 1840, she wrote Jackson how privileged and delighted she had been to host her former guardian "beneath my own roof." She prayed that a servant's carelessness in exposing the Old General to the night air on a long walk had not made him suffer. Caroline hoped that "my dear Edward saw you the night you left this [place]" and referred to Frances as "the child of sorrow and affliction."[44]

The years 1839–40 marked a turning point for the Lewis-Butler family. The Butlers could not determine whether their future at Dunboyne was safe. After almost a decade, they had not approached their goals of wealth and high social status, and the recent family illnesses and deaths bore heavily. Both Frances and Edward Butler were worried, and the home atmosphere was charged with emotion. Before the major's death, the Lewises had come to a virtual eclipse. Unable to stem losses at Woodlawn and missing the chance to move to Louisiana, their lives were darkened. Major Lewis's passing seemed both a symbol of the family's decline and an omen of its future.

Nelly Lewis traveled to Louisiana soon after her husband's death to visit the Butlers and Charles Conrad and his two children. Lorenzo Lewis wrote Conrad in April 1840 and urged Conrad and his children to bring Nelly back to Virginia in June: "Your warm climate is death to her in summer." Lorenzo thought that Conrad and his sons likewise would benefit by "the advantage of Audley air." Lorenzo wanted Nelly to have adequate money for her stay in the South and arranged with Conrad for a transfer of $250 out of her yearly $1,000 pension. Whether Conrad accepted Lorenzo's invitation is unknown. We know that

Nelly, living discontentedly by herself at her increasingly neglected Woodlawn mansion, decided to make a second trip south in 1840 to see Frances and the grandchildren. She may have intended to move permanently to Louisiana to be with (or at least near) them. Her visit caused a fateful change in the family's relationships.[45]

5

A Taste of Success

Dunboyne, 1840–1847

Eleanor Parke Lewis was staying at Dunboyne in December 1840 when an argument ensued between her and Edward Butler. The sort of fracas that all families dread, it shattered their friendship and brought Nelly Lewis only more sadness and grief, adding to what she already felt. Nelly either decided or was ordered to leave Dunboyne immediately. Boarding a steamer to New Orleans, she remained the month with Charles Conrad and his two children, Charles (1837–92) and Lewis (1839–83)

Nelly's letter to Elizabeth Gibson on December 20, 1840, bared her soul and all her anger. The misgivings and resentments harbored ever since the Butlers' marriage, and particularly since their decision to move to the Deep South, burst forth. Nelly accused Butler of ungentlemanly behavior, of insults to her, and of "brutal treatment" and cruelty to Frances and Sonny, who then were ill. Edward Butler, charged Nelly, gave the *appearance* of being "soft and gentle" but in fact was violent and unkind. Frances wished that Nelly might "pass the winter with her," but Butler resolved "to prevent it." He claimed that her name was ridiculed throughout the state and accused her of having "made my Husband miserable & shortened his days." In Nelly's view, only "the power he has over her poor children" prevented Frances from "leaving him forever." Butler made the life of Frances one of agony, and "he has the most selfish malignant mean disposition I ever knew." Echoing the many earlier sentiments about Frances being "buried alive" in Louisiana, Nelly pronounced that her "only remaining daughter suffers a *living death* & cannot pray to be released because she is the only stay her poor children have." Unsparing of Butler's relations, Nelly continued, in contradictory fashion: "He is the worst possible example (except that he is *strictly honest & moral*) his Sisters are his counterparts, as mean as selfish, as little addicted to *truth* telling as he is." Furthermore, not only did the Bells overprice the plantation they sold the Butlers in 1833, but "as soon as B. was *master* he pressed Mr L

& myself & my darling Angela to pass the winter with them, & tried to persuade Mr L to settle near him, so much for his veracity."[1] Eleanor Parke Lewis never visited Dunboyne again, retiring to live with her son, Lorenzo, and his family at Audley Farm.

Reading this letter, brim-filled with regret, despising, anger, and grief, one well might consider poorly the actions if not the entire character of Edward G. W. Butler. Was he such a cruel, even brutal, husband and father? Recent works on Eleanor Parke Lewis—in particular the introduction to Patricia Brady's edited collection of Nelly's letters, *George Washington's Beautiful Nelly*, and David Riblett's 1993 biography, *Nelly Custis, Child of Mount Vernon*—give that impression.[2]

We may never know exactly what sparked the eruption between Nelly Lewis and Edward Butler. Butler's succeeding missives infrequently speak of her, and hers only briefly of him and always with scant regard. Except for a notable series of letters to her husband during his Mexican War service in 1847–48, those of Frances Parke Butler that remain for scholars to review are relatively few in number, and none yet has been found that details the fracture in relations in December 1840. When the family history over a longer time is examined, however, some understanding emerges.

A major conflagration had been in the making since 1826. Never at peace with the decision of her daughter Frances to marry a soldier of limited means, Nelly Lewis grew ever anxious and unhappy. After the Butlers' move to "foreign" Louisiana, she missed her family and found them inaccessible. Believing that the education and talents of Frances and of her grandchildren were wasted in Iberville Parish, that there was minimal likelihood of the Butlers securing appropriate social and economic status, and that Edward Butler failed sufficiently to provide for his family, Nelly waxed increasingly pessimistic. The Butlers' match contrasted with the marriage Angela made with the wealthy Charles Conrad, and Nelly's worries were sharpened by her own and Major Lewis's worsening financial futures as productivity at Woodlawn declined. She persisted in improvident habits of living and spending, of which both Frances and Edward Butler were aware at least from letters of Major Lewis. It was no secret that Lawrence Lewis had been forced to sell off many of the Woodlawn slaves in 1837. Might Nelly have stated openly her reservations and misgivings about Butler during her and Major Lewis's visits? Proud and of an independent mind, it is unlikely she hid completely her opinions. Enough of his mother-in-law's concerns approached truth that her statements would have touched Butler's nerves. He possessed a thin skin. His own honor challenged, his long-held insecurities wounded—Butler experienced distress from Nelly Lewis's pronouncements.

Unlike most southern women, Frances Butler married outside of normal geographic and social boundaries. Her union with Butler lessened the chances of enhancement of the Lewis family unit. It had been risky from the viewpoint especially of Nelly Lewis, a revering descendant of her country's founder. Frances Butler's existence in Louisiana admittedly was very different from the one she enjoyed during her youth. She later acknowledged that "no Lady . . . had been so indulged before marriage" as she. Added to the drudgery at Dunboyne, as the Butler children matured, was time-consuming schooling. Frances Butler accomplished it mostly alone at least until 1839–40, when after a long search the couple hired a tutor, James Young, from Boston.[3]

If Frances Butler resented her life in Louisiana in their early years at Dunboyne, however, it remains to be demonstrated. As has been noted already, she proved resilient, strong, determined, and talented. Unlike many women of the evangelical antebellum South, she inwardly grew and kept her resolve even within the context of life's trials. She was not a complainer, although her experiences chastened her enthusiasm for Louisiana. Not only did Frances relish her life there, she and Edward *each* attempted repeatedly and sincerely to persuade her parents to join them. After the 1835 marriage of Angela Lewis, both daughters and many grandchildren lived in the Deep South; but their presence *still* proved insufficient to induce Lawrence and Nelly Lewis to abandon Woodlawn.

Among the helpful qualities of Frances Parke Butler were her interest in and ability to learn about the economy of sugar planting and production and about what was involved with successful plantation management. She came to know and associate with her husband's business contacts. The Panic of 1837 and ensuing economic depression had fewer consequences for the Butlers than for their commission merchant Thomas Barrett. Frances expressed her sorrow and concern, regretting that she and Butler were too poor to assist him. Soon Butler changed factors to Harrison, Clegg and Co., or C. Clegg, followed by A. LeDoux and Co., and ultimately Alphonse Miltenberger, who remained their factor. Her experiences now broad, Frances shared with Major Lewis some of the lessons she had learned as a plantation mistress, writing him in March 1837 to discourage her brother, Lorenzo, who was considering becoming a sugar plantation investor, in absentia:

> I deeply regret the continued failure of the crops in Virginia—yet my dear Father *experience* has taught me that to make a plantation profitable at *any time*—a purchaser must *live on* it—devote his whole time to it—economise in every way and then the high rates of interest and the failure of one or two crops will make it hard enough for him to pay for it and difficult enough even to meet his common wants.—provided he is a good planter, a prudent man and has a *good overseer* (& the most difficult of all things to procure) he may get along in time—If not he certainly brings ruin and misery upon himself—.[4]

Edward Butler had occasional misgivings about his life in Iberville. Vowing never to become so indebted that he could not extricate himself, Butler was unable to operate a plantation without constant borrowing. It galled him. In a letter to Lorenzo Lewis in April 1841, in which he enclosed the last payment of Valery Hebert for the purchase of the Lewis slaves, Butler confessed to Lorenzo his permanent state of indebtedness: "If I could once get out of debt, I think I should be disposed to play the gentleman one summer, as I think a trip to the White Sulphur Spring would benefit both Frances and myself. But I cannot yet consider myself a free man."[5]

Much like modern-day man's enslavement to his work and his desire for a "real break," Butler was admitting his own shackle—continual debt. Hearing his mother-in-law criticize his own regretful obligations made them all the more painful. For the Butlers there also was loss of financial independence, which Nelly wished for her daughter and children, and the constant, year-in, year-out necessity to remain home and to oversee the work at Dunboyne. They would miss out on fraternizing with finer society in New Orleans and summer trips to far-off spas or extended vacations on the Gulf Coast, which Frances's sister and her family enjoyed. Owning a growing plantation and numbers of slaves thus far, in 1840, had not propelled the Butlers to the level of wealthy elites. Although most Louisiana sugar planters of modest means led hard lives, the couple aspired to better things. The failure to attain more economic success during the 1830s frustrated them and affected body and soul.

The omnipresent and long-smoldering combination of emotions, added to economic worries, came to a flash point after tragedy struck. After multiple deaths in the family occurred in late 1839, only a small spark was needed to set off the flame. Whatever the statement or act may have been that constituted the spark, it occurred when Eleanor Parke Lewis visited the Butlers at Dunboyne early in December 1840.

Despite the trying events of 1839 and 1840, life at Dunboyne carried on. The area of the Butlers' house fronting on the River Road then contained nine white people, who must have included the overseer and his kin. The slave force numbered an impressive one hundred people, seventeen of them children under age ten. Of the slaves, Frances used seven household servants. Both of the adjacent properties up and down river included slaves among the population count.[6] A considerable amount of land and effort was devoted to raising food crops and animals, but the principal cash crop of the plantation was sugar cane. The sugar crop of 1841, sold mostly through August 1842, was less productive than that of the prior year, and perhaps as a result Nelly Lewis's hopes to have Frances and her children visit her at Audley went unfulfilled. The breach between her and Butler caused no apparent effect on other members of the family, however, and Butler maintained cordial communications with his brother-in-law Lorenzo, the Butler children wrote their grandmother, and the Conrad children spent Christmas 1841 with the Butlers. According to Nelly, with whom Frances remained in close touch, both Charley and Lewis Conrad slept in "P's room," and they were well behaved.[7]

After a dip in crop returns of 1841–42, the yields and returns evened off at a relatively good level. The Butlers seem not fully to have comprehended it, but Dunboyne had entered a time of overall improvement. The first two months' sales of the produce from the 1842 crop, beginning in November, brought $8,726.81, and 1843 sugar and molasses sales through September netted almost $10,000 more, making a decent total return. The sugar of the following crop, sold through June of 1844, brought in approximately $16,150. And the 1844 crop, between October 1844 and July 1845, came in at $17,552.[8]

It is helpful to examine a likely cause for the bettering situation. All planters of size relied upon their overseers for management. As Frances Butler observed to her father, qualified overseers were scarce, and their pay high. Locating good ones demanded Butler's attention and time. In 1834–35, John Campbell received $800, but he was replaced in 1835 by Jon Martin, who was paid $600. Martin remained only a year before James Johns Jr. came on the plantation, at a wage of $800. He worked through 1839, when the Butler Record Book shows that Joachim Cox "commenced" at Dunboyne on January 1, 1840, with pay of $700 a year. Cox and his family stayed unusually long, until 1848, and he had a major effect on the efficiency and productivity of the plantation. Butler commonly included in the employment agreement some provision for domestic help and food allowances along with salary. Cox also received "the services of Grace, 1 Bl [barrel] Sugar, 1 Bag Coffee, 20 Bls pork & 2 Bls Flour, for Johnson & himself, & an allowance of meat for workmen." A valuable and almost permanent fixture of the plantation, the carpenter George Johnson worked from 1833 until 1856. In 1840, he received a cash salary of $400, increased by 1856 to $550. Johnson's personal servant was named Sophy, with whom he may have fathered a son, named Byron. Butler sold the child to Johnson in 1839 for $410.80. Young boys often assisted in house chores, like the five-year-old slave boy Eugene, whom Cox acquired in 1842 for $340 at an estate sale.[9]

Further indications of change in the Butlers' personal and economic fortunes are evident. In 1842, and with much irony considering his objections to banking institutions, Butler became president of the Plaquemine branch of the Union Bank of Louisiana. The position, which he held until 1847, eased his ability to finance and refinance land purchases and his plantation operations. And it was a natural step to take in furthering his goals: Edward Butler ventured into planting and forsook the military precisely to gain more respect and wealth. He followed the political scene and enjoyed friendships with several men who were prominent in the Jackson administration. Jackson's long-time advisor and friend John Eaton was present at Butler's wedding and invited him to his own with Margaret O'Neil Timberlake, known as Peggy, on January 1, 1829. In the next few years, the refusal of Washington society to accept Peggy Eaton and the rumors surrounding her created much distraction in the Jackson administration. Butler and his sister, Caroline Bell, shared concerns about the effect on their former guardian of the so-called Petticoat Affair. They also sympathized with and worried about Butler's old West Point comrade Andrew Jackson Donelson, who served Jackson as a personal secretary and who disagreed with Jackson's support of the Eatons. (After Donelson's first wife Emily died, the Butlers in January 1837 offered him and his children their home as a sanctuary.) Even closer, two brothers-in-law became U.S. senators. First, in 1840 the Democrat politician Robert Carter Nicholas, a devoted friend of the Butlers and the Bells ever since Butler's posting at Pensacola, married Butler's half-sister Susan Adelaide Vinson. He had been chosen to the Senate in 1836, and served until 1841. Nicholas eventually became Louisiana's secretary of state and then its superintendent of public instruction before retiring to a plantation in Terrebonne Parish. Additionally, the widowed Charles Magill Conrad served in the U.S. Senate from 1842 to 1843 and became the secretary of war in the Fillmore administration.[10]

Butler's active interest in Louisiana politics commenced at least by 1842, perhaps partly inspired by renewed ambitions in military affairs. A friend, Edward Delany, wrote Butler from Clinton, Louisiana, that June about the prospects for election of Alexandre Mouton for governor. He referred to Butler's having received unjust treatment in the recent legislative session, controlled by Whig party members, "in respect to the election of Generals by that body." Butler clearly did not forsake his military aspirations; but only in October 1846, when Democrat Governor Isaac Johnson was in office, was he successful in gaining the position of major general of the 3rd Division of the state militia. He served briefly, until he received an appointment in February 1847 to command the U.S. Army 3rd Dragoon Regiment in Mexico.

Ever defensive of his old guardian's reputation, Butler became embroiled in a dispute with Charles Conrad. While a Whig party U.S. senator, Conrad opposed remitting the $1,000 fine levied against Jackson in 1815 when Jackson disobeyed an order of Judge Hall to restore civil law in New Orleans. Conrad lost his election bid based largely on the resultant unpopularity within both the Democrat and Whig parties over his action, and he took offense to what he contended was Butler's active opposition to him. Although Butler denied personal involvement in the defeat of Conrad, he admitted having "expressed hope that our Legislature would not ratify or sanction" Conrad's position. Butler offered Conrad his opinion that both parties had shown "disapprobation of your conduct towards the Savior of Louisiana." Differences between brothers-in-law would resurface after the Civil War. Butler also ran unsuccessfully for a state judgeship in 1844.

He remained busy with plantation affairs. In early 1845, the Butlers acquired from Mrs. Arsine Breaux, a widow, an additional downriver tract that was one and one-half arpents wide by forty deep, in area approximately 136 superficial arpents, for $5,000. By April 1846 it was fully paid. Butler was searching for iron rails to erect a plantation railroad and "skids" for storing the milled cane stalk residue, known as bagasse, to be used as fuel in the mill. In order to improve the efficiency of his manufacture, he contracted to buy a new "Steam Engine and sugar Mill," from Niles and Co. of Cincinnati, to be installed in the summer of 1845 in time for the harvest and grinding time that year. Half of the total cost of $4,620 would be paid when the new engine arrived, the rest in March 1846.

Niles had contracted in 1844 to furnish a new mill to a recently settled downriver landowner and friend of the Butlers, John Hampden Randolph, of Forest Home Plantation. The company offered to supply "a competent Carpenter and Engineer" to help Butler, who was to furnish at his expense "all the mason work and materials, all the timber hewed and squared," and laborers for assembly of the machinery. Butler agreed to house and feed the workers.[11]

Butler's new mill remained mostly intact through the Civil War, and was still there in 1871 when he sold Dunboyne. It appears that Butler acquired at least some of the important and economically valuable sugar mill improvements of the time. A report written in 2009, following archaeology on two plantations upstream from and near Dunboyne, is helpful in determining what changes were made in the 1845 renovations. Like those neighbors, he installed a condenser and pump-type horizontal steam engine with its typical crank and wheel construction. Instead of vertical rollers, he replaced the old ones with three horizontal rollers next to the steam engine. The mill may have gained a second set of sugar kettles, four to six kettles long, with one cane grinder. The layout of the mill was typical of others in the 1840s, a rectangular main building of four rooms or "sheds" in a row, about 216 feet long by forty to forty-five feet wide. Each of the rooms performed a different function, first grinding the cane, then boiling the juice, cooling it in vats, and finally purging the finished product. A rough plat of elevations of the plantation from the antebellum years affirms that a large, rear wing was joined, and there probably also was a much smaller wing for additional cooling space, creating an F-shaped structure. The wings were approximately fifty by forty feet and twenty feet square, respectively. Most mills built or improved in the 1840s continued to use wood as fuel, as did Butler, with added fuel in the form of bagasse. A few mills began to install the newly tested Rillieux process, by which vapor created by the evaporation of the sugar cane juice in one vacuum pan was used to boil juice in a second, connected pan. Butler was aware of the innovation, but he installed neither vacuum pans nor the Rillieux process. After 1850, some mills converted to coal, and a few even switched exclusively to using bagasse as fuel. Both conversions required changes to the kettle train. A means of removing and storing the bagasse waste definitely was provided, because in 1844 Butler was searching for iron rails "to create my Bagasse Skids and Rail Road." The mill used lime as a separator agent and acid neutralizer, and then probably also sulfur. Finally, the mill specifications provided for "gearing for a corn mill," in order to upgrade the processing of slaves' food.[12]

The educations of their young gave the Butlers much concern. Raised on the plantation, the Butler children received careful supervision, unlike many in similar situations in the antebellum South. The Butlers knew that they could not offer by themselves the classical and foreign language training they wished for their offspring, and hiring tutors from far away was not an uncommon practice in the neighborhood. Finding appropriate teachers proved difficult. Butler searched the North, choosing James Young, who possessed knowledge of French. Recommended by Yale professor Benjamin Silliman, Young remained as tutor only a year. For their daughters, Frances Butler and the tutors gave less emphasis to teaching "Christian usefulness or domestic virtue" than in many other southern areas.

The Butlers may have feared what the extended exposure to slavery might lead to morally in their four impressionable youths. The influences of the institution often worried cultivated southerners, according to the historian Frederick Law Olmstead. The oldest son, Edward Jr., now in his teens, attempted school in nearby Baton Rouge; the place offered an unsatisfactory solution. His father considered sending him to Centenary College, in Jackson, Louisiana, but instead, at age fourteen, Sonny entered Georgetown College in Washington, D.C. There, he joined his first cousin Edward Butler Donelson, son of Butler's sister, Eliza, and John Donelson IV. On the way to school in August 1843, Sonny visited his grandmother and cousins at Audley Farm. None of the other Butler children made the trip to Audley that summer. Nelly was placated by the responsibility of having the Conrad children stay with her for a while when Charles Conrad left them on his way to Europe on an extended tour. According to their grandmother, the Butler girls benefited from a French music instructor who taught them at home, Frances Butler handling other disciplines "as usual." Nelly also arranged for Angela Lewis Conrad's remains to be moved to Mount Vernon and placed near the tomb of George and Martha Washington.[13]

In 1843, a fortuitous event occurred to relieve Frances Butler of some of the obligation of educating Isabel and Caro. A place to school the girls became available when a new Episcopal priest and his wife came to minister to the recently established St. Mary's Church parish at Bayou Goula. Along with many other Episcopal churches in south Louisiana between 1840 and 1860, Saint Mary's was created through the energetic leadership of Bishop Leonidas Polk. A graduate of the U.S. Military Academy, Polk forsook the army to become an Episcopal priest. Charles Fay of Savannah served as the St. Mary parish's initial rector, and his presence in the neighborhood constituted a blessing for the Butlers, who Nelly Lewis noted had been "so many years without religious services." St. Mary's contained only twelve plantation families; even so, local Roman Catholic priests resented the presence both of Fay and the church parish. Elsewhere, Episcopal churches were flourishing, among them St. James in Baton Rouge, St. John's in Thibodaux, and St. James in Alexandria. Fay's congregants, however, had no physical structure, in spite of there being "so considerable a Protestant community as that in the vicinity of Bayou Goula, and one so amply provided with wealth and worldly means." To the delight of the Butlers, the rector and his wife agreed to house Sissy and Caro during the week. Mrs. Fay, a daughter of Episcopal bishop John Henry Hopkins of Vermont (1792–1868) and an experienced teacher, opened her home to ten pupils. Butler pronounced her as "certainly, a most accomplished woman," and was pleased that "my little girls . . . are making very satisfactory progress." They evidently remained through the year 1844 and possibly longer, as the school operated until the end of 1845. It closed much to Bishop Polk's lamentation when Fay resigned from the parish to become the priest at "The Mission Church" in New Orleans. Frances continued caring at home for her youngest, Lawrence, and Sonny thrived at Georgetown: "My child rejoices much in his being there," gratefully wrote Nelly Lewis.[14]

If one may say with fair certainty that the Butlers' fortunes bettered in the first half of the 1840s, Butler's beloved sisters, Caroline Bell and Eliza Donelson, underwent trials. Having removed to St. James Parish when Robert Bell sold out to Butler in 1833, the Bells became financially pressed by the last quarter of the 1830s. With his factor Thomas Barrett, they jointly owned property in Iberville that was mortgaged to the Citizens Bank to secure a loan by the bank to Bell in 1837. Due no doubt in part to Barrett's economic problems, it was seized and sold at a judicial sale. Butler held an interest in the matter, having obtained an earlier mortgage on the land in the amount of $14,400 by the Bank of Louisiana. The Bell family misfortune weighed upon Butler, adding to his many other problems of the years between 1838 and 1840. Surrendering White Hall Plantation, the Bells joined Susan and Cary Nicholas in a half-interest in property in St. James Parish, referred to as the "Nicholas & Bell Plantation" in the annual *Statement of the Sugar Crop Made in Louisiana* by Champomier. They moved into a small house two miles above the Nicholas residence, but by late 1842 Robert Bell was dead. Assisted by Nicholas in managing her affairs in Louisiana, Caroline traveled to Nashville, staying with Jackson at the Hermitage. She eventually settled in the city and, despite being hampered by a lack of servants, was soon engaged in making repairs to her new home and garden. From late 1843 she was to share her house with Eliza, following the deaths of both Eliza's husband, John Donelson IV, and her daughter, Mary Isabella Donelson. Eliza retired from the Donelson residence in Florence, Alabama, to live out her days with Caroline in Nashville. Eliza Donelson died in 1850, and after the death of Robert Carter Nicholas in 1856 Caroline Bell lived with her niece Susan and her family, until Caroline's own death in Nashville in 1864.

In the meantime, once more called upon by his family, Butler helped Eliza to afford the education of his troublesome nephew, Edward B. Donelson. Donelson had entered Georgetown College with Sonny and wished to quit the college. In October 1843, "Uncle" Jackson, still amazingly alert, complained to Butler of difficulty writing. He was "much debilitated, greatly afflicted with shortness of breathing," yet continued to involve himself with the Butler sisters' and his relatives' welfare and with politics. In correspondence the following February 1844, Jackson explained to Butler that he had dissuaded Eliza's son from leaving Georgetown and expressed delight with the Louisiana elections having returned the state to "the flag of young democracy," which would never again be destroyed by "the monied aristocracy of New Orleans." The Old Warrior, soon to leave this earth, pleaded with Butler to pay him a visit en route to Baltimore, where Butler planned to go as a delegate to the Democratic Party Convention in 1844. The visit occurred in the spring of 1845, and Butler found Jackson talking "brilliantly. When [Jackson] became excited he would lean over and support his head on one hand." Butler reported on May 12 to another of Jackson's devotees, Sam Houston, that "I have just returned from a pilgrimage to the Hermitage, where I left our dear old General in great bodily affliction; yet calmly awaiting the close of his earthly career which may he now daily expect."[15]

Within a month of Butler's letter to Houston, on June 8, Jackson died and was buried next to his beloved Rachel. He and Butler had remained notably close. In Jackson's last years, Butler acknowledged to Jackson his pride in and appreciation for the man he considered as near and dear as his sisters. Sending congratulations on Jackson's seventy-sixth birthday, Butler remarked that Jackson continued "unsullied by dishonour, and devoted to the care and protection of the orphan, and the advancement of the interests, the honour, and the glory of your country." Following Jackson's death, Butler wrote to Andrew Jackson Jr. that history would remember Jackson as "*the savior of his country*" once "the bitterness of party strife has ceased to poison the minds and to confuse the vision of a portion of his countrymen." Butler and his sisters owed Jackson a personal debt, as well, for having "been to us all a kind father."[16] The "Old General" remained Butler's ultimate earthly hero.

With the acquisition and installation of a new sugar mill in 1845, Edward Butler was able to dispose of his old one, to Anastasie Hebert Comau, a widow, for $2,900. She acquired the steam engine and sugar mill, the cane carrier and its timbers, the running gears and frame of Butler's corn mill, water cistern pipes, fixtures of the bagasse carrier, a boiler attached to the steam engine, and an additional boiler. Butler secured the sale with a mortgage on the Comau property (a tract four arpents wide by forty deep) and on the mill to be erected there.[17]

Illustrative of the many facets of the Dunboyne operation that year (and most others) is a portion of a memorandum or diary of Butler's manager Michael Moore. Written during Butler's absence with the U.S. Army in Mexico in the late summer of 1847, the journal portrays a constant, busy scene of varied, preharvest tasks:

> Memorandum
>
> 107. Loads of fodder—saved—the piece of new ground corn fodder pulled today & will make another stack—22 Acres of Corn pulled & in the Corn House—gave 45 loads of 22 Bbls. Produces equal to 30 Bbls average to the acre . . . & Cox—expects the new ground to yield better. 3 loads of grass cut & saved on W. Butler road below the sugar House—Crop roads being cut—also down at the old rain house—Turnips—sowed twice—& another patch will be sowed this full moon—The juice receivers—finished—& shed weather boarded as far up the boards held out—will be finished next week—the water receiver will be removed the moment the posts are ready—*then the sugar house will be all ready* for rolling—Fully one half the wood hauled & piled up—About 50000 brick arched up ready for burning. About two days more work to make the kiln—70—Harmanson nominated for Congress—[18]

For the previous fourteen years the Butler properties measured a total of twelve and one-half arpents fronting on the Mississippi River. The lower one and one-half arpents were separated from the rest above by a tract of land one and one-half arpents wide by forty deep owned by Francis Evan Bush, or, in 1845, by his remarried widow, Caroline Landry Breaux. In mid-summer of that year, Butler found a way to close the gap, persuading Caroline Breaux to exchange her land for his of equal size located a distance of seven and one-half arpents downriver. Butler had acquired his downriver parcel earlier from the widow of Arsine Breaux. Butler additionally sold off to other members of the Landry family a small "back tract" of twenty-six and one-half arpents in area. By these transactions, Dunboyne became entirely one continuous plantation of fourteen arpents, more than a half mile, fronting the Mississippi.[19] When, in 1846, Butler arranged for a mortgage renewal with his bank, the mortgage document incorrectly described Dunboyne as having eleven arpents front by fifty deep, amounting to six hundred superficial arpents. It stated a total of seventy-five slaves, forty-two being males age eleven and older, and sixteen females age twelve and older.[20]

What were the results of Butler's improvements? His new mill and his consolidated property along the Mississippi River coast paid off. The *Statement of the Sugar Crop Made in Louisiana in 1845–6* recited that the Butlers produced 264 hogsheads of sugar weighing 280,000 pounds. The plantation Crop Record showed that on June 29, 1846, 250 hogsheads of sugar were sent to Philadelphia, in addition to 350 barrels of molasses. The net receipts after insurance costs were $19,046.27. Other, smaller amounts of sugar and molasses amounting to about fifteen hogsheads of sugar and 172 barrels of molasses were sold or bartered locally and in New Orleans from the 1845 crop.[21]

The recent economic successes eased the way for Frances to receive permission to visit Virginia. The occasion was her enrollment of Sissy and Caro Butler in Miss Mercer's Belmont School for girls near Leesburg. The distance was far, the girls would have to remain in the area throughout the year, and the cost was high at roughly $250 a year for each child. Miss Mercer's provided not only room and board but instruction in most of the subjects that the Butlers desired for their daughters—"all the English branches, Latin, Greek, ethics, and mathematics." For an extra charge, the school offered "French, drawing, music, chemistry, and philosophy." The departure of Reverend and Mrs. Fay from Bayou Goula had lent urgency to the Butlers' search for a way to educate the girls, then ages fourteen and twelve. And Frances, desperate over the lack of educational opportunities for her children, resolved that they all leave Louisiana and acquire decent schooling. The girls still lacked adequate foundations for first communions, for which Frances required assistance from her aunt at Arlington, Mary Lee Fitzhugh Custis. When Sonny left home in 1843, he carried with him a message of thanks from Frances to her brother, Lorenzo. In it, her relief at Sonny's (and by inference, the girls') release from Louisiana is expressed strongly, raising some question about her commitment to the life that she and Butler chose. It reflected a change from her initial optimism and eagerness for the Iberville area and revealed a rare display of misery in the role of a sugar planter's wife: "The first wish of my heart, the most fervent prayer upon my lips, has ever been for the power of my removing my children from Louisiana—. . . . I cannot tell you how happy it will make me to have him located among my own dear Friends—and have him placed in a situation so favorable to his mental and moral improvement as the one at Georgetown." Frances held special concern for Sonny; she described him as wild and "self-willed" by reason of his being "so little controlled at school." She expected him to remain away for four long years, which constituted a great personal sacrifice for her. Frances Butler's worries were not unusual; many families living in the Old Southwest voiced such feelings about their children's upbringing and behavior and over the separation from relatives and friends.[22]

On her way to deliver the girls to school in August 1846, apparently accompanied as well by nine-year-old Lawrence, Frances Butler visited the Custises at their Arlington home, and friends in Alexandria, renewing old contacts. She had not seen her beloved friends and family for fifteen years. Turning down an invitation to travel to Newport, Rhode Island, Nelly Lewis gladly remained in the Shenandoah Valley in order to be with Frances and the Conrad grandsons. Prospectively having the Butler children so close at school provided her with much delight and anticipation. Frances "was hoping to return the next summer to visit" the girls at school, and she planned to stay with Nelly at Audley at least until October, probably much longer, taking Lawrence and Sonny home with her. Her oldest child now had been gone from Louisiana for three years and the next year proposed studying at South Carolina College, in Columbia.[23]

Nelly's scheme to keep Frances with her through Christmas 1846 was unfulfilled. By December, Frances departed, leaving Nelly at Audley with Lorenzo and his wife, Esther, and their six children. The war with Mexico was under way. Edward Butler supported the annexation of Texas to the United States even with almost certain military opposition from Mexico. He now wanted to be a part of the American forces that, under Zachary Taylor's command, were achieving victories. He anticipated becoming a high-ranking officer in the U.S. Army and soon departing for Mexico. Meanwhile, Conrad had removed his own sons from Audley to return with them to New Orleans, leaving Nelly worrying about "dreadful accidents by steamboats" and protesting about Frances having "left us earlier than she would have done" because of Butler's appointment as a commander of volunteers. Many Butler relatives were to serve in the war, notably Major General William Orlando Butler of Kentucky, a son of Edward Butler's uncle Pierce Butler and a prominent Democratic politician. In Nelly's view, her son-in-law, "like the rest of the Butlers . . . is Mexico mad. . . . I think it is a great folly on his part." She knew that Dunboyne's 1846 crop had been disappointing and that Frances must oversee the plantation while Butler was gone. When Frances could not travel to Virginia in 1847, however, Nelly's slant on the matter remained bitter: "He considers unnecessary expense, visiting young Daughters & a mother 68 years old besides other dear friends."[24]

Butler's U.S. Army commission was not formally delivered until June 1847, but he received the news of his assignment the previous February. In late May, Butler was on his way to Texas as a colonel commanding the 3rd Dragoon Regiment. Frances gratefully responded to his letter informing her of the safe arrival "on the Brazos" and sent him the best wishes of friends and of "Coxe," the overseer. She once again took charge of Dunboyne Plantation and commenced a weekly report on events at home: Cox was planting potatoes and laying by the sugar cane and had pronounced the recent rains as good for the corn; Lulu, the nurse for the sick slaves, was attending only a few "patients," who are "doing well"; the carpenter Johnson made and installed shutters for the parlor window; Sissy and Caro wrote home and anticipated a rest from school; Frances wanted Butler to write Caro, who was becoming a flirt; and their old friends, the Henry McCalls, of Evan Hall Plantation near Donaldsonville, were visiting and would stay "some time." Frances ended her letter with a plea for Butler not to be concerned that she write to him all of her "troubles." After all, admitted Frances, "I have no one but you to aid me, our interests are the same—and you are the Proper person to advise with." For the rest of the Mexican War and until his return in late July 1848, Frances Parke Butler wrote her husband with the plantation and family news, informed him of neighborhood happenings, sought his advice, fretted about whether she could handle the challenges, and sent Colonel Edward Butler her love and encouragement.[25]

6

With the 3rd Dragoons

The War with Mexico, 1847–1848

In spite of Zachary Taylor's military successes in 1846, the United States failed to subdue the Mexican government. Official opposition remained, especially in the politically strategic, heavily populated parts of central and southern Mexico. In the United States in early 1847, the political promises of a quick, decisive victory encountered disappointment. General Winfield Scott depleted Taylor's army in northern Mexico in order to begin preparations for the invasion at Vera Cruz, with the objective of capturing the nation's capital. The undermanned forces led by Taylor were to be challenged in late February 1847 at the Battle of Saltillo-Buena Vista. No one knew that this battle would be the last of the major fighting in northeastern Mexico.

Mexico was divided by class, race, and politics. With diminishing allegiance of the populace to a national purpose, the war in the northern sector was becoming a guerrilla contest. The fighting was sanctioned partly by the Mexican government but assumed a local, unofficial character. Mexicans fought the United States and also among themselves. As a result, by the end of 1847 the Mexican nation approached chaos. Pervasive and rapacious atrocities were committed against Mexican civilians by poorly disciplined American volunteer troops. In the north, the struggle evolved into one of revenge, reprisal, and viciousness between Mexican guerrillas and the U.S. volunteer and regular armies. In March 1847, Mexican general Antonio Canales proclaimed martial law and ordered the citizens "to give no quarter to any American . . . even though they be unarmed." The initial U.S. enlistments were ending, forcing the War Department under Secretary William L. Marcy to issue a second call for volunteers during late 1846. Toward the end of this effort, on February 11, 1847, Congress created the 3rd Regiment of U.S. Army Dragoons, eight infantry regiments, and one of voltigeurs (skirmishers). As an incentive, Congress made available to volunteer and regular soldiers, excluding officers, bounties of 160 acres of land. The result was that most of the new regiments rapidly filled their quotas of men.[1]

The new dragoon regiment was commanded by Edward G. W. Butler of Louisiana. Volunteers to fight in Mexico possessed complex reasons for leaving their families, but the desire for military fame and action were common incentives among the officers. Even though Butler finally had gained moderate wealth as a sugar cane planter by 1847, his earlier army career had failed to provide him with the sort of fame that his Revolutionary era family attained. Butler also maintained an interest in the fate of Texas. In his later years, he spoke of a commitment to the dying Andrew Jackson. He promised to obtain Sam Houston's support for the annexation of Texas to the United States and for abandoning any alliance with France or Great Britain. Butler naturally championed the expansionist Democrat James K. Polk for president as the conflict with Mexico approached, and he hoped that his military training would be in demand. He soon was in communication with Zachary Taylor, offering opinions and advice. After Louisiana's Governor Isaac Johnson made Butler a major general of the 3rd Division of the Louisiana militia, Butler sensed an opportunity for glory should he serve with Taylor. Upon hearing of his designation as colonel of the 3rd Dragoons, his immediate reaction appears to have been disappointment at not receiving a higher rank. The war with Mexico, however, would be Edward Butler's chance, perhaps a last chance, to join the many Butler kin to serve their country, to fulfill a deep and burning wish for military fame, and to make his own mark as a warrior.[2]

The 3rd Dragoon Regiment's first headquarters was Chalmette Plantation, downstream from New Orleans. In January 1815, the site witnessed American forces under Andrew Jackson defeat an experienced British army. Located near the Mississippi River, it was the gathering place for volunteers from across the United States before heading off to Mexico. Fields of misery and disease, the plantation flooded from frequent rains; provisions were inadequate, and proper medical care was almost absent. Unrest thrived among the volunteers destined for Mexico, and many sickened and died. Writing home about the experience in July 1846, an Indianan observed: "We are almost deluged in water and mud, as it has rained almost every day since we left home. Having pitched our tents, several of us not particularly delighted with our new quarters, sought more congenial lodgings in the city. . . . Having arrived [at camp] we were forced to wade from the river to our tents, nearly to the knees in mud and water. . . . Some of the more enterprising in camp have greatly improved their conditions, by laying hardwood in the bottom of their tents. . . ." The outdoor tent accommodations appear to have been reserved for volunteers. The regular army soldiers found relative comfort in brick and wooden structures closer to the city, in the military post known as Jackson Barracks. Few of the officers in the army shared the encampment, but instead stayed in New Orleans. Named second in command under Butler initially was Lieutenant Colonel Thomas P. Moore, a Virginian living in Kentucky who served with Illinois volunteers in the 1832 Black Hawk War. Under Moore was Major Lewis Cass Jr., appointed from Michigan. Cass was the son of the future 1848 Democratic presidential candidate against Whig candidate Zachary Taylor.[3]

The recruitment of volunteers for the ten companies of the 3rd Dragoons, undertaken mainly by their captains, occupied much of the spring of 1847. Unranked soldiers received enlistment compensation, and physicians determined their physical fitness for service. The list of ranked commanders first assigned to the companies in the regiment was provided to Butler by the office of the army's long-serving adjutant general, Brigadier General Roger Jones. It was a varied group, some foreign-born, a few with prior experience in the military:

John Butler of Philadelphia [kin to Butler's relative Pierce Butler]
Richard T. Merrick of Maryland
Lemuel Ford of Indiana
John S. Sitgreaves of South Carolina
William H. Duff of New York City
Greene W. Caldwell of North Carolina
James Hagan of Alabama
Alphonse W. Duperu of Louisiana
Edgar B. Gaither of Kentucky
Andrew T. McReynolds of Michigan

Most of the commanders initially had been assigned to infantry units but by April were officially part of Butler's dragoons. Once the company ranks filled, the regiment was scheduled to move to Point Isabel, Texas, located on an inlet separated from the Gulf of Mexico by Padre Island. It served as the main base of operations and supply for Zachary Taylor's army in northern Mexico. Colonel Butler, who received permission to remain at Dunboyne Plantation until the regiment was organized, ordered his captains to requisition the horses and the necessary "horse furniture." By April 20, only five of the companies had assembled, and only one numbered over one hundred men. Butler reported to General Jones the likely readiness of the companies to "take the field" by May 31. He stressed the need for tents, horses, and equipment for the anticipated full complements of 110 men per company and noted that Major Cass was to sail for Point Isabel on May 18. His destination was Palo Alto, the site of the battle the previous May. There, he was to join Lieutenant Colonel Moore and meet the regiment. Butler planned to unite with the 3rd Dragoons once all of the companies had gathered.[4]

Within the structure of the U.S. Army of the time, dragoons constituted one of the three parts—along with infantry and artillery. They were "light cavalry," capable of fighting on horseback and afoot, armed with pistols, carbines, and sabers. Each dragoon regiment consisted of alphabetically lettered companies of roughly one hundred privates, each company commanded by a captain, a first and a second lieutenant, and several sergeants and corporals. At the regimental level was a full colonel, with a lieutenant colonel and a major as additional senior officers. Serving as the colonel's secretary to assist in writing official letters and orders and to make reports was an officer-level adjutant. His duties also might include training the regiment's noncommissioned officers and managing its band. Each regiment was to have a "surgeon" and two assistants. The quartermaster's unenviable task was arranging for food provisions for the regiment as well as for draft animals, horses, and mules, for clothing, knapsacks, and other necessary items, and for shelter for the men. Butler's adjutant until the end of 1847 was Second Lieutenant John V. S. Haviland of Pennsylvania, succeeded by Second Lieutenant Edward McPherson of Maryland. Appointed in April 1847 to the important position of regimental quartermaster was Second Lieutenant Charles Radziminski. A forty-two-year-old native of Poland, veteran of the Polish Revolutionary Army, and resident of Washington, D.C., he proved to be invaluable. After October 1847, Radziminski was assistant adjutant to the regiment and assumed the role of regimental adjutant in March 1848. Butler's most trusted and reliable assistant, he and the colonel worked closely. The friendship between him, Butler, and all members of the Butler family was to last for the rest of Radziminski's all-too-short life.[5]

Colonel Butler almost immediately experienced problems in assembling his regiment in full strength. As the companies gathered in New Orleans, some were still undermanned, and "recruiting funds" were requested. Like so many other volunteers encamped at Chalmette, men began to sicken. Clothing and stands of arms were needed, and the horses supplied for Captain Sitgreaves's still-absent company were "inferior in quality and in a condition which disqualifies them for service and reflects no credit upon the Quartermaster Department." A blow to the pride and aspirations of Butler was the decision of President Polk and the War Department in May to remove five companies from the 3rd Dragoons that were intended for General Taylor's command. They instead sailed to Vera Cruz to join General Winfield Scott's army heading inland to Mexico City. Butler did not know that by then Taylor, having lost faith in the Democratic administration in Washington, no longer cared to command U.S. forces. To no avail, Colonel Butler complained to Adjutant General Jones about the troop reduction. He expressed to Taylor his "mortification and regret in not being allowed to take to you, as I anticipated, my entire Regiment." Taylor equivocated. He told Butler definitely that "your command would largely share" in "forward movement to San Luis [Potosi]." In the same message, however, Taylor expressed his hope for a quick peace, following which he anticipated "the pleasure of your company in Louisiana."[6]

From New Orleans, the typical means of reaching Texas was by ship. After experiencing the disease and distressing conditions at camp in Chalmette, the soldiers often fared unhappily on board. For many, the voyage was their first time at sea. The *Southern Sentinel* of Plaquemine, Louisiana, repeated an illustrative and comical story: an innocent, piney-woods Alabama volunteer aboard ship applied salt water to rinse his long, dirty, and unruly hair after having rubbed in a soap of turpentine base. The chemical result of the mixture of salt water and turpentine caused his hair to rise, "stiff as the quill of a porcupine." Suspecting that "'some of them thar Louisianians has played tricks enuff on me,'" the enraged man pulled out his Bowie knife. "'Now if any one dare, lit him fetch me the one that put salt in this ere water!'"[7]

Butler arrived on June 12, 1847, at Point Isabel, the small village just north of Padre Island that Taylor employed as the army supply depot. Its harbor "filled with hundreds of vessels," Point Isabel appeared to Butler "more like the levee at New Orleans." Teamsters and laborers and acres of wagons and army stores crowded the scene. His destination was nearby Matamoros, the headquarters of the Lower Rio Grande District commanded by Colonel William Davenport of Pennsylvania. Reflecting a common practice for U.S. Army officers, two dependable slaves from Dunboyne Plantation accompanied Butler. Named Dennis (age twenty-eight) and William (thirty-three), they attended his needs for proper uniforms, clean quarters, and healthy food. They also groomed his horses and handled other chores. Butler received extra pay for their expenses. Dragoon commanders like Butler also brought their own horses, whereas noncommissioned officers and privates were "issued mounts." Butler's four companies, or the regiment "right wing," were assembled at Matamoros with companies of the 10th and 13th Infantry Regiments. He found them "encamped and in a good state of discipline." The level of instruction was commendably high, and Butler congratulated his men for "their Soldierlike manner and Gentleman like deportment." Still expecting the arrival of a fifth company under Captain Sitgreaves, who had been diverted to Vera Cruz, Butler anticipated proceeding on to "join the commanding general," with whom the Butlers had enjoyed a long friendship. (Delighting Frances Butler and her neighbors on his way home in early December 1847, Taylor's steamboat docked at Dunboyne for a visit and drinks. Evidently with trepidation, she had a friend "dr[a]w some old Bramiss, and Pale Sherry neither of which nor any of your best wines had been touched since you left.") Butler's goal of serving personally with his friend was not to be: instead, the 3rd Dragoons, the 13th Infantry Regiment, and other regiments were ordered to the newly established "camp of instruction" near Mier. It was a town on the supply route from the Gulf Coast to Monterrey and located near the Rio Grande River above Camargo, which was the head of navigation for large, shallow-draft steamboats. They did not arrive at Mier for months, during which the men would be subjected to the perils of the climate and to disease in the camp at Matamoros. It was the beginning of a painful experience for the troops and their commander, who came to love and respect the men of his regiment.[8]

The grave dangers to army volunteers in the Mexican War from disease have been well documented. Soldiers often arrived already sick with measles and small pox, or weak from their exposure and living conditions in the camp below New Orleans. In the crowded, lowcountry military camps of Mexico, they caught influenza and malaria and became infected with diarrhea and dysentery. Yellow fever broke out in Vera Cruz the summer of 1847. For the survivors, months passed before soldiers became acclimated and resistant. Most of the regular army soldiers already had been exposed to many ailments that thrived in the camps, and unlike the volunteers, most were vaccinated for smallpox. When hospitals finally were organized, they were undermanned, and the treatments were inadequate or incorrect. Referring to the hospitals in Matamoros, an Illinois volunteer, Private Thomas D. Tennery, commented: "It presents quite a sorrowful aspect; there are some five or six places [around the city] where they are kept; these though large and spacious are crowded with the sick from all parts of the Union." Colonel Butler encountered the problems immediately. Among the quandaries he faced was resolving "whether the heirs of the deceased Soldiers are entitled to compensation for articles of clothing to which they were entitled but which they had not drawn at the times of their deaths." News of the sickness among his regiment and others came both through newspapers and by letter from him to Frances. It added to her anxieties about her own numerous ill friends and neighbors that summer and about the sick, weary, and sometimes recalcitrant plantation slaves for whom she was responsible. The cane and corn crops at least appeared in fine shape.[9]

Throughout the summer of 1847, Butler's 3rd Dragoons languished in the camp near Matamoros. Their regimental complement of horses remained below the needed count, and many of the horses supplied from New Orleans were unfit. They were "in so poor a condition," wrote Butler, "as to render it necessary for the Quarter Master to send them to pasture." As a result, the regiment was hindered from undertaking its important training task, "the drill on horseback." Even the arrival of the long-delayed company under Captain Sitgreaves, which suffered through a forty-day voyage from Charleston, South Carolina, somehow routed initially to Vera Cruz, was disconcerting. Sitgreaves reported the death from yellow fever of one of Butler's most esteemed original company captains, William Duff. In addition, because the company arrived at Matamoros infected with mumps and measles, Butler reported that "I have encamped it . . . beyond my chain of sentinels." A number of men had not received medical inspections, which disqualified them from service.[10]

The prospect of moving his regimental headquarters from Matamoros to Mier appealed both to Colonel Butler and to Frances. New Orleans and other city newspapers sent correspondents to Mexico and kept the American public informed. Frances searched the papers for word of the war and the regiment and sought news from other sources. Situated on the edge of the Rio Grande Valley and within distant sight of mountains to the west, Mier upon approach brought into view "white washed grave yard walls, and white stone houses, added to two large churches near the center of the town: . . . the appearance of a beautiful city." Reputed to be healthy, Mier was near the juncture of the Rio Grande with a smaller stream. The commander of the Upper Rio Grande District at

Mier, Brigadier General Enos D. Hopping, in late July reported inaccurately to his superiors that it contained no death-causing disease that was indigenous to the location. He added that clean water was available both for bathing and for drinking, and close to Mier there also was a hot spring with healthful qualities. But Hopping, a "political" appointee from New York and an officer of volunteers, beginning March 1847, could not deny the difficulties that the men in camp near Mier were undergoing. They suffered from "excessive heat," diarrhea (attributed by Hopping to "imprudence in . . . diet"), and measles. He still had no decent hospital and lacked a trained field surgeon. The position was supposed to be occupied as a matter of course at any large camp. The general's command in mid-August included eight companies each of the 10th and 13th Infantry Regiments, seven of the 16th Infantry, and ten companies of the 4th Indiana Volunteers—all told, more than twenty-five hundred men. Over one-fourth were reported sick on August 22. He anxiously awaited the arrival of Butler's full complement of dragoons in order to quell the ever-bold attacks on traders and the military supply wagon trains by guerrilla bands. Several occurred in August and September 1847, and the U.S. Army began to tighten its control over local Mexicans and their political leaders.

One of the companies of the 3rd Dragoons was captained by John Butler of Philadelphia, the son of Philadelphian doctor James Mease. His grandfather, John Mease, was with Washington during the crossing of the Delaware River in December 1776. Captain Butler's maternal grandfather was Pierce Butler, uncle of the 3rd Dragoon Regiment commander. He already was scouting in the vicinity of Mier and recovered a large number of wagon-loads of goods captured by the partisans. A squadron of thirty dragoons had killed fifteen "robbers." When he wrote his superior on August 8, however, the captain was suffering from "an attack of the worst kind of the prevailing disease of the Country"—probably dysentery. He reported seven hundred or more men sick at Mier; in understatement, "I cannot think the encampment healthy." The conditions at Mier eventually received acknowledgment, but on September 1 General Hopping was among the dead. Until the arrival of the main body of 3rd Dragoons, his place temporarily was occupied by Brigadier General William G. Belknap, a veteran of earlier battles of the Mexican War. Still at Matamoros and awaiting horses, Colonel Butler reported on September 3 of having 150 men on the sick list, a number of them becoming fatal. The situation could not have been more worrisome, and Butler prayed for a change of air and for health-giving exercise for his men.[11]

Their long wait ended on September 8. Butler wrote to Colonel William Davenport at Camargo of his planned departure with four companies, "without their pay," and still "without their compliment of horses." Belknap ordered Butler to assume command of the camp at Mier and of the Upper Rio Grande District. The colonel's charges not only were his own dragoons, but the infantry regiments already at Mier as well as a regiment of Arkansas cavalry volunteers. His responsibilities suddenly much enlarged, Butler showed no hesitation. He kept his men occupied with drills and with attendance to animals and other duties from 5:00 A.M. to 8:40 P.M. daily.[12]

Instructions from General Taylor's headquarters in Monterrey to Colonel Butler were explicit: The regiment's main duties were to escort mail and supply wagons westward to the town of Cerralvo. It was a "pretty place situated in full view of the mountains which now begin to show their rough and majestic grandeur," on the way to Monterrey. Availing himself of any soldiers in his command, Butler was to use his discretion to explore and patrol the country north and south along the Rio Grande and inland from Mier toward Cerralvo. His men were charged to "suppress guerrillas or robber bands which infest the roads." In addition, the merchants sending goods inland must receive protection from the wagon train escorts. In order to accomplish the scouting, Colonel Butler would have "to keep one company of Dragoons [constantly] in motion through the country below Cerralvo." Each roving company of at least sixty men was relieved at the end of one week. The assigned tasks were challenging. Wagons must be repaired and made good for the long haul to Monterrey. Horses, still in short supply, along with the mules or oxen to pull the wagons, must be cared for properly. The regiment fortunately found a man, Palmer, a self-proclaimed veterinarian, whose knowledge of horses and mules proved sufficient to allow him to join and serve the regiment. Forage was scarce or damaged and unfit for horses and draft animals. Threats from the guerrillas, mainly led by the ex-politician and self-appointed irregular General Canales, required frequent dispatch of detachments. The always dangerous countryside was unfamiliar, the terrain wild, and the locations and quantities of water uncertain. During escorts, Butler's captains were in total and strict command of their wagon trains. The wagon masters were held responsible for teamsters and "sutlers [civilian shop keepers] and others . . . allowed to accompany the train, with or without their wagons." Each train proceeded along with an artillery piece. The manner of march generally was "a Company of Dragoons in front and one in rear of a train; the two companies of

Infantry in the center, with the articles between them; and an advance guard and flankers." Butler's orders of November 1, 1847, to Captain Richard T. Merrick of Maryland for an escort serve as an example of the tasks for which a detachment of dragoons was held responsible:

> At Sunrise to-morrow you will take command of the escort, (to be composed of thirty men of your own Company and the Arkansas Cavalry), and proceed with the train to Aldemas.
>
> After the waggons are loaded with corn, you will continue your march in the direction of Serralvo taking with you your own and thirty men of the Arkansas Cavalry, and directing Capt. Enyart to return with the remainder, in charge of the waggons.
>
> You will be furnished with a sketch of the Country which you are to traverse, and tho' the main object of your expedition is to ascertain the strength and position of the Guerrilla bands, and to destroy or to disperse them, you will, nevertheless, examine the Country minutely, noting the distances between the several places on your route, and the points at which water can be obtained; also the positions at which Forage can be obtained, and in what quantities.
>
> You will subsist your men and horses upon the Country, thru' which you pass, giving orders upon the Quarter Master's Department for the amount of supplies which you may obtain.

Butler was obligated to supply Taylor's able assistant adjutant general, Major William W. S. Bliss, with detailed monthly reports of the many duties and activities of his and other regiments. There is no indication that Butler's mode of command was harsh, but he enforced strict discipline in a perilous zone and in a camp where disease was certain to occur. His family wondered about his handling of the troops and whether he was severe with them. Because Butler was exacting, his mode of command differed from that of most other units in the war with Mexico. There was little room for the more common "obsession with democracy in U.S. volunteer camp life." Partly tongue-in-cheek but tellingly, Frances asked him soon after Butler arrived at Mier: "Did you ever ask Mr. Radziminski if he had found you a strict disciplinarian? You recollect I told him you would be."[13]

The apprehending and suppression of bands of guerrillas and robbers being major reasons for the assignment of the 3rd Dragoons to Mier, any success was cause for celebration. A report of Lieutenant J. Harris Maddox, of Maryland, provides an example. After a dangerous raid in Guerrero, situated north of Mier, on the Rio Grande, Maddox related his adventure directly to Butler:

> I have the honor to report that this morning before day break I surrounded the Town of Guerrero & after much trouble succeeded in taking as prisoner Cap Don Jose Maria Gonzales. He was secreted in a dark loft & I entered sword in hand with a soldier following me with a candle, collared him & dragged him from his place of concealment—Canales is within my Chain of Sentinels, & without an accident, I will have him with his excellency Gonzales to you in a day or two—In trying to find a place to ford the river I was near losing one of my men—The river was rocky in its bottom & the horses & mules for some time were lost from sight—I got him out—& he is doing well—
>
> I have completely tamed the town & have got every thing ready for an attack which is expected to be made by some two or three hundred men belonging to Canales & Gonzales' companies now reported to be in here.—
>
> I may fail to take Canales but dead or alive I will deliver Gonzales to you.[14]

The outcome of the capture was unexpected. It turned out that the Canales mentioned in the report was only a captain (who escaped capture), not the guerrilla commanding general. And instead of almost certain execution, the prisoner was exonerated by his military tribunal on February 24, 1848, and released. Gonzales, who had been paroled from an earlier taking, rather than violating that parole had been forced by General Canales to resume duty with the guerrillas. Near the end of his life, during an interview for the *St. Louis Globe-Democrat*, Butler recounted the incident and gave credit to the intervention of a priest who was Gonzales's friend and mentor and who supplied the proof of innocence:

> After his release on parole Canales had sent him an order directing him to come to and settle up his regimental accounts, after which he would be permitted to keep his word to the Americans. Gonzales, like an honorable soldier, refused to do any thing of the kind, and one night a squadron of lancers carried off Capt. Gonzales, who was forcibly retained by Canales until his capture. I shall never forget the look of gratitude upon the priest's face when I issued the order setting Gonzales at liberty.[15]

Catching the elusive enemy within the large area to be covered required that Butler establish command posts in several places around Mier. In October 1847, for instance, Butler received approval for posts at two picturesque old towns, Reynosa, to the south on the Rio Grande, and Agua Leguas, inland to the west of Mier. Part of the challenge for the dragoons was overcoming collaboration between the guerrillas and local traders, politicians, and others. Much of the tribute paid to Canales had been forced on the populace under threat. The U.S. Army attempted to counter local opposition or collaboration with the bandits by taxing towns, imposing collections on people who assisted the enemy, executing any guerrillas who were caught, and even burning villages suspected of harboring bandits. General John E. Wool became Taylor's replacement at Monterrey. His adjutant was Captain Irvin McDowell, a graduate of West Point destined to become a major general for the Union in the American Civil War. McDowell issued Order 11, making Mexican town officials personally responsible. The effects of such extreme measures have been the subject of debate among historians, but the efforts of U.S. authorities increasingly were directed toward dividing Mexicans in order to prevent a united opposition. The armistice of March 6, 1848, would bring an end to official violence. The gradual submission of Mexican rancheros to the U.S. Army led to the virtual elimination of highway robbery by May.[16]

Surrounded by sickness and disease among his men, and by their too-frequent deaths, Butler somehow escaped harm in Mexico. However, numerous company commanders and other close associates were not so fortunate. A recorded case of serious illness provides an example of Butler's concern for his command. Among his most cherished and respected captains were John Butler, Richard Merrick, and John Sitgreaves. They all sickened with influenza or pneumonia worsened by dysentery "owing to the very cold weather" during December 1847. They eventually were taken to the army hospital in the town of Mier. Assistant Surgeon (and future surgeon general of the Confederacy) Lieutenant Colonel Samuel Preston Moore cared for them. Colonel Butler wrote Adjutant General Jones to allow Captains Butler and Merrick, the most ill, leaves of absence "to enable them to recover their health at my plantation in Louisiana" under the watchful care of Frances. So grim became John Butler's condition that his commander wrote Captain Butler's wife, Gabriella Manigault Morris Butler, on December 16 and 19 to report on her husband's condition. Before the letters and request for leave of absence could have reached their destinations—correspondence taking as long as three or four weeks en route to the East Coast of the United States—John

Butler expired on December 23. Informing General Wool, the colonel lamented, "as a Gentleman and Soldier [he] left no Superior behind him." The colonel proceeded to issue a statement to his troops praising Captain Butler and stating the all-too-obvious common pain of the regiment: "Since his [Colonel Butler's] arrival in Mexico, it has been his sad fate to see his officers prostrate and his brave men falling around him, not from the Sword of the enemy, whom they have sought in vain, but from inglorious and unrelenting disease." The address was published in a Philadelphia newspaper, which described it as "extremely and pathetically beautiful; it comes from the very heart of a Commander who deplores the death of so many officers and brave men, the victims of a cruel war, in which climate kills more than the enemy."[17]

Upon receiving the sad news, John Butler's younger brother, Pierce, dispatched the family's plantation physician, Dr. Sam Wilson, from South Carolina to retrieve the body. He also was to bring back to Philadelphia the deceased captain's manservant and a "favorite horse" that Captain Butler took with him to Mexico the previous spring.

Eventually both Merrick and Sitgreaves recovered. Although Merrick was allowed to return to the United States to recuperate, he never visited Dunboyne Plantation.[18]

Further medical problems in the 3rd Dragoons followed John Butler's death. In early January 1848, over twenty men of the regiment caught smallpox, apparently after a dragoon detachment camped overnight at a ranch where infected inhabitants dwelled. Some eight others were found ill when they arrived at Monterrey in attendance to a wagon train. They were isolated, and the surgeon in charge, Nathan Jarvis, vaccinated those of the detachment who had not earlier received protection. The disease problems remained.[19]

While he was in Mexico, Edward Butler's family sought after and fretted over news of the war and of his sector in particular, and eagerly awaited letters from him. Frances Butler worried whether her management of Dunboyne complied with her husband's wishes and whether the crop would be good and make a profit. She also assumed the task of arranging in New Orleans and Philadelphia to have the regimental standard made. The flag, painted on silk, took months to finish and ship to far-off Mier, but after it was received she was given the regiment's effusive thanks. Her act was noted in newspapers, to which Frances's reaction was embarrassment in having her role made public: "*Women* are best in the *shade* & I regret publicity even though it is complimentary." Letters of

Butler's son at South Carolina College and his adoring daughter Isabel, or Sissy, at Belmont School in Virginia were forwarded from home. Butler provided the family with photographs of himself; a rare one survives showing Colonel Butler in his service uniform and sporting a mustache, which was a mark of his dragoon regiment. Sissy gave thanks that he was spared having to participate in the fighting in central Mexico. News arrived that "two of your officers had been wounded"—referring to the companies that had been diverted to Vera Cruz and to Scott's army.

Frances, too, remained concerned, her feelings about his quest for glory conflicted. Thankfully, she could rely for comfort upon old and new friends from her Iberville neighborhood. Most of them living downriver within less than a thirty-minute buggy ride, they included Christopher and Harriet McCall Adams, of Alhambra Plantation; John Hampden Randolph and his wife, Emily, on Forest Home Plantation; Samuel T. Harrison, on Annandale Plantation; Paul (later Louisiana's governor) and Cora Wills Vaughn Hebert, on White Castle Plantation; and John and Ann Montgomery Thompson, living on Claiborne Plantation. Frances attended their family weddings and other special events and exchanged visits when she had time. The men kept watch on the crops and goings on at Dunboyne, and their wives provided much needed society. Frances delivered their good wishes and prayers for his safe return and regularly forwarded messages of love from the wives and children of Butler's two manservants, Dennis and William.[20]

Although she needed her husband's advice in fulfilling her oversight during his absence, Frances feared his temper should she make a misstep. She dealt with her sometimes recalcitrant field laborers and house servants and navigated the endless hazards of the critical fall sugar cane harvest. Aside from the valuable assistance received from the plantation overseers, Cox and Moore, among her most trusted workers was the slave driver, Watt. A diligent and intelligent slave, Watt saved Frances many a worry. While she performed her innumerable duties, Frances wrote Butler at least twice weekly; he sent her equally frequent instructions on plantation management and news of his life with the army in far-off Mexico. They arrived long after the fact—if at all—and with mixed welcome.

Two major events occurred that tested her endurance as well as her relationship with Butler. The first was an accidental fire during the early part of grinding that threatened to destroy the sugar mill. At the time, Frances was quite ill from malarial ague accompanied by chills, fever, sweating, and high pulse rate, but she accepted blame for the fire and delivered praise to those who saved the day. The plantation carpenter, Johnson, "who was at his post, discovered the fire, & by the greatest exertions succeeded in keeping the fire under [control] until assistance reached him." The damage did not materially delay the mill operation, but Frances was mortified to have to report the situation. By the time she had a letter off to him and began to receive his worried responses, Butler was suffering through the illnesses of many in his regiment and the eventual death of Captain Butler. She was unaware of his torments until January 20, 1848. On New Year's Day, 1848, Frances sat at home, exhausted from her exertions during the extremely successful grinding. She was lonely, with no friends or family; even young Lawrence had left her to visit friends in New Orleans. Writing her husband, she spoke of how hard she and her crews worked to save and mill the sugar cane crop. She was grateful for the good results. Although she wished for Butler to be home "this time 1849," she countered his latest reproof and rebuked him. Frances stated in no uncertain terms that "*you know in your own conscience* Mr B— that *I do not deserve it*—I have most anxiously tried to do my duty *always*—and you know that although no lady in this Parish had been so much indulged before marriage—that not one has spent as little—or laboured so much as I have done—If you will only treat me with the consideration and respect due from a Gentleman to a Lady, I will be content—."[21] The reply from Butler may have been sympathetic and calming, and Frances wrote next with love and affection, understanding for the loss of Captain Butler, and gratitude for her husband's approbation. She regretted her expression of anger, however heartfelt. But in some ways, that outburst—a shriek of pain, or of regret—marked a turn in the Butler marriage. Notwithstanding occasional differences between them, there is little indication that Butler ever again was overly faultfinding or made excessive demands upon Frances.

Only six weeks later, while Frances hosted Eliza Donelson, another incident occurred that again tried her resolve and raised different concerns. It involved the death of a young slave whom Caroline Bell had leased to the Butlers' friend Samuel T. Harrison, on Annandale Plantation. The happening touched on how the Butlers perceived their duties to and relationships with their workers in bondage.

The assistant overseer on Dunboyne, an Irishman named Michael Moore, was in the process of acquiring a plantation of his own and had bought eight "young, active, strong, men" in the New Orleans slave market. Frances understood and accepted that the sugar economy and their personal lives were supported by slaves. By this time in her residence on Dunboyne, however, she was in retreat from her and Butler's optimism when they acquired their first plantation properties. Referring to Moore's actions, she reflected to Butler on the "baseless . . . expectations founded on a planters life— . . . almost always one of debt and difficulty." Even so, they both firmly believed in white superiority. They supported other slaveowners' critical views of abolitionists and of their growing, ever frightening drumbeat. They thought of their roles to the Dunboyne Plantation slaves as those of loving, kind parents. After she watched Butler depart for Mexico the previous June, for instance, Frances described for her cousin Mary Custis Lee the goodbye gathering of Dunboyne's slave families: "I never saw anything more touching than the parting between Mr. Butler & his negro's—who are all devoted to him—even the youngest infants were brought forward to be noticed before his departure—it would have afforded the best refutation of the Abolitionists had they witnessed it—for had they been his children, they could not have evinced a grief more deep and sincere."[22]

The slaves on Dunboyne maintained frequent social contact with others on nearby plantations, and an effective grapevine operated to spread word of any incident affecting them. News of a brutal whipping death of a young slave, Yellow Boy, by an overseer named Sowers on the Harrisons' land passed quickly through the slave workers and came to the attention of Frances. No doubt because Harrison was away, and because the slave was Caroline Bell's property, Frances and Eliza took personal action. They immediately sent both the Dunboyne physician, Augustus H. Mears, and overseer Michael Moore to investigate. The body of the slave had been buried hastily in a failed attempt to conceal the evidence, and the examination indicated the true nature of the injuries. All of the information was reported to Frances and Eliza. After Harrison returned, however, and with a threat from Sowers of a defamation suit against Moore, "Dr Mears denied all that they had said, gave a statement . . . that induced him to say the Boy *might* have died of dropsy." Harrison also defended his overseer and had others "sign some paper which saves Sowers from prosecution—and there the matter ends—but it does not end with me—." Frances and her sister-in-law were indignant and distressed, and Frances promptly dismissed Dr. Mears. She sent him a forcefully worded letter accusing him of denying his original statement despite clear proof of death from "*injuries inflicted by the lash.*" A copy of the Mears letter accompanied her missive to Butler, both dated February 15. Already having had some problems with Mears, whose dubious treatment of several Dunboyne workers raised issues, Frances explained: "I did not plague you with these things before, because I knew you liked Mears—but *this last business is too bad*—It was *before* this that our negros were not allowed to go under shelter in the rain, and I have not sent them out since I heard that they were not—." Having already taken on the formidable task of replacing her overseer, Cox, with one named Tirsenie, Frances now hired a new physician, Alfred Hall. She found Hall's treatment of the slaves quite satisfactory and had little inclination to alter her decision: "I think I have made a most happy exchange—Dr. M[ears] and Mr. H[arrison] are very anxious to explain away all my impressions with regard to the affair I mentioned, but I see no good reasons—for changing my opinions about it."[23]

Little documentation exists to show Butler's reaction to the decisions regarding their plantation physician. The couple's letters crossed, some were lost, and he raised issues—which Frances addressed as well as she could, never relenting. Her actions truly were unusual. They challenged some concepts of southern honor, the hierarchy of authority, the role of the male in disciplining slaves, and the personal reputations of persons of respect in the community, particularly those of friends. On the other hand, the Butler and Lewis families had no history of barbarous cruelty to their slaves, and the beating and death of Caroline Bell's young slave touched a raw nerve. The subsequent lies of Mears and Harrison, in an attempt to cover over the facts, affronted even more so Frances's own deeply held honor, based especially upon the traditions of her distinguished family. During Butler's absence, she was accountable for the well-being of her family—which to her included their slaves—and for the plantation. The incident was a threat. It pushed her to fix improper working conditions that her own overseer and the plantation physician had condoned. One cannot help but remark upon the developing character of Frances Butler and her determination to act with a sense of moral right despite far-off Butler's questions: "I wrote to you twice last week and explained your mistake with regard to Dr Mears—." There is no indication that Sowers ever received punishment for his murder. Butler remained a friend of Samuel Harrison and even served as an executor of his estate when Harrison died in 1856, but the reputations of all of the involved men suffered in Frances's eyes.[24] Could the events have contributed further to Frances Butler's disenchantment with life on Dunboyne?

The wartime letters of Frances brought Butler news of family and friends and of the plantation and carried words of love and sympathy for him and his men, but they were seldom happy. Even as her letters described with growing confidence her management of plantation affairs as 1848 progressed, a cloud of possible disapproval from her husband pervaded. Frances's isolation from her family and her increasing responsibilities of managing the plantation added strain to her worry over Butler's and her children's welfare.[25]

From the start of his tour in Mexico, Colonel Butler corresponded not only with his army superiors in the nation's capital, but also with figures of political importance. Among the latter was a longtime family friend, from 1844 to 1849 the U.S. senator from Louisiana, Henry Johnson. An experienced politician, Johnson had served formerly both in the U.S. Senate and House of Representatives, and as governor of Louisiana. While acting as U.S. senator in the early 1820s, Johnson was a suitor of Frances Parke Lewis. Writing her friend Gibson, Nelly Lewis dismissed Johnson: "He is much like a monkey . . . & *murders English & Grammar.* Of course, *wont do.*" He nevertheless constituted a well-placed contact for Colonel Butler, and the two exchanged letters. At least as early as July 1847, chafing over the inactivity in Matamoros and over the progress and handling of the war, Butler wrote Johnson. He recommended that Johnson counsel the president and others to put the Mexican people and the Roman Catholic Church in Mexico "under contribution." Johnson helpfully passed along Butler's ideas to President Polk, who appeared receptive at least to some of the suggestions (although not to that of taxing Mexico's national church).[26]

Butler hoped to earn distinction in action with the enemy, yet he was not even able to join his friend Zachary Taylor in Monterrey, much less enter into direct battle with the Mexican Army. He viewed the dragoons' opponents as robbers and murderers. His letters home to Frances and others made plain his desires, but as one associate observed, Butler had "taken the wrong road to get the active, & exciting service he wished." With the death of the commanding general of the Upper Rio Grande District at Mier, Enos Hopping, Butler visualized improved chances at least for promotion to brigadier general. He again enlisted Johnson's assistance, but both the War Department under Marcy and President Polk were inclined to pass him over for someone else. Johnson's response to Colonel Butler must have been disheartening: Secretary of War Marcy favored promoting "one of the officers most distinguished in the battle of Mexico." Another opportunity arose in January 1848. Butler believed that he had been chosen one of the members of a court of inquiry to handle a difficult and disagreeable dispute between General Winfield Scott and his junior grade generals, William Worth and Gideon Pillow. Instead, the veteran Lieutenant Colonel William Belknap was finally chosen.[27]

General Antonio Canales posed a constant threat, but he also presented to General John E. Wool a conundrum illustrative of the strange war in which the United States was engaged. Canales, discontent with the actions of the governing Mexican military, wanted to seek independence for his own base of operations, Tamaulipas State. Angling for support among his own people as well as from the United States, Canales wrote Wool in late January. He offered to "cease all hostility to the Army and American citizens" in return for Wool's cooperation in his independence effort. Wool appeared receptive. He informed Gonzales that he would pass along the offer to superiors but only would respect the declarations of the guerrillas if they first laid down their arms and returned to their homes, and if their acts were confirmed by proper authorities. Because of the discussions, Butler missed out on another opportunity for action. General Wool cancelled an earlier command for the 3rd Dragoons to occupy Victoria, in Tamaulipas, a move intended to counter the threat from Canales. Wool instead promised to protect Mexicans who declared their neutrality and then gave "an indulgence" to Canales and other guerrillas who laid down their arms.[28]

There were to be no further chances for glory: peace negotiations between Mexico and the United States had commenced. By mid-February 1848, even before her husband had official knowledge, Frances reported to him information about a "peace signed by Genl Scott & Mr [Nicholas] Trist, with the Mexican Authorities" and the general terms of the agreement. She and the family could begin to rejoice and to hope for Butler's safe return home; he and others still at their posts in Mexico could only wonder and wait.[29]

In spite of an armistice agreed to by March, its terms and effects on Butler and his 3rd Dragoons remained unclear. A curious correspondence ensued between Butler and General Wool, and Wool's adjutant, McDowell. It illustrates their mutual confusion over developments in the peace effort. The communication commenced after contact between Butler and his adversary, General Canales, regarding cessation of hostilities. Thinking that Colonel Butler knew of his peace overtures with Wool, Canales requested that Butler respect the "arrangement" he had with Wool regarding the end of fighting. Butler responded, indicating that he had not received official instructions and would continue "to disinfest the neighborhood, its roads and places of concealment." He coldly reminded Canales of the command the previous April for Mexican soldiers to undertake "indiscriminate massacre of my [U.S.] countrymen," and suggested that if Canales wanted to avoid capture and punishment, he surrender "unconditionally." The exchange between Butler and Canales was reported to Wool, who disputed Butler's handling of things. Butler explained that he remained uninformed of any amnesty and expressed disagreement with any "guarantees" to Canales, in whom Butler held no trust. "It has been my constant effort," wrote the colonel to Captain McDowell, "since entrusted with the command of this District, to ascertain the character, habits, and intentions of those lawless men; and, as they are guerrillas, in fact, opportunity is all that is wanted to recall them to their accustomed and favorite pursuits—indiscriminate robbery and murder." Butler pressed General Wool, at Monterrey. Wool assured Butler that he remained watchful over Canales and that Butler, too, should maintain vigilance over the guerrillas, not to let up on them unless they laid down their arms and returned to their fields, but to not permit the execution of prisoners without following due process. "I take it that you will not let them surprise you," Wool also cautioned his colonel, no doubt unnecessarily. Wool, confused about the general treaty progress and also baffled by a lack of clear orders, expressed dismay about any amnesty: "The whole procedure . . . is to me incomprehensible . . . it would seem to be without the authority of the President," and the Treaty of Guadalupe Hidalgo still had no approval by Mexico or by the U.S. Senate. Time gaps in contacts over the long distances between Mexico and Washington led to uncertainty and rumors and to unrest among Wool's officers. Some of them believed that unless the armistice was followed quickly by a ratified treaty, fighting surely would recommence. In late April Butler received instructions from Wool to hold his position with no "forward movement or . . . any material change in the disposition of troops." Butler would receive his orders, Wool cautioned, only when the final political decision was definitely known.[30]

Between February and May 1848, as the 3rd Dragoons remained restless in camp, the routines and drills at Mier were to be maintained, strict order was to be kept, and the authority of the U.S. Army respected. Butler's Daily Orders and Letterbook both reflect the varied events and challenges of an occupying force in Mexico: A U.S. citizen, a murderer who fled to Mexico to avoid capture, was arrested and returned to Corpus Christi; armed deserters of a Texas battalion who placed the town of Lampasas under contribution were ordered apprehended; Mary O'Doherty, a laundress and the wife of an imprisoned army private, was banned from her husband's post at Cerralvo (Butler appealed to the humanity of the post commander not to "turn her out upon the world, in a strange country, whatever might have been his [the private's] offenses, a helpless and unprotected female"); and two bars of silver, carried on a wagon train escorted by the 3rd Dragoons, were stolen, and the thief was caught and jailed. By April, Butler was faced with some trouble within the camp involving Arkansas mounted volunteers. Those troops, along with the Texas Rangers, were allowed unusual independence of movement in their roles mainly as scouts for regular troops. Earlier in the war, both units participated in indiscriminate killing of Mexicans, contributing much to the deterioration of the war. Generals Taylor and Scott feared a popular revolt against U.S. military forces. Butler, wary of the volunteer units, exercised caution and did not allow them or anyone else to cause problems with the local population. He worked the volunteers hard, and they consequently complained. Butler informed General Wool's adjutant Irvin McDowell that a number of his dragoons not only suffered from the smallpox, but that the men and their horses were exhausted by constant detachment duty. Butler explained that the volunteers simply had been too idle and into mischief and were owed some activity. A sorrowful event of the last few months in Mexico was a duel in March between Lieutenants J. H. Maddox and Edward McPherson, Butler's adjutant. The duel and McPherson's death prompted the arrest of Maddox, the hero of the capture of Captain Gonzales the previous month. Colonel Butler requested that he receive a general court-martial.[31]

The wind-down of the U.S. occupation of Mexico after official treaty ratifications took several months. Ever present was fear of renewal of hostilities because of abusive and illegal behavior on the part of insufficiently disciplined American soldiers. Butler's frustrations with his superiors, the difficulties of managing restless, bored, and sick troops, and his own inactivity tempted him to resign. Frances, now well in charge of Dunboyne, discouraged any such course. He had incurred too many sacrifices and still "had no opportunity of winning Laurels for" himself. She cautioned him that "should the War be renewed, and further opportunity for fame escape you" before any lasting peace treaty was ratified, he would regret prematurely coming home "to look after things." "You could never cease to lament a step of the sort," Frances wrote. Only in mid-June would Butler receive a notice from Wool that "peace has been definitely settled." Before Butler could leave, General Wool ordered Butler to "put all . . . troops, except Captain Hunt's Company, en route for Matamoros." One hundred sixty-two wagons were on their way to Camargo, located at the head of steamboat navigation, and they were available to the regiment. Still in Mier on June 20, and after having to deal with "a few of my Dragoons" who "became mutinous," Butler reported the final departure of his regiment and a company of the 10th Infantry. Five companies of North Carolina volunteers left for Camargo, and another remained at Mier. There also remained "about fifty sick Dragoons," who were brought by wagon to Mier and loaded onto a steamboat. Butler pleaded with Wool that "as the Dragoons are without tents, I hope they will be discharged or ordered to New Orleans at once." On June 14, in an order that described much in brief fashion, Captain John Sitgreaves announced a meeting the following day of a Council of Administration "for the purpose of disposing of clothes of deceased soldiers."

In his Order 164 to the regiment to turn over their horses, arms, and equipment before embarking for New Orleans, General Wool commended the men: "In parting with this Corps, the Commanding General cannot omit expressing his admiration of its discipline, and the obedience and promptness, with which all the duties required of it, have been performed, which reflects the highest credit in the Officers and men, as well as upon their able and efficient Commander." The respect between Wool and Butler was mutual. When Butler caught up with the remainder of his regiment in Palo Alto, he also wrote an eloquent farewell to soldiers with whom he had formed a close bond and shared both deep sadness and a sense of accomplishment. Through his adjutant, Charles Radziminski, he addressed the regiment on June 30, 1848:

> The war is ended, and the officers and men of the 3d. Dragoons, having honorably acquitted themselves of their duty to their country and their obligations to their Government, are about to return to their homes, and to resume their respective positions in society.
>
> The Colonel Commanding would, therefore, do injustice to them and violence to his own feelings, were he to allow them to depart without bearing evidence to their claims upon the respect and gratitude of their countrymen.
>
> They have experienced much hardship and suffering, and have been decimated by disease; and yet, the heavy requirements of the service have been promptly met, and subordination and discipline have continued to be their characteristics.
>
> Pride, therefore, commingled with pain and with pleasure, is the predominant feeling with which their Colonel takes leave of them; and, wheresoever their lots may be cast, and whatsoever fortune may attend them, his prayers and best wishes will accompany them.

In one of her last letters to her husband before he left Mexico, on June 15, Frances Butler advised him to acquire some of the dragoon horses and mules for the plantation; they had become scarce due to the war needs. Following his regiment's official disbanding at Jefferson Barracks, Missouri, Butler and his servants, Dennis and William, were back at Dunboyne Plantation by late July or early August 1848, safe and healthy. The colonel soon received from his Iberville friends a "large cut and thrust sword" with a gilt scabbard, an honored gift that he retained throughout his life.[32] It recently was rediscovered, was acquired from a dealer, and is preserved at the Historic New Orleans Collection.

Edward Butler's arrival home must have been joyous, but surely he felt chastened by his experiences in Mexico. Despite Frances's watchfulness and adept oversight, Dunboyne had been a major concern. An exacting husband for whom wealth and social advancement long seemed unreachable, Butler cast an ever-sharp eye on her management. Was his thirst for military distinction quenched? We cannot know for certain. Butler's aspirations to glory in battle and to the rank of general were thwarted. By the time he arrived in northern Mexico, the main thrust of action was in central Mexico. American forces soon were under a different commander than the friend, Zachary Taylor, whom he chose to follow. Long months of waiting in Matamoros followed by the "camp of instruction" at Mier proved rarely active militarily. But the posts exposed him and his dragoon charges to illness equal to any that the war wrought upon American soldiers. The disease-related loss of many good friends and comrades grieved him. Still, Butler achieved the respect of his men and superiors, carried out his responsibilities with diligence, and maintained discipline firmly but humanely in the midst of danger and with little reward. Once Butler was home and delivered his final report, Adjutant General Jones wrote to express his personal admiration and appreciation:

> Colonel:
>
> . . . In taking official leave of you, Colonel! I would do injustice to my feelings did I not express the regret I feel on your again returning to Civil life. A soldier by education, and I might say by inheritance as so many of the name have distinguished themselves in the Army, you cheerfully offered your Services when your Country needed them. As the Colonel of one of the Regiments raised for prosecuting the War with Mexico, you were ever found ready to introduce order and to enforce discipline, and in exercising so responsible a Command, no doubt your own example had the happiest effect on those acting under you.

> I sincerely hope that on leaving the Army, you may find in the bosom of your family that repose and happiness that you merit.
>
> I am Col. Etc. R. Jones Adjt. Genl.[33]

In 1875, Butler penned a letter to one of his former volunteers, William Louis Schley of Baltimore. Only in 1881 did Schley send a much-belated reply and report on the whereabouts of a number of the members of the 3rd Dragoons with whom he served. He also reminisced: "I remember you, Col., with much pleasure and shall ever feel kind towards you—you were ever a kind, indulgent friend & your confidence was never lost in me. . . . Accept my warm esteem."[34]

For the remainder of his long life, Edward Butler remembered the wartime experience and cherished the fellowship he shared with his men. In spite of the many disappointments, he could take satisfaction in having performed his duty well and in achieving the goal of service to his nation equal to that of his father and uncles during and after the American Revolution. As for the much challenged but indomitable Frances Butler, her life could resume a more normal course: "I cannot tell you what a relief it will be to me to have no one to govern but myself." Once again and finally, she handed over to her husband the burdensome responsibilities of Dunboyne Plantation.[35]

Colonel Edward George Washington Butler (1800–88) in the uniform of the 3rd Dragoon Regiment, U.S. Army, 1847–48. Throughout his life Butler retained his trim figure and military bearing. The mustache, an identifying symbol of dragoon service during the Mexican War, was shaved off later. The oil portrait is attributed to Jacques Amans and hangs at the Historic New Orleans Collection (HNOC) Research Library. The Historic New Orleans Collection, Gift of David D. Plater and Ormonde Plater, acc. no 2007.0310.

Frances Parke Lewis Butler (1799–1875), circa 1850. Photograph/daguerreotype located at Woodlawn Plantation, Virginia, her childhood home. The portrait shows Frances in her finery, perhaps for a daughter's wedding a few years after her husband's return from army service in Mexico. Courtesy of Woodlawn, a National Trust Historic Site.

Lieutenant Lawrence Lewis Butler, C.S.A. (1837–98), youngest child of Frances and E.G.W. Butler. Photograph by Thuss, Nashville, probably in 1861. Located at HNOC, MSS. 102, in Folder 1594. Lawrence Butler served as an aide-de-camp for Confederate generals Leonidas Polk and Marcus Wright in the Civil War. He assisted his father at Dunboyne following the war, and after his marriage he worked for Edward J. Gay, his father-in-law. The Historic New Orleans Collection, Gift of Richard C. Plater, Jr., acc. no. 76-48-L.

Dunboyne Plantation house. This 1956 photograph shows the house after it was moved back from the Mississippi River and lowered from eight-foot walls to four-foot-high pier foundations sometime around 1893. The house was constructed in 1833 and demolished in the 1960s. Photograph by E. W. McDonald of Dry Prong, Louisiana.

Edward G. W. Butler, circa 1835. The oil portrait, now located at Woodlawn Plantation, Virginia, depicts Butler at a time when he struggled to make Dunboyne Plantation profitable. Courtesy of Woodlawn, a National Trust Historic Site.

"Doremus' Mississippi Views," circa 1875. The town of Bayou Goula, Louisiana. Located about one mile downstream from Dunboyne Plantation, the town was a center of commerce and an outpost for the Union Army in the Civil War. St. Mary's Episcopal Church, which the Butlers attended, is shown. Courtesy of Denis Murrell, of Tally-Ho Plantation, Bayou Goula.

Joseph Erwin, circa 1761–1829, ancestor of Mary Susan Gay Butler. Photograph/carte de visite of a portrait. Erwin, who was important in the development of sugar planting in Louisiana, owned Home Place Plantation (later renamed St. Louis Plantation), near Plaquemine, Louisiana. He played an influential role in the Butlers' move to the state. Author's collection.

Edward James Gay (1816–89). Photograph/carte de visite taken in 1870 by Scholten, of St. Louis. Gay, the father-in-law of Lawrence Lewis Butler, was involved in Butler family affairs from the time of the Civil War onward. Author's collection.

Mary Susan Gay Butler (1845–82), wife of Lawrence Lewis Butler. Black and white photograph/carte de visite. "Sue" Butler provided a home and assisted in caring for her father-in-law E. G. W. Butler from 1877 until her death in 1882. Author's collection.

The purported Butler/McCutchon house in Pass Christian, Mississippi. The Butlers, who rented the house from 1871 until about 1877, found peace and happiness there after the sale of Dunboyne. The Butlers, their son Edward, Jr., and daughter Caroline are buried in nearby Live Oak Cemetery. Undated photograph provided by Jessie M. Heitzmann, of Pass Christian. Courtesy of the Collection of Billy Bourdin, Pass Christian Historical Society.

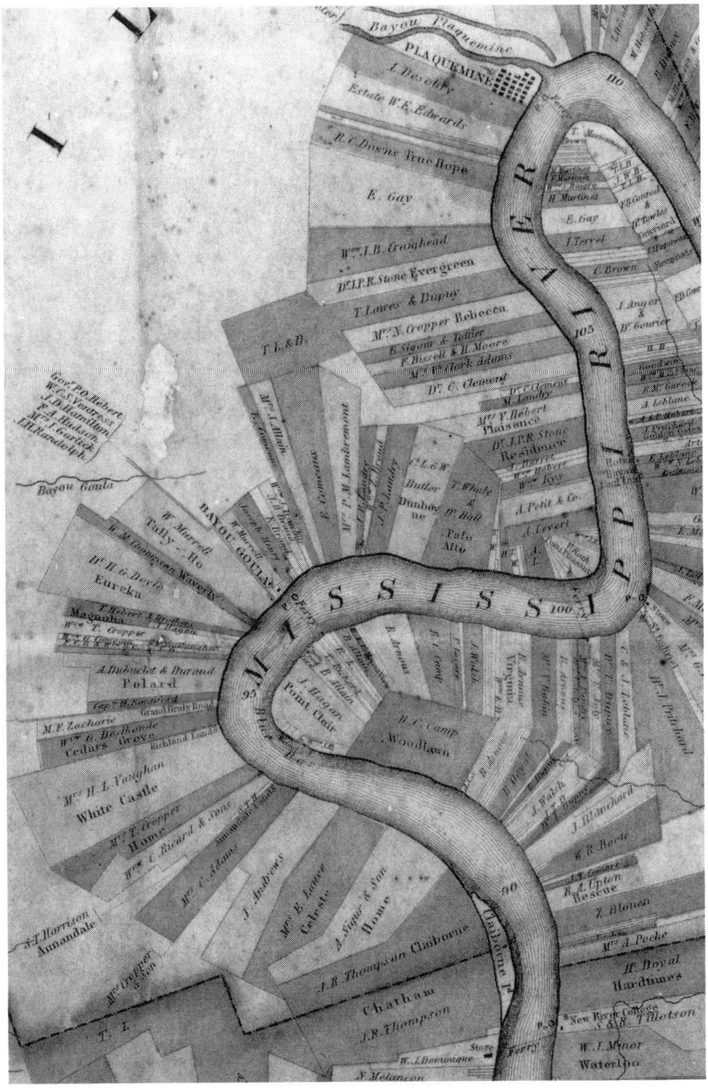

M. Adrien Persac, *Plantations of the Mississippi River from Natchez to New Orleans* (Norman's Chart). Photograph courtesy of Judith Bolton and the LSU Special Collections Library.

Caroline Swanwick "Caro" Butler Turnbull (1834–76). Photograph, circa 1855. Caro Butler Turnbull and her two sons lived with her parents after her husband's death in 1856 through the Civil War until Dunboyne was sold in 1871. Courtesy of Colette Endrizzi of Tucson, Arizona.

Major Lawrence Lewis (1767–1839). Oil portrait by John Beale Bordley in 1841 from an original painted in 1832. Lewis, father of Frances Parke Lewis Butler, assisted the Butlers financially after their marriage and move to Louisiana. Courtesy of Elizabeth Plater Cropp.

Eleanor Parke "Nelly" Custis Lewis (1779–1852). Oil portrait by John Beale Bordley in 1841 from an original painted in 1832. Nelly Lewis was the mother of Frances Parke Lewis Butler. A granddaughter of Martha Washington, in 1799 she married Lawrence Lewis, George Washington's nephew and his personal secretary after Washington left the presidency. Growing resentful of Butler, Nelly Lewis fell out with him in late 1840. After Woodlawn was sold, Nelly resided at Audley Farm, Clarke County, Virginia. Courtesy of Elizabeth Plater Cropp.

Eleanor Isabella "Sissy" Butler Williamson (1832–66). Tinted photograph, circa 1860. Isabel was the first daughter of E. G. W. and Frances Parke Butler and the first of their children born in Louisiana, at Dunboyne Plantation. Reproduction photograph of the original by Chris Bartol. Courtesy of Philip Eugene Morehead.

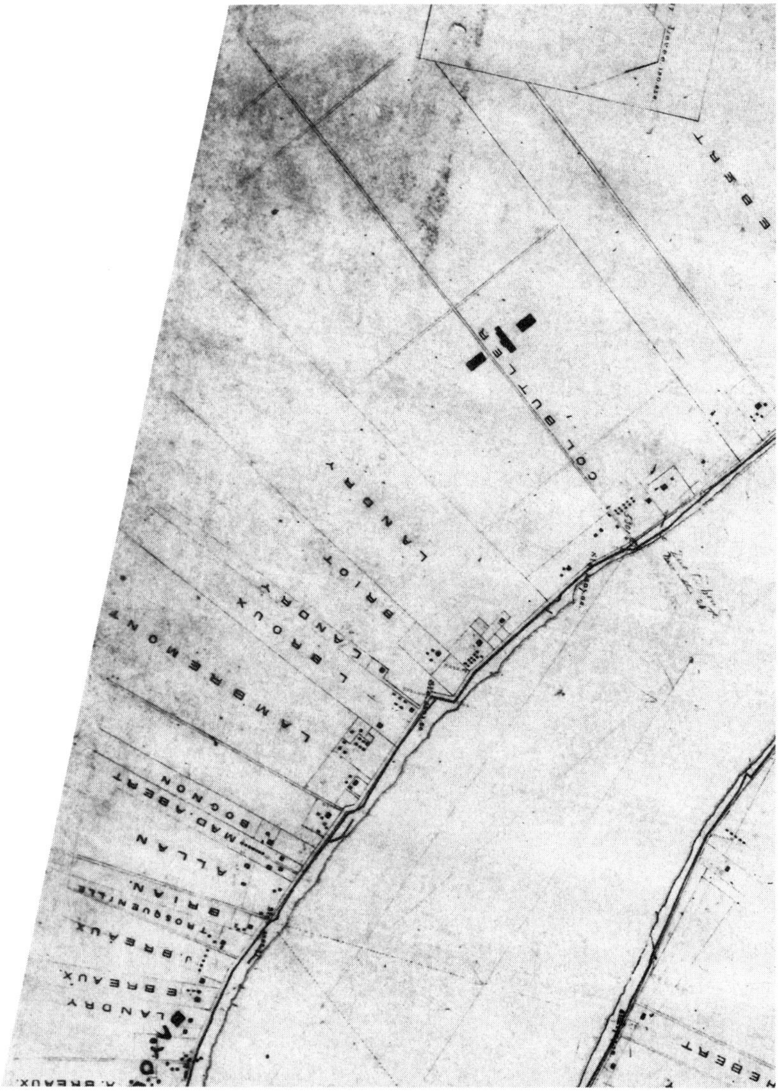

The 1851 map of A. A. Humphreys and H. L. Abbot of the Mississippi River depicts Dunboyne Plantation ("Col. Butler") with its buildings and cabins. The map of the plantation shows the locations of the Big House, slave cabins and other nearby structures, the sugar mill, and the Mississippi River. The map original is at NARA, Record Group 77, MD1-30.

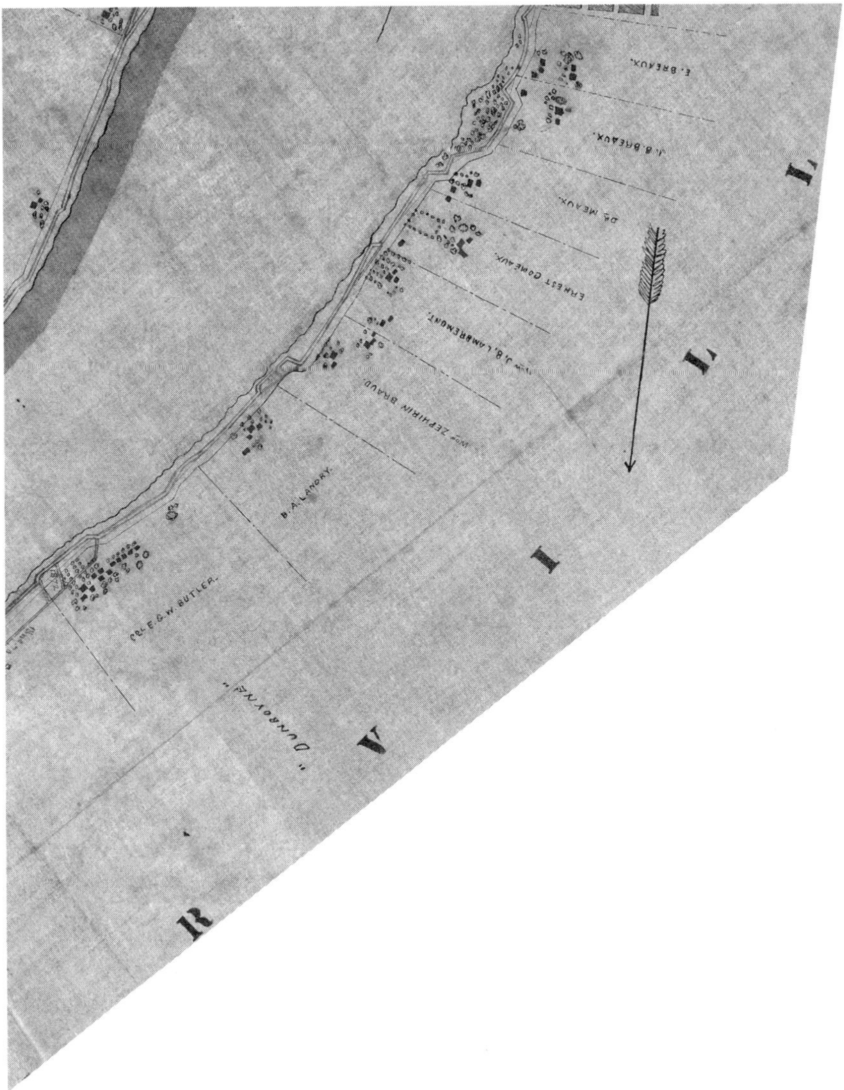

Louisiana Board of Public Works 1866 map entitled *Mississippi River Levees from Thomas Point to Carrollton (New Orleans)*, Chart 11-U, Map LD 5 Z001, from Louisiana and Lower Mississippi River Collections, LSU Libraries. The map shows the Plaquemine Bastion Fortress (built by the U.S. Army in 1864), the town of Plaquemine, and Bayou Plaquemine.

Major Edward G. W. Butler, Jr., eldest Butler child. Elevated to a major in the Confederate Army in the 11th Louisiana Regiment, Butler was killed at the Battle of Belmont, Missouri, on November 7, 1861. A young man of great promise, he served as secretary to the United States legation in Berlin before the Civil War. His death intensely grieved Frances Butler. The Historic New Orleans Collection, Gift of Richard C. Plater, Jr., acc. no. 76-48-L.

7

"A Proper Sense of One's Obligations"

Fulfillment, 1850–1860

At the end of the war with Mexico, Dunboyne was well-established. On its 550 improved acres, and nearby the Butler residence, mules, horses, and over a dozen cattle grazed. Sometimes, as in 1860, the cultivated land was reduced, perhaps due to crop rotation or to weather conditions. Aside from sugar cane, the crop selections said much about the diets and other needs of those living on the place or of the livestock. The 1860 census, for instance, counted 7,500 bushels of Indian corn, 50 bushels of peas or beans, 100 pounds of butter, 20 bushels of Irish potatoes, and 100 pounds of flax, as well as 150 bushels of sweet potatoes. Maps from the time show that the plantation was shaped in a wide, irregular rectangle fronting on the Mississippi River and reaching back over a mile. Edward Butler increased his holdings by 520 acres through a patent acquisition under the Swamp Lands Act of March 1852, which allowed for the purchase of warrants of government-owned "swamp and overflowed lands." Probably intended to ensure a supply of wood fuel for the sugar house, the newly bought land was situated behind the Randolph and Doyle plantations to the south of Dunboyne. The increase in size made Dunboyne a medium-large plantation in Iberville Parish. On Dunboyne's upstream side in the early 1840s, Louis Baugnon initially owned the property; by the time Butler was fighting in Mexico, Valery Hebert owned the plantation, which he named Palo Alto. It grew in the 1850s because of a merger with the plantation just upriver from it belonging to Dr. Alfred Hall and Thomas Whaley. Dunboyne's neighbor downriver was Pierre Joseph Landry, whose family maintained ownership through the Civil War.

The sugar mill complex required access both to the swamp for wood fuel and to the river for receiving and shipping goods. It was located well to the rear of the Dunboyne residence, close to the boundary between the former Thomas/Bell/Butler parcel and the Henry/Butler tract. A well-traveled dirt road connected the back of the plantation and mill directly to the "Dunboyne Landing" on the riverbank downstream from the Butler residence. Like most planters whose property faced the Mississippi River, the Butlers resided at "the front" of the plantation. Although Nelly Lewis wrote during her 1833 visit of a public road separating the home from the flood protection levee, a grove of trees faced the public road. The Dunboyne residence was situated at the back of the grove within hedges or picket fencing sufficient to keep out large animals that on occasion may have been pastured in the grove. On each side of the Butler home there was open space utilized for pasture. Inside of the protective fencing, a garden flourished; it grew vegetables for the Butler kitchen and probably some of the slaves, as well as flowers, ornamentals, and fruit trees. The kitchen structure was separate from and to the rear of the Butlers' house.

Along the Mississippi River in southern Louisiana, building arrangements reflected the time of establishment and, to some degree, the culture of the plantation owners. Dunboyne's layout was similar to many earlier plantations that lined the river. It appears to have been established by Philip Thomas, who owned the eight-arpent tract that Robert Bell acquired in 1826, and lasted throughout the nineteenth century. Maps throughout the decades show that at least two rows of slave cabins faced the river perhaps 100 to 150 yards downstream from the "big house." The square-shaped cabins were regularly spaced and graced by trees planted riverside of the front row. In 1841 there numbered ninety-one slaves; in 1850, the census found ninety-six slaves making their homes in the quarters. Two families likely shared one gable-sided structure, raised off the ground on wood blocks or brick piers. Frances Butler referred to the slave residence area as the "gallery" when she greeted the slaves there following Christmas 1847. Each side of a double slave cabin contained a front door. A shared central chimney allowed for heating the two sides, and the front of each house featured a built-in porch. In recent times, cultural geographers have referred to such structures as "small Creole quarter house" types.

The complex of residential and farm buildings featured a variety of sites and arrangements, with clusters of buildings on the two sides and to the rear of and near the Butler home. Although there is little mention of dependencies around the Butlers' home in family letters, there were barns, a carriage house, livery stables, sheds for horses, cattle, and mules, probably a small infirmary, perhaps a smoke house, and other structures necessary to the functioning of the household and plantation. There does not appear to have been any specific slave dining house. The overseer lived somewhere near the quarters, his house larger and better maintained than the slave cabins. Usually styled similar to slave cabins, Dunboyne's overseer house may have been one of the earlier homes from the Henry or Allain times. The slave driver Watt probably lived in a prominent cabin at the upstream end of the quarters. While some of these outbuildings could be quite substantial, made of brick, most of Dunboyne's probably were simple, wood-frame structures.[1]

No photographs exist of the Butlers' home from the 1840s and 1850s. The house was elevated and sat on brick foundation walls eight feet or so high. The ground-floor basement was employed for food and wine storage, weather-protected clothes washing, and perhaps a servant's room. The home was moved back from the encroaching river around 1893 and was repositioned on four-foot-high brick piers. Photographs taken before its demolition in the 1960s show a simple but refined gable-ended structure in the Greek Revival cottage style. A central hall dividing bedrooms and parlor served probably for a cold or rainy weather dining area, as well as a space for social occasions and to promote circulation of cooling breezes from the Mississippi River. No full description exists of the floor plan, although there was room to handle visits from the Lewises and others and to house the four children. A Greek key-shaped front doorway frame with sidelights and transom—all topped with a simple pediment—and four tall, Greek key-framed shuttered windows extending to the floor faced onto a broad veranda the width of the house. Square porch columns supported the steeply sloped, overhanging roof. The rear also may have had a full gallery, perhaps with a *cabinet* (for storage or bathing) at each end, and the porches may have been used for dining in fair weather. During the era of the Butlers, there was no ell wing off the rear. The front and side walls were covered with lapped boards. The front roof was broken by two simply-shaped dormers, each with two window sashes of six lights to allow for air and daylight. Undoubtedly the Butlers collected rainwater from the roof for drinking and washing, the earlier receptacles likely to have been hogsheads. Eventually cisterns set upon solid brick foundations or walls were constructed. They were made of brick and/or of cypress wood, each shaped like a "huge barrel with staves and metal bands" to hold them tight. Two internal chimneys arose from the roof ridge. Their placement indicates that each chimney had a double hearth to heat two rooms. How the broad hallway was heated is unclear. At the attic level, each of the gable-sided ends displayed three centered and closely set windows with double sashes of six panes. One might assume from their presence that part of the attic had been converted to living space.

A 1956 photo of the Dunboyne house reveals that screened sitting and sleeping porches with tin shed roofs were eventually built, one on each side of the front gallery. Insect-prevention screens were not invented in the antebellum years, however. Because Frances Butler renovated an older Acadian home to what became the Dunboyne house, no doubt much of the heavy timber from that earlier structure was retained. It is not known whether the house utilized bousillage as fill between the timbers on the main floor. In front of the house a picket fence enclosed a flower garden. It may have been a continuation of the Butlers' garden, established in part to satisfy Frances Butler's love of flowers: "You tell me to procure all the flowers and shrubs possible—this I shall surely do," Caroline Bell assured Frances the summer before they arrived in Louisiana in 1831. In addition to the six Butlers, the census of 1850 listed the overseer, William Crabtree (age thirty-five), a native of South Carolina, his Louisiana-born wife (thirty-two), and their five children, three boys and two girls (fourteen and under). The only other white person noted was the long-employed carpenter George Johnson, born in Pennsylvania. Besides land and slaves, the substantially valued assets on Dunboyne were the Butlers' residence and the brick sugar house, with its steam engine, kettles, and open pan "apparatus." In all, the plantation received a census value totaling a quite respectable $130,000.[2]

Upon returning from the Mexican War, Butler was greeted by the overseer hired by Frances Butler. "Mr. Tirsinie" worked for the 1848 and 1849 grinding seasons. His salary of $700 remained the standard for the Dunboyne overseers for a number of years. From that salary, each overseer was expected to "find" (provision) himself. Typically, the costs of supplies such as molasses, sugar, pork, ham, and beef were deducted from the overseers' payments. The driver, Watt, remained a valuable asset. As an example of her own deep obligation to him, after the 1847 harvest Frances Butler rewarded him with a payment of $100. Other slaves were compensated for occasional extra services, such as felling timber and hauling the cut wood. After Tirsinie left Dunboyne, William Crabtree and successive men oversaw the place each for only a year or two, through 1853. Joachim Cox had been working for a while for J. D. Murrell at Tally-Ho Plantation just below Bayou Goula. When he re-signed as overseer with the Butlers in January 1854, he was forty-four years old. Butler, who realized what a treasure Cox was, retained him at Dunboyne through the difficult Civil War years, until March 1865. Cox and his wife and three children may have continued to live on their own land nearby instead of on the Butler place. His salary was $1,000 yearly, "he to find himself and Johnson & to place two Negro men on my plantation." Cox's "two Negro men" may have been his own slaves, for whom he received compensation for their use on Dunboyne in the form of a higher wage than the norm. The last year of his employ, and after the emancipation of Butler's slaves, Cox's wages were drastically reduced to "$400, & no hire." Like other places in the war-torn Sugar Belt, Dunboyne found it hard to retain and pay essential employees.[3]

The carpenter Johnson, whose efforts Frances Butler credited for saving the sugar mill from destruction by fire in 1847, may have shared housing with the overseer, and he had had a yet-unclear bond with the house servant Lucinda. Butler valued Johnson enough to increase his annual salary to $500. His discharge at the end of the grinding season in December 1856 gave no reason. At age fifty-six, perhaps he was "played out," or the dismissal may have been instigated by Cox, who was responsible under his hiring arrangement to "find" Johnson.[4]

How successful was Dunboyne as a sugar cane plantation? Its economic achievements provided some measure of how well the Butlers' attained their hoped-for social position and wealth. The absence of a personal plantation record from the 1850s is a hindrance, but some observations on sugar yields and productivity are possible. Sugar prices had been depressed arbitrarily by the Tariff Act of 1846, by which duties on imported raw sugar were reduced. They remained relatively low through 1855, when Cuba, the principal exporter to the United States, experienced a production decline. In addition, if there was an unusually large crop region-wide, sugar prices tended to drop, as in 1853, reaching only an average of 3.2 cents a pound. Freight rates on the Mississippi River, the quantity and quality of the crop, and the availability of credit also affected prices. If severe weather occurred, as during an 1856 summer drought followed by early autumn freezes, prices tended to increase. Although the sugar import tariff was reduced further, prices held from 1857 through 1860. The highly productive year of 1861 put pressure on prices, but freight costs for shipping to New Orleans had declined substantially in the 1850s. They favored sugar producers especially along the Mississippi River and Bayou Lafourche. In addition, the Butlers apparently paid off their mortgages by the early 1850s and remained free of additional debt, avoided serious legal troubles, and acquired no expensive land. Butler relied on a stable and efficient workforce to which he did not add through acquisitions of high-priced slaves. In the late 1850s, he made more improvements to the mill, which increased its efficiency. He elaborated to his fellow planter and then-relative Daniel Turnbull on how they helped the harvest prospects. Writing in the autumn of 1858: "I am making prettier than usual, by Carson & Kearny's 'Sugar Clarifier,' and Shelby's newly inserted Bagasse Furnace is the admiration of all beholders. . . . It does not consume ½ a *Cord* per day, & furnished Steam enough to run the mill & granulating pan."[5]

From the 1840s until the Civil War, sugar production statistics were printed annually in New Orleans in the *Statement of the Sugar Crop Made in Louisiana,* by P. A. Champomier. The analyses of the crop are helpful in determining what was happening in Iberville Parish and on Dunboyne in particular. As indicated by table 1, there was no definite trend of increased production beginning with the 1849 crop, but there were years of good returns. For example, after the two relatively steady years of 1849 and 1850, the plantation's yield was drastically reduced, an effect (according to Champomier) of a regional drought that created a light crop, low sucrose, and poor-quality sugar. (Even a disappointing sugar yield might allow for decent molasses production, as it did in 1851.) Dunboyne's showing, however, was not reflected in all of the neighbors' yields. A few of them increased returns from the 1850 harvest. The outstanding grinding season of 1853 on Dunboyne was also the case for most (but not all) neighbors. Evidently, the large supply of sugar statewide caused such a drop in prices that many small cane farmers abandoned sugar for cotton. Weather always affected a plantation's yields, and toward the end of the decade it played a determining role. Superior quality sugar was produced in 1858, followed by a drought stretching from late spring 1859 through the grinding season. The water shortage that year was so severe that many mills in the Sugar Belt could not operate at all, and others had to haul water to use in the milling process. Then, severe frosts came in November and freezes in December. The Dunboyne crop was less than half that of the prior year. In summary, the Butlers survived several tough years during the 1850s, when sugar yields and prices were low.

At the dawn of the Civil War, the plantation fared unusually well. In 1861, the weather was so favorable that grinding not only began early, but the crop stood with no freeze into the beginning of winter. The results must have astonished the Butlers. At the average price of 8.75 cents per pound, Dunboyne probably was able to profit handsomely, before the effects of the Union coastal blockade took hold and many plantations were abandoned due to war. Given Dunboyne's production of 420 hogsheads, the gross for the Butler crop in 1861, using 1,150 pounds of sugar per hogshead, could have been almost $42,500. That contrasted with the year of 1854, when the plantation produced 282 hogsheads, and the

TABLE 1. Sugar production figures for Dunboyne and nearby plantations in 1849–1862 (in hogsheads of sugar)

	Dunboyne	Palo Alto[a]	Landry	Evergreen	Moore[b]	Hynes/Gay[c]
1849–50	216	160	220	300	125	236
1850–51	215	145	200	312	86	548
1851–52	165	173	250	238	65	495
1852–53	343	220	310	435	96	830
1853–54	405	250	268	520	180	1,113
1854–55	282	250	292	420	126	728
1855–56[d]	150	14	119	165	78	635
1856–57[e]	88	115	32	106	-	(not listed)
1857–58	268	405	248	500	-	523
1858–59	370	403	304	670	-	1,275
1859–60[f]	175	72	165	326	-	425
1861–62[g]	420	422	335	604	-	1,385

Notes:

[a] Palo Alto was property of Mrs. Valery Hebert, but by 1856 it was sold to or combined with property of upriver owners Thomas Whaley and Dr. A. Hall.

[b] Michael Moore, the Dunboyne manager in 1847–48, disappears from the list after 1855.

[c] The Hynes estate, renamed St. Louis Plantation, by 1852 came under management of Edward J. Gay and by 1858 his ownership.

[d] Champomier, *Statement of the Sugar Crop Made in Louisiana in 1855–56*, notes, 43, "The quality of the crop is inferior to the previous one."

[e] Champomier, *Statement of the Sugar Crop Made in Louisiana in 1856–57*, vi, comments relative to the disastrous harvest, on the "killing frost" of October 1855, especially in Iberville and West Baton Rouge Parishes. It may have destroyed the cane used for planting for the 1856 season.

[f] The year 1857 experienced a severe summer drought followed by an early frost in late October, then a freeze with ice in mid-November. Champomier, *Statement of the Sugar Crop Made in Louisiana in 1857–58*, vii, viii.

[g] Unlike the dry summer of 1860, followed by bad storms, the 1861 season was unusually favorable, produced a large crop, and allowed grinding to begin early. Fearing cold, planters windrowed much cane, but the winter proved mild. However, by the time he reported in early 1862, Champomier expressed concern for the future: "A considerable portion of the Cane-growing country has been disturbed, while some plantations are left almost entirely bare of working hands." Champomier, *Statement of the Sugar Crop Made in Louisiana in 1861–62*, vii, viii.

price was closer to 4.75 cents a pound, bringing an estimated gross return of $15,400. Definitely, higher sugar prices toward the end of the decade eased problems—even in less high-yielding years, such as 1858.[6]

Butler found little time to rest upon arriving home safely in the summer of 1848. In addition to his oversight of the plantation, Butler took a leadership role among his planter neighbors in opposing a combine of steamboat companies that increased freight charges. The additional costs posed a serious threat to profitability on plantations. Evidently, too, Butler occasionally was tapped to assist the local police jury. In 1858 he served with Paul Hebert and Lucien Landry on a committee charged with supervising and financing the clean-out and enlargement of a stream near Bayou Goula.[7]

In the effort to bestow on them an appropriate education, the Butlers' teenage girls, Sissy and Caro, remained at Belmont School into 1849. In September 1847, Frances had relayed to her soldier husband a compliment from one of her old Virginia friends, Betsy Mason. It illuminates something of the social graces that the Butlers tried to attain for their daughters. The girls, wrote Mason, had "'created by their beauty & sweetness an interest in all who saw them, and an *approbation* as entire as your heart could wish for them." They were "discreet, elegant in their habits, affectionate & modest in their manners, graceful in their movements, and with a development in their minds which promises all that your fondest hopes & prayers could ask for.'" At some point during 1849, possibly in time for Mardi Gras festivities, the girls were home again and, along with Lawrence and Sonny, attended schools in New Orleans. When the census taker visited in 1850, all four children were counted at Dunboyne, perhaps on vacation. Frances Butler continued her role as plantation mistress. Her duties provoked Nelly Lewis to accuse Butler of "always [having] some excuse" to keep Frances and her children from visiting. Nelly suffered her first stroke in 1850, and her resultant paralysis gave Frances anxiety. While Butler was away on business in New York during the summer of 1851, sickness attacked Dunboyne, felling the Butler children and field workers. The house servants succumbed "at a time," according to Nelly, "when [Frances] most required them." Most of the Butlers' friends were away, and the lot of Frances and her charges had been a "bad crop, excessive heat & suffocating drought, myriads of mosquitos—." Unable to leave Louisiana to visit the failing Nelly Lewis that autumn, Frances fretted about her mother.[8]

Frances was alone at home managing responsibilities when she wrote Nelly. She probably let slip some expression of frustration at Butler's absence during her need and at his lack of sympathy. She may well have regretted having said anything, because the news jarred Nelly's emotions. In late October 1851, Nelly conveyed her intractable detestation of Butler to her old friend Elizabeth Gibson:

> My Darlings are much improved in health but *happiness*, or even *peace* I fear is not for my poor child *in this world*. She is unhappily under the control of a selfish, tyrannical, & deceitful Being and will never be anything but a curse to his family—I suppose he is at home again after enjoying the healthy north in the society of old friends, & writes to my child that he is displeased with her for saying that "the coast has been sickly this summer" when she knows that he thinks La healthy. He is astonished that she should contradict his statement & writes this when all his family[,] many of his negroes some of his neighbors have been ill, & he knew & left La to save his life—can any one be happy with such a man—candidly confess that to hear he was *dead* will be a relief to me—may be he will make his peace with Heaven before he goes, but that is all I can wish for him.[9]

Nelly did not know, and would not have cared, that Butler arrived in New York in a state of illness. After recovery, he left for home, planning a stop in South Carolina to visit Rawlins Lowndes, his former army comrade. He missed attending a reunion with Alexander Duncan, the Yale schoolmate and friend of Anthony Butler. Duncan was one of the "old friends" to whom Nelly Lewis referred. Following Anthony's death, Duncan consoled Anthony's fiancée, Sarah Butler of Providence, Rhode Island. Their friendship led to marriage in 1827, and Duncan, a native of Scotland but by now a naturalized citizen of the United States, established residency, took up business, and practiced law in his bride's hometown. The business expanded to banking in New York City, and Duncan soon accumulated a sizeable fortune. The couple frequently traveled to Scotland and England and eventually moved there. The resumption of relations with Anthony Butler's old friend proved fortuitous for the Butlers during and after the Civil War; Duncan saved them from destitution. Nelly Lewis died at Audley on July 15, 1852, ever-resentful and unforgiving of her son-in-law for separating her from her "darlings."[10]

A comfort to Edward and Frances Butler was the construction of St. Mary's Episcopal Church. Bayou Goula had no Episcopal church and seldom a priest since the parish was founded in 1844. The planter family Episcopalians in the vicinity must have given thanks to see the edifice, designed by the eminent Irish-American architect Henry Howard, become a reality. According to Bishop Leonidas Polk in his report at the annual diocesan convention in June 1851, the church was consecrated on the eighth Sunday after Trinity, July 21, 1850. It was "an exceedingly neat gothic edifice, built of brick, and sufficiently large for the accommodation of the Congregation." Because "an ample fund for the support of the ministry has also been provided," the church soon had its first rector, Reverend Henry T. Lee of Virginia. Within a year, the church served ten communicants, and Lee reported that "the condition of this church is, in all respects, encouraging; a decided increase of interest in the service and institutions of the church has been manifested." The record is incomplete, but the Butlers participated in the initial funding and attended the church, along with other residents in the vicinity, such as John R. Thompson and John Hampden Randolph.[11]

Although Reverend Lee resigned in 1852, not to be replaced until January 1855, by J. G. Downing, the Butlers maintained their loyalty to St. Mary's. Butler served in 1853 as one of three diocesan convention delegates and in 1855 subscribed with other communicants to the Protestant Episcopal Association. It was set up to provide a more stable source of income for the bishop. During most of the 1850s, however, the church lacked a parsonage to house the priest. That problem finally was remedied by 1857, in time for the January 1858 residency of James Philson. Reverend Philson had a decent place for him and his family to live: "A comfortable and commodious Rectory has been purchased, and almost paid for . . . effected by the liberality of a vestryman, and a lady, residing in the vicinity, who, though not a member of the church, has in this and many other instances, shown her good will to it." The charitable lady certainly was Harriet Winn, whose husband, E. G. Winn, sold the land for the church and with John Hampden Randolph paid for its construction. Philson quickly stimulated the church's growth. By the time of the annual convention in mid-1858, the church counted twenty-one communicants, of whom twelve were black. Butler still supported the Protestant Episcopal Association, pledging $20. Reverend Philson served at St. Mary's through the Civil War, when the church and the fortunes of its parishioners suffered severely.[12]

Butler continued to assist his sisters and their families. Eliza Butler Donelson firmly supported Frances during Butler's absence in Mexico. When she died in 1850, her passing saddened the Butlers, prompting Nelly Lewis to report the event to Elizabeth Gibson and referring to Eliza Donelson as "my child's best friend in *that* family." Eliza willed her property to her worrisome son, Ned, and named Butler coexecutor of the estate. He appears not to have fulfilled the request of Eliza to erect a monument intended to mark her family tomb, for which she allowed a princely amount of $8,000. His aging sister Caroline still owned slaves in Louisiana. Butler asked his nephew to assist Caroline, who was indebted to one Judge Maury, by buying the slaves. Donelson rather stiffly complained, citing the need to handle his own deceased mother's "pressing" obligations. He did agree to purchase Caroline Bell's "Negroes to the extent of that debt and wiping it off from against her."[13]

Butler loved his contemporary kin and possessed a keen interest in his forebears. He honored his personal connections to the nation's founding and its defense, and he revered Andrew Jackson and his family. After his return from Mexico, Butler increased his correspondence with relatives and his research into his Irish roots. His interests no doubt were stimulated by a distinction bestowed upon him in 1853 in the form of a gift of a battle saber of Butler's uncle, General Richard Butler. The weapon was owned by William Lingan Gaither, the president of the Maryland State Senate. Gaither was the great nephew of Major Henry Gaither, the last fellow American officer to see General Butler alive after his mortal wound at St. Clair's defeat on November 4, 1791. In presenting the sword to Butler, Gaither noted that it was "in the full assurance that, if used, it will be only maintaining that freedom and nationality which your gallant uncle died in supporting." Butler added the sword to and kept it safely in his collection of swords until his death in 1888.[14]

In antebellum southern plantation society, the institution of marriage was central for both men and women. It "provided a standard against which they expressed their own lives," and for women their lives during marriage constituted "the fulfillment of their official roles." If lucky, a woman chose a mate who also brought about "the realization of . . . personal dreams of happiness."[15] By the early 1850s, Isabel and Caroline Butler were of marriageable age. Their choices would prove both fortunate and fateful to themselves and to their parents.

After Sissy and Caro returned from Virginia, the Butlers searched for a nearby institution for Caro—Sissy having completed her schooling—that offered not only an appropriate education but useful contacts. They chose the school of "Madame Desrayaux," who since 1840 operated a "Day and Boarding School for Young Ladies" in New Orleans. Advertised in the *Daily Picayune* in early 1849, it was located on "Burgundy Street between Custom House and Bienville Streets." The school was housed in a structure "recently built, and which can accommodate sixty boarders . . . erected for the express purpose of a Seminary for Ladies." Entered there, Caro received training in music, French, and other subjects, the intention of which was to maintain the "family circle" and to give her "the right connections."[16]

On visits to the city during the 1849 Mardi Gras and Lenten seasons, and at parties and balls, the girls received rapid, exciting introductions to society. Between the War with Mexico and the Civil War, New Orleans contained a mix of cultural groups and enjoyed "flush times, high wages, high profits, and high prices." Its buildings showed splendor, and the city offered fine theater, music, and opera. Two large opera houses existed. The Butlers had relatives in and near the city and enjoyed wide contacts among the commercial classes. Planters and their wives and families took advantage of the slack time after the end of grinding to visit the city. It offered social benefits, shopping, and entertainment, and planters arranged financing there.[17]

Caroline Butler almost certainly met her future husband through family acquaintances among the wealthy planter class, and possibly while in New Orleans to complete her education. Although younger than Sissy, Caro married first, to William Barrow Turnbull. The ceremony occurred on the evening of May 12, 1853, at Dunboyne Plantation, performed by Bishop Polk. Turnbull was the eldest of two children of Daniel Turnbull and Martha Hilliard Barrow of West Feliciana Parish. Living at Rosedown Plantation and combining fortunes of two families, the Turnbulls owned tracts of land in the Feliciana parishes and across the Mississippi River. Daniel Turnbull ably managed the properties. Built in the 1830s, near St. Francisville, the Rosedown house possessed size and grace, its grounds adorned by Martha Turnbull's colorful and exotic gardens, which already claimed renown. William Turnbull was a strikingly handsome young man, portrayed by the noted artist Thomas Sully in 1852 while the Turnbulls visited Philadelphia on their accustomed getaway. He constituted quite a catch for Caroline Butler. Living in New Orleans initially, they soon moved to his property, DeSoto Plantation, on Turnbull (or Red River) Island at the confluence of the Red and Mississippi Rivers. Surviving merchant receipts provide evidence that the couple was surrounded by and clothed in the accoutrements of wealth. On one shopping adventure in April 1855, Caro acquired house furnishings totaling $2,534.87 from the well-regarded New Orleans firm of P. Mallard and Co., at 67

Royal Street. The purchase included a crib for her one-year old son, William B. Turnbull Jr., born in 1854 at Dunboyne, four draperies for $300, a bedstead at $200, and an armoire for $200. Such furnishings would help make livable their plantation house, which contained three bedrooms, a parlor, a dining room and pantry, a library, hall, and wine room. That same month, Caro on two occasions visited "Mrs. Ferret," located at 71 Royal Street. She was described as "Dress Maker and Milliner," and there, Caro charged $596.69 for clothes.[18]

Caro gave birth to a second son, Daniel, in May 1856, also very likely at Dunboyne under the care of Frances Butler. Turnbull worked to improve his plantation and to make it viable, adding structures to the property and slaves to the workforce, all of which were expensive. In June 1856, for example, the builder J. J. Seiders presented an invoice for constructing twenty-two cabins, a driver's house, extra flooring and windows, and for "embrasing" windows and floors. The cost: $6,786. The bill was paid off by August. At least twenty-five of the nearly 150 slaves at DeSoto were Caro's personal property. They represented a bequest from her aunt Eliza Donelson after Eliza's son, Edward Butler Donelson, died in 1852 without issue while living in St. James Parish. Twenty-three slaves had been acquired by the couple after marriage. Most of them, numbering 109, belonged separately to William Turnbull. The DeSoto Plantation was worth almost $200,000 by 1857, but it also carried debt of well over $100,000.[19]

Barely had Caro Butler married William B. Turnbull than her elder sister Eleanor Angela Isabella Butler became engaged, in the summer of 1853. Her fiancé was George McWillie Williamson of Shreveport, the son of South Carolina-born Thomas Taylor Williamson and Tirzah Anne McWillie. Again, the circumstances of the meeting of the young lovers are undocumented. They may have been introduced by Sissy's brother Sonny, who attended South Carolina College at the same time as Williamson; or they may have met during the wedding festivities for Caro. Following strict formalities, George Williamson first requested her father's permission to marry Sissy. Then, his father wrote Butler to acknowledge that the Butlers "favorably entertained" the "proposal of [George Williamson] to become connected with your family." The association delighted Thomas Williamson, who "can only express my pleasure at so favorable a termination of a matter so interesting to my son—indeed to all of us—and to assure yourself and Lady that the proposed alliance is one in every respect agreeable to me."[20]

Held at Dunboyne on the ninth of May 1854, and celebrated by Bishop Polk, this marriage also was socially and economically favorable for Edward and Frances Butler. Thomas Williamson, one of Shreveport's founders in 1835, in the 1840s operated a steamboat on the Red River. It kept the river clear of the log "raft" that so often blocked navigation. He later became a planter in DeSoto Parish. His son George practiced law following college graduation in 1850 and became the Caddo Parish district attorney. The newly married couple took up residence in Shreveport in March 1855 following a visit to Sissy's parents. Butler relayed to Lawrence his daughter's delight "with the improved appearance of her house, by the addition of her new articles of furniture." In November 1855, Sissy gave birth to Isabella Butler Williamson, the first of six children.[21]

Frances and Edward Butler could not have wished for more for their daughters than their marital pairings. Two new southern dynasties had been confirmed. The matches appeared destined to support the Butlers' social aspirations and bettering economic status, aspirations that had been present since they determined to move to Louisiana. Frances and Edward now wished to help their sons find livelihoods and their own spouses.

Once Sonny left South Carolina College, he returned to Louisiana. Before long, however, he was enrolled at Harvard University in the study of law. The profession was honored in southern society, especially among the more schooled and affluent. Butler respected the law because of his successful uncle Thomas Butler and brothers-in-law Charles Conrad and Cary Nicholas, not to mention Andrew Jackson. "Son," as Sonny was often later called, remained away at least until 1854, but even into his mid-twenties young Butler lacked employment. His father began to explore on Son's behalf a position in the U.S. Army. In early 1855, he contacted Jefferson Davis, who held the post of secretary of war in Franklin Pierce's administration. Butler provided Davis with suggestions concerning frontier defense and recommended for army service both his son and Charles Radziminski, a former dragoon comrade from Mexico. Receptive to forming the "new cav. rgts." that Butler endorsed, in June 1855 Davis appointed Radziminski to be a first lieutenant in the 2nd U.S. Cavalry. Meanwhile, Butler was investigating a different, no doubt more suitable position for his son in the arena of diplomacy. He persuaded Louisiana congressman John Perkins Jr. to influence President Pierce to offer Sonny a position in the Department of State. In late 1855, Edward G. W. Butler Jr. was nominated as the secretary to the U.S. legation in Berlin. His parents relished seeing his appointment take place the following January, and Son remained abroad until the outbreak of the Civil War.[22]

Educated primarily by his mother, Lawrence Butler had reached an age to leave home, and New Orleans was the initial destination for him. In December 1850, his teacher Matthias Hare reported that he performed "most favorably" in general studies and conduct, led his class in "most of the English branches," and excelled in arithmetic, French, and handwriting.[23] The arrangement soon changed. Probably on a visit in 1853 to New York to the Livingston family, Lawrence expressed a desire to Mortimer Livingston, brother of Butler's old flame Julia, to attend school in Boston, near Sonny. Butler made inquiries, and through connections with the Livingstons, or using his commercial agent Gustave Miltenberger, he contacted a prominent Boston businessman, James S. Amory. Instead of Boston, Amory recommended that Butler place Lawrence in the school in New York City where his own son attended. Butler agreed, and Lawrence immediately began classes at "Mr. Peugnet's School." On the Butlers' behalf, Amory supervised Lawrence, who (despite some discipline difficulties) by late 1854 received praise from Amory for his nobility and natural character. Amory found him happy and content but inclined to be too generous and "fond of making presents."[24]

In early 1855, Amory advised Lawrence's parents that the youth should employ the coming summer to prepare for entrance exams to Harvard. Butler agreed to the recommendation; Lawrence, however, began to have second thoughts about Harvard—perhaps partly because his brother would no longer be there. By May, Butler instead allowed Lawrence to apply to the University of Virginia. Now thoroughly involved with Lawrence Butler's education, Amory expressed regret at Butler's decision to follow Lawrence's wishes. He believed that with "the association of the young in different parts of the Union . . . one of the strongest bonds of the Union is formed." From seeing different places and people, Amory wrote, one could take a "comprehensive view so essential to every man who is truly a patriot." Disregarding this sound counsel, Butler allowed his son to matriculate in the South. In late June 1857, Lawrence Butler received his "Certificate of Proficiency in the Class of Political Economy" at the University of Virginia. He presently was on his way north to see "Uncle Custis" at Arlington, to present his respects "to the President [Buchanan] and [Vice-President] Genl. Cass." He then intended to "visit friends in Balt., Mrs. Livingston & Mrs. Lowndes, on the north River, and Mr. Amory, near Boston," before heading home to Louisiana.[25]

The Butlers were happy with their children's progress into adulthood, but a tragic event would change their lives. On November 11, 1856, during a crossing of the Mississippi River near Turnbull Island, William Turnbull's rowboat capsized from the waves of a passing steamboat, and he drowned. The blows of sorrow fell hard on the Butlers and Turnbulls, and the young father's death endangered the families' fortunes and futures. Caro particularly faced immediate decisions about how and where to live and how to manage DeSoto Plantation. Needing funds to buy the personal property in which she owned an interest, Caro promptly sold fifteen of the slaves left to her by her aunt. They went to her first cousin Edward B. Donelson's widow, Jennie Donelson, who bought them for $2,197.33. The price represented a bargain and an act of concern for Jennie, but it also provided Caro with some cash. Her desire to be independent and to live on and manage DeSoto on her own, however, was unacceptable to the elder Butlers and Turnbulls, who feared for her safety. She was in a difficult situation. In spite of his responsibilities on Dunboyne, Butler began to assist Caro in managing the Turnbull Island property. He reported to Daniel Turnbull in July 1857 that he had engaged one "Gomez" at DeSoto for $500 to "make up the crop of sugar" and remained on the lookout for a mill engineer.[26]

Caro alternated extended visits to the Butlers and Turnbulls, and her boys delighted their grandparents—perhaps the one saving grace of their father's death. During the fall harvest of 1857, the Butlers introduced the children, Dan, one year old, and Will, three, to the joys of chewing sugar cane. Lawrence, by then home again and planning to study law, took them to see nearby friends. "He and the boys had a gay time of it," reported Butler to the Turnbulls. Butler, by all accounts a strict father, now relaxed and had fun with his grandchildren. "Dan, tho' very willful, is a glorious fellow, and I often please myself with [the] idea of seeing him at the head of a squadron, illustrating the propensities of the Butlers." His news to Turnbull, who eventually became administrator of his son's estate, included word on the cane crop and advice on the harvest and grinding at DeSoto. To relieve her of her responsibilities "and to place Caro and her children in a *Safer position*," Butler recommended that Turnbull sell DeSoto. Its debts threatened the loss of the children's inheritance.[27]

The challenge of securing her and her children's long-term welfare involved Caro in decisions regarding the estate, which initially was administered by a Turnbull family advisor and relative named John Towles. Although she was reasonably assured that her father-in-law would provide for his grandchildren, Caro had misgivings about giving up DeSoto. Uncertain and only slowly convinced that it should be sold, she considered disposing of the property in one block rather than "in detail," or parts, to get a better price. In a procès-verbal of the estate, the property received a value of almost $200,000, but that included community property in slaves, the house, and its furnishings, worth roughly $41,000. The debt on the property now came to over $129,000. Even if it were sold at its value, Caro and her children would be left with too little. She also wanted to retain a usufruct on the productive plantation, to maintain her autonomy. She did not wish to become reliant on her children, the Turnbull in-laws, or her parents. Butler appealed to Turnbull: "Knowing her pride and independence of character, I was anxious, if possible, to avoid such a state of things." She ultimately acknowledged that a proper "master" should run the place and endeavor to pay off the heavy debt.[28]

At Caro's request, the district court in West Feliciana Parish directed the Butlers and Turnbulls to hold a family meeting in order to determine the best course of action. It took place in January 1859, attended by Daniel Turnbull, various members of Martha Turnbull's family, and Butler as "under tutor" of his grandchildren. The outcome, agreed to by Caro and so ordered by the local judge, was the sale at auction of DeSoto Plantation, in one block. The only bidder, Daniel Turnbull, acquired 2,256 acres of land for $200,000, slightly above the $198,000 appraisal. The proceeds paid off William and Caro Turnbull's plantation debts of $118,567.18. It left $81,932 owed in the form of a seventeen-year bond, at 8 percent interest, in favor of Caroline B. Turnbull as the children's tutrix. The bond was secured by a mortgage on DeSoto, and Daniel Turnbull was not to alienate the property to the prejudice of the bond. His plantation acquisition included ninety-five slaves age twelve and over, the ten-room house and its furnishings, assorted farm implements, one hundred cattle, sixty hogs and other animals, a sailboat, one lot of brick, fifteen hundred bushels of corn, seven stacks of fodder, four thousand "hoop poles," and 150 barrels of "mess pork." It constituted a major transaction, all intended to keep the family unit solvent and to protect the heirs of Daniel Turnbull's only son.[29]

The arrangement pleased Caro, who trusted her father-in-law. She was grateful to retain her personal slave Rebecca, "as a servant for my children." She also could rest easy at not having the plantation slaves with whom she was "so nearly associated in the past" fall into the "hands of strangers." Within a year, Butler arranged for Caro's slaves inherited from her aunt to be sold on credit to her brother-in-law, George Williamson, for $30,000. Caro was to receive payment in yearly installments over seven years at 7 percent, secured by a mortgage on the slaves. Presumably the slaves, who were picked up at Turnbull Island by Williamson, would be used on his plantation in DeSoto Parish near Shreveport.

Again through the efforts of Daniel Turnbull, by early 1860 Caro and her boys acquired a permanent home, probably in New Orleans, where her sons could receive schooling. By all counts, Caro achieved as high a degree of protection from further misfortune for herself and her children as she could hope. The settlements lifted a weight, too, from Frances and Edward Butler.[30]

Joyous grandchild sharing continued between the two families, and Frances Butler finally managed to travel away from home. Her presence was essential to Sissy in early 1859, when she visited the Williamsons for the birth on February 22 of Evelyn Angela, the third of Sissy's brood of six. The trip to and from Caddo Parish took as long as five days by steamboat and coach. While she was away, Frances counted on Caro to look after Butler. General Winfield Scott paid a visit during her absence, prompting Frances to comment on how things were handled: "I trust that my dear daughter asserted herself to talk a little, and that therefore I was not too much missed—and I am sure that the Genl. never saw such *boys* as ours." Butler bragged to Frances about the proceeds from a good sale of sugar and commented favorably on their eldest son's usefulness in Berlin. "*No agent*," replied Sonny's most ardent promoter, "of this or any other country, carries to her Service a more pure and patriotic *desire* for his Countrie's welfare and honour than Edward does."[31]

Having finished his time at the University of Virginia, at the urging of his father Lawrence Butler began the study of law with a family friend. Like others of his age, Lawrence had "somewhat neglected his opportunities." But, his father wrote to the jurist-historian Charles Gayarré in November 1857, he would "prove himself worthy of being a Butler—." Lawrence evidently found the law wearying: He "wants self-reliance, and is too easily discouraged," Butler reported to Gayarré a few months later.

". . . I will take it as a great favor if you will commend to him the study and practice of the Law, and encourage him by your friendly advice; as I am very desirous that he should adopt and pursue it, as a profession." The topic led Butler to express his beliefs about personal character and the heritage he wished for his family: "I attribute much of what is good in my own character to a proper sense of one's obligations (imposed on their descendants by a distinguished ancestry). I have consistently endeavored to impress it upon my children."[32]

Gayarré's compliance with Butler's plea had the desired effect, and Lawrence completed his law studies. With urging from his mother, Lawrence determined to visit Son in Europe before commencing a law practice. He traveled along with the Butlers' friend Alexander Duncan on the latter's return trip from New York to England, arriving in June 1859. While there, an opportunity arose to perform the duty of dispatcher to the U.S. legation in Paris, and it is possible that during his stay there Lawrence took a short course in civil law. He was in Germany in August, traveling with Son and visiting art galleries and acquiring a porcelain gift for his mother.[33]

As the 1860s commenced, Edward and Frances Butler enjoyed relative prosperity. Their children's futures, even that of the widowed Caroline Turnbull, seemed definite. Feeling a stuffed wallet from the 1859 production of sugar, Butler contacted George P. A. Healy, the noted portraitist, to order for Frances a copy of the Gilbert Stuart portrait of Nelly Lewis. Along with the frame, it cost a handsome $275. "I hope . . . that the surprise was agreeable," Healy wrote in presenting Butler the bill.[34] Appearances of peace and plenty, however, were beginning to be overshadowed by the nation's political problems and the South's reactions to fundamental challenges to its way of life. The Butlers' lives were about to transform dramatically.

8

"I Am No Submissionist"

Toward the End of Union

The politics of the day furnished much of interest to Edward G. W. Butler. An historian of antebellum Louisiana, John M. Sacher, concludes that although slavery always was a delicate sectional issue, by the time of the 1848 presidential election one main question dominated Louisiana's politics: which candidate would or would not better protect the institution. In support of their man, Lewis Cass, Democrats charged that Zachary Taylor would not fight for slavery and protect white liberty despite his plantation heritage. The *Southern Sentinel* of Plaquemine, favoring the Whigs' candidate, Taylor, criticized Cass for being an opponent of slavery and even supporting its abolition. Secure in its support of Taylor, the local press promoted his vice presidential candidate Millard Fillmore, a northerner, as being consistent in not opposing slavery and in disavowing any desire to interfere with it. The extreme tendencies of the campaigns alarmed a number of the Butlers' friends, including Charles Thornton, Norbert Lauve, and John Hampden Randolph. They created an organization called the Bayou Goula Rough and Ready Club to support Taylor. Its club members lauded him as "the only man in the United States capable of allaying the strife which exists in the different parts of our country." He, alone, could "lull to peace the wild and threatening storm which now menaces our safety, and threatens to dissolve our glorious Union."[1] Their worries were prophetic.

It is unlikely that Butler, a Democrat ever faithful to the traditions of Andrew Jackson, voted for his former army commander. His own cousin, General Robert O. Butler, ran for vice president on the Democratic ticket. Even so, Taylor and Butler continued their friendship. By the time of his election, Taylor and Nelly Lewis had formed a friendship and were correspondents. Taylor reported to her of receiving a visit in Baton Rouge from the Butlers: "My old acquaintance and valued friend, your excellent and accomplished daughter Mrs. Butler; who with the Col. is now with us, on a short visit, in excellent health, which fact affords me much pleasure to communicate." After the election, Taylor answered a query of Butler to comment on his expectation that the newly elected Senator Henry Clay would be conciliatory. In addition, Butler asked, had he chosen John C. Crittenden of Kentucky to be a cabinet member in order to assist the inexperienced new national chief executive? The former army general and sugar planter answered candidly, if pathetically: he admitted having little knowledge of "the prominent men of our Country. I only know them by report."[2]

The 1850s brought political upheaval in Louisiana and elsewhere in the nation. Given their keen interest in and extensive reading about the topic, Edward and Frances Butler could not help but be concerned. Butler began to communicate with a number of old associates in order to gain information and to articulate his own beliefs. Soon after Taylor's inauguration, he was in touch with Rawlins Lowndes to sound him out on the slavery issue. Lowndes, who with Butler was an aide-de-camp to General Gaines in the 1820s, lived in South Carolina but resided part-time near his wife's family in New York. Lowndes acknowledged his old comrade's worries about the increasing hostility toward slavery. Fearing the nation's dismemberment and torn between contradictions concerning slavery, Lowndes declared to Butler his personal conflicts. Black people, said Lowndes, were incapable of training "for a freer form of Government," unless they submitted to "domestic servitude as it exists in this Country." But he also realized that slavery was not "the spirit of the age." The country's destiny, Lowndes told his Louisiana friend, was to bring about emancipation.[3] Butler must have blanched.

Before long, the nation was embroiled in the debate over slavery expansion into the lands newly acquired from Mexico. Charles Radziminski, Butler's trusted assistant from the 3rd Dragoons, finally accepted the Butlers' long-standing invitation to visit. Their long discussions turned to slavery and politics. During 1850, Radziminski, familiar with the high-pitched contentions in the nation's capital, informed Butler: "Clouds seem to be gathering on this fair land of ours," which may portend a war "far more disagreeable than that of Mexico has proved to be." The issues tended to die off for a while, and the Butlers turned their attentions to their daughters' marriages and sons' educations and careers. Toward mid-decade, however, the crisis over the determination of slavery expansion in Nebraska and Kansas again stimulated Butler to seek out the views of old northern friends. In 1855, James Amory, who had guided Lawrence Butler through his school years in New York City, responded to a letter from Butler raising questions on the issue of race. Defining their separation in attitude, Amory pointed out to Butler that "it is impossible for those born in free states not to desire for all mankind the same blessing which they appreciate so highly. We do not see the blacks in the same relation to them that those born in the South do." Still hopeful, Amory pleaded for "calm and steady reasoning, and consistent obedience to all the laws of the country," in order to avoid the dire consequences of "a *real* alienation of the North from the South."[4]

The Butlers' doubts about the arguments being made for emancipation were founded in deeply held paternalistic views; their attitudes originated in their heritage and experiences with slaves. A series of letters from the early 1850s illuminates their thinking. Not long after Butler completed his military duty in 1848, the family was visited by Charles Gayarré. Serving as Louisiana's secretary of state, but working on a history of early Louisiana, Gayarré sought help with sources and became interested in the couple's families. In 1853, sometime after the early meetings and correspondence developed into a strong friendship, the Butler house slave Lucinda contracted tuberculosis and died. Her passing, which caused much family grief, coincided with Gayarré's research and writing on slavery in Louisiana. Butler suggested his friend use Lucinda as an example not only of slave devotion to Butler's "entire household," but as well to the "poor slaves" for whom she also cared. Lucinda demonstrated her love in many ways, including a bequest of $76 to her former charge, Isabel Butler. Her master depicted Lucinda to Gayarré as "one who, in the performance of her duties, and in exemplary conduct, is unsurpassed by any living being,—white or black,—and who experiences for every member of my family those considerate and devoted attentions to which She has established so many claims." Lucinda, Butler pointed out, had declined freedom several times, even while in Cincinnati and subject to the terms of the Northwest Ordinance.[5]

The Butlers perceived that Lucinda's happiness stemmed from her dual, if contradictory, role as house slave and member of the Butler "family." They represented their version of the correctness of the institution through a recounting of the fates of George and Martha Washington's slaves. As told to Butler by Lawrence Lewis, who was Washington's nephew and secretary: Before he died, the master of Mount Vernon consulted Lewis on the wisdom of freeing his slaves after his death. Lewis opposed the act; yet Washington, "against his own convictions, as to the best mode of promoting their happiness," but "in deference to public opinion," "liberated *his own* Negroes." In the long, carefully written will, Washington "made ample provision for their support; which . . . Lewis (his executor) faithfully applied." The result was that the freed blacks became "a nuisance both to [Lewis] and the neighborhood," and "nearly all . . . disappeared." In contrast, Butler wrote, the slaves of Martha Washington, who remained in bondage after her death, enjoyed "health and happiness" and retained their good manners and dedication. The lesson to Butler for opposing emancipation and its supporters was clear: "Such are the people, and such the community of feeling and interest, which a set of miserable and unfeeling fanatics, in this country and in *England*, would destroy."[6]

Edward and Frances Butler increasingly tussled with the dilemma of how to support an ever slave-unfriendly Union. Their forebears had sacrificed so much to create and defend the nation, but that nation was supposed to uphold the indispensable institution of slavery. A middle ground was becoming difficult to maintain, given the Butlers' thinking that their family's welfare and freedom depended on the maintenance and expansion of slavery. There is no evidence, also, that Edward and Frances Butler ever were able to shake the racial convictions on which they justified slavery. They accepted the almost universal southern creed in the benevolence of the institution: "That the slave labored for his master was the least he could do for the many blessings showered on him."[7]

Butler's friend Andrew Jackson Donelson ran for vice president in 1856 with the nativist American Party (also called the Know-Nothing Party). The party evinced a political bias against immigrants and Catholics. Butler resisted such extremes. His beloved childhood guardian, he told the economist-editor J.D.B. DeBow, would have had contempt for the mid-1850s political group: Jackson rebuffed anyone promoting "anti-masonry" and "Native Americanism."[8]

Butler's relationships with Andrew Jackson and Jackson's old supporters, as well as his own nationalist heritage, compelled him to resist secession, at least until the end of the decade. He knew how strongly Jackson opposed "nullification" in 1832, believing it to be simply a pretext to form a southern confederacy. But angered by the increasingly strident calls for emancipation, and by the trends toward violence in accomplishing abolition, he struggled with the idea. Butler wrote Martin Van Buren, perhaps using an earlier connection through Jackson. He asked the former president, now back in Kinderhook, New York, to use his influence on New York Democrats. Although Van Buren was long retired from public life, Butler considered him familiar with southern sentiment. The elder statesman would respect southerners' determination "to resist all further interference with their affairs." Butler urged Van Buren to help dissuade northern Democrats from forming "the miserable combinations and factions which disturb [the] powers and threaten [the] existence" of "*our Glorious Union.*" Again using his connections with Andrew Jackson in order to obtain an introduction, Butler initiated correspondence with John Slidell sometime around 1854.

An influential U.S. senator from Louisiana, Slidell was a wealthy planter; his holdings in the 1850s included thousands of acres in Iberville Parish. He became the force behind the election of James Buchanan to the presidency in 1856 and eventually swung to the cause of secession from the Union. In a tenor of friendship, Slidell and Butler wrote each other off and on, and as the election of 1860 approached, with some frequency. Discussing the nation's political problems with Slidell in 1857, Butler thought that he might admit of a peaceable secession. But in reality, he wrote, a "Civil War and its concomitant horrors, will be the immediate and unavoidable result" of dissolution of the Union. Butler's inward strife accelerated following the Kansas and Nebraska controversies and the Dred Scott decision of the U.S. Supreme Court. His ambivalence paralleled that of John Hampden Randolph, then residing at his grandiose Nottoway Plantation home. Randolph urged that "we must abide by the Constitution and the Union," however dark the horizon, and follow George Washington's advice to maintain the unity of government. That could change, however, forcing southerners to self-protection, "should the time unhappily arrive when there is direct oppression from the free states upon the South."[9]

As the end of the decade approached, Butler focused more on political events. Aware of Slidell's backing of Buchanan, and again using mutual connections with Andrew Jackson, Butler corresponded with the future president. He wanted to explore Buchanan's prospects in 1856 and to seek his position on the Kansas constitution controversy in 1857. The communications with John Slidell expanded. Slidell, who assisted President Buchanan in selecting his cabinet and remained his close advisor, was considered part of the pro-Union wing of the Democratic Party. Having failed to unify the party in order to oppose the Republican candidate in 1860, however, Slidell became more pessimistic about the nation's future. "Political prospects are gloomy," he wrote Butler in August 1860. "I see little chance of defeating Lincoln's election." He blamed Stephen Douglas for purposefully attempting "to break down the Democratic party; and elect Lincoln, & place himself at the head of the Anti-Slavery Party in '64." Like so many in Louisiana, Butler dreaded the prospect of a Republican victory and sought advice about what to do. Slidell cautioned Butler against "precipitate action," should Lincoln be elected, but Slidell could not conceive that "the Union can be preserved for many years." He was uncertain what specific course was proper but began to urge southern states to prepare for unity and counseled holding a southern conference in order for the states to discuss "ideas as to the mode of action."[10]

How then to act when faced with a split Democratic Party and the likelihood of a president of the United States whose views so conflicted with the Butlers' own? Shortly before the 1860 presidential election, Butler was in communication with Paul O. Hebert, their friend and neighbor and the former Louisiana governor. On October 23, 1860, from New York City, Hebert reported finding virtually no one who was sympathetic to the South. He urged that "the different States, acting upon their *sovereign* right to do so, *go out of the Union one by one*, and . . . see what *other* sovereign power there is under this Government that will dare say, '*They shall not.*'" Butler made the letter and his own reply of November 1 available to the *New Orleans Daily Delta*. Both were reprinted in the secession-leaning *Plaquemine (La.) Gazette and Sentinel* on November 10, after Lincoln's election on November 6. The local newspaper described Butler as one "of the famous, heroic family which has figured so gloriously in our military history." Butler in his letter held himself to be "conservative" and evoked his upbringing by the sainted Andrew Jackson. He stated his willingness to act "as a true and dutiful soldier, whenever and whatever Louisiana commands." Leery of the state's leaving the Union, however, he believed that too many were deluded into thinking that the split could be peaceful. The northern states had already broken the constitutionally lawful Fugitive Slave Act. If Louisiana attempted to leave the Union without an "overt act" of provocation by a new administration, the result would be "a border war . . . unequal in its horrors by those of the Scottish borders [or] the French revolution." Should a victorious Lincoln commit such an "act" (which Butler left undefined), the appropriate response even then should be a convention of slave states to determine how to protect "our rights and honors."[11] So far, Butler was following the cautionary words of Slidell against "precipitate action."

His relatively mild words had been expressed before the reality of Lincoln's election. Iberville Parish voted heavily for the southern Democratic favorite, John Breckinridge. The final tally in the parish was 535 for Breckinridge to 229 for the Constitutional Union Party candidate John Bell. Stephen Douglas received only 101 votes. Breckinridge's victory margin over Bell within the Bayou Goula area was even greater, 64 to 23, and Douglas came in second with a close

59 votes. The *Gazette and Sentinel* on November 10 celebrated Breckinridge's local win, but "all the news which we give our readers this morning is of the gloomiest character." They would have to accommodate "to the melancholy fact of Lincoln's election, and prepare . . . for the worst that may follow."[12]

The waters would not remain calm. Within a few weeks after the presidential election, John Slidell's own thinking grew more radical. He expressed sympathy to President Buchanan over the delicate role he must have but now believed that preserving the Union was impossible, "'nor do I consider it desirable to do so if we could.'" Already, Louisianans had begun military training to defend themselves. In Iberville, as elsewhere, local governmental authorities tightened control over movement and assembly of slaves, and a group of Iberville citizens formed a "Minute Man" organization. It assumed two objectives: first, "to promote concert of action with the Southern States," and second, to pursue at a State Convention "the withdrawal of the State of Louisiana from the present Union" and the establishment of a Confederate government of the southern states. By mid-December, a number of Bayou Goula men convened to create a "military company," and Butler addressed the group, ostensibly to advise it on particulars. The leaders of the meeting were friends of the Butlers, Paul O. Hebert, Dr. J. P. Stone, and W. M. Thompson. The elected officers of the company were Captain Gustave Lauve and First Lieutenant Nathaniel Cropp. By the end of the month, a constitution and bylaws had been drafted. Preparations for disunion and war quickened.[13]

After Lincoln's election, Louisiana governor Thomas Overton Moore converted to supporting immediate secession and in December assembled the legislature. It called for a January 7, 1861, election of delegates to a statewide convention scheduled to meet on January 23 in order to examine the issue of secession. They would be chosen in each parish according to state legislative representation. Iberville was to receive one for its senatorial district, and each parish could choose two delegates as their "representatives."[14]

With evident instigation from the *Plaquemine (La.) Gazette and Sentinel*, a sizeable group of Bayou Goula residents formed to select appropriate delegates. Headed by John A. Sigur, Dr. P. M. Lambremont, and F. A. Hudson, they wrote to ask Butler to be a candidate for one of the two Iberville representative delegates to the January convention. The other candidate was forty-five-year-old New York native Theodore Johnston, a landowner with seventy-seven slaves. Johnston had been a former postmaster in Plaquemine and later became quartermaster of the

3rd Louisiana Infantry in the Civil War. The senatorial candidate was Augustus Talbot, a one-time Sixth Judicial District Court district attorney and Plaquemine town mayor and city councilman who owned five slaves. Receiving the letter on December 4, Butler accepted the nomination but wanted to make his position known: "Though most anxious for the co-operation of the slave States, *ab initio*, I deem it our duty to defer to their opinions and action under the circumstances which surround them; and should the adjacent States retire from the Confederacy, I do not think Louisiana could occupy an isolated position, consistently with her duty, her rights, or her honor." Butler was simply exercising another note of caution about the need for unity among Louisiana and her neighbors. His response, however, elicited much discussion throughout the remainder of the month. The newspaper's Tennessee-born editor, William P. Bradburn, asked Butler to clarify his "ambiguity of . . . expression." Butler replied, "I would much have preferred united and preconcerted action on the part of the slave states; but, they have decided separately, and I would not have Louisiana occupy an isolated position." In Bradburn's view, the matter thus was decided: because five other states had already seceded or were about to, Louisiana had no choice. "No one would have Louisiana secede if her immediate sister States had previously decided not to do so."[15]

Butler was gradually nudged into a stronger line in favor of immediate secession for Louisiana. During December, the lineup of candidates to the January convention had been on the basis mainly of how immediately they favored secession and under what circumstances it would be justified. Immediate secessionists favored no delay, cooperationists favored secession but only after consultation and in unison with other southern states, and conditional unionists would not secede before some compromise was attempted with the national government. As the month progressed, those who spoke for cooperation slowly became branded by newspapers and citizens of more radical tendencies as being "submissionist." The term was understood to mean willingness to give in to demands of the Black Republicans. The effect of such marking of dishonor was to push moderates toward immediate secession.[16]

Sometime during the last week or so of December, other candidates desiring election as delegates to the convention turned up the heat on Butler. They attempted to paint him as being less than an immediate secessionist, thus in fact a cooperationist, if not completely willing to submit to northern demands. Probably his earlier statements, all of which were published in the local newspaper, gave his opponents what they deemed an opening to confuse the electorate by distortion. They publicly invited Butler to join them in their moderate stance, as he must be one with them. Dr. Lambremont, one of the initial petitioners for Butler's candidacy, raised the issue. Butler deftly and somewhat humorously responded in the December 29 issue of the *Gazette and Sentinel*: "Learning that I am placed in a false position, by a misapprehension, I will not say a misstatement, of my conversations and by the alleged determination of those politically opposed to me to place me on their ticket for the Convention. I deem it proper to say that I am no submissionist, or Unionist in that sense of the word; and that, whilst I feel flattered by the confidence implied in the proposed nomination by my political opponents, I prefer to occupy the position assigned me by my friends on the ticket with Messrs. Talbot & Johnston."[17]

Bradburn pronounced Butler in accord with "the ticket" (which Bradburn had created and supported). But the editor took care in the edition published just before the election to give a clear summary of the position of the three candidates: They were for secession by "*separate state action*," not only as their "duty" to maintain Louisiana's "honor and welfare," but out of necessity. Acts of secession were anticipated by five other states, all of which were having separate secession conventions. Louisiana could not "take a contrary course." The candidates, continued Bradburn, loved the Union but believed "that all hope is gone for living happily and honorably in it." "They are for Louisiana falling back on her reserved rights." Those, the editor held, allowed dissolution of "a copartnership which, apart from the name, is little else than a source of evil at present to our State, and undisturbed, must be a curse to her future." The options offered to Iberville constituents left little room for any choice other than for immediate secession, given the newspaper's view of no alternatives. Butler's once-cautionary views were fully replaced by those much more akin to the positions of the radical secessionists.[18]

As expected, the three candidates whom the newspaper supported won. Augustus Talbot, the senatorial candidate, handily beat the cooperationist Joseph A. Breaux, 390 to 329. Butler's parish representative ticket-mate Theodore Johnston polled 381 votes to come in first. For Butler, however, the vote was quite close. He won by only four votes, 323 to 319, over the next highest candidate, Gervais Schlatre, a cooperationist. Statewide, the secessionist candidates won a majority of the votes, but the never-revealed "real returns" showed a close race. Secessionist votes counted 20,557, as opposed to 18,651 cooperationist votes in the representative districts. In the senatorial districts, the tally was even closer, 20,214 to 18,451. Sentiment in Louisiana was less in favor of immediate secession than its supporters claimed, but the convention still would be heavily tilted toward Louisiana's fast exit from the Union.[19]

Not wanting anyone to have misapprehensions after the election of the three delegates, Bradburn reassured his readers. Now, "Iberville sustains the principle of *Secession and separate State action.*" To Bradburn, Lincoln's election in effect was "annihilation of slavery in the Union" and war upon slaveowners until it was accomplished. By a secession of all slave states, including the border states, a destiny of liberty was upheld. The choice of the Iberville ticket meant having delegates "in point of ability, experience, and position" in whom "the interests of our State and Parish may be confidently confided."[20] Whatever doubts Edward Butler may have had before his election to the Louisiana Secession Convention, he was now considered a hardline secessionist for whom the United States no longer held any fealty.

The 1850s may have misled Butler to minimize concerns for his future prosperity. How could the good times possibly end? Perhaps, even now, he saw no contradictions. He arrived at the Secession Convention in January 1861 fully devoted and committed to the principle of immediate separation from the Union. Butler had long worried about the problems and criticisms of slavery. With many others, he pondered what would happen should the call to secession advance. He knew what war's violence brought and that loss of control over slaves might be an unwanted result. His choice for secession departed from Andrew Jackson's forceful opposition to a similar course in 1832–33. In Butler's eyes, though, the forced emancipation of black slaves seemed inevitable after Lincoln's election. It was an unacceptable threat to a cherished way of life and to a democracy that could be upheld only by the institution of slavery. Like others in the immediate secession camp, he endorsed at any and all costs what effectively was a revolution. Would we today say that he was blinded?

At the convention, Butler assisted in defeating first the "Constitutional Unionist" faction and then the "Cooperationists," each of which wanted to delay if not avoid secession. On January 26, the convention voted officially to dissolve the state's union with the United States of America and to reassume those rights that had been delegated to the United States. For the present, although not for long, Louisiana was an independent nation. Having military experience in the state militia and U.S. Army, Butler gained an assignment on the convention's

Committee on Military and Naval Affairs. It was chaired by the future Confederate general Richard W. Taylor, the son of Butler's Mexican War commander, Zachary Taylor. Among his important decisions, which further stamped his radical course, Butler cast votes for a resolution to admit all arms and munitions free of duty charges, to transfer the regular army of the state to the Confederate States of America (once Louisiana joined the Confederacy), and to cede to the new nation the right to possess and occupy those facilities that already had been seized by Louisiana from the United States. Consistent with his secessionist philosophy, Butler also voted for Louisiana to reserve the right to withdraw from the Confederacy, once it adopted the new nation's constitution. Intriguingly, he may even have received an offer, through Jefferson Davis's brother Joe Davis, to a high rank in, if not to assume command of, the military forces of the Confederacy. Butler recounted the event late in life in an interview with a St. Louis newspaper reporter. He had replied to Davis that as "a member of the State Convention of Louisiana which took the State out of the Union . . . his allegiance was first due to his own State, and he could be controlled by the wishes of his State." Butler thought that Davis interpreted his answer to the offer as a refusal, and "nothing more was said of it."[21]

In the midst of the convention, an alarmed U.S. Army officer, Captain C. C. Kilburn, relayed to his superior in Washington his impressions of the dark mood in New Orleans: "I am astonished to find a most marked and determined change of feeling toward the Government at Washington. Under all circumstances I consider that any purchase of subsistence for and on behalf of the United States would run great risk of seizure for the use and benefit of the troops now in arms in this State."[22] The concerns of Captain Kilburn accurately reflected a determination and spirit of resistance of city residents that quickly spread to other areas. By early April 1861, Iberville Parish appropriated funds for various militia units, including $500 to the "Bayou Goula Guards." Like other parishes, Iberville tightened its rules governing slaves. No slave, for instance, was allowed to own a boat and "traffic with his fellow slaves whatsoever." If a slave worked away from "his home place," as was common, he must be accompanied when in transit "by the overseer or another white person employed for the purpose." Fears of abolitionist sentiment among slaves and of slave rebelliousness in general spread across the South, and slaves came under much stricter control and were subjected to harsher punishment for violations. Everywhere, preparations were made for armed conflict.[23]

By 1861, most southerners lacked faith in the ability of the United States to guarantee their rights—particularly the right to hold slaves. Louisiana favored maintaining the Union more than many of her sister states, but those ties contracted over the 1850s. The election of Lincoln and the prospect of national power by an uncompromising and rhetorically extreme political group fed long-held fears and created a determination to protect what the entire South perceived as a sacred institution. Edward Butler grew up amid intensely patriotic family and friends, but he eventually weakened in his adherence to the Union. His use of the term "honor" so frequently in connection with his changing position indicates the personal affront that he felt in connection with actions of northern radicals. To Butler, they wanted to overturn principles that he believed were constitutionally supported. Additionally, he adhered to slavery as an underpinning of his culture and of his personal life. A forced ending of the institution constituted a threat to his family's well-being and also to its honor. Interestingly, the extant letters of Edward Butler contain little directly showing how fully he, his family, and friends economically depended on slavery. The well-chronicled attempts to save Caro's family fortunes after William Turnbull's death come close. Without the institution, the Butlers' dream for themselves and their children to become wealthy and to achieve high social positions would have been evanescent. The recorded sentiments of Frances Butler, as closely tied by heritage to the formation and preservation of the Union as her husband, are fewer. But there can be no doubt that she held views similar to his. The Butlers had experienced the dangers of civil war in Mexico and were warned by friends in the North over the previous decade. Notwithstanding, Frances and Edward Butler succumbed to the radical advice of politicians like John Slidell and to the growing proslavery propaganda and coercion. The Butlers could not withstand the increasing forces of secession and its consequence, war. More than others, they might have realized the anxiety and suffering that would result.[24]

9

"Soil & Liberties Have Been Invaded"

The Trial of War

A discussion of Frances and Edward G. W. Butler during the American Civil War necessarily involves the parallel stories of their two sons and of their son-in-law George Williamson. The fates of the three young men, who abandoned careers to join the Confederacy, were joined with the Butlers.

After the fall of Fort Sumter in Charleston Harbor, formal war commenced between the Union and the Confederate States of America. Edward Butler busied himself, even writing Confederate President Davis, to secure appropriate army officer commissions for his sons and his son-in-law. Then age sixty-one, he made no further attempt to obtain a commission for himself. According to the account of his life written in the *St. Louis Post-Dispatch* at his death, "physical infirmities," probably referring to malaria, kept him from the struggle. In spite of periodic illness, the likely more important reasons may have been his responsibilities to oversee property and protect family.

Even with the onset of the Union blockade at the mouth of the Mississippi River, the mood across the state was decidedly optimistic for a short while. Life proceeded almost normally, and few people thought that the Sugar Belt would ever face the enemy. Historian Charles P. Roland observed that in 1861 sugar planters in particular held an "unquenchable faith in the military powers of the South," which "was matched by a high regard for the genius of President Jefferson Davis." Butler, however, retained a proper regard for the strength of the North; and, from experience, his wariness about civil war may have influenced his decision not to pursue a military position. Few details of the effects of war appeared in the *Statement of the Sugar Crop* for 1861–62. By the time the report was compiled in August 1862, however, Champomier included a pessimistic note. Owing both to floods "and the disasters attending the war, the crop will fall very far short of that of last year. . . . A considerable portion of the Cane-growing country has been disturbed, while some plantations are left almost entirely bare of working hands." From the beginning, Butler harbored some doubts about his family's future, and he needed confirmation of the wisdom of the Confederacy's course. Soon after the surrender of Fort Sumter, he sought John Slidell's advice. What, asked Butler, was Slidell "doing in these stormy times"? Slidell's response: "Nothing." After all, the people were unified and he was confident of a victory won with foreign assistance. Reverend James Philson, Butler's rector at St. Mary's Episcopal Church, encouraged Butler as well. He wrote his parishioner that the South's "soil & liberties have been invaded & therefore to my mind there never was a clearer case in which it was a nation's duty to take up arms."[1] Did such assurances calm the Butlers' fears? Only a few years earlier Butler had fretted over what energies a war might unleash. He now may have been cheered by close friends, but he knew that the floodgates were open.

Edward G. W. Butler Jr., in Berlin as secretary of the U.S. legation when fighting broke out in April 1861, was delayed in his efforts to reach home. Assigned to the 11th Infantry Regiment of Louisiana Volunteers, formed in August, Son received the rank of major. He served under Colonel Samuel F. Marks and Lieutenant Colonel Robert H. Barrow, both of West Feliciana Parish. Lawrence Butler and he soon were united. Lawrence volunteered in April and initially achieved the rank of corporal in Company D of Rightor's 1st Special Battalion of Louisiana Infantry. Then, after becoming second sergeant, Lawrence received a promotion to second lieutenant on a "tour of instruction" in Richmond, Virginia. While stationed in September at Camp Moore near Tangipahoa Station, Tangipahoa Parish, Louisiana, he was ordered to Union City, Tennessee, to join the 11th Louisiana Infantry Regiment. Raised to first lieutenant, effective August 28, Lawrence was assigned command of Company K. Formed in Caddo Parish, it was known as the "Shreveport Rebels." Lawrence, age twenty-four, thus would be under the watch of his older brother—a welcome resolution for their concerned parents.[2]

According to Son, writing home on September 27, Lawrence had been sick and unable to report to the regiment, which by then was in garrison in Columbus, Kentucky, and comprised part of the forces under General Leonidas Polk. The culprit may have been measles, to which Son also succumbed after nursing his ill servant, Charles. Following the arrival of the 11th Louisiana in Columbus, others sickened, and there already had been a few deaths. Son wrote his parents that two thousand enemy soldiers were encamped across the Mississippi River from Columbus, the enemy had clashed with "our cavalry," and federal gunboats shelled the town. The prize was the neutral state of Kentucky. Both the Confederacy and the United States vied for its commitment and saw the Bluegrass State as crucial for success in the upper South. The enemy threat appeared to recede during October. Sent to Nashville to recruit, Son was present at the death by diphtheria of his cousin Maggie, the youngest child of Susan Nicholas. A friend, Mary Knox, reported the death to the Butlers and asked Butler to assist Susan with business affairs at the Albemarle Plantation, in Assumption Parish.[3]

Major Butler soon was back with his unit in Kentucky, and on November 7 the lull in the action ended. Southern forces became engaged in the Battle of Belmont, Missouri, with Union troops under the command of General Ulysses Grant. In Grant's first Civil War engagement with the Rebels, Union soldiers carried by boats converged on the low-lying fields and woods opposite fortified Columbus the night of the 6th. They hoped to take a garrison of Confederates there. The Confederate troops, however, mustered a counterattack, their steamboats ferrying men across the river. The Rebel transports often came under fire from other Union gunboats or from Union troops on shore, but they managed to land their men. The 11th Louisiana Regiment was sent across in the late morning of November 7 to reinforce the Rebel soldiers under General Gideon Pillow and to attempt a "flank movement" in order to attack the enemy's rear. The report of Colonel Marks, the regiment commander, to Polk described confusion on the identity of the enemy. Marks "ordered Major Butler to advance to the edge of the woods, to ascertain what [Union] regiment" they were facing. "As soon as they discovered the major the main body opened fire on him. I then ordered my men to commence firing."[4] Possibly from his own men's mistaken fire, Butler suffered a deadly wound.

Butler was discovered first by a Union Army physician, John H. Brinton. Brinton later wrote of finding the Confederate officer while riding his horse among his troops during the battle. "Lying on the ground in a fence angle of a clearing," Butler "called to me, asking me to dismount and help him, 'if you are a gentleman.'" Despite danger to himself, Brinton complied and determined that Butler had a mortal wound in the liver. New to warfare, Brinton found the experience heartrending:

> "Major Butler of Louisiana" [told me] that he had formerly been Secretary of Legation at Berlin, and that he was a grandson of Mrs. Lewis Washington, or Washington Lewis [Eleanor Parke Lewis, granddaughter of George Washington], of Clarke County, Virginia. . . . He asked me how long he could live. I

> answered "but a very short time." He then said to me: "Please send a message to my father,—by the first flag of truce,—tell him how you found me,—and that I died as he behoved me, at the head of my men." I did all that I could for him, stimulating him from my flask. He was very grateful and said, "Oh, Doctor, I wish I had met you before this." He begged me to remain with him, and when I told him that our troops were on their way to their boats, he offered to protect me while he lived, if I would only stay. I assured him that his own people would find him, and that I must go. So I mounted and reluctantly left him on the ground.

Brinton subsequently received assurance that Butler was taken by Confederate troops to the town of Belmont, where he died. No one in the Butler family learned about Brinton's act of humanity on the field of battle.[5]

Son was transported to Polk's own headquarters "on a trestle." In addition to internal wounds he suffered a shattered arm. A volunteer who nursed him pled with the attending physician to administer morphine in order to ease Son's pain. Her request was refused. According to Polk's dispatch to young Edward's father, the wounded soldier commented before death that "he fell, as he chose to say to us, 'as a Butler ought to fall, in the discharge of his duty.'" From Columbus, Polk informed Butler, "I send you his remains." Lawrence was present as his brother died, and because the Mississippi River still was open to navigation he was allowed to provide "escort to his remains" to far-off Dunboyne. There, Lawrence acted "as consoler to my deeply afflicted family."[6]

The Battle of Belmont was no skirmish, even though the numbers seem minuscule in comparison to later clashes. Confederate casualties amounted to 105 killed, 419 wounded, and 117 missing. The extent of Lawrence Butler's participation is unclear, but he had some involvement. He afterward contributed briefly to answers to Polk's formal follow-up procedure, referred to in official records as interrogatories. He commented mainly on the timing of departure of the regiment from the Columbus side of the river over to Belmont. He also might have assisted in recovering Son's body. A former Dunboyne house slave, Clarissa, was in Nashville after Son's interment attending to Caroline Bell and Susan Nicholas. Having heard of Son's death when his father informed his relatives, she wrote with singular articulation to comfort the elder Butler. "To have the precious deposit so near you, where his poor Mother can go daily with her tribute of fresh flowers, fit emblems of the pure spirit of her departed boy," penned this sensitive domestic servant, "must be an unspeakable consolation." Clarissa was glad to know that "Master Lawrence will have the companionship of Master [George] Williamson at Columbus," which would please Isabel as well. Butler had complained to Clarissa of the growing scarcity of coffee, and Clarissa replied that "since the scarcity, we have resorted to use old plain of parching meal—& find that it gives unusual satisfaction."[7]

Lawrence Butler held the rank of captain at the time of the battle. For a short while during the war, letters reached Lawrence bringing news from home. His fearful mother wrote him soon after Sonny's death to send her love and fervent prayers for his well-being. Lawrence's personal attendant, the Dunboyne slave Dennis, left behind a wife, Betsy, and Frances forwarded Betsy's love to Dennis. At Dunboyne, his sister Sissy Williamson and her children were visiting; and Caro Turnbull and her two sons were living with the Butlers. They provided needed distraction for a grieving Frances. "The *boys* still think of nothing but military affairs—and are all prepared to *rise* in rank, as *you* may do," observed Frances.[8]

The following April, the 11th Louisiana Regiment was in Corinth, Mississippi, preparing for the Battle of Shiloh. Newly assigned to Polk's staff, Lawrence and his brother-in-law Williamson served together. Williamson began the Civil War in April 1861 as a first lieutenant along with Lawrence Butler, in Rightor's 1st Special Battalion of Louisiana Infantry. As an experienced lawyer, Williamson was tapped by Polk in August 1861 to become a "legal counselor." The elder Butler assisted in placing both men in the same battalion. When Secretary of War Judah Benjamin delayed, Butler wrote Adjutant General Samuel Cooper to push the assignment along. Williamson joined Polk's staff by January 1862 and became Polk's assistant adjutant general, receiving reports following the Battle of Shiloh. With Williamson's influence, young Butler joined him as an assistant adjutant general with the Confederate 1st Army Corps, Western Department. He still held the position in December 1862, at Murfreesboro, Tennessee, when he was recorded signing directives for his commander. Sometime in early 1863 Butler was reassigned, but Williamson remained with Polk. Williamson soon received a severe shoulder wound in the Battle of Stones River, Tennessee, following which he moved to the staff of General Edmund Kirby Smith of the Trans-Mississippi Department. Then promoted to major and located in Shreveport, conveniently near his home, Williamson was an inspector general and, by late 1863, Smith's adjutant general. One of his duties was traveling to San Antonio, where he oversaw impressments of cotton on behalf of the Confederacy. In February 1864 he was in charge of a prisoner exchange between the Department and the Union Army in Arkansas. Again promoted, to lieutenant colonel, Williamson remained in Shreveport with Smith until the war's end, much to the relief of his family.[9]

Lawrence Butler soon had new duties. In October 1863, and now a major, he was one of a number of Confederate officers attempting to crack down on stragglers, absentee conscripts, and deserters. Faced with mounting manpower problems caused by battlefield losses and by fiscal ruin and a worthless currency, the Confederacy was desperate. It had too few resources to pay its soldiers. In order to alleviate the lack of able men to fight, in the late summer of 1863 the central government instituted the Volunteer and Conscript Bureau of Tennessee, Alabama, and Mississippi. It had been under way only a month when Butler's assignment took place. The bureau operated from Marietta, Georgia, and its insufficient supporting force of two thousand men was commanded by Brigadier General Gideon Pillow. The roundup occupied a month and reportedly brought in 7,336 conscripts, mostly from Alabama, Mississippi, and Georgia. Pillow counted on sending many of the men to Mobile, Alabama, and others to the Army of Virginia. Butler's contribution to the haul of men was 116 stragglers in Georgia and three from Alabama, of a total of 489 collected from the state of Georgia.[10]

Lawrence Butler's war record dims beginning in late 1863. It is unlikely that he could have made it home safely, the Union forces having returned to the Dunboyne neighborhood soon after the fall of Port Hudson in July. If he visited, he found the family well but economically stressed, fearful of depredations from both sides, and Frances still in mourning for Sonny. Although an invasion of Louisiana by Union forces did not occur until April 1862, the war soon affected planters like Butler. Sugar makers began to experience difficulty marketing their bountiful 1861 crop, because the Union blockade hindered coastal and foreign shipping. Transport of troops and military supplies increasingly occupied railroads and steamboats. Sugar planters sought markets in Texas and with plantations that grew only cotton. Normal life dissolved, and the disruptions forced citizens to concentrate on their home lives and on the means of limiting any threat to slavery; the institution's possible disintegration concerned everyone and caused much anxiety. Besides luxuries, necessities such as pork, beef, and salt became scarce. From Thibodaux, where Confederate General Braxton Bragg lived at Bivouac Plantation facing Bayou Lafourche, Elise Ellis Bragg wrote her husband in April 1862. She noted that "the good old Doctor" was "sending two boxes of delicacies," and "we would have done the same if we had anything—but we are out of all dainties & many necessities." In addition, the Union capture of New Orleans late that month commenced a serious loss by planters of draft animals, which were confiscated by both the Union and Confederate forces. After areas became occupied by the Federals, many growers felt compelled to take the oath of allegiance to the United States in order to escape plunder. Their operations, however, remained hampered.

Enduring the emotional blow from the loss of Sonny, Frances Butler tried to put on a good face. Her letter to Lawrence Butler in mid-December 1861 expressed both defiance of Lincoln and hope for aid from England and France in breaking the blockade. But the news of enemy advances was worrisome. Earlier in 1861, her first cousin Mary Custis Lee, the wife of General Robert E. Lee, wrote of Union army pillage committed in Virginia. Despite protection from General Winfield Scott, Yankees invaded homes of close relatives. They were Anna Fitzhugh, of Ravensworth, Fairfax County, and John Augustine Washington III, former owner of Mount Vernon then living at Waveland, Fauquier County [killed in battle in September 1861]. Frances lamented Son's death—"so full of promise as his life had." Protective and supportive of him, she experienced Son's death particularly hard. Unlike the many who mourned their dead later in the war, she was able to conduct a decent ceremony for young Edward. She took comfort from the presence of two vivacious Turnbull grandsons and her walks to visit Son's grave nearby their home. Still, she could not accept his fate. Two and a half years' later, Butler reported her in a state of grief: "Frances has never been out . . . since the death of our Son."[11]

With men and materials consigned far away to other parts of the South, Louisiana found herself unprepared for the loss of New Orleans. Iberville Parish was positioned north of and upriver from the region termed the "Valley" of Bayou Lafourche, a distributary of the river originating at Donaldsonville. The Dunboyne neighborhood and towns of Bayou Goula and Plaquemine nevertheless became a part of the Union-controlled area known as the Lafourche District. The war activities soon commenced at Donaldsonville, southward along the bayou, and to the west. They would weigh deeply on Dunboyne and the Butlers. Shortly after the fall of New Orleans, and in a show of overwhelming power, Union forces captured the strategically important New Orleans, Opelousas, and Great Western Railroad. It ran between New Orleans and Brashear City on the Atchafalaya River. They also marched north on Bayou Lafourche to Donaldsonville and steamed up the Mississippi River to capture Baton Rouge and Natchez. Numerous fearful planters readied to flee their homes and properties. The invaders noted that in order to prevent crops from falling into Union hands, planters threw hogsheads of sugar into the Mississippi or burned bales of cotton. Some planters, in particular those inclined to the old Whig Party, thought of the United States more as a protector. Others who were sympathetic to the Confederate cause determined to await Rebel assistance.[12] The shock to the South of having lost New Orleans bore heavily. The Yankees, "emboldened by no resistance whatsoever . . . will prove troublesome. . . . We can get nothing from the City," Elise Bragg complained. Once territory was taken by Union forces, "we have never regained a foot of ground lost." Bragg reflected a loss of hope that came early to southern supporters in the Sugar Belt. What future for their new republic could there be, asked many southerners, given the surrender of its most important city and port? Almost as soon as the news reached England and France, on whose recognition the Confederacy counted, the enthusiasm of the two nations for the South's cause dampened. The effects of New Orleans's surrender to the Union were devastating.[13]

Slow in responding to the Union invasion into the Bayou Lafourche region, Louisiana militia troops in the summer of 1862 retook Brashear City. They pushed the Yankees back along the railroad to Des Allemands, closer to New Orleans. Louisiana's Governor Moore, however, found minimal support for the Rebel cause in the area. The local populations remained distrustful of the state government's ability to raise and equip a force sufficient to meet that of the Union and feared inviting retribution from the occupying army and navy. The Lafourche region's defense remained weak until Richard Taylor was appointed major general of the Confederate District of Louisiana. The district was a part of the larger Trans-Mississippi Department under General Edmund Kirby Smith, with jurisdiction over the vast territory of Louisiana, Texas, and Arkansas west of the Mississippi River. Taylor quickly assigned General Alfred Mouton to take charge in the Lafourche and to reassert control. Based in Thibodaux, Mouton began organizing and training a Rebel army to defend the region, where the residents greatly feared another, worse invasion of the enemy forces.[14]

The Rebels' build-up of manpower so close to New Orleans and their attempts to disrupt the Federal control of the Mississippi River provoked Union forces to action. General Benjamin Butler, then commanding the Department of the Gulf headquartered in the city, ordered Brigadier General Godfrey Weitzel to commence a full offensive. The Ohioan Weitzel had roomed at the U.S. Military Academy with future Louisiana governor Francis T. Nicholls. Both men quickly rose in their respective armies, and Nicholls was then serving with the Confederacy in Virginia. Landing at Nicholls's hometown of Donaldsonville on October 25, 1862, Weitzel's army moved with dispatch. Despite strong resistance from Mouton's Confederates, especially just above the village of Labadieville, the Federals reached Thibodaux by October 28. Mouton's army barely escaped and retreated west of the Atchafalaya. The Union Army once again controlled the Lafourche District.[15]

In September 1862, just as Weitzel began his preparations for the Lafourche offensive, Lincoln's Emancipation Proclamation set a date of January 1 for freeing slaves in areas still controlled by the Confederacy. Its effect was to encourage already restless slaves to leave their plantations. Seeking freedom, these destitute people deluged the frequently unwelcoming occupying armies. Planters found it difficult to maintain discipline, and many attempted to recover their runaways from the Northern authorities. The melting away of the labor force in the district, initiated by the invasion of Weitzel's army, coincided with the planters' gearing up for the all-important sugar cane harvest. At the northern end of the district, along the river, Union forces raided plantations in September; prior to Weitzel's arrival on the Lafourche, Union vessels and shore parties landed at Plaquemine. On the return voyage, U.S. gunboats retaliated against Rebels firing from positions along the levees.[16]

In addition, colored troops began to serve in the Union Army in Louisiana, despite Weitzel's opinion that they constituted an unneeded encouragement to slaves to scavenge and steal. In his view, their inclusion led to even more resentment among the planters, whose support Weitzel hoped to attain. Dunboyne received its first visit from Union forces that fall, and Butler found it necessary to plead in writing to Weitzel for the safety of his family and property. Replying to Butler, the Union commander acknowledged the distinguished family kinships of Frances Butler, and for Colonel Butler, the "services you have rendered the country in previous wars." But Weitzel would not agree to protect Dunboyne, especially if "required for military uses." Butler's liquor stash had been raided, however, and Weitzel promised to punish the offenders.[17]

The exchange between Butler and Weitzel, documented by the latter's response to Butler's plea, illustrates problems that all planters encountered as Federal troops invaded and took control of portions of the South. They were justifiably anxious for themselves and their wealth through their landholdings and slaves. Frances Butler's heritage and Butler's own distinguished military record afforded limited protection. Although some Union Army resources were spent on guarding homes and farms of citizens, the dedication to such efforts diminished as the war intensified. The army's needs included crops and livestock. Depending on the circumstances and time of the conflict, the war focused increasingly on the capacity of private property to produce any and all crops. Although the Union Army officially avoided destruction and taking of southerners' property in most of 1862, the policy began to evolve. The Emancipation Proclamation attacked the military advantages that slavery gave the South. It signified a change toward a "directed severity" policy applied by military forces against the rebellious southern civilians. In addition, hard-core secessionists and members of the planter class, who were mostly blamed for the national conflict, were selected for harsh treatment. As a locally prominent supporter of secession, and one closely involved with military decision-making when the state joined the Confederacy, Butler qualified. Iberville escaped much of the broad destruction, foraging, and pillaging that occurred along Bayou Lafourche both during and after Weitzel's invasion in 1862, especially to properties whose owners had fled the area. But the dangers were there. To illustrate, after the surrender of Port Hudson in July 1863, in a fairly typical sweep of the country, Federal troops of the 49th Massachusetts Volunteer Regiment marched upriver from Donaldsonville. They arrested "all overseers and such persons who would likely give . . . information of the strength and whereabouts of the enemy." The troops later "went up to the McCall's [Evan Hall] plantation about three miles distant, and secured a boat load of corn. Our associates, the Second Louisiana, well acquainted with the neighborhood, pilfered a considerable quantity of jewelry." It might prove difficult for the Butlers to avoid severe losses without remaining strictly neutral, but impartiality was a sentiment foreign to Edward and Frances Butler. They would have to rely on luck and prayer that the active conflict would not beset their own neighborhood.[18]

The Butlers' hopes for a quiet existence were destined to collapse; the situation in Iberville and other parts of the Lafourche District worsened. General Butler used the U.S. Congress's Confiscation Act of July 1862 to sequester properties that were in Union-controlled areas west of the Mississippi River. Intended to punish "disloyal" persons, the measure forced many reluctant planters to sign the oath of allegiance to the United States in order to avoid losing their property. The edict fell particularly hard upon landowners who abandoned their homes, and their lands were confiscated and sold at auction in New Orleans. One may conclude that Edward Butler reached the decision to agree to an oath of allegiance. He could not otherwise preserve his land and provide for his family. In some respects, taking the oath mattered little, as both armies did not hesitate to use private property. While the petty vandalism about which Butler complained to General Weitzel occurred more frequently than burning and wholesale looting of plantations, both sides considered crops such as corn, hay, or sugar to be fair game. After landing in Plaquemine from boats in February 1863, a regiment of Union troops was assigned the duty of clearing obstructions from Bayou Plaquemine. The temptation to steal molasses, available from the recent harvest, was too much. Most of the soldiers' time was spent stealing it, cooking it in kettles, and pulling candy. As 1862 ended and the new year began, the Butlers, caring for Caroline Turnbull and her two young sons, surely felt imperiled and wondered how they would survive.[19]

In addition, guerrilla warfare increased and affected the lives of everyone along the Iberville "coast." The confiscation of citizens' properties and the conscription of "loyal" white men had been ordered in January 1863 by the newly appointed Union general Nathaniel Banks. The policy led to active resistance. Now angered, men prepared their return to the Confederate cause, and the families of those who did fight for the Union suffered reprisals from Confederate irregulars. The Union forces were aware of the strategic value of the land between the Mississippi River and Bayou Grosse Tête on the western side of Iberville Parish. Supported by gunboats, they occupied towns along the river. But to the west, the guerrillas controlled the morass of swamps, lakes, bayous, and rivers, which were interspersed with roads and trails along the high ground, known as "ridges." Originating from a mixture of Cajun, Anglo-American, and —curiously—even slave backgrounds, the young fighters survived off of the generosity of locals. The sympathetic natives included steamboat captains, barge polers, and pirogue owners who were experienced in the secrets of navigating "the unobvious routes connecting Louisiana's Attakapas Prairie parishes to the Mississippi." The terrain provided a perfect cover for the raids of mounted guerrillas. In late December 1862, close to Dunboyne, conflicts had occurred between them and Union forces under Captain Solon Perkins of Company A, 2nd Massachusetts Cavalry Battalion. Fearing what they thought was to be a massive invasion from the west, Union soldiers in January 1863 abandoned the recently occupied town of Plaquemine, upriver from the Butlers.[20]

As the Confederate Army retreated up Bayou Teche and on to Alexandria in late 1862 and early 1863, General Kirby Smith moved his headquarters to Shreveport. The populace there, fearing Union invasion, almost succumbed to panic. Relief came in the spring when Union armies concentrated at Vicksburg and Port Hudson, but Smith failed to support a Confederate reinvasion of the Lafourche country. No doubt unsuspecting of any great danger, the Iberville area received a reminder of its vulnerability in mid-June. A brigade of Rebel troops under Colonel James Major marched from Washington, Louisiana, crossed Bayou Plaquemine late in the day on June 18, "and at 6 p. m. started down the Mississippi River." By remaining behind the levee, Major avoided detection by "three large [Federal] gunboats" patrolling in the river. The Rebels no doubt traversed the front of Dunboyne. Did the Butlers celebrate their presence? It is hard to imagine that the passage of such a large armed force on the road in front of the Butlers' residence went unnoticed. No written record exists of their awareness, however, and indeed the presence of the Rebels may not have been appreciated. Arriving on June 19 at Bayou Goula at daylight, Major surprised the enemy, captured the Union "commissary and quartermaster stores; destroyed Federal plantations [those confiscated and operated by Union authorities and their designees]; recaptured over 1,000 negroes" who were confiscated "by Banks from planters living in St. Landry and Rapides Parishes, found them starving and in great destitution, kept the men." The Confederates "left the women and children," with no one to care for them, and headed to Thibodaux, where they were welcomed, en route to Brashear City. Taylor's army was unable to dislodge the Union forces, made up primarily of ex-slave soldiers, in a fierce battle at Fort Butler in Donaldsonville. With the fall of Port Hudson to the Union, the Confederates could not retain control over the Lafourche District. Once again they retreated across the Atchafalaya to the Teche country.[21]

The strategic town of Plaquemine had been surprised by repeated incursions of Confederates during 1862. As a consequence, the Department of the Gulf began construction of a "bastion fort" there in late 1863. Located about four hundred yards south of the town and twelve hundred yards from Bayou Plaquemine, the fort took a year to build. The Union commanders requisitioned men and animal teams from the town's citizens and from plantation owners in the vicinity. At its highest strength, the fort's armament included a thirty-pound Parrott gun, four eighteen-pound siege guns and siege carriages, and nine thirty-two-pound garrison guns with barbette carriages. Each gun had one hundred rounds of ammunition, "giving the proper proportion of round shot and canister or grape."

However, the fortress commanders found their complement of men insufficient. Of the approximate 450 men available, 131 served on "provost guard" and other duties at the fort. The remaining men, who stood picket duty along a three- to four-mile stretch, came under frequent attack by guerrillas. Initially the fort lacked ability to counterattack, as only twenty-one cavalrymen were available. Of those, twelve were "*unreliable and entirely worthless*" riders. As a result, the Plaquemine post could not defend planters like Butler who lived "immediately outside the lines who seemed to be working their plantations in good faith." Such planters "are continually applying for protection against the marauding bands" numbering between one hundred and five hundred.[22]

At the same time, owing to concerns about goods and persons that slipped through to the enemy, the Department of the Gulf undertook to improve supervision over the local provost marshals. In the Union scheme, the provost marshals "played a role similar to military government officers in modern war." They "held power to destroy planters, controlling the labor supply and sometimes exercising judicial functions in plantation affairs, to the extreme annoyance of the owners."[23] The department increased the number of regiments of Union cavalry assigned to larger towns like Plaquemine, Donaldsonville, and Thibodaux, the latter being the Lafourche District headquarters. The action strengthened protection of the area. Smaller forces were based in settlements such as Bayou Goula and Labadieville. Beginning in 1864, the district command transferred from General Weitzel to Colonel Edward Molineux of the 159th New York Infantry. He was succeeded in March by Colonel Nicholas W. Day, in May by Brigadier General John McNeal, and then in June by Brigadier General Robert A. Cameron of Indiana. Cameron remained until the end of the war. The military buildup in the district was to protect New Orleans, which Union commanders recognized was insufficiently defended against guerrilla activity west of the Mississippi. In addition, Union leaders wanted to be sure of maintaining lines of communication in the offensive march toward the Red River Valley that was being planned by General Banks.[24]

As the Butlers came under the threat of vandalism and plunder from both Union and Confederate activities, their plantation operations were in jeopardy. Correspondence to and from Dunboyne was difficult, adding to the household's anxiety about Lawrence Butler, who at the time was with the Rebel army in Georgia. If privately delivered, mail occasionally got through. Establishing a contact with General Banks, Butler managed to send word of his family's wartime plight to Alexander Duncan, in England. A message reached Duncan sometime in 1863, because Duncan's reply, dated December 22, 1863, referred to Butler's letter, "enclosed to me by General Banks many months ago." The exact contents of Butler's letter are unknown, but Duncan expressed concern about how Butler was "managing to keep your people together, under the new order of things." He offered to lend Butler $5,000, drawing on an account in New York, the sum "to be repaid when you found it convenient."[25] By the phrase "the new order of things," Duncan referred not simply to the military occupation of the Butlers' world, but to the changes that were occurring to the system of slave labor.

The Confiscation Act of July 1862, the Emancipation Proclamation in September 1862, and the Union takeover of the country parishes west of the Mississippi that autumn had created labor unrest. Unemployed slaves immediately challenged the plantation system. Some from Dunboyne Plantation probably fled to the Union army. The invading forces not only had much difficulty handling the large number of escaping slaves, but also were troubled at the prospect of angering slaveowners. Although excitedly anticipating freedom, slaves experienced confusion and hardship. Ellen M. Pugh of Bayou Lafourche was one of many slaveowners who attempted to reclaim their slaves who fled to New Orleans and the Union encampment "near Carrollton." Families often were split. The wife of "Nathan" deserted her husband and refused to return to him: "Nathan is very anxious for you to bring his wife and child," wrote Ellen Pugh to her husband, Alexander, but "if you cannot get his wife he says bring his child."[26]

In response, both General Benjamin Butler and his successor, General Banks, began issuing a series of military edicts to set rules for hiring and managing labor. A new approach to the labor challenge, the regulations were ever changing and bewildering, an "irreconcilable contradiction" in an environment of uncertainty between slavery and free labor. Planters seldom found satisfaction with the prescriptions. Under General Butler's Order 91 in November 1862, slaves were required to return to their former owners or be subject to arrest for "vagrancy." Planters, however, were bound to pay slaves behind Union lines a monthly salary, at first set at $10, less $3 for rations, and give laborers housing and medical care. Corporal punishment was prohibited, but military patrols were assigned to keep slaves at work on the plantations. The result of this rule was that production fell drastically. Planters bridled at surrendering physical control over their laborers or paying cash wages, and often they simply did not harvest the cane. Or slaves refused to perform their chores. In early 1863, after replacing Benjamin

Butler, General Banks in Order 12 amended the arrangements, making them less favorable to slaves but allowing for pay to slaves according to their duties or for a share of one-twentieth of the crop. The amount varied with the importance of the work or the skills required. Slaves also received a clothing allowance, food, and shelter. On abandoned plantations controlled by Federal authorities, contractors paid black laborers $1 per day. The planters who now "employed" their slaves, however, became unhappy about using invalids and elderly workers and appealed for more control over the labor force. They could not adjust to surrendering full control of their laborers, and the laborers no longer would work unless they were "treated properly." Cash payment for workers required that planters have available cash and credit gained from the marketing of their crops, and both forms of money became scarce. The war left few banking institutions available to finance operations. In addition, the marketing of crops fell completely under U.S. Army regulation at New Orleans, the sole remaining port after the blockade closed off other venues.[27]

By January 1863 a "sequestration commission" was established to run the labor system. The instructions for Iberville, dated February 5, 1863, serve as an example of rules for affected parishes. They required "officers of the Government" to "induce the Slaves to return to the Plantations where they belong." For their labor, the slaves received food and clothing and a share or cash payment. If paid in shares: mechanics, sugar makers, and drivers, three shares each; able-bodied field men, two shares per man; and field women and house servants, one each. If wages were paid: mechanics, sugar makers, and drivers, $3 daily; able-bodied field men, $2 a day; and field women and house servants, only $1. Planters signed up many workers but found it difficult to elicit work from them. The crop of 1863 was endangered due to insufficient numbers of laborers. Planters, forced to hire white laborers, again were unable to harvest the crops on their once productive lands. In September 1863, General Banks commenced the conscription of black males from age twenty to thirty for army service. The action aggravated the scarcity of labor on plantations. Congress enlarged the pool the following February to those between the ages of eighteen and forty.

Further exasperating planters, in January 1864 General Banks suspended the slavery laws of Louisiana. In February, General Order 23 replaced the prior rules on planter-laborer relations. Monthly wages were raised from $2 to $8 for first-class male workers. If shares were used, workers received one-fourth of the proceeds of the sales of the crop, up from one-twentieth. Hours of labor were defined. The authorities ordained garden plots of up to one acre for laborers. Workers were allowed to choose their employers but forced to contract for the year's work and to remain on the plantation. Planters no longer had physical control of their workers and could not inflict corporal punishment, but the orders permitted employers to withhold half of the monthly wages until the end of the year in order to ensure that laborers would not leave before the end of the harvest.

Planters like Butler remained irreconcilably supportive of slavery: in their view, the army's efforts to regulate labor relations did not allow employers to exercise sufficient control over the workers. The rules amounted simply to deficient understanding or ignorance of the society and economy of the sugar region. Planters believed that they brought about only problems and financial disaster. By 1862, state sugar manufacture already had declined to 87,231 hogsheads, down from almost 460,000 in 1861. The trend continued, and production dropped further in 1864–65, when the Sugar Belt generated only 10,387 hogsheads. By 1865, in Iberville Parish, the number of sugar cane plantations was 23, from 121 in 1861. In Louisiana overall, fewer than two hundred sugar plantations survived of the original 1,291. In the words of one historian, "the plantation economy fell apart."[28]

In the midst of this deterioration, how did the Butlers and Caro Turnbull and her children at Dunboyne fare? The family managed, although like all plantations, Dunboyne's labor supply felt the blow, and Butler reluctantly adjusted to cash wages or shares. Despite a dearth of wartime records, those in existence show that Dunboyne made and marketed both sugar and cotton. The latter, unlike sugar, provided some assurance of good yield and price. An indication of the state of things is available for the dark year of 1864–65.

Planters then operated under the final set of General Banks's instructions, General Order 23. Instead of wages, Butler chose to use a shares system. He paid his remaining forty-three workers (less than half the force of 1860 and consisting of twenty-nine men and fourteen women) by crediting them each with an equal portion of their one-third share of the twenty-five bales of cotton sold at 33 cents per pound. Fourteen of the field hands, including three women, assisted in bringing in a sugar cane crop in 1864 on only twenty-eight arpents (less than twenty-four acres). Each hand received a credit of $43.45 on the share he or she was owed at $200 per arpent. Seven other workers appeared on the plantation by June 1865. They included the servant Dennis, who attended both Butlers in their respective wars. Besides the active workers, one woman named Sylvia, described as "not employed," was charged with "Preservation of Garden Seeds" such as sweet pepper, eggplant, and tomato. Many workers received cash "under apportionment by Bureau Agent," a reference by Butler to the Freedmen's Bureau established in March 1865. The amount, $2.29 or $2.55, depended on whether the worker was "1st Class" or "2nd Class." Every employee's account was debited for varying expenses incurred with Butler. Employees bought pork, flour, tobacco, items for clothing, and $7.75 for the "portion of 1/3rd plan[tation] Expenses for Articles Consumed," all of which exceeded the value of their shares. The shares system was complicated. The workers' yearly accounts showed substantial debts owed to Butler; he was not only their employer, but a merchant and banker for them. The debts of the disgruntled workers revealed problems, especially with the shares manner of compensation. By the war's end, Dunboyne Plantation had fifty workers who remained or returned to the plantation and who constituted a solid base of labor. The Butlers theoretically could move ahead to restore their wealth. Their futures depended on finding available buyers who would pay prices high enough to cover expenses, keeping a labor force that was sufficient in number and would work, and securing capital to restore the mill and neglected fields.[29] Those conditions would be difficult to achieve.

Other essential employees, like overseers, continued to work at Dunboyne during the war, but the conflict caused disruptive changes in their makeup and compensation. Economics played a large part. Restrictions imposed on planters in their management practices with their black laborers caused white workers to leave. Butler's records are illustrative. As noted earlier, the overseer Joachim Cox found his wages in 1864 drastically "reduced to $400, + no hire," from $1,000 (which also paid him for the two workers he supplied). Even then, he was discharged after the 1864 harvest, in January 1865. Butler found no replacement until the following August, when James Adamson, also paid at $400 yearly, "+ find himself," was hired. Taking George Johnson's spot as the plantation carpenter in 1857 was Emmanuel Nate, at $400 a year, a sum that Butler raised to $600 in 1860. By 1863, however, Nate received only $300. In addition, Butler hired Adolph Arceneaux in 1863 to perform the duties of both gardener and general hostler. Paid $3 monthly, Arceneaux probably was a former slave, and his important duties included providing the household with fresh produce. The only other major services that the Butlers apparently afforded were those of Dr. B. Hall, a neighbor on Palo Alto Plantation. His $200 annual retainer was reduced to $100 by January 1, 1864. The Butlers simply had too little money to pay him and others their original stipends. Their labor force and the Dunboyne Plantation's productivity had declined. Hard times prevailed. The Butlers' resources were few, and they borrowed coal from Dr. Hall in the winter of 1864–65 to heat the rooms at Dunboyne.[30]

The Confederate forces of General Richard Taylor repulsed the Union army under Nathaniel Banks in the Red River Campaign in the spring of 1864. Success there, however, lent no opportunity for Taylor to reoccupy the Lafourche District. Supplies for another offensive were unavailable, and the Confederacy's Trans-Mississippi Department commander, General Kirby Smith, lacked the will to try. Even so, the Union command *believed* that New Orleans was still vulnerable to the Rebels and reinforced the Lafourche area.[31] Its fears may have been exaggerated, but there is no doubt that military activity by Confederate guerrillas was expanding. Provoked by the Union destruction of property in the region, by robberies committed by Union troops, and by bad treatment of Confederate prisoners, the local population increasingly resisted Union occupation. Guerrillas hid in the swamps and on bayou and river ridges, and often surprised the Federals throughout the district. When Union troops were dispatched to catch the small bands, their attempts usually fell short. The Rebels melted into the shallow bayous, lakes, and bays, where boats carrying the Federal troops proved insufficient. Union couriers traveling between Donaldsonville and Plaquemine were particularly in danger, and attacks on them occurred in the Butlers' neighborhood. Even reinforced military posts in Plaquemine and Bayou Goula remained susceptible. In early August 1864, one hundred Union pickets defending the fort at Plaquemine found themselves under attack by mounted Confederate infantry. The Rebels drove in the pickets, and fifty Rebels entered the town. Three Yankee soldiers were killed and four taken prisoner. Following the fierce fight, the Rebels retreated west to Indian Village.[32]

As the fortunes of the Confederacy disintegrated, so did the "constraints of law." The discipline of workers deteriorated further. Guerrilla activities increased, along with the bands of scavengers and deserters from the Confederacy known as Jayhawkers. Nightriders overran parishes not closely supervised by Union forces. Their targets included Pointe Coupée, adjacent to Iberville Parish. The guerrillas, notably those led by Captain U.M.C. Brown of the 17th Arkansas Cavalry, indulged in "raiding and bushwhacking along the Mississippi River." They attacked often, especially between Donaldsonville and Bayou Goula. The murderous bands particularly troubled civilians who were considered Union sympathizers. Lieutenant Charles Parkhurst, of the 3rd Rhode Island Cavalry, recalled that one of his major distractions was protecting "the Northern men who had leased the abandoned plantations and who were trying to make their fortunes using the labor of the freedmen." Those hopefuls, noted the skeptical Parkhurst, sought riches in the conquered areas but may have found only frustration. "They either had to employ some old resident called a Union man, who had been in neither army—a stay-at-home who had the vices of both armies and the virtues of neither—or to rely on their own judgment." Parkhurst observed that "whichever conclusion was adopted was quite sure to result in financial ruin." In January 1865, companies commanded by Colonel Willard Sayles of the 3rd Rhode Island Cavalry at Napoleonville and companies of the 8th U.S. Colored Infantry from Bonnet Carré were instructed to "take post at Bayou Goula." Combined with forces at Plaquemine, they were ordered to "throw out all their available cavalry upon the roads leading north into the Grosse Tête country and south into the avenues to the lower Grand River, to intercept the guerrillas, etc., who may have escaped you." The cavalry discovered Rebels, some at the rear of the plantation belonging to W. M. Thompson and near the Forest Home Plantation of John Randolph. No sooner had the 3rd Rhode Island Cavalry arrived than they were attacked "about one mile above Bayou Goula" by twenty-four guerrillas under Captain John Williams. The Rebels made off with eleven Union captives. A Union soldier, "Sergeant Dodge," found himself reduced in rank for "disgracefully" surrendering. This action took place less than a mile from Dunboyne Plantation.[33]

Clashes between guerrillas and Union forces and chases into the swamps at the rear of plantations around Bayou Goula continued until April, when Union naval and land forces coordinated their efforts. They succeeded in extending Union control to the waterways, which were the essential escapes and hideouts of the guerrillas and provided the mail routes and other supply passages to and from the Attakapas areas. Except for a few holdout guerrillas located in the vicinity of Houma, the surrender of Captain Brown at Donaldsonville on May 16, 1865, ended most of the problems.[34]

Defenseless in the midst of military activity, Butler sought assistance from Edward J. Gay. A fellow planter and a commission merchant, Gay lived at St. Louis Plantation, upriver from Dunboyne and just below Plaquemine. The families may have been socially close even before the Civil War, and they shared many of the same friends. Wartime trials brought them together.

Gay was a long-time resident of St. Louis, with extensive business interests there and in New Orleans. In 1840 he had married Lavinia Hynes, whose family owned the estate of her deceased grandfather, Joseph Erwin. It was the very same Home Place Plantation, later named Hynes Plantation, on which the Butlers shared a first mortgage with Lawrence Lewis in the 1820s. By 1856, Gay had bought out his wife's family and was the sole owner. He renamed the plantation St. Louis, after his home city, and in 1858 constructed a family mansion facing the Mississippi River. In 1860, Gay changed his domicile to Iberville Parish. Although Gay held strong secessionist positions, which clashed with those of his St. Louis family members and business associates, he was a realist. Early in the Civil War he recognized the futility of the southern cause. In order to hold on to his family's lands and to continue his mercantile business with New Orleans and St. Louis, Gay took the oath of allegiance to the United States and developed a working relationship with the Union Army provost marshal in Plaquemine. His plantation labor force and animal teams were conscripted repeatedly in 1864 for construction of the Union Army fort at Plaquemine, but Gay assisted "more . . . than any other Plantation in the Parish," reported Union major Richard Shaw at the Plaquemine headquarters. As a result, General Banks ordered that "any interference with his [Gay's] labor or his property, is hereby forbidden." With a few notable exceptions, and despite the Gays' eldest son Andrew Hynes Gay serving in the Confederate Army, the family lived quietly in their sumptuous St. Louis Plantation home. Their younger children, together with most of their friends and relatives in the vicinity, enjoyed a brisk, unfettered social life. Their seventeen-year-old daughter, Mary Susan, wrote in her 1863–64 diary about the children's frequent visits back and forth to Rosedale and Bayou Grosse Tête. They were the very areas where Rebel guerrillas were active. She and her friends and relatives befriended members of the Confederate forces in the vicinity. Yankees and Confederates clashed in or near Plaquemine, and Mary Susan recorded the events. Seldom, though, did the war interrupt the visits, the dinners with friends and family, and the short trips in the neighborhood of Plaquemine. Edward J. Gay appears to have been free to travel on business to New Orleans and St. Louis. In August 1864, Mary Susan made a note of the departure of her elder sister, Sophie, on the steamboat *Mollie Able*. Sophie spent the next year away at school in St. Louis. Once the Union forces opened up commerce on the Mississippi River, Gay thrived. The family retained much of its prewar wealth, while others completely lost theirs.[35]

Butler's need for assistance from Gay resulted from the strict regulations that the Union command imposed on the area. The Department of the Gulf remained suspicious of the populace in the vicinity of Plaquemine. Locals sympathized with the roving Confederates and slipped provisions to them. After the army required citizens to take new oaths of allegiance throughout the district, the requirements expanded to include support for the U.S. Constitution, Congress, the president's slave proclamations, and even the president personally. The department tightened authorization to travel on business or to shop and required permits for firearms and boats, which could be lent to or appropriated by guerrillas. Already, Butler had appealed to and gained some sympathy from General Banks, but he remained on the Union Army's list of those unworthy of protection. In May 1864, facing danger to his family, Butler asked Gay to help him with the provost marshal in Plaquemine. He wanted to obtain a license, perhaps to arm himself or to travel into or beyond Plaquemine. Gay by now had permission to carry a pistol and, later, a shotgun. He did argue on Butler's behalf but failed to persuade the provost marshal; nonetheless, Butler profusely thanked Gay for taking the trouble. He remained dissatisfied, grumbling that "I . . . think that, if he would grant me permits and explain to his Superior, the grounds on which he acts, and the course of Gen. Banks toward me, all his difficulties would be obviated."

The Butlers additionally suffered from the excesses of black Union troops and freed slaves who trespassed on and abused their property. "Cannot the Provost relieve me," asked Butler of Gay, "of negro Horses & Hogs? They have burned my fences & turned their livestock upon me; and when I am compelled to shoot the Hogs which enter my yard & garden, apparent dissatisfaction is the result." One must wonder how Butler escaped punishment for shooting hogs destined for Yankee cooking pots. In addition to such offenses on his land, Union couriers riding between Donaldsonville and Plaquemine frequented the Butlers' property for rest and became a problem. The commanding officer at Plaquemine reported that Butler complained about the couriers. They were "in the habit of loitering around his yard, stealing money and other articles from the negroes, and obliging him to feed them, although on account of the closing of the lines, he is unable to get supplies for his [Butler's] own family." The Butlers were still grieving, lonely, and helpless. "Mrs. Butler & my daughter, Mrs. Turnbull," Butler further implored his friend Gay, "are without the means of transportation, and the former has never been out since the death of our Son; but they desire me to say that they would be very happy to see *Mrs.* Gay, at any & all times; and, should you pass in this direction, I hope you will call to see me." Some relief came only toward the end of the conflict, when the commander in Plaquemine extended the downriver boundary for granting permits "for those needing to travel to obtain family supplies." Dunboyne now was within the zone of protection, and the Butlers finally could get away on errands and visits.[36]

At the end of May 1865, however, the Butlers remained unable to travel. Having a permit to carry a weapon was of no use now. Everything had been stolen, protested Butler to Union major Edmund C. Burt. Burt and his 3rd Rhode Island Cavalry rode out from Plaquemine to Bayou Goula looking for boats in which Rebels could invade the neighborhood or escape capture. "Colonel Butler . . . ," recorded Burt, "has two skiffs owned by his colored hands, the largest of which will carry eight persons with ease. Colonel Butler informs me that he had a permit from Captain Wells, of the Navy, to keep this boat [and] . . ." of groups across the river who came and stole everything they could, "including the last horse he had to ride." In the view of Major Burt, the culprit was the guerrilla "thief" Captain Brown, who with five to ten men had "infested the vicinity of Bayou Goula for a long time." The Butlers' plantation was not the only one that suffered from guerrilla raids. In late March, one sally occurred at "Madam Randolph's plantation," and another in late April, "at the Andrews plantation," homes of friends. The thievery does not appear to have embraced Caro's and Frances's heirlooms. Despite the sporadic occupation of Dunboyne by black Union soldiers, the presence of both black and white men on the plantation may have tempered the women's anxiety concerning black soldiers.[37]

At the end of the Civil War, the Butlers' prospects were poor. Badly damaged and neglected, the sugar mill and the slave cabins, which still housed workers, were sorely in need of repair. The availability of labor was questionable, and Butler considered freed blacks to be unreliable. As early as 1863–64, he had inquired of Alexander Duncan about the possibility of importing workers from abroad. Duncan, who visited Dunboyne before the war, now resumed communications and repeatedly discouraged Butler from trying to hire workers from Great Britain. He commiserated with the freedmen: "Poor creatures! They have been the means of raising a terrible war . . . and, now that it is over . . . they are, as a people to suffer from the change and . . . freedom will scarcely pay them for giving up the parental care of their late masters." But on the positive side, the Butlers retained their land and home, and the promise of Lawrence's safe return cheered them. With them, also, were Caroline Turnbull and her sons, Will and Dan. Caroline had a legitimate claim on their behalf to the estate of Daniel Turnbull. Finally, the Butlers' friend Alexander Duncan committed to help Butler make a new start. Duncan already had advanced funds through his company in New York City, and he wanted "to hear from you how you are to get on, now that the end has come."[38]

10

Hardships and Sorrows

Dunboyne Endings

Near the war's end, in 1864 and 1865, Lawrence Butler again was an assistant adjutant general, this time to Brigadier General Marcus J. Wright. Wright gained notoriety after the Civil War when he assembled the records of Confederate officers for the future publication of *The War of the Rebellion*. As the conflict was ending, he commanded the District of West Tennessee-Northern Mississippi, based in Grenada, Mississippi. Wright probably knew Major Butler from their participation in the Battle of Belmont, in which Wright commanded the 154th Tennessee Infantry. After Lee's surrender at Appomattox Court House in April, various Confederate forces engaged in the formalities of their own surrenders. On May 1, acting on Wright's behalf, Major Butler undertook his last wartime assignment. He delivered to Union Army major general C. C. Washburn in Memphis an armistice agreement between General Richard Taylor, Wright's superior, and Union Army major general Edward Canby. Washburn refused any arrangement other than the terms which Lee and Grant had agreed to and sent Butler back to his command. The surrender was accepted on May 5, in Citronelle, Alabama, and Butler, paroled as a prisoner of war on May 17, soon made it home. His safe return from that cruel and wasteful war must have been joyous. Lawrence now would have to pitch in and help his parents and sister. Looking over the old place, he surely wondered whether Dunboyne ever would recover its prosperity.[1]

On top of the state of deterioration brought by war, floods came. Although none directly affected Dunboyne, Iberville and surrounding parishes suffered extensively. The Mississippi River deluged the region in 1866, 1867, and 1868. The impacts fell hard upon the economy. Many freedmen and whites were destitute, even near starvation, and to survive they required repeated intervention by the U.S. Army. In May 1866, the army shipped 19,600 rations from New Orleans for the three adjoining parishes of Iberville, West Baton Rouge, and Pointe Coupée.

The following April, numbers of planters were compelled to remove, by skiff, from their flooded homes in "interior Iberville." Most affected were the poor of both races. "Surrounded with water for three or four months and . . . scarcely able to get out of their houses for a month after the water goes down on account of the mud," they endured "sickness and continued debility; as for cultivating anything it is utterly impossible." In the spring of 1867, the Iberville Parish Police Jury sent Lawrence Butler, then a juror, to New Orleans to plead for rations again. The army shipped food and supplies multiple times during April, May, and June. Six thousand rations arrived in Iberville and West Baton Rouge, and an additional "16,020 Rations, for distribution to the destitute," were provided in March 1868.[2]

The devastation to Louisiana's sugar industry, its labor difficulties, and the lack of requisite capital to recover presented tremendous challenges. Conditions tested the survival abilities of everyone. Two years after the end of the Civil War, the Lafourche planter David Pugh articulated the general unhappiness of his class when he reported to his wife, Ellen. She was visiting relatives in New York for the first time in years: "In private business there is no chance at all, from the fact that nobody is doing anything. Money is more scarce than at any time since the war commenced. The banks are beginning to fail, and everyone dreading a terrible crash before long."[3] Matters could not have appeared worse.

During the war, Louisiana planters situated in the Union-controlled parts encountered slave emancipation sooner than other southern agriculture operations. Both employers and laborers expressed discomfort with their situations. Few planters held much confidence in the freedmen and retained their old opinions about white superiority and black inferiority. For their part, freedmen remained suspicious of their former masters and unhappy with many of their accommodations. The U.S. Bureau of Refugees, Freedmen, and Abandoned Lands maintained district offices in many Louisiana communities. Known as the "Freedmen's Bureau," its office in Plaquemine covered the parishes of West Baton Rouge and Iberville. Bureau officials often found difficult the task of serving as go-betweens in former slaves' transition to freedom. They kept in place some military rules for a while, but military oversight diminished in the year or two after peace. Enforcement of civil and criminal law devolved to civil authorities, whose effectiveness and fairness often came into question. Laborers became dissatisfied with the shares payment system, an arrangement that planters preferred because of their cash flow problems. As workers pressured employers, compensation in cash gradually took hold, but the sugar industry only reluctantly adjusted to wage labor. Laborers pressed for more autonomy via negotiated cash wages and improved working conditions. Planters, threatened both economically and politically, pushed back to retain physical control of their laborers. They wanted assurance that workers would be available and fully involved in all of the important phases of crop growing, harvesting, and milling.[4]

Dunboyne Plantation struggled as an ongoing sugar cane growing and milling concern in the postwar years. The plantation structurally survived but did not undergo the sort of major upgrading needed to produce a profit. An 1879 legal description depicted a plantation that was materially unchanged since the 1850s. The land was "cultivated in cane and corn. The improvements consists of dwelling House, sugar House, Quarters for Laborers, Corn House & all necessary appurtenances for a Sugar Farm. It has a front of . . . 10 or 12 acres. The Sugar House & all the Buildings are situated just about in Centre of the place. The Dwelling House & Cabins being in front & Sugar House farther back. The Sugar House looks rather dilapidated. But is worth something like $5000 or $6000. The dwelling House is worth something like $4000."[5] Like most of its neighbors of larger size, the Dunboyne sugar house was of "brick and shingle" construction and remained a steam-and-kettle operation. Much in need of repair and upgrading, the mill barely managed. The plantation moved back to sugar cane and away from cotton, which Butler mainly produced in the final year or so of the war. Between 1867 and 1871, when reports once more were published, sugar prices ranged between 11¾ cents and 13 cents per pound, with molasses between 55 cents and 75 cents a gallon. Seemingly high, prices could vary. Insurance premiums, taxes, freight, commissions, and other costs reduced the returns. Observers disagree on what growers made; across the Sugar Belt, the spread of receipts for sugar after expenses was 9½ cents to 11¾ cents per pound between early 1867 (for the 1866 crop) and December 1868.[6]

In the midst of unsettled labor conditions, Butler fought to raise yields and to hire affordable and reliable workers. He was paying a thirty-man, fourteen-woman field workforce in 1864 and 1865 using shares of the crop, after expenses. They received compensation based upon crop prices set at 33 cents per pound for cotton and $200 an arpent for sugar produced. Clothing, food, and other items such as tobacco were deducted from the amounts credited to each worker, and all of Butler's workers became indebted to him. The plantation operating expenses in 1865 included the costs of cotton seed and the seed plant cane, which

Butler may have acquired from another plantation and planted on fifteen arpents of Dunboyne. Amounts for nails, castor oil, and the salaries paid to the Butlers' overseer, carpenter, engineer, and plantation doctor were among many other expenses. Corn, in which the plantation once was self-sufficient, was acquired from freedmen working on or leasing the property of the Ricard family. Its members were prominent free people of color and former slaveholders. Their property was located downriver from and near Bayou Goula.

The continuing stagnant economy and the difficulties Dunboyne faced with its now free labor created turnover among the non-field help, and their wages fluctuated. For example, the overseer, hired in August 1865 at $400 yearly, only lasted until December 1866. Butler no longer could afford such a salary, and the new overseer, Green Freeman, worked for one-eighth of the crop, plus his personal requirements of sugar and molasses. He also had "to find himself" (furnish the costs of his own sustenance). After a gap in the overseer record, perhaps when Lawrence Butler was handling the duties, Joseph Cointment came to work on January 1, 1868, and remained until October 1870. Cointment received a higher wage, $800, less sugar, molasses, and corn. The carpenter Emmanuel Nate, who began work in 1857 at $400 and was "to find himself," received $500 in 1860, halved to $250 in 1863. His wages changed in 1865 to $30 a month less his house rent of $50 per year. Nate's employ ended February 1, 1868. His replacement, James Harrison, was paid only $24 monthly, except $30 a month during grinding time, for the two years that he remained with the Butlers. Harrison's varied duties, besides carpentry, involved working on tools, cooperage (such as making hogsheads), and splitting poles. Other contract workers appear on Butler's books, normally receiving $1 a day, although Toby West received $1.50 daily in 1868 and John West, employed as the Butlers' "hostler," began work for $8 monthly on February 25, 1868.[7] White laborer tasks embraced some that formerly may have occupied slaves. The hire of whites tended to be irregular and temporary, other than the overseer, carpenter, and engineer positions.

After 1866, Butler mainly recorded household workers and failed to list field laborers. Several house servants typically received pay every three months of between $6.25 and $7.50—or $25 to $30 yearly—through 1870. Even with the bad times, the Butlers continued to employ five or six household and yard workers. Among them was Dennis, who returned in 1865 after serving Lawrence Butler for the entire Civil War. Except for Dennis's fairly constant pay of $72 yearly, most of the servants' wages were reduced over time from $65 a year to under $30 by 1870.[8]

In spite of Butler's poor documentation of field laborers after 1866, the records of the Freedmen's Bureau shed light on his labor problems and on his intransigence in the face of an evolving society and economy. The local bureau representatives in Plaquemine and those at the headquarters in New Orleans wrote and exchanged reports, comments, requests, and instructions, all of which are preserved at the National Archives.

By the spring of 1866, when for some unknown reason the bureau listed Lawrence Butler as owner, Dunboyne had experienced attrition in its field labor. The number dropped from forty-four workers as the war ended the previous spring to thirty-three, consisting of twenty-one men and twelve women. Sugar cane was raised on only ninety-five acres, and the plantation still grew one hundred acres of cotton, in addition to 105 acres of corn. All of the field workers were paid on crop shares. A year later, the number of workers declined slightly, to nineteen men, eight women, and three male children. Additionally, one male and one female described as "aged and helpless" inhabited the quarters, but no evidence is available to state whether and how they were supported by Butler. Butler's workers by then no longer received shares: seven received housing, fuel, and wages, and twenty-three were paid in rations and wages, evidence of a reduction in the resident population on the place. Paying at the low end of Iberville and West Baton Rouge Parish salaries, Butler compensated his workers at an average of $9.23 a month. Although some cotton still was cultivated in the two parishes, it no longer grew on Dunboyne. In the spring of 1867, 106 acres were in cane and one hundred in corn, a reduction in the total acreage farmed.

Eighteen months later, at the end of October 1868, Dunboyne still had thirty freedmen working, made up of twenty men, seven women, and three male children. The plantation maintained another three "aged and helpless" adults and seven male and fourteen female children. The workforce then cultivated 150 acres of sugar cane, two hundred acres of corn, and five acres of "cereals." With a larger resident population to support in late 1868, the plantation also afforded workers more pay than registered the prior year. Wages were in the middle of the pay rates for the two parishes, averaging $11 per month, plus rations. During the height of grinding, however, Dunboyne suffered a critical loss of laborers, when almost half of the force quit. The likely cause was Butler's overreaction to a wage dispute on the plantation, when the workers were "charged for more lost time than they actually lost." As a result, "they left, after being [paid] in full for what they had already earned."[9]

The difficulties with Butler's field laborers began during the Civil War and never ceased, a situation made clear in records of the army provost marshals and Freedmen's Bureau officials. The agencies dealt with a staggering breadth of local problems and ruled extensively over private and commercial affairs. Among the issues was lawlessness. At the war's end it was common, symptomatic of the upheaval occasioned by war and by the floods, which worsened already unsettled conditions. The number and seriousness of "petty theft" arrests grew so large that the authorities were at a loss what to do with the thieves. As the army provost courts ended, the Freedmen's Bureau and civil authorities found themselves sharing law enforcement responsibilities. The bureau agents were directed to protect and guide the freedmen. They received instructions to bring suits for redress in state courts and not to make arrests on their own. Freedmen held little trust in the civil authorities, who only reluctantly provided them legal relief. Military intervention remained a possibility. Reacting to the local planters' unrest about and reluctance to adjust to manumission, the bureau headquarters pleaded that the civil courts "act justly and temperately towards the freedmen." The bureau wished for the judges to "render them the kind assistance that is required by a people who having been lately manumitted, are, to a great extent, ignorant of the laws and customs that govern free persons."[10]

In 1867 Dunboyne experienced labor trouble that, if it had happened during antebellum years, would have been handled on the plantation. One difficulty began on John Randolph's Nottoway Plantation. Two laborers refused to sign a new, year-long work contract in January 1867. They repeated an untrue story that anyone who signed "would be put into army and persecuted in divers ways." The rumor "created the greatest dissatisfaction, uneasiness and injury among the Freedmen" on several plantations, including Dunboyne. Perhaps affected by the gossip, the Dunboyne freedman Andrew Parker quit "without giving notice or explanation of any kind." When Lawrence Butler reported the problem to the local bureau officer, F. A. Osbourn, Osbourn ordered Parker to "be brought to this office at once for examination and trial." Found not to have a reasonable excuse for breaking his employment contract, Parker lost his job and also any pay he was due.[11]

Yet another Dunboyne incident, which formerly would have required no governmental permit, occurred with the freedman Charles Turnbull. He was accused of theft and beating and abusing his consort, Patsy Garnett. Lawrence Butler obtained permission from Osbourn to ban Turnbull from the plantation and to order him "to have no further intercourse with said Patsy Garnett." Turnbull, however, continued to be a thorn in the Butlers' side.[12]

On occasion, planters like Butler needed help for their former slaves who were sick or too feeble to work or even to live on the place. The Freedmen's Hospital had been established in New Orleans, and in 1867 Butler requested transportation for his former slave Peter Goodall to the hospital. Goodall, born in 1814, was acquired by Butler in Richmond in 1833. Now an invalid, he was "old and entirely unable to move," reported Assistant Subassistant Osbourn. He "has been supported for the last twenty years by Col Butler, who represents him as an honest man, worthy of the attention of the Bureau." The bureau furnished Goodall a steamboat ride to the city and the hospital.[13]

Bureau officials watched closely the state of affairs in their districts. The reports noted relations between newly freed slaves, planters, and other whites, the improvement or lack thereof of morals of the freedmen, and the conditions of the freedmen's schools and their participation in the educational process. The share payment system, which was poorly understood and disadvantageous to the hands, gradually gave way to the annual wage contracts normally negotiated shortly after January 1. Communicating between plantations, freedmen often resisted making new contracts in order to achieve higher wages, but Butler, for one, could ill afford to pay high wages. As freedmen organized to achieve unity in demanding better wages, their interest in politics also increased. From the planters' view, as well as that of the local bureau officials, too much time was being occupied by freedmen in "Politics and Political Clubs." Their meetings caused neglect of work and often evolved into raucous parties. When the freedmen meetings were held on Sundays, they drew particular criticism from planters and the bureau officials.[14]

Edward Butler held a low opinion of manumission and despised the lack of self-control in so many of the freedmen. Finding the situation intolerable, he protested. Unemployed hands on Dunboyne who simply loafed around the premises highly upset the discipline-minded former U.S. Army colonel. He lodged a strong complaint with the bureau office in Plaquemine, which ordered the irritants to "quit the place or be liable to the action of the Civ. Authorities as trespassers." Butler continued his representations about Charles Turnbull, whom he accused of stealing a cow. Further, jolly men returning from the "Moses Club," "swearing, singing and whooping as they passed [the Butlers'] residence," disturbed the peace and quiet to which the Butlers long had been accustomed. In frustration and overreaction, he even expressed a fear of "collision of races." Other loudly vociferous meetings that the freedmen held across the Mississippi River, at which guns were discharged, excited the residents of Dunboyne. Butler charged the civil authorities with incompetence and failure to act to prevent his family's "ruin and destruction." Butler traveled to New Orleans to voice in person his concerns about the problems with black workers and lax law enforcement. He met with the U.S. Army Fifth Military District commander, the distinguished Civil War general Winfield Scott Hancock. Afterward, the general wrote Butler soothingly on "the subject of the Negro element in your vicinage, and to the embarrassment you experience in consequence of the failure of crops and the peculiar disposition of the laborers." He noted that he had been receiving other protests. His hope was to relieve "the embarrassing necessities of those to whom, in great measure, must be committed the task of recovering order and prosperity in Louisiana." Hancock requested reports on Butler's case from both the commissioner of the Freedmen's Bureau as well as the state commandant.[15]

The local bureau agent and the justice of the peace were directed to investigate Butler's charges. The inquiries and interviews with Butler riled both sides. The officials took offense at Butler's appeal to higher authority and at what they considered his high-handed and exaggerated requests. In addition, when asked to point out the miscreant Turnbull, the Old Colonel grew recalcitrant. According to the new bureau agent Charles E. Merrill, Butler displayed a hands-off attitude and a too-dignified manner. The agent reported angrily at Butler's inclination not "to give a negro the benefit of the law. But [he] wants to see them dragged and drove about like dogs under his lash at his calling or command. I also learned that he has been trying to hire laborers for six dollars per month to work the coming year, which would almost compel them to steal or starve. . . . If Mr. Butler would throw aside all prejudice against the Negroes & poor white people in general, he would live a much happier life in the future." Merrill requested that Iberville's justice of the peace, G. Hebert, make an investigation and take statements to determine whether Butler's accusations had any foundation. Hebert also was instructed to see "as to the necessity of the Military to save [Butler] from destruction and ruin caused by the Freedmen and incompetent Civil Officers." Merrill ultimately found that Butler's remarks regarding the conduct of the freedmen were exaggerated and undeserving of any military intervention. He did agree that political meetings tended to be loud and a nuisance, particularly when held on a Sunday.[16] The authorities' deficient support reinforced Butler's already critical sentiments of them.

Freedmen throughout the Sugar Belt commenced political action and resisted planter efforts to keep them under tight control. The workers increasingly showed their independence. Discharging an employee who preferred to participate in political activities instead of working might result in his fellows striking. Such an event came in 1867, on the Belle Grove Plantation of the Butlers' friend John Andrews, as statewide elections approached. Plantation owners normally resisted overt violence against their increasingly independent-acting workers, but they could and did use more subtle intimidation in their efforts to force their workers to attend to business. Wary of the situation, Butler shortly after the war's end asked Alexander Duncan about substituting foreign workers for former slaves. Duncan had just arrived in New York and hoped finally to hear from Butler, "now the last war is over." He advised Butler that he still did not think that European emigrants would "go to the South." More likely, help would come from New York rather than from England. Planters continued to search for less expensive and less troublesome labor alternatives in place of what local sources could furnish. Their freed slaves, in the opinions of Butler and other planters, simply could not be trusted to perform. His old friend Andrew Jackson Donelson even blamed local whites at his Mississippi operation for putting "it into their [former slaves'] head that something is due to them for service in past years." Donelson was forced to pay higher wages and to "deal liberally" with his workers. And in late 1865, the Lafourche planter David Bryan Pugh complained that the diminished value of his rich land signified a need for "a change in the labor system, of which we have no reasonable prospect." The stakes were high, and adjustments by both employers and workers were painful and hard to understand. But laborers often achieved beneficial changes from their former masters. The historian Fox-Genovese has written that the end of slavery and subsequent difficulties "laid the foundation for future victories." Now free, men and women were able to "ground the relations between people in institutions." Without them, "no people could hope to determine its destiny, shape its young, and define its own virtues."[17]

A diligent correspondent, Edward Butler recommenced writing old friends once the war ended. If for no other reason, he wanted to sound out their thinking on how to face the challenge of being a postwar sugar cane planter. In addition to Duncan and Donelson, Butler communicated with former President

James Buchanan, under whose watch the country unraveled in the late 1850s. Butler, of course, would not hold him responsible for the war. Hearing of the problems in Louisiana and elsewhere, Buchanan sympathized with those who suffered from the springtime Mississippi River flooding of 1867, but he had little to say about Butler's labor difficulties. John Slidell, Butler's prewar advisor, mirrored Butler's "gloomy" expectations concerning "the experiment of free African labor." Like most other southern whites, Slidell could not conceive of them, "even under the most honorable circumstances," performing with ". . . sustained and continuous industry, when left to follow, uncontrolled, their natural instincts." Robert E. Lee, occupying the presidency of Washington College in Lexington, Virginia, exchanged long letters with Butler. If somewhat less racially strident than Butler, Lee also was not entirely hopeful. Butler complained bitterly to his old friend about his problems with labor and with local officials. Responding in January 1867, Lee urged patience with the "difficulties" that Butler described. Southerners needed to "sustain our State Governments & maintain our elevative standards of morals, religion & literary culture." Concerning the Turnbull boys, over whom Butler retained a guiding influence, Lee counseled postponing for a few years sending them away to school. In the meantime, "teach them Self Control & Self Denial." Later that year, after military control tightened over Louisiana's government, Lee reflected to Butler "that, notwithstanding our boastful assertions to the world, for nearly a century, that our government was based on the consent of the people; which we proclaimed, was the only rightful foundation on which any government could stand . . . it rests upon force; as much as any government that ever existed."[18]

Many southern white women had been accustomed to almost complete dependency on slaves for all of their domestic needs. That held true for Frances Butler, but little correspondence exists to show how she handled problems with her freed servants. She employed several, who worked in the house and garden, and managing the house was not easy. With little money, how could the Butlers afford necessary supplies, schooling for their grandsons, and the wages of the servants? Frances still grieved the death of their beloved Edward Butler Jr. In May 1866, she also lost her eldest daughter, Isabel Williamson. Isabel's good fortune was to live near her husband during much of the Civil War, and Sissy gave birth to two daughters during the war, adding to her brood of two sons and two daughters. Within months of the birth of the last child, named Caroline, in June 1865, Sissy began to experience symptoms of an illness that eventually claimed her. Writing her mother in late October 1865 that she had caught a cold, Sissy also complained of having a cough and a "wound in my cheek," which broke out in blisters. Her physician informed Sissy that her "lungs are severely affected," and he advised her to seek a doctor's cure in San Antonio or even to travel to Cuba for treatment. The decision was difficult: she wanted to remain with her children, and she did not want to travel to Cuba without the company of her sister, Caro. There was no resolution for what in fact was tuberculosis. Isabel's death came on June 9, 1866, following several weeks in which Sissy "knew of the grave . . . just before her." She voiced no complaint, but only displayed calm fortitude and serene faith, according to her obituary. Within two years George Williamson remarried, and he sired an additional five children before his death in 1882. Differences developed between him and the Butlers, and the cousins visited only on occasion. The Butlers and Williamsons slowly pulled apart.[19]

Their growing family strains arose mainly due to the failure of George Williamson to repay a large debt to Caro Turnbull. It was based upon the promissory notes executed when Williamson acquired slaves from Caro in 1860. Williamson took the position that inasmuch as he no longer owned the slaves after their emancipation, any binding financial obligation relating to their acquisition was void. To the Butlers, the emancipation of the slaves during the war provided little excuse for his denial of the debt. Especially because he was part of the family, Williamson should live up to the debt; it was a sacred financial duty and a matter of family honor. It also represented money that Caro much needed.[20]

Not only would she wait in vain for a payment from Williamson, but Caro had become ensnarled in another disagreeable family dispute, with her mother-in-law, Martha Turnbull. Expensive and time consuming for Caro and for Butler, who assisted her, the arguments involved Daniel Turnbull's debts to her as tutrix for her two sons. The Civil War forced Caro and her children to seek the protection afforded by her parents, but she could not have foreseen that the war would come to their doorstep. She probably also did not know of the destruction suffered by the DeSoto Plantation on Turnbull Island, in which Caro retained an interest as a creditor on behalf of her children. Witnesses recounted later that during the "siege of Port Hudson [in 1863] the Yankees, Negroes etc. took away all the Mules, stock, killed all hogs, Wagons broke open store rooms" on DeSoto. The dwelling house and sugar mill were destroyed. Bales of cotton also had been taken "to pack Mrs. C. B. Turnbulls' furniture & I never saw any of it." With no opportunity to remove her possessions, Caro lost them forever. Could she manage to save her children's interest in the land itself?[21]

After war's end, and once able, the Butlers began to stir in order to salvage what they could for their Turnbull grandsons. The effort would prove daunting. Upon his death in 1861, Daniel Turnbull left a will giving his entire property to his daughter Sarah, recently married to James Bowman. He thus excluded his Turnbull grandsons as heirs. Among the debts on Daniel Turnbull's estate, however, was the obligation on the mortgage held by Caro Turnbull following the sale of DeSoto Plantation to Daniel Turnbull. Martha Turnbull became administratrix of her husband's estate and thus responsible for its proper management and the settlement of its debts. As income from the estate and payments to Caroline fell off during the war, the friendship between the Butlers and Martha Turnbull declined. In January 1865 she filed an accounting of her administration during the years since her husband's death. In the view of Caro, the Butlers, and Caro's legal advisor, the account figures were inaccurate and irregular. They requested a second account of the administration, and this time it included the Turnbull children as creditors for the amount of their grandfather's bond, plus interest. Caro's attorney, Charles M. Conrad—her uncle and a former U.S. senator and secretary of war in the Fillmore administration—argued that certain aspects of the estate had been conducted improperly: Martha Turnbull failed to furnish a required security bond, and Sarah Bowman, her daughter, had not accepted the succession. Conrad believed the estate to be insolvent. He asked the 7th Judicial District Court in West Feliciana Parish to appoint Caro as administratrix in the place of Martha Turnbull. Because she lived in Iberville Parish and had claims to the succession, Caro opened a succession record there. The distrust and split between the families widened. By 1867, when matters appeared hopelessly tangled, Caro even considered renouncing the succession on behalf of her children, fearing they might be overburdened by their grandfather's debts.[22]

The emotional and financial costs of the endless disputes added to the Butlers' insuperable problems with their plantation. Martha Turnbull blamed Butler and Charles Conrad for instigating their court suit, which she considered unnecessary. Caro and her parents no longer allowed the children to visit their Turnbull relatives. When the boys began college careers in 1870, Martha Turnbull complained icily to Caro: "Your letter advising me of the departure of my grandchildren Willie & Dan Turnbull is before me, & however odious I may have been represented, I should like to say farewell to the sons of my dear William

& have them at Rosedown." The boys found their away-from-home allowances to be insufficient, and in June 1870 Will appealed to Martha to "send me some money—as I cannot get any from home and am very hard up for some."[23]

A settlement of the long-standing issues finally was reached in 1871. After reciting the history of the conflict, the document filed with the Turnbull succession record set forth the details of a compromise. By it, Martha Turnbull abandoned her claims on her husband's succession, and Sarah Bowman, who also opposed the Turnbull children's claims, now recognized them. Martha and Sarah agreed to a sale of DeSoto Plantation, the proceeds paid to Caro in discharge of the debt of the estate to her children. Certain accounts of the estate were ratified. Caro agreed that, following a deduction from the amount due on Daniel Turnbull's bond, any balance remaining from the DeSoto Plantation sale was joint property of Caro's children and of Sarah T. Bowman. At a family meeting attended by Lawrence Butler, his new father-in-law, Edward J. Gay, and others including Edward G. W. Butler as under-tutor, each attorney recommended and the parties all agreed to the settlement. By the year's end, using funds borrowed from Frances and a credit owed to Will and Dan by their father's estate, Caro purchased the 2,256-acre plantation on their behalf, for $5,000. For an additional $13,000 she bought the nearby, 2,400-acre Styopa Plantation on Turnbull Island. Sarah Bowman acquired Rosedown, other Turnbull lands near St. Francisville, and the personal property of her father.[24]

If both Frances and Edward Butler experienced dark days after the Civil War, most of their friends were affected similarly. As the historian Drew Gilpin Faust has written, now "this was a world without slaves." The "loss of the property that had provided the foundation for privilege undermined the wealth and position of formerly slaveowning families." The Butlers' adjustment to the new order involved what John Rodrigue has referred to as "a profound psychological and ideological transformation," and they needed "no small amount of good fortune." But the Butlers, and so many other southerners, built their "new selves"—in Faust's words referring mainly to women—atop their "elitist assumptions of the old." They changed, but they would not change their fundamental thinking.[25]

Amid all of the difficulties of the postwar years—life and work at Dunboyne, family grief over deaths of two children, and the trials of assisting Caroline Turnbull—there were a few bright spots. One was the solid friendship of Alexander Duncan. In late 1867, long after Duncan twice offered financial aid in the midst of the Civil War, Butler finally asked to borrow $5,000. His true friend responded unhesitatingly in March 1868 that he was "most happy to give you the loan at 5 pc and . . . trust that it may be of some use to you." The news lifted Butler's spirits. In the first of a series of letters, Duncan in April wrote that he was glad that "your letters have been more cheery, about matters towards you." Duncan then resided in England and Scotland but traveled to New York and Providence on business and to visit family. Although sympathetic to Butler's plight, he advised Butler to follow Lee's counsel on "Christian fortitude" and not to place faith in the "Paddy of Ireland," but in the more reliable Negro. "For you must recollect—they [the former slaves] have been terribly tampered with" since emancipation, continued Duncan, "and I trust they have seen what fruits they must reap from following the Blackguards who care not a farthing for them." He believed that the freedmen would "return to the guidance of their old friends." In Duncan's thinking, no doubt also applicable to Butler, the example of the southern "gentleman" was what the ex-slave must follow. That surely involved the maintenance of obeisance, black to white. Learning of the proceedings to impeach Lincoln's successor, Duncan pessimistically concluded that he would not survive. But Duncan rejoiced when Johnson prevailed and prayed for "an utter routing of the Radicals." The South was "in a terrible position," he told Butler, and "we are passing through a revolution no one can doubt." When General U. S. Grant was nominated to succeed Johnson, Duncan preferred him over the Democrat candidate, thinking that Grant would "take a conservative course." Duncan later confessed to Butler that his favorable opinion of Grant had been misguided.[26]

Thankfully, Edward and Frances Butler could resume attendance at St. Mary's, with which they closely associated in their pre–Civil War lives. The spiritual needs of local Episcopalians had gone unmet during wartime, and the comforts of St. Mary's and its society had been lost. "Services were much interrupted during the war," stated Reverend James Philson in 1866, in his report to the Diocese of Louisiana. "This parish has been reduced to the verge of extinction on account of the heavy losses sustained by its members." Fairly regular services resumed by 1867, but the parish still had only eleven communicants, with fifteen having "removed." Philson accepted another position at St. Matthews in Houma. He was soon replaced, and the Butlers were able to avail themselves of the church's services.[27]

During these years Lawrence Lewis Butler was assisting his father with the difficult tasks of plantation management, and he was living with his parents at

Dunboyne. He additionally achieved distinction serving as a local public official, especially helpful with flood disaster efforts in the parish. His marriage with Mary Susan Gay, a daughter of Lavinia Hynes and Edward J. Gay of St. Louis Plantation, proved to be the most significant family event of the post–Civil War years. The history of the Butlers became entwined thereafter with that of the Gay family.

The wartime friendship established between the Butlers and the Gays grew closer, and the families enjoyed occasional social gatherings. During the conflict, Gay had taken an oath of allegiance, obtained permits for firearms, and furnished men, teams, and drivers to build the army fortress in Plaquemine. He, his family, and his property received official safeguard and right to U.S. protection. Unlike Butler and others prominent in the Secession Convention and other Confederate activities, Gay in late 1866 received a full pardon from President Johnson. Once he renewed his oath of allegiance to the Constitution, it allowed him to "claim any property . . . sold by the order, judgment, or decree of a court under the confiscation laws of the United States." Gay escaped many of the wartime problems that fell upon his fellow Iberville planters, and his resources far outmatched those of the Butlers. He handled similar labor issues on his several plantations and came to advise Edward Butler on matters of sugar agriculture, manufacture, and commerce.[28]

The couple's well-educated, lively, and beautiful daughter, Mary Susan, returned home from her school, LeQuat-LeRoi Institute, in New Orleans in late 1866 or early 1867. Lawrence Butler and she soon became engaged. After they married at St. Louis Plantation on March 11, 1869, Lawrence and Sue took up part-time residence with her parents. Recognizing that his future lay not with Dunboyne but with his father-in-law, Lawrence entered into a management apprenticeship with Gay. He worked in a variety of roles, Gay evidently wishing for Lawrence to become an integral part of the family's commercial world. Edward Butler having been ill much of the year, however, the newlyweds moved full-time to Dunboyne in October 1869. There, Lawrence could superintend the fall harvest and milling. The Butlers "are all so kind and good," wrote Sue to her younger sister Nannie Gay, "I am really more attached than ever to them." Referring to Dan and Will Turnbull, "The boys are studying very hard to prepare themselves to go to Bishop Quintard's College [in Sewanee, Tennessee] this winter." Now pregnant, Sue took refreshing walks with the Turnbull boys while awaiting a visit from her parents. She reported that she was "getting fat, fatter—fattest, but I have to work hard too for I have nothing but those braided petticoats." In the drive by carriage between Dunboyne and her parents' home, Sue Butler enjoyed the autumn air and lovely colors: japonicas all abloom and orange trees loaded "with their tempting fruit" in front yards along the way. The couple's first child, Frances Parke Butler, nicknamed Fannie, arrived on December 27.[29]

By the end of 1868, the Butlers' plantation had produced only 77 hogsheads of sugar, 5,980 gallons of molasses, and 2,000 barrels of corn. In 1861–62, for a comparison, 420 hogsheads of sugar came off of Dunboyne. All plantations in the area struggled, but Dunboyne hung on an economic precipice. The plantation supplied a mere $1,370 of the family's $2,300 income, and its expenses added up to $1,146, leaving little from the plantation to use for improvements. Occasional labor received 75 cents per day, and field hands made upward of $13 a month, or more if they worked regularly. Butler retained a core of old hands, despite his interest in replacing them with foreigners. Meanwhile, the labor market tightened. Edward J. Gay had resisted hiring outsiders but before long looked to Virginia for workers. When that option failed, Gay sent Lawrence Butler to Chicago, where Lawrence arranged with agents for a mix of Scandinavian, German, and English immigrant laborers to be shipped south. The effort proved an expensive experiment and also failed. Finally, Gay turned to San Francisco to bring Chinese coolies to Louisiana. None of the efforts proved successful.

Although Butler equally wished to rid himself of black labor, unlike Gay he lacked the necessary capital to try to substitute outside labor for his former slaves. The Dunboyne Plantation mill also required costly repairs, if not complete rebuilding. Like other planters in the neighborhood, Butler found it necessary to contract out much of the expensive work. By 1870, Dunboyne Plantation was foundering. The seventy-year-old Edward Butler chafed over his labor problems and local politics, he was suffering from eye disease, and the family lacked sufficient money on which to live. Butler applied once again to Alexander Duncan, whose charity to his Louisiana friends saw no bottom. Having already lent $5,000, Duncan agreed to arrange for another loan, handled through Butler's agents and secured only by Butler's personal note or bond. Concerned about the earlier debt, Butler hesitated. "It is only $5000," replied Duncan. "Let it come just when you find it convenient; &, if that never comes, no matter—." There is no evidence that Butler ever did repay his friend; in effect, the loans became gifts. In 1870, in spite of money problems and no doubt thinking of cheaper access to markets, Butler granted a formal servitude of passage to the New Orleans, Mobile, and Chattanooga Railroad for only $1. The grantee only was required to keep the drains open, build bridges where necessary, and pay for any damages to crops and buildings.[30]

The enlarging perils that the Butlers faced, together with the Old Colonel's growing incapacitation, contrasted with their outward behavior. In 1870, while Sue and Lawrence resided much of the time at Dunboyne, little Fanny gave joy to both sets of grandparents. Lawrence took time from his demanding work to deliver Will and Dan Turnbull to the University of the South (later, Dan transferred to Washington and Lee University). Frances Butler and Lavinia Gay became godmothers to their new Butler granddaughter, Frances. And Edward J. Gay was chosen her godfather at a baptism in late April 1870. The occasion, at St. Mary's Episcopal Church, gave Sue Butler an opportunity to be confirmed as an Episcopalian. "She has joined the Church of which my family for many generations have been members," Lawrence Butler happily recounted to Nannie Gay. The Butlers entertained a large entourage after the packed services: "Your family, together with the Bishop, Mr. & Mrs. Barrow & Mr. Dillon, our Pastor, dined with us. . . . Sue & I hope to have baby's photograph taken in time to send to you by your Mother, & shall expect a good one from you in return." The elder Butler sent a barrel of pecans from the 1869 crop to Mary and Robert E. Lee, who shared them with "our young friends who call in the eve's, to whom they have afforded pleasing employment if not Conversation." Lee remained concerned about Butler and about Louisiana's apparent perpetual concentration on sugar cane as a main crop. He disliked the tendency of his fellow southerners to focus on their political problems and offered his opinion on the current southern center of attention: "I am more than ever impressed with the necessity of the people of the South attending to their material prosperity; building up their individual fortunes; taking care, less of Federal politics, & more of their own affairs." Southerners, according to Lee, should develop their own resources and replenish the white population so depleted by war and the economic trials following it.[31] Butler soon lost his distinguished friend and correspondent, who died in October of that year.

In spite of some happy times and a remarkable ability to continue writing, Butler was pushed to sell out. He appeared frail, and eye ailments nearly blinded him. Quietly, Frances promoted a sale of Dunboyne and sought the advice and assistance of Lawrence and Edward J. Gay. Butler reluctantly signed a deed of sale of his beloved Dunboyne Plantation on February 27, 1871. The place had been his life's hope for prosperity and distinction, but by 1870 it constituted a millstone that threatened to sink the family. The details of the sale are significant: The buyer was Henry D. Fales, "late of Cuba." He was the brother of Carlota Fales, the wife of William Glasgow Jr., of St. Louis. They were connected to the Gays through Edward J. Gay's mother, Sophia Mitchell Gay, whose sister Sarah married William Glasgow Sr. The Glasgow son, William Jr., who married (a second time) Carlota Fales of Cuba, had associated in business with Gay; and Gay steered Fales, his cousin's relative by marriage, to the Butlers. From the beginning, Glasgow would be an investor (and Gay a silent financier), and he ultimately came to run the operation completely. The sale was for a total price of $52,090, and Fales paid $10,000 cash to the Butlers. The balance due of $42,090 was handled through promissory notes, at 8 percent interest, payable at one-year intervals. The first note of $2,572 and the second of $5,122 were owed by Fales. The third note, due in three years, for $12,256, was drawn on Glasgow, who thus helped Fales finance the purchase. The final payments, due in the fourth and fifth years for $11,465.29 and $10,674.58, respectively, also were based on promissory notes signed by Fales. Butler retained a mortgage on the plantation, and the sugar house was to be insured continually for no less than $10,000.[32]

Prospectively, the Butlers achieved financial security through the sale of Dunboyne. Their economic futures, however, depended on the operational prosperity of the new owner. If successful, Fales would pay off the sale gradually and provide income on which Frances and Edward Butler could live comfortably. As unhappy as Butler might be, perhaps this was the best way.

11

The Pass

"A Place to Suit"

Once the sale of Dunboyne Plantation was signed and recorded, news of it traveled rapidly. Lavinia Gay reported a week afterward that the Butlers "were looking for another home in the same neighborhood. Mrs. Turnbull wants very much to go on to see her boys this summer. They receive good reports from the boys and Mrs. T. looks much happier." Unsuccessful in their search for a "place to suit them" nearby, however, and Fales already having arrived in Iberville from abroad, the Butlers began looking for a house in Pass Christian, on the Mississippi Sound. "The Pass," as it was called, long had been an attraction to Louisianans and to others from the South. Providing a spot to visit as early as the 1820s, by 1831 Pass Christian boasted a fashionable hotel, and in 1839 steamboats departed every day for New Orleans. Many cottages constructed in the 1840s and 1850s housed families who came to escape the summer heat, mosquitoes, and fevers of New Orleans and elsewhere. Pass Christian became a home to Edward Butler's cousin and friend Samuel McCutchon Jr., who descended from his uncle William Butler. Not long after the Civil War, the Mississippi Gulf Coast attracted Jefferson Davis, and especially fortuitously, Butler's old boyhood friend, retired U.S. Army general William Selby Harney.[1]

The prospect of moving some distance and to smaller quarters immediately motivated Frances Butler to set about a cleanout of family heirlooms and furnishings at Dunboyne. Sue and Lawrence received many items, among them treasured relics of Martha and George Washington from their lives in Philadelphia and at Mount Vernon. They included a silver candlestick by which Washington had "signed all his letters, & used until his death"; an old-fashioned teapot of Martha Washington "used before her marriage to Gen'l. W."; and "books, pictures and . . . an old fashioned bookcase that Genl Washington gave to Mrs. Butlers mother when she was a young girl."[2]

As the Butlers prepared to move following the sale of Dunboyne, Frances made a decision that she must have been advised to undertake by her son or by Edward J. Gay. On numerous occasions over the years, Edward Butler had made use of his wife's "paraphernal" (or separately owned) assets. The employment of her personal property to acquire and improve their land or to buy slaves constituted a legal claim by Frances. Now, in order to protect her lifetime investment in Dunboyne, she determined to put matters into her own hands. Pressed on the matter, on May 17, 1871, Butler cosigned with Frances a formal deed of transfer. It bestowed on Frances the sole ownership of and rights to the four promissory notes executed by Fales at the time of the plantation sale, totaling $42,090. In addition, Butler assigned to Frances his Iberville Parish "swamp land," which Frances claimed but he had retained, of 120.24 acres and valued at $21,799.65½. The total value of assigned land and notes came to almost $63,900. The agreement documented carefully Frances's other ancient but unforgotten "paraphernal rights and claims," which had to be accounted for by the transaction. It bears quoting fully:

> . . . Edward G. W. Butler, received and applied to his own use the following sums, which were the paraphernal of his said wife to wit: Amount of note of Captain Erwin, given to the said Mrs. Frances P. Butler by her Father, Major Lawrence Lewis, and her Mother, Mrs. Eleanor P. Lewis (born Custis) and Collected during said Marriage by said Edward G. W. Butler, say nine thousand three hundred and thirty three 33⅓ dollars $9333 – 33⅓.
>
> Amount of one half of another similar note given to the said Mrs. Butler, by her father about the year 1833, say four thousand and sixty-six 66⅓ 4666.66⅓
>
> Amount of a debt due by Robert Bell to Major Lawrence Lewis, and by the latter donated to his daughter, the same Mrs. Butler, which debt, was assumed by the said Edward G. W. Butler, as part of the price of a plantation by him purchased from said Robert Bell, in the Parish of Iberville, say twelve thousand Dollars 12000.00
>
> Amount of the price of a Certain tract of land on the Kenawha River State of Virginia, belonging to the said Mrs. Butler, by gift from her mother, and Sold about the 1835 or six, say, six thousand three hundred dollars. 6300.00
>
> Amount of legacies, under the Will of Mrs Martha Washington, great grand Mother of the said Mrs Butler, received by said Edward G. W. Butler from the Executors of Mrs Washington, from account of his wife, in two in-

> stallments, one of six hundred dollars, and one of six hundred and twenty nine Dollars, say in all twelve hundred and twenty nine Dollars. 1229.00
>
> Said Severals items Constituting together the total sum of thirty three thousand five hundred and twenty nine dollars. $33529.00
>
> Liquidated Amount to which the said Edward G. W. Butler acknowledges himself to be justly and truly indebted to his said wife on account of her paraphernal rights and Claims, and without prejudice to such other rights and Claims as the said Mrs. Butler may set up for other items not herein Specified, such for instance the value of Certain Slaves and their naturel increase owned by her, previous to the year 1860.

Frances then acknowledged "that her said husband has accounted to her and has replaced in her hands the aforesaid sum of [$21,799.65½] [for the swamplands] on account of her paraphernal rights and Claims, and therefore, grants unto him a partial receipt and acquittance, as to said amount and a release to that extent only, of the legal mortgage by which her said rights and Claims are secured."[3] The remarkable agreement between the couple contrasted with customary arrangements between man and wife in those times. It was the second of the family's recent major legal actions; the third would be Frances's will, which she was to prepare and write the following year.

By 1870–71, Frances Butler wished to perpetuate her family. The settlements that Caro reached with Martha Turnbull and her daughter, Sarah, did not convince Frances that Caro would or could manage the properties well. Frances trusted herself, as long as she had assistance from Charles Conrad, Lawrence Butler, and now Edward J. Gay. Although Butler had overseen much of Caro's business, Frances no longer had faith in her husband's abilities. She believed him to be infirm, his energies failing. In the undoubted discussions between Edward and Frances Butler about the proposed assignment, would she have asked for his permission and willing consent, based upon her fears for her family's financial welfare? Beforehand, Lawrence probed his father's imperfect recollections concerning Frances's claims; Butler advised Lawrence to rely on her excellent memory for details of her property. In the preliminaries leading up to drafting a document, would she have instructed him that he must acquiesce, and that was that? The expectations under the circumstances are that his opinions were consulted; and legally, there seems no doubt of Butler's ultimate consent. But uncertainty remains about the extent to which Butler acknowledged any incapacity and the necessity for the sale of Dunboyne; even more doubtful is his ready concurrence in the assignment of his claims to the interest and principal on the notes. Iberville Parish records and Butler's own store of documents of earlier transactions were available, and Frances may have consulted them. If not, she managed to recall the details of every occasion during their long union in which her husband financed Dunboyne using her personal assets.[4]

In their early years at Dunboyne, Frances appeared willing—even eager—to contribute from her resources. As their marriage lengthened, her approval may have been given more reluctantly, despite her outward legal assent. She may have understood that her ambitions for wealth and high social status were not easily attainable. Perhaps she was considering, then: Should she have made all those sacrifices? A cloud hovers over the business, which is reminiscent of Nelly Lewis's resentment of her son-in-law for having deprived Frances of the expectations, however evanescent, to which a scion of the Washington family was due. Was Frances Butler saying that the deprivations, the criticism by and demands of Butler, the anxieties of two wars, and the waste represented by the loss of Sonny simply were unnecessary? With the limited documentation of the moment, one can read only so much into her motivations. One thing is certain: the assignment of the notes, representing Edward Butler's lifelong material accomplishments, stripped him of property and left him virtually helpless.

In June 1871, the Butlers moved into a temporary house in Pass Christian, followed soon by a more permanent cottage. It was on the corner of Red Creek Road (now Menge Avenue) and East Scenic Drive, a short distance from the village center. The house was raised a few feet on brick piers and situated on a high sand dune landscaped with ancient, twisted live oaks. It still stands, after much storm battering in the twentieth century and more recently from Hurricane Katrina in 2005. From a description in an 1868 lease advertisement, the "Handsome Dwelling" sat on a large lot, one arpent wide by fifteen deep, facing the Gulf of Mexico. It was "very convenient to the new wharf" for people and goods leaving from or heading to the Mississippi back country. Built to catch the refreshing ocean breezes, the cottage contained four high-ceilinged rooms. Each room was eighteen feet by eighteen feet, two on each side of a twelve-foot-wide hall that extended the full depth of the house. Galleries were mounted front and back, the rear one with two "cabinets," each twelve feet square. Onto the front gallery the tall, front-room windows opened half-way to allow for air circulation and direct access to and from the gallery. Apart from and to the rear of the dwelling there existed "a large kitchen, servants' rooms, store rooms, stables, etc."

A fence enclosed the front five acres, which boasted an abundance of "fruit—apple, pear, peach, plum and orange trees, and two large scuppernong arbors yielding an abundance of grapes for making wine." Family lore relates that Frances Butler introduced her favorite camellias to the yard, beginning a coastal horticulture that took hold and continues to the present. They may have been given her in the 1850s by Martha Turnbull from the gardens at Rosedown—still ornamented in the twenty-first century with old camellia bushes—and then transplanted from Dunboyne. A conspicuous and long-lived camellia bush planted in front of the house even was named "Martha," after Turnbull, or perhaps for Frances's famous great-grandmother. Water for the house came from "the finest spring on the Coast," apparently located on the bluff slope to the beach, and "supplying 300 to 400 gallons . . . per day, in the yard, by means of a 'water ram.'"

Thus suitable either for vacation life or for more permanent existence, the house had been occupied since the McCutchons acquired it from Victor Burthe of New Orleans in 1853. McCutchon removed his family to Belize after the Civil War, leaving the house vacant. Now assisted by Thomas Herndon, married to Jane Krumbhaar, another Butler cousin, Edward and Frances Butler arranged to rent it. No sooner were they settled than Frances communicated with friends and relatives, praising life at the Pass: "This pleasant winter Climate would do my dear Esther [widow of Lorenzo Lewis] so much good," Frances wrote her nephew Dainger Lewis, in Virginia. Not only was the winter climate warmer than at Dunboyne, but the Mississippi Gulf Coast at Pass Christian was quiet and "peaceful, the Society excellent, and most friendly—the fish, oysters, crabs be most abundant." She and Butler were "pleasantly situated."[5]

The Butlers regretted leaving their friends and relatives in Iberville. They longed for the eight-month-old Frances "Fannie" Butler and her "little pattering feet and bird voice," as her grandmother described her. Soon, though, they were immersed in arranging their new house and paying bills. Frances was pleased that her July charge for fish was only $5.75, and that her supply of eggs, chickens, vegetables, and so on cost only $9.75. Dennis, the long-time servant at Dunboyne who moved to Pass Christian with them, received $12 for the month of July. Frances made certain that all "back demands," including moving expenses and house cleaning, were paid off. The new Dunboyne owner, Fales, acquired from the Butlers some household items—such as their large glass decanters and individual pieces of furniture, but most of the Butlers' possessions came by boat to the Pass. Praise of locally available supplies notwithstanding, the cost of living was high. Fireplace coal was shipped in by sailing vessels, and other items came by rail.

Frances paid $44 for a servant in October, and soon she needed carpenters to mend a rotted roof. There was "present indebtedness to Mr. Gay and the Miltenbergers for our fuel." Anxious to begin life at Pass Christian without having to "dip into the small income that remains to us," Frances announced to Lawrence that she required more "means." She urged him to sell the Dunboyne swamplands, so that she might settle the debts. As for Caro Turnbull, who remained a concern, Frances bucked at the unwillingness of her former son-in-law, George Williamson, to honor his long-standing debt. It was an obligation that Williamson ungraciously informed Caro he would not meet "if he can help it." Caro owned Styopa Plantation, adjoining DeSoto Plantation on Turnbull Island; but her mother, having financially assisted in the purchase, urged Lawrence to buy a half-interest in the place and assume management. Frances even offered to advance money to make the payments in order that Lawrence could buy mules and implements. Lawrence, however, would decline her suggestion and offer, as he then was heavily involved in the employ of Edward J. Gay at St. Louis Plantation.[6]

Comfortably fixed at home facing picturesque Mississippi Sound but fretting about their finances, about Caro Turnbull, and about the education of Caro's sons, Frances decided that she needed a last will and testament. She planned and wrote it by hand at her beachfront home. The four-page document was dated March 3, 1872, and it was another window into her concerns. In her will, Frances gave her property entirely to Caro Turnbull and to grandsons William and Daniel Turnbull. The will listed portraits, books, relics, and bonds and notes—a reference to the debts owed to her by the new owner of Dunboyne. She purposely excluded her son Lawrence Lewis Butler, because he "is a man of much business capacity, and he has made a most desirable marriage, and . . . my said dear daughter Caro Butler Turnbull is poor, and from her modest nature is incapable of helping herself; and her physical strength is entirely unequal to hard labour and that she will be called upon to take care of her Father whose infirmities render him incapable of helping himself." The decisions to exclude Lawrence and to depend solely upon Caro Turnbull for the care of Butler left absolutely no contingency plan in case something should happen to Caro. They reflected the lack of legal counsel when she was writing the will. And they would prove crucial. Her festering anger against George Williamson then began to spill out:

> . . . I also give her [Caro Turnbull] all the little that remains to me, because she has been deprived of nearly all the property belonging to her deceased

> Husband and that Col. George Williamson has refused to pay her either the principal or the interest of the sum of thirty thousand dollars which he owes her for negroes sold by her to him before the Confederate War, under the plea that as the U.S. has deprived him of the said negroes, that he is not bound to pay for them, or even for the time during which they remained in his possession, and were labouring for his benefit, which was until after the surrender of Genl Kirby Smith.

Naming her brother-in-law, Charles M. Conrad, and his son, Charles Angelo Conrad, as her executors—the "truest friends [Caro] has on earth," Frances ended with a declaration: she had consulted "*no one,*" and the will was "my own act and deed."[7]

Because much of Frances Butler's evident disillusion and resentment in this important document are directed at her once beloved son-in-law George Williamson, his story is worth examining. No letters from Williamson to the Butlers were located in the examined manuscript collections. The Butlers and the Williamson children seldom were in contact following Isabel Butler Williamson's death in 1866. There evidently were many occasions for correspondence over the years, and Williamson had helped Lawrence Butler to receive advancement in the Confederate Army during the Civil War. Following his wartime service, last under General Edmund Kirby Smith, Williamson resumed his law practice in Shreveport. After Isabel's death, he was elected to but was refused a seat in the U.S. Senate. He remarried and had another five children by his second wife, Mary Lee Marshall of DeSoto Parish. In 1872 he aided the faction of the Republican Party supported by President Ulysses S. Grant in defeating Governor Henry Clay Warmoth's candidate for governor, John McEnery. Evidently as a reward, Grant appointed Williamson to be the U.S. minister in Central America, where he moved his family. Serving in the State Department from 1873 to 1879, Williamson encouraged expanded trade between Central America and the United States. He particularly furthered the exportation to Central America of goods manufactured in the United States and the importation of inexpensive raw materials from Central America to the United States. During the early 1880s Williamson became the general counsel for the Texas and Pacific Railroad. He died in Shreveport in 1882. His obdurateness in honoring his debt to Caro Turnbull thoroughly soured any friendship between Williamson and Frances Butler. Both Edward and Lawrence Butler agreed with her views of Williamson, their disapproval bolstered by his decision to support and serve under the despised Ulysses S. Grant.[8]

As Frances Butler occupied herself with domestic matters and with the welfare of Caro, the Old Colonel recovered amid the pleasant society and surroundings of the Mississippi Sound. He used his time to correspond with friends and to add to his knowledge of his cherished Butler family. Besides communicating with cousins in Pennsylvania and elsewhere, one of the friends with whom he renewed contact was Hal Thompson, of Baltimore. A one-time U.S. Army comrade and fellow surveyor of Pensacola Harbor in the early 1820s, Thompson lamented Butler's "reverses in your latter days." He did not know that Butler's move to Pass Christian was permanent. Thompson, who left the U.S. Army to become a banker, could not bear to revisit regions south of Maryland, only to see the "sad & wanton destruction of the . . . plantations by the Yankees." They, in the opinion of Butler's friend, simply were "selfish" and jealous when "seeing such comforts & high culture" of the South. But Thompson remained confident that the "recuperative energies of your People" ultimately would "restore you again, in some measure, to your old condition."[9] If such sentiments encouraged Butler, fate would create a long wait.

An economic reality for Frances and Edward Butler was their continuing dependence upon the success of Dunboyne Plantation. Frances held the mortgage represented by the notes used to finance the purchase by Henry Fales. Troubles followed the new owner of the plantation from the very beginning. Expecting a cash infusion from his mother, who was due to arrive from Cuba, Fales encountered delays. He also proved to be woefully inexperienced in sugar cane agriculture and processing and immediately recognized a need for a reliable manager. "Not being myself confait in Louisiana planting," wrote Fales to Edward J. Gay in early May 1871, "I require a man who has practical knowledge." William Glasgow Jr., Fales's brother-in-law and the endorser of one of the purchase notes, soon realized that money to run the plantation was short. Not only was Fales poorly prepared, thought Glasgow, but he also might lack the ability and energy to manage the place. Glasgow already was embarrassed at having influenced Gay to advance funds to Fales. He appealed to Gay, however, to lend additional money to pay off the hands, "unless his mother should arrive soon" bringing financial assistance. In June, writing from St. Louis, Glasgow asked Gay to "go down to Dunboyne and ride over the plantation with Mr. F., when you will be able to form a better idea of his progress." Cash would be needed until January 1, 1872, with the completion of sugar making, to meet various expenses, including payment on the note due then. By mid-June, Fales was in a "dead lock," and Glasgow found himself pressed into buying a half-interest in Dunboyne. Advised by Gay, Glasgow arranged for Fales to live on Dunboyne, attend to it, secure additional financing, and keep accounts without charging for his services. The men would be equal partners. They would use Glasgow's company in St. Louis as their factor and commission merchant. Of significance to the interests of Frances Butler, "I am to give my note to the old lady [Frances] for ½ the cash pay't plantation expenses to date. Henry is to do likewise—." Gay, who drew up a formal agreement and provided expertise to both men, surely regretted having so involved himself, his family, and the family of his daughter, Sue.[10]

Henry Fales's experiment with sugar cane quickly wrecked upon the shoals of inexperience and overoptimism. By 1872, Glasgow was solely in charge, accompanied by his young son, Eddie, whom his father hoped "would take a fancy to planting." Glasgow's wife joined her family, and as of January 1873 all were "getting the [Dunboyne] House cleaned etc & will be more comfortable soon." The 1872 fall crop came in poorly, however, and the mill house lacked much-needed repairs. "We did not make all the steam required last year," confessed Glasgow to Lawrence Butler the following July, and the grate bars and fire bed had been "left under the boilers which impeded the draught from the burner." The problems were almost total in scope: "I have to have more system about the Sugar House than last year," admitted Glasgow, in addition blaming poor growing conditions for losses to the corn crop.[11]

William Glasgow somehow managed to hang on for a while longer, but by the 1874–75 harvest Gay—the creditor of both Fales and Glasgow—was in charge of the plantation and had hired a competent manager, Major D. C. Hubbard. A native of Alabama, Hubbard had moved to Pointe Coupée Parish with his father, a former congressman and the Confederate commissioner of Indian affairs. The payroll for June 1875 shows that forty-four regular field workers and two "contractors" tended the plantation. Lawrence Butler originally trained to run Gay's Iberville plantations after his marriage to Sue Gay. In September 1872, he instead joined Edward J. Gay, Gay's brother William, and Richard Hanenkamp and Co. in a St. Louis business described as "dealers in staple groceries." Lawrence and Sue, now parents of a son, Edward Gay Butler, desired better educational opportunities for their growing family. They departed Louisiana in the spring of 1873 for St. Louis, where they remained permanently.[12]

Illness felled Frances Butler in June 1875. Despite the attendance of Caro, a physician, and a nurse, by June 23 she was desperately sick and Lawrence was sent for. She appeared to recover, allowing him to leave, but after a turn for the worse and before Lawrence could make it back Frances succumbed on June 30 at her home in Pass Christian. By that time the entire family had become reliant upon Edward J. Gay. Forced to handle both their grief and the discovery of Edward and Frances Butler's financial difficulties, the family members were in a scramble to manage everything. Lawrence Butler was in such debt to Gay that he required "further pecuniary aid" to pay for the funeral and undertaker. Edward and Frances Butler had received substantial financial assistance from Gay simply to pay 1874–75 living expenses, for which they owed him over $2,200, plus interest. Gay paid the bills of their grocer Solari Sons in New Orleans, agent Thomas Herndon for house rent, merchant C. Courteney, coal suppliers for heating, freight for casks of pecans and barrels of sugar and syrup, for property taxes in Iberville, and more. Frances's burial casket was made by W. Bothic, an undertaker in New Orleans at 221 Camp Street. It cost $150, plus shipment to Pass Christian. The undertaker's invoice described the casket as "metallic . . . 5 x 9 full glass full Satin lined Rose Ornaments 8 Bar handles and full Ornamented." The charges for the burial plot at Live Oak Cemetery, to the rear of Trinity Episcopal Church, and a physician's bill for attending Frances were part of Gay's loan, advanced to her estate. Sue Butler's intention was to assist personally in the funeral and burial by acquiring and paying for the cast iron surround fence for the plot, the design for which was chosen jointly by her and Caro Turnbull. Gay, however, lent the funds for the handsome railings, corner posts, and gate—only portions of which remain after massive destruction to the cemetery during Hurricane Katrina. As her debts mounted, Frances Butler assigned to Gay the Dunboyne sale notes due her by Henry Fales as "collateral security for advances made or which might be made" to the Butlers. Gay thus became a major creditor of the Butlers and shared directly in their claims against Fales for nonpayment of the mortgage and liens against Dunboyne Plantation.[13]

Other woes piled up. Daniel Turnbull by now was home from college in Virginia and found work. At the time, he impressed his uncle Lawrence Butler with his sense of responsibility. In contrast, Will Turnbull had forsaken college and remained unemployed and poorly prepared for life. Not only was he in debt, reported Lawrence Butler to his father-in-law, but he was in "danger of . . . being made the dupe of some designing person." Lawrence determined to prevent Will from any action "to make away with his own property" and in so doing to discredit his mother and brother. The details of Will's foolish actions may not have been known to his grandparents before Frances became ill, but his misconduct definitely became part of the burden that Caro Turnbull carried, adding to her sorrows over her mother's passing. She was short on funds and forced to borrow $1,000 from Gay. Caro wrote Gay that she was advised by Lawrence to prevail on her sons to renounce their claims to Styopa Plantation, "in consideration of the money advanced for their support and education." By doing so, "I might be able to give you security for all advances made upon the place, and they both say they will." The continual refusal of George Williamson to honor his debts to Caro, who had borrowed $6,300 from Frances Butler to buy Styopa Plantation, further angered Lawrence Butler. To Lawrence, Williamson was only "a demagogue & a sharper & his treatment of my Sister Mrs Turnbull justifies my opinion of him—."[14]

The financial and other predicaments in the Butler family and a need to avoid paying more rent and expense at the Pass also dictated that choices be made about Edward Butler's future. Now seventy-five years old, Butler might return to Dunboyne. There, Lawrence suggested, he could "use the little 2 Room house . . . should he like to go . . . during the winter—." Gay was asked to consult the occupant of the Butlers' former Dunboyne home, Major Hubbard, about the feasibility of that move. In addition, Lawrence opined, "Dennis & his family wish to return to Dunboyne as soon as Sister breaks up housekeeping at the Pass & they would take care of Father if the Major would board him—." By October, Caro determined to remove furniture from Pass Christian to New Orleans, where she would reside. She proposed sending her mother's "personal effects" back to Dunboyne, or "to be disposed of for Father's benefit—." Lawrence planned "to arrange for [Edward Butler's] support in such a way as to require the least expenditure possible."[15] One needs little imagination to understand what feelings the elder Butler was experiencing during these months. Uncertain of his future, insecure as a result of his loss of financial wherewithal, ashamed of and unable to comprehend his grandson Will's behavior, and grieving over the death of his wife, Butler was in a sad state. Thankfully, he would not be called upon to move away from his beloved Pass Christian just yet.

In order to protect its interests, the Gay Company had assumed operation of Dunboyne Plantation and paid Hubbard's salary and other expenses, even before the death of Frances. But Gay was not legally the owner. Soon, Lawrence Butler filed suit in the Fifth Judicial District Court in Iberville Parish to foreclose on the plantation and to sell it at a sheriff's sale. The place was badly deteriorated: only seven mules and seven carts remained, along with a "baggage cart, 6 one horse plows, 1 old corn planter, 1 corn sheller, 2 small harrows." Its debts had ballooned, and only one of the sale notes was redeemed, in 1873, for $2,572.13. Additional mortgages burdened the plantation, including one to Marie Ann Fales (Henry Fales's mother) for $12,690.22. Another debt was to Glasgow Bros. of St. Louis for $25,000, and a final one was to J. B. Peltier for $347.50 for unpaid "work done on the sugar house and engine" in 1872. The bidder on and buyer of the property, on June 26, 1876, was Lawrence Butler, as expected. He paid $7,856.35, of which $4,501.09 remained after all costs were deducted. Those costs included $2,853.07 owed Gay & Co. for "cash and supplies furnished to carry on said plantation while under seizure." Other debts to Gay were for advances for the Butlers' personal expenses and for Frances's funeral, plus commissions and interest. Symbolic of the plantation's deterioration, after the court's proration, no one received all that was owed.[16]

A few years following Frances Butler's death, Edward Butler began communicating with a well-known author of the times, L. U. Reavis, of St. Louis. Referred to Butler by Jefferson Davis, Reavis was researching and writing about the career of Butler's friend William Selby Harney. Butler gave Reavis information on Harney and their friendship, and he used the opportunity as well to provide the writer with his own family story, including the pedigree of Frances. As described by Butler, she was "my gifted and illustrious wife, who died at Pass Christian, Mississippi, June 30th, 1875." Her obituary, which Butler may have written, described Frances as "one of the most gifted and distinguished women of her time." Throughout their long marriage, Butler greatly respected Frances's honesty and determination, her reliability in their household, and her devotion to her family. He found support in her Washington family heritage, and many of her relatives became his friends. Butler enjoyed Frances's companionship and loved her. Their marriage underwent many strains, however, some resulting from their financial situations during the 1830s and 1860s. It additionally suffered from the divisive, bone-deep, and bitter enmity that developed between Frances's beloved mother and Edward Butler. The couple's physical separation and the stresses of her responsibilities during Butler's Mexico military service, in 1847–48, caused additional tensions, although the experience developed Frances Butler's character and abilities. Their union appears at times to have been happy, but Frances's concentration on having her children raised to a state of refinement, to succeed in wealth, and to be married well suffered disappointments. The circumstances of civil conflict took their toll on her, particularly when Edward G. W. Butler Jr. died at the Battle of Belmont. Her mother-worship of Sonny and the dashed promise that he held crushed her. Convinced of the inferiority of emancipated slaves, the couple struggled after the Civil War. They became embroiled in seemingly endless attempts to recover Caro Turnbull's family fortunes and to regain for her the money owed by George Williamson, debts which they considered matters of honor. The sale of Dunboyne and their move to Pass Christian gave Frances Butler hope that the Butlers' final years would be peaceful, passed in comfort, and warmed by the company of friends and of family during visits. She underestimated Caro Turnbull's abilities and the degree to which Caro succeeded in achieving a reasonable settlement from the Turnbulls for her sons. The arrangement for Frances to assume sole ownership of the debt from the plantation sale to Fales may have seemed far-sighted, but Frances's miscalculations and the absence of legal counsel led her to make unwise provisions in her will. At the time of her death, Edward Butler realized neither the extent to which Dunboyne was threatened with collapse under its new owners, nor that she excluded him. He unknowingly had been placed in a precarious and vulnerable position.[17]

12

"Are You Afraid to Die?"

"No Daughter—I Am a Soldier"

In thinking that Caroline Turnbull was to care for her father in his declining years, Frances Butler assumed that Caroline would be able to handle that responsibility. Giving Frances credit, there should have been no reason to think that Caro could not meet any such familial obligation. The property settlement reached in 1872 between her and Martha Turnbull and Sarah Turnbull Bowman was considered both by Edward Butler and Caro's attorney Charles Conrad to be "an excellent bargain for Caro." Probably to ensure Caro's and her sons' future, Frances financed the acquisition of Styopa Plantation adjoining DeSoto Plantation on Turnbull Island. Caro soon found a suitable tenant to lease Styopa for one year, for $1,000.[1] She retained her parents' belief that land was the core of wealth.

Will and Dan Turnbull had been a comfort to their Butler grandparents during the Civil War. The documentation of their teenage years following the war indicates that they were handsome youths, short on experience, typically playful, and somewhat irresponsible. They had become friends with their new aunt, Sue Gay Butler. "Will gave me a copy of Longfellow's 'Golden Legend' for a birthday present and Dan gave me a beautiful little glass Bohemian paper stand," Sue recounted to her sister Nannie when Dan and Will joined her and Lawrence for a weekend in July 1871. "The boys are going to Bayou Sara next week. I enjoyed this visit to Dunboyne more than I had before—they were so good & kind."[2]

By 1870 the boys were anxious to commence their college careers, Will at the University of the South and Dan at Washington and Lee. The colleges were intended to polish and ready them for life, but maturity eluded Will. He remained at Sewanee only one semester. Perhaps intending to return there, instead Will did nothing. He received but declined an appointment to West Point that Butler helped arrange for him in 1873. The particulars of Will's life in the ensuing few years are sketchy; he in essence remained unemployed, alternated stays with his Butler and Turnbull grandparents and in New Orleans, and ran up debts that

Caro was obliged to pay. Finally, at some point in 1875, he became romantically entangled with a relative, Sarah Louise Barrow, of West Feliciana Parish. She no doubt was "the designing person" described by Lawrence Butler to Edward Gay. A member of the extensive Barrow family that included Martha Turnbull, Sarah was born in 1849. She was the third child of Robert Hilliard Barrow Jr. (1824–78) and Mary Eliza Barrow (1825–1920). After the Civil War, Sarah married a cousin and ex-Confederate, Robert James Barrow Jr., born in 1848. It is unknown precisely how Sarah, widowed in 1871 when her husband drowned, became involved with Will Turnbull. Probably during a visit to Rosedown, Will met and befriended Sarah. The lonely, young widow was attracted to the strikingly handsome and well-connected William Turnbull. Their friendship became a passion and led to results that the families never could have imagined. An account in February 1876 was given to Lawrence Butler from his father's cousin, Anna Butler, living at her family home, the Cottage, not far from St. Francisville. By her report, Will inaccurately boasted to Sarah Barrow of his family wealth, thus misleading Sarah. When the couple engaged in a sexual liaison (only hinted at by Anna Butler), Sarah's family forced him to agree to marry her. Turnbull secured a license on January 1, 1876, and the event took place on January 3 before A. Gordon Bakewell, rector of Grace Episcopal Church. The ceremony was witnessed formally by other male Barrow kin and W. W. Semple. Then, as related by Anna Butler, the following day Will Turnbull abandoned Sarah and fled to New Orleans.[3]

News of the marriage and of young Will Turnbull's desertion reached his grandfather Butler and his mother well before Anna Butler's recounting to Lawrence. Butler wrote of it to Alexander Duncan in January 1876, prompting Duncan to commiserate. He was "sorry to learn . . . that you and your Daughter had been sorely tried by Will Turnbull marrying, as you think, unwisely. I trust that it may turn out better than you anticipated."[4] Not only did the marriage not "turn out," but the scandal and Caroline's shame and grief piled on top of a much direr problem for her.

In September 1875, following Frances Butler's death and before any inkling of trouble, Caroline Turnbull determined to leave the house in Pass Christian. Her preference was for her father to live with Lawrence and Sue Butler, who had offered to take in the Old Colonel. Caro also was agreeable to an arrangement for her and her father to "board with Mrs. Hubbard," the current Dunboyne manager's wife, "if he wanted to return" to the old plantation.[5] Before the end of the winter of 1875–76, however, and soon after receiving the news of Will's misdeeds, Caro became ill. She was medically diagnosed with "tubercules on the womb," Lawrence Butler informed Edward J. Gay, and "her sufferings are intense. . . . Her trials have broken her body and heart but . . . she bears them with real Christian fortitude." In the absence of her father, who continued at the Pass pending a final decision on a permanent residence and who had become aware of Caro's condition, young Dan Turnbull remained with his mother. Caro thankfully also received help from the Conrads, and Lawrence Butler soon was en route from St. Louis "to aid in giving her proper attention."[6]

Even as the news broke of Caro's life-threatening illness, the contents of the last will and testament of Frances Butler finally became known to Lawrence and to his father. Both were astounded and upset, Butler writing Gay that "tho' divested of my property, I fancied that; even under the laws of Louisiana, I was recognized as one of the heirs of my deceased wife." He suspected Charles M. Conrad, the named executor, of misadvising Frances. When Gay wanted to know whether Frances sought Butler's consent to having Gay acquire Dunboyne, a distraught and perhaps forgetful Butler complained that once he was "disposed . . . of my property; which I had acquired by hard labor and economy," he thereafter "was ignored, in all transactions, relating to it, and *incidentally* learned of your arrangement with Mrs. Butler." Only after months of waiting for information on Frances's will had he found out "that I was ignored" in it, and "you can see, therefore . . . that my sanction or approbation would be superfluous." Already decided on a return to Dunboyne, Butler "could not avoid a feeling of embarrassment, as an *intruder*." In addition, he was short on funds. Frances Butler even earlier had sent to a family friend in Baltimore, William G. Harrison, many family relics to auction, including a dinner ring, jewels belonging to Caro, and a set of Cervantes's *Don Quixote* that had been given to George Washington by the minister of Spain to the United States. Harrison was having no success. Facing a life with little resemblance to his accustomed comfort, Butler arranged with friends in the North to sell his extensive stash of wines, the proceeds from which he could use to pay expenses. He also asked Louisiana congressman R. L. Gibson to present a claim for "articles taken by the officers of the Government in the Civil War." Butler seems not to have been able to provide the requisites for claiming loss of his property.[7]

At the time, neither Butler nor his son Lawrence fully appreciated the legal and familial ramifications of Frances Butler's last will. She had acquired all rights to Dunboyne through Butler's assignment to her of the notes from the Dunboyne Plantation sale to Fales. The Fales notes then having been assigned to Gay as security on her debts, the property essentially, if not legally, belonged solely to Gay, who also helped finance the Fales-Glasgow purchase of Dunboyne. After Charles Conrad received from Lawrence Butler the sealed will, Lawrence awaited word from Conrad on its meaning. Lawrence as well now had to assist Caro Turnbull, who was in debt to Gay. Caro's verbal instructions to her son Dan to care for his grandfather after her death notwithstanding, Lawrence could not count on him, and no such provision was written into Caro's will. The Old Colonel faced the possibility of dependence on his Conrad nephews, which was a prospect too dark to consider. Writing Gay, Lawrence expressed his concern and searched for solutions: "I see but one hope for my Father & that is in buying Dunboyne cheap & getting an account allowed for my services as agent if no provision can be obtained for my Father's support." When the will was probated in early April, Lawrence vented his frustration to his father-in-law. No one, including Caroline Turnbull, had ever "led me to understand that she was the sole heir, & no one but Conrad may have known its real provisions." Further, he predicted bitterness on the part of the children of his deceased sister Isabel and that "Caro's death will promote a state of affairs which my poor Mother little appreciated." Not only was there cause for worry about his father's support, but William Turnbull's "worthlessness" simply made a bad situation intolerable. At least Gay was moving to seal up ownership of Dunboyne and putting it in Lawrence Butler's name, an act for which Lawrence expressed gratitude. Lawrence provided Gay with his power of attorney and asked him to "explain to [Dan Turnbull] the mode of settling his mother's indebtedness & the best mode of depositing the balance. I know you will allow my sister the most reasonable discount of her notes consistent with a business transaction."[8]

Even Dan Turnbull's judgment and intentions were in doubt. Reporting to his brother-in-law about Caroline Turnbull's illness, Edward Gay Jr. remarked: "As Dan took such a peculiar position in regard to money, I did not go any more to inquire how she was . . . I don't know who Dan's advisers are but consider them a disadvantage to him."[9] The concern over the Turnbull boys was general. Their grandfather, who for so long had assisted in their raising, felt sympathy for their plight. He remembered well his own youthful despair and loneliness over the loss of close relatives. Writing Lawrence Butler in May, once Caro's fate seemed certain, Butler considered what the future held for his grandsons following

Caro's death: "My poor little Boys will be left alone, in this cold and selfish world; like their Grandfather, at a much earlier age; & I have no fears for Dan; but poor Willie is very incapable of taking care of himself, & I cannot avoid a feeling of deep anxiety, on his account. I hope, however, that God, in his mercy, will protect him."[10]

Lawrence arranged for the colonel's residence at Dunboyne Plantation, and the Hubbards agreed to board him. Still in Pass Christian in April, Butler relied on Samuel McCutchon to move his effects, and he requested that his servant "Dennis assist in caring for him, if Dennis is not needed as a gardener." In Butler's opinion, Dennis's care only required a half-hour each morning to get his old master moving.[11]

Nearly penniless, isolated from friends and family, helpless to do anything for his daughter Caro, Butler experienced a marked change in his circumstances. Reporting to Lawrence after his arrival at his old home, he had received from Nannie Gay a red flannel shirt that he wore to help with arthritis in an arm and shoulder. Major Duncan provided him with "oil of sassafras" for the pain, and the couple "was very kind to me; . . . tho' not *refined,* they seem to be very estimable persons. Poor things, they are very poor & very economical." Butler found the accommodations almost primitive: "Tho' they have had little furniture, they *might* be more neat. They have made a *kitchen* of *your* little room; adjoining the small dining room; and the hogs, sheep & calves being admitted into the yard, the flowers have disappeared." Not only were animals allowed into the yard, but "three cows, five calves, seven hogs, one grey horse, one black horse, and a stove" occupied "Downstairs store rooms" of the home. In consequence, "the house is filled with *fleas,*" Butler complained to Lawrence. He expected to receive sheets and pillow cases from Sue and asked Lawrence's help in making for him "a pair of black, strong & cool pants, & a thin black coat; as I have none to fall back upon, in case of accidents. Let the vest be long, & straight, in front, and the pants large around the hips, and nearly as long as yours." This provides some indication of a body size somewhat fuller and shorter than his son's. With no money to spare, his wines only having just arrived in New York to be sold, and at that, "badly ruined," Butler could be of no assistance to Caro. He asked his friend Charles Gayarré to write Caro's obituary, "and his dear little girls, at the Pass, will put flowers upon the Coffin of my poor, unfortunate child, when she is called home; and I shall be left, for consolation, the Consciousness of having done all in my power in respect for her memory."[12]

Caroline Swanwick Butler Turnbull died on September 11, 1876; her illness, according to Gayarré, was one of "long agony and indescribable suffering" but borne with calm and resignation. The official record of her death gave its cause as "Cancer of the Uterus." Of family, only her sons and her uncle Conrad attended the funeral and burial at Pass Christian two days later. On behalf of Edward Butler, Edward J. Gay's New Orleans–based manager Charles Cranwill transmitted to Gayarré the request to write a long and loving obituary. It revealed also that during her last months Caro had been living at the residence of Marie Isabella Burthe, a daughter of Robert Carter and Susan Vinson Nicholas, and near Dan and Will. The Burthe home then was in "Greenville," a part of the old Foucher Plantation subdivided after 1836 and located in the present-day University section of uptown New Orleans between Audubon Park and the Carrollton district.[13]

During her remaining days, Caro therefore mercifully had been offered asylum by loved ones, her cousins. Susan Vinson Nicholas's child, Marie Isabella, was born in 1846, in St. James Parish. Following the death of Susan's husband in 1856 at his sugar plantation in Terrebonne Parish, and after the onset of the Civil War, Susan established residence in Nashville. There, she provided a home to Caroline Butler Bell (Butler's sister and her half-sister). At some point, Marie Isabella Nicholas met and in 1863 married the Confederate soldier and New Orleans native George Joseph Frederick Burthe. In the 1870 census he was listed as a farmer in Orleans Parish, in Ward 7, which New Orleans city ward maps locate on the northeast side of Esplanade Avenue extending from the Mississippi River all the way to Bayou St. John. By the time she provided succor to Caro Turnbull in the summer of 1876, however, Marie Burthe had been widowed a year and evidently changed her residence to the Greenville area. The Burthe household included a new baby son and six other children. Marie's charity would have been a difficult task, but evidently she carried it out with good spirit, and Caro Turnbull was blessed to have her help.[14]

Neither Lawrence nor his father was in a position to comfort or advise Caro's sons, although the boys' relatives with the Conrad law firm apparently handled Caro's will. Sealed in an envelope, it was delivered to the Second District Court in Orleans Parish within weeks. The will, the original of which is missing from her succession record in New Orleans, was promptly proved. In the petition to be placed in possession, the Turnbulls stated that the twenty-seven hundred-acre Styopa Plantation and Caro's few personal belongings remained to be divided. Daniel received 75 percent and Will 25 percent—the unequal treatment probably due to Will's debts that Caro had paid off. DeSoto Plantation was unmentioned, as it was a direct inheritance of the Turnbull boys from their father's estate; nor was mention made of any familial obligation toward Butler. By October 4, 1876, Dan and Will were in possession of their inheritance. Within a year and a half of Caro's death, her sons sold both properties for $23,000 to Joseph Torres of Pointe Coupée Parish and John J. Giddens of New Orleans. Little reference to Will occurs thereafter, and he soon established residence in New York; Dan remained to contend for a share of Dunboyne. Sue Butler agreed to buy from Dan any furniture of Caro that he wished to sell, apparently thinking that Caro still owned a number of Washington heirlooms. But Dan attempted to lay claim to Dunboyne, meeting firm resistance from Edward Gay and Lawrence Butler, who had been careful to document their rights to it. Lawrence from afar was embarrassed by his nephews and apologized to his father-in-law: "You have my thanks for statement with reference to status of affairs in settlement of my Mother's estate—I regret exceedingly that you have been so much troubled and annoyed by the conduct of the Turnbulls & hope my title to the Plantation may be sustained—."[15]

At Dunboyne during that spring and summer of 1876, before Caroline's death, Butler sought to adjust to life back on his old sugar plantation. His companions were Dennis and his wife, Susan Anna, born in 1828 or 1829. Butler expressed their gladness "to hear from 'Master Lawrence,' & [they] send much love to all. He is gardner & She is Laundress, & they both find time to attend to 'Old Master.'" He wanted to be sure that portraits of his father Edward, his brother Anthony, and E.G.W. Butler Jr. all were set aside for him from the house cleaning at the Pass. Butler also expressed great interest in the forthcoming Democratic National Convention in St. Louis. Arrangements had to be made with Mrs. Hubbard to pay her $20 a month for board, but having no money, Butler authorized her to draw on Gay & Co. in New Orleans. By the year's end he finally realized the proceeds, $168.38, from the sale of his Madeira and sherry wines through his New York contact, Alexander Hamilton. Many bottles remained unsold; even with old friends acquiring some, the demand for the wines was minimal. Their disposal hung over Butler until well into 1879, when he was forced to hire an agent, Thomas Bloodgood. The affair ended up costing him money when he had the remaining bottles packed and shipped to him at St. Louis, where Butler then resided.[16]

Butler's letters from Dunboyne in 1877 dwelled on politics and spoke optimistically about the prospects for the country's relief from corrupt politicians. Although adjusting to his new existence, he suffered much from the winter's cold temperatures, due partly to a scarcity of carpets in the old raised house. The red flannel shirts and thick coat, which Sue and Lawrence sent, "have saved me from freezing." Living off the meager returns from sales of his wines, Butler pined for Pass Christian and hoped somehow to return there in the summer along with Lawrence and Sue and the children in order that they and he might avoid sickness. But Sue Butler was pregnant with the future Anna Margaret Gay Butler, to be named for her mother's close sister, Nannie, and they were unable to leave St. Louis. In a pleasant summertime interlude at Dunboyne for the colonel, his granddaughter Isabel, along with her step-mother Mary Lee Marshall Williamson, George Williamson's second wife, came to see Butler. She was a "sensible and fine woman," Butler wrote Nannie. "We are all charmed with her." He applauded Mrs. Williamson's decision to move from Shreveport to New Orleans "next month, for the education of the children. I am very glad of it; as they are too much out of the world." His grandson Pierce Williamson intended to enter the U.S. Naval Academy, and George Williamson Jr. was doing well at Baltimore Medical College.[17]

In August, news came of the death of his U.S. Army friend Rawlins Lowndes. For much of his life, Lowndes oversaw his rice plantation on the Santee River in South Carolina. He and his wife, Gertrude Livingston, spent summers at Staatsburg, New York, her old family home. At the outbreak of the Civil War, Lowndes, who strongly disagreed with secession, acquired his own estate on the Hudson River and lived there permanently. Despite their political differences, the loss of his friend much grieved Butler. By early September 1877, Butler's health began to worsen. Writing Lawrence, he was evidently troubled: "Tho' my sight is nearly gone, I will endeavor to write, to say that I am very low down." He was unable to eat. "My tongue is like a file," Butler wrote, but he could not afford to see a doctor. He pled with Lawrence: "Dennis & S. Anna insist upon [Hubbard] taking me to Pass Christian, & giving me some nice warm Salt Baths," and would Lawrence arrange for him to move back to the Pass? Living there cost $40 a month, but Dennis also might be hired as a servant and reduce the expense. Unable any longer to survive on his own, even with the assistance of Dennis, and in view of the impracticality and expense of moving to back the Mississippi Coast, Edward Butler soon was on his way to St. Louis. He thereafter resided with his son and daughter-in-law and their growing family.[18]

Having engineered what turned out to be a relatively short tenure for the colonel back at Dunboyne, Lawrence Butler at a judicial sale in July 1876 acquired his old home plantation. Heavily in debt to Gay and experiencing what seemed to be increasingly and uncontrollably high living expenses, Lawrence hoped that he could rely upon the Louisiana property to augment his family income. The choice of Major Hubbard to run the plantation had been a good one, and Hubbard and Lawrence in effect operated as a partnership. Hubbard intended to buy him out for half of the value of the plantation, payment to come from Hubbard's share of its receipts. The place was "doing well," thought Lawrence. But another twist of fate would intervene. By late October 1878, blessedly long after Edward Butler departed for St. Louis, both Duncan Hubbard and his wife, Adine, were dead, victims of the yellow fever epidemic of 1878.[19]

After his post–Civil War migration to Louisiana, Duncan C. Hubbard eventually had entered into a plantation partnership agreement with Joseph A. Erwin, a cousin of Edward J. Gay's wife, in October 1870. Hubbard and Erwin each acquired a half-interest in a sugar cane and cotton plantation of Charles Lefeaux, located on Bayou Grosse Tête. The 716 acres contained a building with a steam engine and boiler, a sugar mill, and a cotton gin. The $5,000 cost of the property was to be paid for in five promissory notes of $1,000 at 8 percent interest, "payable at the Counting House of Edward J. Gay & Co. of the City of New Orleans." Following the death of Erwin, Gay, who then owned William Glasgow's half-interest in Dunboyne, contracted Hubbard to work Dunboyne and take Glasgow's portion, for $10,000. When Lawrence Butler assumed the title from Gay, who held Frances Butler's notes from Henry Fales, Lawrence and Hubbard thus associated as partners.[20]

Reports of the 1878 yellow fever epidemic emanated from William Ely, a plantation manager of Edward Gay's son John in West Baton Rouge Parish: by early October "the country is full of it the negroes is jist getting sick and hard to get hands. . . . It is on Increas in this Naberhood. I am afeard we will have hard work to get crops of[f] if this state of things continue." The Gay and Butler families, both away from Louisiana, were aware of the Hubbards' plight, but their attention was distracted by the death of Edward J. Gay's father, John Henderson Gay. News then arrived bringing word of the fever's attack on their elder son, Edward J. Gay Jr., and his subsequent rapid death in New Orleans on September 16. The illness had appeared in the Hubbard household in the middle of September; it missed the Hubbards' young son, Catesby, who either was away visiting relatives or had been sent away to escape the fever. The family included Adine Hubbard's mother, a Mrs. Edmundson, and according to druggist expenses that began on September 17, both women became sick first. They were gone by September 22. The medicine charges continued until October 7, when Duncan Hubbard succumbed. Three coffins, each costing $15, had to be acquired. By the middle of October, the Gay Company representative in New Orleans, William B. Bloomfield, was in communication with the newly appointed plantation manager, John D. Slack, "concerning the necessary proof, etc., for Insurance Claims on the life of the late Major D. C. Hubbard." The prudent Gay, wanting to be sure that Hubbard's debts to him were paid off in the event of his death, had taken out an insurance policy on Hubbard's life.[21]

The death of the able Hubbard meant that the harvest of 1878 on Dunboyne fell to others to manage. The results so disappointed Gay that he complained in December to Slack that the sugar maker, Lanham, failed in making good quality sugar "for that place [Dunboyne] which heretofore made good sugar almost by itself." Sending his son Andrew Hynes Gay to check on things and to provide Slack with sufficient money to pay off the hands, Gay further instructed Slack not to pay Lanham above what he had been receiving under Hubbard: "He has damaged the place more than his years worth in giving it poor sugar and even the molasses is of a dull cloudy muddy colour."[22]

When Hubbard had arrived on Dunboyne during the winter of 1874, his arrangement with Lawrence Butler was for Butler to sell to Hubbard his "one half of Dunboyne Plantation, when the same may be paid for, for . . . $10,000." Hubbard's death threw matters into reverse. In 1880, Hubbard's succession was settled. The interest due on Dunboyne at 8 percent amounted to $4,400, but Hubbard was credited for half the value of improvements that he contributed. At the time that Gay collected $5,000 on the insurance policy on Hubbard, the deceased owed Gay $4,535.88. The succession appraisal placed the total value of Hubbard's share of Dunboyne at $9,318.82½; but in May 1880, in a suit to partition, Butler acquired the succession's half-interest in the plantation for $11,500, payable when the Hubbards' surviving son, Catesby, attained the age of majority.[23]

The situation at Dunboyne was confused and a bother to everyone. Still in St. Louis, Lawrence Butler was ever reliant upon Gay to assist him with keeping the plantation going. In addition, legal challenges had been filed against Frances Butler's will. Charles Conrad was deceased in early 1878, so Edward and Lawrence Butler requested that the Iberville court appoint Andrew H. Gay as executor of the will for her Louisiana interests. The Mississippi-appointed executor, Elliot Henderson, objected, filing suit. The matter finally went to the Louisiana Supreme Court, with the Court, in Case No. 7806, ruling that the will was valid and upholding Andrew Gay's appointment as the Louisiana executor. The Court cited the lack of jurisdiction by Mississippi to overturn an appointment in Louisiana that involved immovable property there. Daniel Turnbull also had challenged the appointment of Andrew Gay. And George Williamson, representing his children by Isabel Butler, opposed the sale of Dunboyne on the basis that the children were creditors of the succession of Frances Butler. Both parties objected to the succession tableau of debts. Neither objection was given credence, but the challenges had been additional troubles to deal with.[24]

No doubt wearied with the oversight of Dunboyne and hoping to avoid any more personal outlay and debt on its account, Lawrence Butler sold the old family plantation in July 1881, to Amedée Hebert. Acting on Lawrence's behalf, Gay accepted a price of $10,000, of which $4,500 was in cash, the balance represented in five promissory notes payable annually over five years at 6 percent interest, due at the New Orleans office of Edward J. Gay and Co. Frances Butler's will finally was settled. However, her hopes that the sale of the plantation to Fales in 1871 and that Edward Butler's assignment to her of the notes of indebtedness would maintain them financially through their lifetimes had been drowned.[25]

Leaving his treasured Dunboyne and his trusted servants Dennis and Susan Anna, Edward Butler arrived in St. Louis in 1877. His move brought Butler to a happy and full life. Finally receiving loving care, near friends, and benefiting from proper nutrition and exercise, Butler thrived. Not only was he amid a lively family in St. Louis, he soon reunited with his old friend William Selby Harney, who lived in the Lucas Place area near Lawrence and Sue. Butler also began to travel to the Harney vacation home in Pass Christian. The place was never far from his thoughts.[26]

Retired following long service with the U.S. Army, the famous frontier and Mexican War army veteran Harney had known Butler since childhood. Schooling together at the original Cumberland College nearby Harney's family home in Tennessee, Butler and Harney thereafter followed different paths in the army. Butler's route was to enter and graduate from West Point, and Harney joined the regular U.S. Army in 1818 as a second lieutenant. The two met again in Baton

Rouge in 1821. Butler had been selected for ordnance duty there with the 4th Artillery Regiment and found Harney serving with the 1st Infantry Regiment. They spent "four months together," noted Butler to Harney's biographer L. U. Reavis, and partook of "the hospitality of the then opulent sugar planters of that country." When the two traveled in unison from Nashville to Washington City on reassignment, Butler experienced "fatigue and exposure" and a relapse of a fever that he had contracted earlier. He confessed to Reavis that Harney "nursed me with the tenderness of a brother." Once again separated, and except for a brief encounter in 1838, the old comrades were not reunited until late 1877, when Butler appeared in St. Louis. There, they gathered to reminisce and to watch out for each other's welfare. Sue Butler reported, for example, Harney's presence at her home in April 1878, suffering from a sore foot, "which necessitates a great deal of care from the Col—."[27]

From his surviving correspondence, one can see how important the relocation to St. Louis was for Butler's welfare. Lawrence and Sue's first home on Lucas Place was in an 1850s era, exclusive, "new money" suburb of the city on its western side. In the 1880s, the Butlers moved to a spacious and elegant new residence on Union Avenue, at the corner of Maple Avenue, on the city's outskirts and at the end of a convenient narrow gauge rail line connecting to the city center. St. Louis presented many attractions and had experienced tremendous growth since 1860, swelling from a population of over 190,000 residents to over 350,000 in 1880. Its commercial and public buildings, churches, and parks were a source of pride for its citizens. Although challenged by other growing cities, such as Chicago, St. Louis still formed a hub for commerce in the Mississippi Valley. In the words of a recent historian, "St. Louis in the 1870s was alive with the magnetic aura of purpose and grandeur." Despite his age and continuing difficulties with his eyes, Butler took advantage of the city's offerings. Long familiar with fine horses, for instance, he could not neglect the races. "This afternoon," Sue wrote her mother in June 1879, "the Col. announced his intention of going over to the race—so Lawrence came on to go with him and I took Toots [Lavinia Hynes Butler] & we remained through two races.—but as he could not see & got very tired, I drove Toots & himself home & L remained."[28]

When Butler was ill, Sue and others were there to attend to him. In early 1879, during a spell of sickness, "the Dr gave us a tonic for the Col. which I think Pa would like as he is so for eggnog, to be taken every morning or night. Beat the white or yellow of one egg together—3 table spoonfuls of cream, 2 table spoonfuls of crushed ice, 1 table spoonful of Brandy, Sugar sufficient to suit the taste—The Col. is getting fat on it—He says it is elegant." At other times the climate of St. Louis, together with any illness, took its toll. Writing again in the summer of 1881, Sue announced: "The Col. is quite feeble with the heat, but still keeps up—taking things quietly & half the time he does not dress himself or come down stairs. He has no fortitude when he is sick & is like a child." Even when suffering from the city's extreme temperatures, Butler relished living with his grandchildren about. Sue described one winter's event shortly after the birth of Mary Susan Butler, her last child: "The Col. suffers from rheumatism such weather, & is deprived of his usual exercise. He is cheerful & seems to take a good deal of interest in the baby, comes down into my room, regularly about five o'clo. to 'investigate her' & she sits on his lap sometimes & seems to really know him."[29]

For now, at least, Butler was determined. "God has dealt harshly with me," he wrote Reavis the May after beginning his new life in St. Louis. But he acknowledged compliments from another friend, who told Butler, "'I envy you, my dear sir, your cheerful and brave concern with which you face the batteries of life.'" Looking forward to Pass Christian and the friends there with whom he could hobnob raised Butler's spirits. Once Harney acquired a second home in the Pass in 1879, Butler again had a vacation place where he could hang up his boots. Even before then, the "Old Seminole," as Harney had become known, associated with a female companion, "Mme. [Mary] St. Cyr." As a widow in her late forties, she hired on for Harney in the early 1870s to be his private secretary. Eventually termed Harney's "general manager," St. Cyr took on the function of his nurse as he aged, and in 1884 she became his second wife. Butler liked and respected her, and he particularly felt sympathy for the neglect Harney suffered from the children of his first marriage. She filled the family void for Harney and was a great blessing to him. Harney once jokingly left an order for Butler "to report at my House, at the Pass, without delay; and if he dares to destroy my order, I will bring him before a court of Inquiry. . . ." Undoubtedly having to borrow funds from Lawrence to travel, Butler was glad to oblige such "invitations" to the Pass. Others in the circle of friends there included Confederate general Braxton Bragg's widow, Eliza Ellis Bragg, and Jefferson Davis. Davis and Butler commenced a spirited correspondence, and in January 1882, while on the Mississippi Coast with Harney, Butler acknowledged receipt of a copy of Davis's *Rise and Fall of the Confederate Government.* Perhaps unable to read it, he gave the book to Prince Leopold, Duke of Albany, a member of the family of Queen Victoria of England, and told Davis: "I find [Harney] quite as blind as myself, and very deaf." Butler also was able to reunite with Alexander Duncan, his cherished old friend and his benefactor from the difficult postwar days. Duncan jestingly urged Butler to write a "history of your reminiscences," but, "no swearing."[30]

Butler possessed a reputation as a family historian from long years of correspondence on the subject with friends and relatives. In late 1882 he was approached on the topic by Reverend Joseph A. Murray, a Presbyterian minister and scholar of Carlisle, Pennsylvania, the American home of Butler's ancestors. In addition to his pastime as a divine, Murray engaged in such endeavors as preparing an essay for the Pennsylvania *Historical Register* on the Butler family. Seeking information, he received it in copious amounts from Edward Butler. The colonel was cheered by the request and delighted in furnishing Murray with lore on the five famous Butler brothers whose Irish immigrant parents settled in Carlisle. Written in uncommon detail, the article was a testament to Butler's knowledge and to the organization and care of his personal records beginning almost from the completion of his years at West Point. Many of the old letters were copied and sent to Murray. He also was able to provide Murray with details of his sword collection. One sword had been worn by his uncle General Richard Butler at the time of his death at St. Clair's Defeat in 1791. Another prize was the Toledo blade of Colonel Thomas Butler, with its inscription etched on one side—"NO ME CAQUE SIN RAZON" (Draw Me Not Without Just Cause), and on the other side—"ME EMBAINES SIN HONOR" (Sheathe Me Not Without Honor). The growing friendship between Butler and Murray lasted until Butler's death and encouraged Butler to relate to Murray the many twists and turns of his long life. Despite the energy and vivacity reflected in his correspondence, and although confident of having lived an honorable life, Butler again expressed his sadness. "I have been very unfortunate," he allowed to Murray, and listed the losses he had suffered from the time of his father's and mother's deaths early in his youth, on to his most recent heart-rending loss. His daughter-in-law, Sue Gay Butler, was dead, "leaving me alone with my youngest son and only living child."[31]

Butler was visiting Harney in Pass Christian when Sue Butler died on March 26, 1882. It followed a brief illness, the mysterious and debilitating symptoms suggesting either influenza or pneumonia, but pronounced to be "septicaemia" by the City of St. Louis Register of Deaths. To assist with the family's loss of a wife and mother, the Gays immediately stepped in; during the fall and winter the children—the youngest of whom, Mary Susan, not yet two years old—were brought to Louisiana to stay with their grandparents. Butler remained in St. Louis with his grieving, lonely son Lawrence. They received care from a "Miss Willis," Lawrence wrote Nannie, by then married to Andrew Price and living at Acadia Plantation near Thibodaux, Louisiana. She was "doing all in her power for Father's & my comfort." Father and son planned to spend "Thanksgiving with Mrs & Mr Cummings." As the first anniversary of Sue's death approached, both men had reason for sorrow. Life must have seemed a repeat of the experiences following Frances's death in 1875. Butler recited their woes to Murray and to Nannie Price. In addition to his own family losses, Gertrude Livingston Lowndes, the widow of his old friend and sister of his first flame, Julia Livingston, had recently passed. There was no alternative but to miss his annual visit to Harney at the Pass.[32]

His poor eyesight notwithstanding, Butler increased communications with many friends and contacts after he moved to St. Louis. Among them was Montgomery Blair, a postmaster general in the first Lincoln administration, who in opposition to Radical Republican rule became a Democrat following the Civil War. They commenced writing in the 1870s, due both to Blair's interest in Andrew Jackson, with whom his father Francis P. Blair had served, and to shared views on politics and race. Blair and Butler followed the national events together, complained of the Republican administration, prayed for Democratic victory in 1876, and bemoaned the election results. At some point around 1880, Butler obtained a reprint of an article Blair wrote and published in the *North American Review* entitled "Views on Negro Suffrage." Blair argued that despite the correctness of emancipation, the black and white races were incompatible in the same society and government. Negro suffrage subverted the American political system, making the former slaves a tool of the military under Republican rulers. In Blair's opinion, based on his understanding of Thomas Jefferson's ideas, one simply could not train them "to the exercise of government." The correspondence ended in 1883 with Blair's death.[33] Butler could not have been more in agreement with Blair's expressions about the innate inequality between blacks and whites. They closely equated with his own racial concepts articulated after the Mexican War and especially when he communicated with John Slidell in the years approaching secession. Butler tread gingerly with friends such as Joseph Murray, but even to him Butler could not resist proclaiming his personal view that Henry Seward's "declaration of the 'irrepressible conflict between freedom and slavery'" brought about the Civil War.[34]

Butler remained able to read as well as write, and he boasted of it to Jefferson Davis, who now lived almost as an icon not far from Pass Christian. He had recently read Gayarré's *Aubert Dubayet; or, The Two Sister Republics,* about the French Revolution; Josiah Quincy's *Figures of the Past*; and Bancroft's first volume of the *History of the Constitution of the United States,* in which Butler thought that the fears of centralized government in the 1780s were "now being justified." Davis and he exchanged memories of U.S. Army service. On Superintendent Sylvanus Thayer at West Point, Butler opined that he "was entitled to great credit for his organization of the Academy but, in his dismissals of Cadets, with and without his drum-head Courts Martial; with other arbitrary acts, were unauthorized and unjustified." Butler informed Davis that he had "an Interminable correspondence on both sides of the waters" and was "keeping up my daily walk of 3 to 4 miles."[35]

In anticipation of his trip south to Mississippi late in 1883, Butler told Davis that he hoped to see him and that Harney was being well cared for by Madame St. Cyr. His "children pay him no attention." Butler recounted having "left [Harney] at school near the 'Hermitage' to go to West Point, in 1816, and, though he [Harney] entered the Army, from Civil life, in 1818, he has the effrontery to put himself on record as *6 months younger than me.*" Harney and Butler were inseparable. Soon arriving at the Pass and while staying with Harney and St. Cyr, Butler reported to his beloved six-year-old granddaughter Nan Butler: "The ladies have all come to see me, & given me . . . kisses; to the amazement & envy of my old Seminole Friend, who attributes my good fortune to my being 'an old fellow.' *Sour grapes!*"[36]

Butler remained in Pass Christian for the winter. A deep January cold snap kept him "confined to my bed during 24 hours," but he otherwise maintained good health and society while a guest of Harney. They paid a visit to Davis at his home, Beauvoir, to the east of the Pass along the Mississippi shore, and Butler and Davis corresponded frequently. The Old Colonel also bestowed his attentions on his Butler grandchildren, who again were brought south to St. Louis Plantation to remain with the Gays. Two unusual visits enlivened Butler beginning in December, when a Williamson grandson, then age twenty-two, came to see Butler at the Pass. "I expect your cousin Willie Williamson tonight," Butler wrote Edward Gay Butler, the twelve-year-old son of Lawrence, "to pass Sunday with me; & am most anxious to see him." And the next month, when Williamson again visited, Butler commented that his grandson gave part of his pay to his sisters, who were "left without means." The contacts with at least some of the Williamson kin contrasted with the absence of word from the Turnbull boys, who had virtually disappeared. Relating to Davis the family history of "my gifted and illustrious wife," Butler lamented, surely referring to Will, "I have heard nothing further of or from my unfortunate grandson . . . and may never more, from him."[37]

Jefferson Davis gave Butler opportunities to discuss politics, always of the closest interest to both. Most particularly, they delighted in the recent recovery of the Democratic Party to national power. The nomination of Grover Cleveland as the Democratic candidate for president provided impetus. Butler wrote Davis in late July 1884 about his satisfaction with the results of the Democratic Party convention, with a tongue-in-cheek exception: "The nominee comes from the 'Empire State,' which, if indulged much longer in furnishing Presidents, will *dominate* the Union." As the election approached, he feared another result as had occurred in the Hayes-Tilden contest in 1876. He even wrote the National Democratic Committee to warn against anyone other than a popularly elected candidate becoming president. Butler supported Cleveland but also expected him to provide patronage in return for southern votes. He was his old political, Jacksonian self and expressed to Davis his lasting appreciation to the Old Warrior, who "was left as my guardian, on the death of my gallant Father, in 1803; and I owe much of what I am to his advice and example." Butler joined Davis in looking forward to having "democratic rule" back and the national government returned "to its primitive simplicity and purity. Then, my dear Mr. Davis, if I am to lose my sight, I can say, in the parting language of my venerated friend and second Father, of the Hermitage: 'Being no longer of use to my Country, my family, nor my Friends; I am prepared to go to my Maker.'" The two friends also could relish a return to Democratic power in Mississippi and Louisiana—both of which, Butler bragged, "carried themselves grandly." And Louisiana had "given 'The Thief and Intruder' [U.S. Representative] Mr. Pitt Kellogg his quietus."[38]

Even as Butler in his correspondence sometimes dwelled on his misfortunes, from the late 1870s until his death he enjoyed notable vitality. Friends remarked on his endurance. Murray acknowledged receipt from Butler of a "photograph of yourself, taken in 1848, when Colonel of the 3rd Dragoons, & which you very obligingly sent me," in addition to a likeness of Butler's "brave son," "whose memory is so tenderly endeared to the father's heart." Murray also complimented Butler on how alive and youthful he was. This, Murray noted, was "while having reached your advanced age with as much health & strength both physical & mental," and in spite of "the loss of so many dear friends."[39] In a joyous turn for Butler, and one that would enrich and may have prolonged his life, Lawrence Butler married again in February 1885, to Susan Anna Mastin, of Huntsville, Alabama.

Lawrence's attraction to Sue Mastin had commenced the previous year through a family friendship. Caroline Levert Mastin O'Fallon, Sue Mastin's sister living in St. Louis and married into one of the first families of the city, made the introductions. Lawrence described Sue, forty-four, as having exhibited "character and great loveliness to all about her, particularly to children," which much appealed to him. He wrote Nannie Price that she also was a "practical, sensible woman . . . , experienced in all that appertains to the management of a house, youthful in feeling but earnest & dignified and *thoroughly refined.*" Mastin would provide what was needed to assist "in the training and education of my children, and . . . she could reestablish our home." He wanted to be certain to convince the Prices and the Gays, all of whom were helping raise the children since Sue Butler's death in 1882. But Lawrence had been lonely while his children spent months at a time in Louisiana in the winters and also felt that they missed having him nearby. He knew that the Gays and Prices joined him in "a common interest . . . in the happiness and welfare of my dear children."[40]

After the engagement and wedding that followed, Butler remained in St. Louis, and he delighted in informing Jefferson Davis that "we have a valued and valuable addition to the household." His exhilaration over the match only slightly exceeded his feelings over Cleveland's recent election to the presidency: "I have read the Inaugural of President Cleveland, and have an idea that he will be the nearest approximation to 'Old Hickory' since the Civil War." By September, Butler could comment happily on the bride's reception in the Butler household: "Lawrence and his new wife are very happy; and the children are devoted to her." That and the fact that "General Harney has taken up his residence near to us; and I go often to see him," capped for the elder Butler a full life.[41]

Even so, Butler found it impossible to continue his annual jaunts to Pass Christian to visit Harney and to see his many friends there. (Harney's health was declining as well.) Despite Butler's defective eyesight and wintertime sensitivity to cold temperatures that kept him constantly to his room, when the weather cooperated Butler remained in sufficiently good form to keep up an amazing "daily three mile walk" past his eighty-seventh birthday. Members of Congress, who then included Edward J. Gay representing the Third District of

Louisiana, brought him a delight. Butler's service in the Secession Convention, his contributions to the seizure of Federal facilities in early 1861, and his support of Louisiana becoming part of the Confederacy had deprived him of the right to hold public office and vote under the Fourteenth Amendment to the U.S. Constitution. The punishment struck hard on one so politically interested and active. After Gay became a member of Congress, Butler asked Gay (or perhaps Gay offered) to assist in lifting the "disabilities." Butler was required to make a formal petition, and Gay introduced the necessary bill in early 1886. On March 4, Butler was notified that "the Bill removing your liabilities became law," by the Act of Congress passed on March 2, 1886. The act allowed that "all disabilities imposed upon and incurred by Edward G. W. Butler, of Missouri, by virtue of the fourteenth amendment of the Constitution, be, and are hereby removed." His citizenship was fully restored.[42]

By now, Butler owned the title of oldest living descendant of his five Revolution-era kin and oldest member of the Society of the Cincinnati. With each birthday, congratulations arrived from friends and relatives, and in 1887 Butler received a visit from former Confederate general Joseph E. Johnston. Johnston complimented Butler as the "'oldest living descendant' of those whom Washington praised, as 'a gallant band of patriot brothers.' No other American family has won as high praise." Interviews with reporters of St. Louis newspapers commenced at least by August 1883, when the *St. Louis Republican* published interviews on his life and reprinted portions of letters from Andrew Jackson to Butler from 1822 to 1826. The series gave Butler the rank of general, perhaps due to his title in the state militia just before his U.S. Army commission in 1847. It was picked up immediately by the *New York Times* and published on August 10 and 11. A later article, entitled "Old Army Officers. Two Venerable Soldiers Who Reside in St. Louis," was written from interviews with Butler and Harney. The story appeared in the *St. Louis Globe-Democrat* on December 26, 1886, and revealed many details of Butler's service for his country in the 1820s and during the war with Mexico. A published image of Butler portrayed a beardless, handsome, and young-looking man, and the reporter found that his "memory is better than that of most men of 60, and his mind remains as bright and keen as ever. While time has impaired his physical activity, it has had no effect upon his mental qualities, and his comprehension of current events is as keen as if he were forty years younger."[43]

The senior graduate of West Point was due the honor of presiding at its annual reunions. By 1885, Butler had become the Academy's oldest living graduate, a distinction he happily added to the list of honors about which he informed friends. When asked to preside at the annual meeting of the Association of the Graduates of the United States Military Academy in June 1887, Butler regretted his absence: "Dear Sir," Butler wrote the association secretary, Lieutenant Charles Braden, "As the time approaches for your reunion, and I am deprived, by age and infirmity, of the honor and pleasure of presiding at your meeting, I send you a toast, which I pray you to present to your honored colleagues, with assurances of my profound regard and abiding good wishes." Read to the graduates at dinner at Grant Hall, the toast reflected Butler's appreciation for his education there and respect for the Academy's ideals, training, and accomplishments: "'The Military Academy: the grandest institution in our country and the Alma Mater of its ablest soldiers and of some of its most distinguished statesmen; the defenders of free institutions, and the protector of law and order." In spite of not having earned glory serving in the U.S. Army, Butler would not fault his training at West Point.[44]

Nannie Gay Price, beloved by Butler, remained a frequent correspondent, and after her marriage Butler added Andrew Price to his letter list. During the autumn of 1887, the Prices at Acadia Plantation experienced a sugar labor strike by mostly black field and mill workers. The long-festering conflict between "elite" planters and sugar plantation workers centered in Lafourche, Terrebonne, and St. Mary Parishes. It originated with complaints of laborers of varied races and classes about low wages and "militarized discipline and economic coercion." Led by the Knights of Labor, the strike ultimately became defined by the white planters and their political allies as mainly a racial affair. In late November 1887, the private and public responses to the strike turned frighteningly violent. Few accounts of witnesses remain, but Thibodaux resident Mary W. Pugh recounted how hundreds of striking workers, chased from their plantations and "having no other place to go come flocking into town," where they occupied every vacant house. Armed whites, including an unofficial militia from outside as well as "companies" of locals, guarded every entrance and exit. The strikers and others, in essence, were cooped up in Thibodaux, creating an emotional tinderbox. A number of the Negroes armed themselves, became loud, and taunted the guards, then marched to the town center for demonstrations. Negotiations resumed between planters and strikers, but suddenly two guards were shot by strikers. The response from the nervous and trigger-happy whites was explosive on November 22. Dozens of blacks—probably over fifty—including many simply considered of "suspicious character," were killed. William Price, brother of Andrew Price, was much involved. By account of Nannie Price, her husband, Andrew, remained active on the plantation and not in town, and the plantation continued its own guards around the sugar house for days thereafter. The event became publicized nationally by the term "Thibodaux Massacre."

Because the Butler, Gay, and Price families were so intertwined, news of the strike quickly reached Colonel Butler and revived long-held racial convictions. He wrote Nannie even before the climax of the strike, fearing that the letter would not reach her "on account of the unquiet condition of the negroes." Butler did "not think that Negroes & Whites will ever amalgamate." He had "written to my faithful Dennis" instructing him to counsel the prominent mulatto local plantation owner, merchant, and politician Theophile T. Allain "to establish a negro colony in Africa." In a follow-up two months later, Butler again alluded to his concerns about "the Negro troubles in your Parish" and advised the Prices to substitute either rice or tobacco for sugar. "As my eyesight is failing," finished Butler, "I must conclude."[45]

Butler's time was nearing, and even though his frailty was evident in a shaky handwriting as the months of 1888 passed, he remained "bright mentally." He spent "much time in a big easy chair in the library of his son's home," as his obituary in the *St. Louis Post-Dispatch* related. Making sure that posterity would know the historical value of his collection of military swords, in March he laboriously wrote descriptions of each of them, their stories, and how they had come into his possession. He still much wanted to see people. "My friends come to my room," he wrote cheerily to Andrew Price, and he regretted having missed seeing two young Louisianans on a visit to St. Louis, Edward D. White and Henry McCall. "'Ned White' & all the McCalls were among the oldest & most revered of my Friends."[46] White, the son of Louisiana governor E. D. White, one of Butler's schoolmates from Cumberland College, became Chief Justice of the United States in 1910; and McCall, of Evan Hall Plantation in Ascension Parish, joined White politically to oppose the Louisiana State Lottery. He was related to the Butlers' McCall friends, among their first after they moved to Louisiana, and probably met White as a student at Mount St. Mary's College in Maryland in 1858.[47]

The end came on September 5, 1888. Official notices following Edward Butler's death attributed the cause to "pneumonia," but Butler in fact experienced other symptoms more akin to heart failure. Lawrence Butler described them in detail to Nannie Price: "Father took his usual exercise on the 1st but was greatly fatigued. He walked around the circle once on Sunday. On Tuesday morning early he had a spell of suffocation and was unwell all day. We sat up with him on Tuesday night and he was again attacked on Wednesday morning on the 5th. He died at 5:45 P. M. on the 5th & was perfectly calm & rational 15 minutes before he died." During Butler's mercifully brief illness, Sue Mastin Butler provided much assistance, and "she read a beautiful hymn to him in the forenoon [before his death]. In reply to her expressed hope that he was not afraid to die," the Old Colonel, faithful to his upbringing and to his Butler family tradition, responded, "'No daughter—I am a soldier.'" Afterward, and assisted by his father-in-law Edward J. Gay in the arrangements, Lawrence took his father's remains "at once to Pass Christian and buried them on the 8th in the presence of those who had loved him there."[48]

Epilogue

No epilogue, I pray you; for your play needs no excuse.
Never excuse; for when the players are all dead, there need
none to be blamed. . . . Let your epilogue alone.
—Theseus, *A Midsummer Night's Dream*

David Brion Davis, one of the most respected historians of the institution of slavery, reminds us that slavery has been part and parcel of the "American experience." For European migrants to America and their descendants, "the grandiose visions of New World wealth—once the Spanish had plundered the Aztec and Inca—seemed always to require slave labor."[1]

There was no doubt: Frances and Edward Butler left the "old" America east of the Alleghenies for the beckoning "new" America to the southwest. They were in search of the wealth that it promised. They were part of that American adventure, which repeated often in different forms in the nineteenth century. The Butlers no doubt planned to attain a high status, as they interpreted the term, by entering the class of planters and slaveowners. Embracing slavery, with its expense and risk and human complexity, the Butlers charted a course that led them to the Civil War and to sorrows, disasters, and reduced fortunes. At the time of their migration, of course, the Butlers could not have known their fate.

People act in accord with ingrained perceptions of the human condition. The Butlers held fixed ideas of racial status, of the rightness of slavery, and of the pursuit of wealth and ownership of property in the southern plantation model. Their views originated in the successful examples of esteemed forefathers, friends, and relatives. In Edward Butler's case, those influences emerged primarily from his father and from his guardian, Andrew Jackson. The attitudes were informed and reinforced by the Bells and to some extent even by Joseph Erwin. The guideposts for Frances Butler were George and Martha Washington and her parents, Eleanor Parke Custis and Lawrence Lewis.[2]

A few observers foresaw the destiny of slavery as early as the 1820s, during the Missouri Compromise. Writing from 1833, the perceptive visitor Alexis de Toqueville noted that "whatever may be the efforts of the Americans of the South to maintain slavery, they will not always succeed. Slavery, now confined to a single tract of the civilized earth, attacked by Christianity as unjust and by political economy as prejudicial, and now contrasted with democratic liberty and the intelligence of our age, cannot survive. By the act of the master, or by the will of the slave, it will cease; and in either case great calamities may be expected to ensue."[3] By the early 1850s, Butler finally sought out the opinions of his friends in the North. Although long aware of controversy over slavery and of the sentiments for abolition, the Butlers little appreciated the intensity of the debate. But, then, the divide was evident. "I do not see blacks in the same relation to them that those born in the South do," wrote his Boston friend James Amory. Butler's comrade and West Point classmate Rawlins Lowndes avowed that slavery was contrary to the country's destiny. The "spirit of the age," he advised Butler, favored emancipation.[4]

Historian Davis acknowledges that "the way problems are conceived and structured reveals much about unexamined assumptions and the issues such as the economic benefits American whites received from black slave labor, that cannot be faced." In part, economics pushed the Butlers to take up lives as sugar planters; wealth preservation drove the arrangements reached by the Butlers and Turnbulls for Caro Turnbull and her sons after her husband's death; and a need to recover the value in Caro's inherited slaves effected the family split when George Williamson broke his contract to pay his debt after the slaves' emancipation. The desire to reestablish a lucrative plantation system caused Butler to search (in vain) for alternate labor for postwar Dunboyne. Like so many white Americans, however, the basis for the Butlers' opposition to emancipation and the introduction of free labor was racial beliefs. These ideas underlay "the growing conflict between a modern ideology of individual freedom and a system of labor that served the interests of millions of landowners, producers, and . . . consumers."[5]

As the war approached in 1860, Butler refused to accept that emancipated slaves were capable of "freedom and responsible citizenship." During and after the conflict, the difficulties with free labor were worsened by his own unchanging attitudes. To the end, Butler could not imagine a full assimilation of blacks into American society, and he may have thought that they had no such desire.

"Blacks and whites will Never amalgamate," he told Nannie Price, writing after his eighty-seventh birthday. In what would appear today as a personal slight to an able and "faithful" friend for over fifty years, Butler advised his former valet Dennis Parker that Americans should "establish a colony in Africa." Echoing long-held opinions, his way of thinking persisted off and on among both races even into the twentieth century. Years before, Toqueville observed of the southern mind, "If it be so difficult to root out an inequality that originates solely in the law, how are those distinctions to be destroyed which seem to be based upon the immutable laws of nature? . . . Those who hope that the Europeans will ever be amalgamated with the Negroes appear to me to delude themselves."[6] The family was fortuitously saved from ruin only by Lawrence Butler's marriage into the Gay family. Edward J. Gay, no less a part of the southern tradition than Butler, evinced a greater facility to change in war and postwar times. His acumen, survivability, and adroitness are worthy of further study.

Ambitious for her family, Frances Butler keenly joined her husband in seeking wealth and status. To a degree, her wishes were fulfilled, particularly by the favorable marriages of daughters Caro and Sissy and of Lawrence Butler. When she was challenged to manage the plantation while Butler was in Mexico in 1847 and 1848, she displayed her best qualities and grew in leadership. She revealed glimpses of doubt about and evidence of weariness with the life at Dunboyne. Was she disillusioned? Nelly Lewis blamed Butler for imposing on Frances a hard and lonely life; whether Frances eventually agreed with her mother may be debated. With the family's tragedies and disappointments, Butler's poor health by 1870, and the anxiety over losing any chance of securing a future for her widowed daughter, Frances's failure of confidence impelled her to abandon Dunboyne. She valued the peace of mind she finally attained when the Butlers moved to tranquil, breezy Pass Christian, Mississippi.

The move eventually pleased Butler, who now could give attention to, if not relive, his family history and his military past. After Frances's death, when almost everything of wealth had vanished, what endured were his remaining family—itself now representing a new dynasty, his experiences from service in the U.S. Army, and the friends and honors it brought him.

One cannot avoid mentioning the omnipresent element of chance. In histories, plain luck is often underestimated. The twists and turns of the Butlers' lives provide us with much of the drama of their story, almost equal to the fascination lent by their personalities. They are part of a grand family panorama.

How Frances and Edward Butler reacted to such events, whether fortuitous or unfortunate, were influenced largely by their beliefs in the special nature of the American South in the nineteenth century. As Davis writes, those attitudes were part good, part evil, ever "colored by human ambivalence."[7]

DESCENDANTS OF EDWARD BUTLER

Thomas Butler (1720–1791) emigrated from Ireland to Pennsylvania in 1748 with his wife and three sons and settled near Carlisle in the Cumberland Valley, then on the western frontier. A soldier, farmer, and gunsmith, Butler made long-barreled rifles for the army, and on January 25, 1777, the Continental Congress appointed him public armorer. He was baptized in Carlisle and founded the Anglican church there. In 1741 he married Eleanor Parker, and they had six sons and three daughters. One son died in infancy, and the other five became officers of the Pennsylvania Line in the American Revolution:

Gen. Richard Butler (1743–1791), married (1) Maria Smith (1737–1824), four children; (2) Catherine Grenadier (?), one child
Lt. Col. William Butler (1744/45–1789), married Jane Carmichael (1741–1834), four children
Col. Thomas Butler (1746–1805), married Sarah Jane Semple (1764–1797), six children
Edward Butler (1748–1748)
Mary Butler (1749–1783), married Jacob Scandratt (1776–1844), one child
Rebecca Butler (1751–c. 1800), married George McCulley (1752–1792), no children
Capt. Pierce Butler (1760–1821), married Mildred Hawkins (1763–1833), eleven children
Capt. Edward Butler (1762–1803), married Isabella Fowler (1772–1821), six children
Eleanor Butler (1763–c. 1800), married James Brown (1761–1815), three children

GENERATION 1

1. Edward Butler (1762–1803), 1788 married Isabella Fowler (1772–1821)
    2. i. Caroline Swanwick Butler (1789–1864), 1805 married Robert G. Bell (1786–1842)

ii. Emmeline Butler (1790–1795)
3. iii. Eliza Eleanor Butler (1791–1850), 1823 married John Donelson IV (1787–1840)
iv. Richard General Butler (1794–1799)
4. v. Edward George Washington Butler (1800–1888), 1826 married Frances Parke Lewis (1799–1875)
vi. Anthony Wayne Butler (1802–1824)

In 1808 Isabella Fowler married William B. Vinson (1770–c. 1815), and they had two children:

William B. Vinson (1809–c. 1837)
Susan Adelaide Vinson (1811–1870), married Robert Carter Nicholas (1789–1856) in 1840, and they had five daughters.

GENERATION 2

2. Caroline Swanwick Butler (1789–1864), 1805 married Robert G. Bell (1786–1842)
i. Robert J. Bell (dates unknown)
ii. George Bell (?–1830)
3. Eliza Eleanor Butler (1791–1850), 1823 married John Donelson IV (1787–1840)
i. Mary Isabella Donelson (1823–1843)
ii. Edward Butler Donelson (1830–1852), married
(1) date unknown Bergondy Lapice (1828–?);
(2) 1851 Jane Harriet "Jennie" Watson (c. 1827–?)
4. Edward George Washington Butler (1800–1888), 1826 married Frances Parke Lewis (1799–1875)
i. Edward George Washington Butler Jr. (1826–1827)
ii. Edward George Washington Butler Jr. (1829–1861)
5. iii. Eleanor Angela Isabella "Sissy" Butler (1832–1866), 1854 married George McWillie Williamson (1829–1882)
6. iv. Caroline Swanwick "Caro" Butler (1834–1876), 1853 married William Barrow Turnbull (1829–1856)
7. v. Lawrence Lewis Butler (1836–1898), married
(1) 1869 Mary Susan "Sue" Gay (1846–1882);
(2) 1885 Susan Ann "Sue" Mastin (1839–1894)
vi. Ormonde Butler (1839–1840)

GENERATION 3

5. Eleanor Angela Isabella "Sissy" Butler (1832–1866), 1854 married George McWillie Williamson (1829–1882)
    8. i. Isabel Butler Williamson (1855–1909), 1881 married Arthur G. Hodge (dates unknown).
    9. ii. George McWillie Williamson Jr. (1857–1936), 1882 married Adine Eatman (1859–1912)
    iii. Eveline Angela Williamson (1854–alive in 1905)
    10. iv. William McWillie Williamson (1861–1894), married Nannie Lemon
    v. Anne McWillie Williamson (1863–?), 1900 married George Herbert Freeman
    11. vi. Caroline Butler Williamson (1865–1919), 1887 married Philip Bernard Frierson (1859–1903)
6. Caroline Swanwick "Caro" Butler (1834–1876), 1853 married William Barrow Turnbull (1829–1856)
    12. i. William Butler Turnbull (1854–1938), married
        (1) 1876 Sarah Louise Barrow (1849–1913), forced marriage, lasted one day and night;
        (2) 1891 Minnie Cleveland "Maude" Hill (c. 1872–?);
        (3) 1904 Lillian Alma Ashley (1868–1916);
        (4) 1915 Sarah Elizabeth "Sadie" Distant (1877–1974)
    13. ii. Daniel Parke Turnbull (1856–1934), 1895 married Catherine F. Mahan (1857–1940)
7. Lawrence Lewis Butler (1836–1898), married
        (1) 1869 Mary Susan "Sue" Gay (1846–1882);
        (2) 1885 Susan Ann "Sue" Mastin (1839–1894)
    14. i. Frances Parke "Fannie" Butler (1869–1929), 1895 married John Ewens (1867–1904)
    ii. Edward Gay Butler (1872–1953), 1898 married Emily Mansfield (1874–1952)
    iii. Lawrence Lewis Butler Jr. (1874–1874)
    15. iv. Lavinia Hynes "Toots" Butler (1875–1955), 1896 married Wyatt Shallcross (1866–1936)
    16. v. Anna Gay Butler (1877–1961), 1904 married Richard Cheatham Plater (1872–1955)
    17. vi. Mary Susan Butler (1880–1958), 1901 married George Armistead Whiting (1879–1947)

GENERATION 4

8. Isabel Butler Williamson (1855–1909), 1881 married Arthur G. Hodge (dates unknown)
    - i. Evelyn Angela Isabel Williamson (1884–1903)
9. George McWillie Williamson Jr. (1857–1936), 1882 married Adine Eatman (1859–1912)
    - i. George McWillie Williamson III (1884–?)
    - ii. Isabel Eleanor Butler Williamson (1888–?), married James Cumming (dates unknown)
    - iii. Sarah Leigh Williamson (1892–?), married Joseph A. Becker (dates unknown)
    - iv. Mary Alice Williamson (1898–?)
    - v. Caroline Butler Williamson (1900–?)
10. William McWillie Williamson (1861–1894), married Nannie Lemon (1870–?)
    - i. Matelle Williamson (died in infancy)
11. Caroline Butler Williamson (1865–1919), 1887 married Philip Bernard Frierson (1859–1903)
    - i. Annie Leigh Frierson (1891–1963), married
        - (1) Thomas Buffington Wilson;
        - (2) John Albert Sewall Jr. (1875–1955);
        - (3) Arnold Marcellus Perkins (1892–1973)
    - ii. George Philip Frierson II (1893–1957), married Lurline Roscoe (1907–1978)
    - iii. Dorothy Witten Frierson (1896–1977), married Daniel Alexander Bogard (1896–1966)
    - iv. Edward Butler Frierson (1898–1961), married Aura Pernell
    - v. Mary Eleanor Frierson (1901–1964), married Lester Cox Morehead (1901–1967)
12. William Butler Turnbull (1854–1938), married
    - (1) 1876 Sarah Louise Barrow (1849–1913), forced marriage, lasted one day and night;
    - (2) 1891 Minnie Cleveland "Maude" Hill (c. 1872–?);
    - (3) 1904 Lillian Alma Ashley (1868–1916);
    - (4) 1915 Sarah Elizabeth "Sadie" Distant (1877–1974)

    William Butler Turnbull and Minnie Cleveland "Maude" Hill child:

    - i. Caroline Butler "Caro" Turnbull (1893–1977), married Hugo Raymond Koonz (1896–1972)

William Butler Turnbull and Lillian Alma Ashley child:

ii. Thelma Olive "Custis" Turnbull (1901–1958), married
(1) 1923 George Alfred Hastings (1895–?);
(2) c. 1923 Richard G. Stern (c, 1890–?);
(3) c. 1933 Clark Foote Hugh (1900–1969);
(4) c. 1952 Arnault Blake Edgerly (1893–1975)

13. Daniel Parke Turnbull (1856–1934), 1895 married Catherine F. Mahan (c. 1857–1940)
i. Daniel Parke Turnbull Jr. (1898–1920)

14. Frances Parke Butler (1869–1929), 1895 married John Ewens (1867–1904)
i. Frances Parke Butler Ewens (1898–1979), 1922 married Edward Francis Twiss (1876–1944)

15. Lavinia Hynes Butler (1875–1955), 1896 married Wyatt Shallcross (1866–1936)
i. Eleanor Custis Shallcross (1898–1959)
ii. Nan Butler Shallcross (1901–1980), 1933 married Cyril Coniston Clemens (1902–1999)
iii. Lawrence Butler Shallcross (1907–1990), 1942 married Helen Lax Clanahan (1913–1996)
iv. Wyatt Shallcross Jr. (1909–1987), 1944 married Katherine Owens (c. 1911–?)
v. Mary Susan Shallcross (1918–?), married Donald C. Beere (c. 1915–?)

16. Anna Gay Butler (1877–1961), 1904 married Richard Cheatham Plater (1872–1955)
i. "Little Wonderful" Plater (1906–1906)
ii. Richard Cheatham Plater Jr. (1908–2004), married
(1) 1932 Eleanore Mundé Leake (1911–1937);
(2) 1941 Pamela Quarles Robinson (1914–1999)
iii. Louise Plater (1910–1982), 1934 married Robert Walter Hale Jr. (1906–1987)

17. Mary Susan Butler (1880–1958), 1901 married George Armistead Whiting (1879–1947)
i. Eleanor Custis Whiting (1902–1949), married
(1) 1923 William Francis Fitzgerald Jr. (dates unknown);
(2) 1949 Leopold Ludwig James Wulff Mogen Baron von Plessen (1894–1971)
ii. Lawrence Lewis Butler Whiting (1906–1950), 1931 married Katherine Ahern Ford (1912–1948)
iii. Betty Washington Whiting (1912–2003)

NOTES

INTRODUCTION

1. Edward G. W. Butler to Frances Parke Butler, March 4, 1831, Folder 543, MSS. 102, Butler Family Papers, Historic New Orleans Collection (hereafter cited as BFP). The Butler Family Papers are arranged with each letter or other item occupying a numbered folder. The papers also are microfilmed, and both the original and microfilmed sources have been consulted. See also William David Butler, John Cromwell Butler, and Joseph Marion Butler, *The Butler Family in America* (St. Louis, Mo., n.d.), 187ff.

1. EDWARD G. W. BUTLER

1. William David Butler, John Cromwell Butler, and Joseph Marion Butler, *The Butler Family in America* (St. Louis, Mo., n.d.), 281, 289–90; Caroline Bell to Edward G. W. Butler, May 13, 1825, BFP 234; Luke Henry Banker, *Fort Southwest Point, Kingston, Tennessee: The Development of a Frontier Post, 1792–1807* (Kingston, Tenn., 1984), 50–51; Edgar Bruce Wesley, *Guarding the Frontier: A Study of Frontier Defense from 1815 to 1825* (Minneapolis, 1935), 46.

2. Caroline Bell to Edward G. W. Butler, May 13, 1825, BFP 234; Francis B. Heitman, *Historical Register and Dictionary of the United States Army, from Its Organization, September 29, 1789, to March 2, 1903* (Washington, D.C., 1903, and Urbana, Ill., 1965), 1:269; Francis Paul Prucha, *The Sword of the Republic: The United States Army on the Frontier, 1783–1846* (Toronto, 1969), 205; Banker, *Fort Southwest Point*, 31–51.

3. Banker, *Fort Southwest Point*, 138; Deed Book A, 100, and Minute Book I, 243, 261, 273, Robertson County, Tennessee, Archives; Caroline Bell to Edward G. W. Butler, May 25, 1827, BFP 367; Andrew Jackson to John Adams, March 5, 1798, and March 22, 1798, in Sam B. Smith and Harriet Chappel Owsley, eds., *The Papers of Andrew Jackson*, vol. 1, *1770–1803* (Knoxville, Tenn., 1980), 185–86, 186 n. 2, and 189; John Sevier to Andrew Jackson, April 5, 1798, in ibid., 191; Isabella Fowler Butler to Andrew Jackson, August 3, 1803, in Harold D. Moser and Sharon Macpherson, eds., *The Papers of Andrew Jackson*, vol. 2, *1804–1813* (Knoxville, Tenn., 1984), 350–51, 351 n. 2.

4. Varina Davis, *Jefferson Davis, Ex President of the Confederate States of America, A Memoir by His Wife* (New York, 1890), 10–11; Pauline Wilcox Burke, *Emily Donelson of Tennessee*, 2 vols. (Rich-

mond, Va., 1942), 1:52. In his role as a guardian of Butler family members and others, Jackson may have been has been partly prompted by a desire to establish a strong kinship network, which he lacked as an orphan. See Mark R. Cheathem, *Andrew Jackson, Southerner* (Baton Rouge, La., 2013), 53–55, 81.

5. Accounts of Andrew Jackson, 1813 and 1817, Papers of Andrew Jackson, Library of Congress 1967 Film, Rolls 6 and 23 on microfilm, Tennessee State Library and Archives; Receipt, November 16, 1814, Series 1, Reel 18, Andrew Jackson Papers, MSS 27532, Library of Congress (hereafter cited as Jackson Papers, LC); Edward G. W. Butler to Andrew Jackson, February 12, 1815, Reel 16, Jackson Papers, LC; Butler et al., *The Butler Family in America*, 281–93; John H. Thweatt, "James Priestly: Classical Scholar of the Old South," *Tennessee Historical Quarterly* 39 (winter 1980): 432, 434f.; Alfred Leland Crabb, "James Priestly, Pioneer Schoolmaster," *Tennessee Historical Quarterly* 12 (1953): 130–34; Mark R. Cheathem, *Old Hickory's Nephew: The Political and Private Struggles of Andrew Jackson Donelson* (Baton Rouge, La., 2007), 13–14; E.G.W. Butler to L. U. Reavis, February 1, 1878, typed copy in author's file; Appointment of Edward G. W. Butler as Cadet, Wm. H. Crawford, Secretary of War, to Edward G. W. Butler, October 1, 1816, BFP 1060; J. C. Calhoun, Secretary of War, to Lieut. Edward G. W. Butler, July 6, 1820, BFP 1061; George Douglas Ramsay, "Recollections of the U.S. Military Academy at West Point, New York, 1814 to 1820," MSS. 257, Special Collections, U.S. Military Academy Library (hereafter cited as Ramsay MSS. 257); Robert V. Remini, *Andrew Jackson and the Course of American Empire, 1767–1821* (New York, 1977), 1:160–61 and n. 57; Butler family genealogy in possession of the author. Jackson's good feelings for West Point, which may have been influenced by Monroe, changed by the late 1820s. See Stephen E. Ambrose, *Duty, Honor, Country: A History of West Point* (Baltimore, Md., 1999), 108.

6. Order of William H. Crawford, Secretary of War, to Cadet Edward G. W. Butler, July 8, 1816, BFP 1059; Ambrose, *Duty, Honor, Country*, 55–56.

7. "Reminisces of General Edward G. W. Butler—Something About His Family," *New York Times*, August 10, 1883; Edward G. W. Butler to J.D.B. DeBow, March 13, 1857, Box 11, Item 121, Letter Book 401, MSS. 156, Charles Gayarré Collection, LSU Special Collections; Ambrose, *Duty, Honor, Country*, 49f.; Ramsay MSS. 257, USMA Library; Edward G. W. Butler to Andrew Jackson, November 20, 1816, Series 1, Reel 22, Jackson Papers, LC; John H. B. Latrobe, "West Point Reminiscences," in *Eighteenth Annual Reunion of the Association of the Graduates of the United States Academy, at West Point, New York, June 9th, 1887* (East Saginaw, Mich., 1887), 1–2, 6, 25–26.

8. Obituary of Edward G. W. Butler, *St. Louis Post-Dispatch*, September 6, 1888 (clipping), BFP 1758; Ramsay MSS. 257, USMA Library; Ambrose, *Duty, Honor, Country*, 66ff., 70–71, 90; *Annual Report of the Board of Visitors to the United States Military Academy Made to Congress and the Secretary of War, for the Year 1819*, http://digital-library.usma.edu (accessed January 4, 2015).

9. *Official Register of the Officers and Cadets of the United States Military Academy, West Point, N.Y. 1818*, http://digital-library.usma.edu (accessed January 4, 2015); *Official Register of the Officers and Cadets of the United States Military Academy, West Point, N.Y. 1819*, http://digital-library.usma.edu (accessed January 4, 2015); *Official Register of the Officers and Cadets of the United States Military Academy, West Point, N.Y. 1820*, http://digital-library.usma.edu (accessed January 4, 2015); Cheathem, *Old Hickory's Nephew*, chapter 2.

10. Account, September 16, 1817, Andrew Jackson Papers, DLC 23, Library of Congress, on microfilm, Tennessee State Library and Archives; Edward G. W. Butler to Andrew Jackson, April 27

and June 5, 1820, Andrew Jackson Papers, DLC 29, Library of Congress, on microfilm, Tennessee State Library and Archives; Andrew Jackson to Anthony Wayne Butler, January 13, 1822, and June 2, 1823, BFP 76, 96; Anthony Wayne Butler to Edward G. W. Butler, July 11, 1823, BFP 109; lists of property of Captain Edward Butler, n.d., BFP 1161, 1162; statement of account for Isabella Vinson by Sarah Earle, April 1, 1818–February 1, 1821, BFP 1256.

11. Edward G. W. Butler to Andrew Jackson, April 27 and June 5, 1820, Andrew Jackson Papers, DLC 29, Library of Congress, on microfilm, Tennessee State Library and Archives; John C. Calhoun to Andrew Jackson, June 1, 1820, in *The Papers of John C. Calhoun*, vol. 5, *1820–1821*, ed. W. Edwin Hemphill (Columbia, S.C., 1971), 165; appointment from John C. Calhoun, Secretary of War, to Lieut. Edward G. W. Butler, July 6, 1820, BFP, 1061.

12. Ramsay MSS. 257.

13. George Blaney to Edward G. W. Butler, August 29, 1820, BFP 1062; James Kearney to Edward G. W. Butler, March 1, 1821, BFP 1063; George Bomford to Edward G. W. Butler, May 21, 1821, BFP 1065; K. Jack Bauer, *Zachary Taylor, Soldier, Planter, Statesman of the Old Southwest* (Baton Rouge, La., 1985, 1993), 41–42; Edward G. W. Butler to L. U. Reavis, February 1, 1878, typed copy in author's file; "Old Army Officers," *St. Louis Globe-Democrat*, December 26, 1886, BFP 1792; Edward M. Coffman, *The Old Army: A Portrait of the American Army in Peacetime, 1784–1898* (New York, 1986), 185; Estwick Evans, "A Pedestrious Tour of Four Thousand Miles, through the Western Territories, during the Winter and Spring of 1818," in Reuben Gold Thwaites, *Early Western Travels, 1748–1846* (Concord, N.J., 1819; reprint, Cleveland, Ohio, 1904), 8:329; Samuel R. Brown, *The Western Gazeteer; or Emigrants' Directory, Containing a Geographical Description of the Western States and Territories* (Auburn, N.Y., 1817; revised ed., New York: Arno Press, 1971), 139–40. The definitive sources for names and origins of Butler's fellow plebes at West Point are the *Official Registers* of the U.S. Military Academy from 1818 through 1820. See note 1.9 above.

14. Robert Bell to Edward G. W. Butler, January 31, 1822, BFP 41; Caroline Bell to Edward G. W. Butler, February 3 and March 20, 1822, BFP 42 and 50; Edmund P. Gaines, Special Order No. 17, to Lieut. Edward G. W. Butler, March 17, 1822, BFP 49; Edward G. W. Butler to Anthony Wayne Butler, July 22, 1822, BFP 63; John R. Fenwick to Edward G. W. Butler, July 22, 1822, BFP 1068. Butler was shifted in 1821 from the 1st Regiment of the Corps of Artillery to the 4th Regiment of Artillery, and he joined the company of fellow second lieutenants Thompson and Turnbull, USMA Class of 1819. They remained together in the 4th Regiment into 1825. *Official Army Register for 1821* (Adjutant and Inspector General's Office, January 1, 1821), BFP 1699; *Official Army Register for 1822* (Adjutant and Inspector General's Office, January 1, 1822), BFP 1700; *Official Army Register for 1823* (Adjutant and Inspector General's Office, January 1, 1823), BFP 1701; *Official Army Register for 1824* (Adjutant and Inspector General's Office, January 1, 1824), BFP 1702; *Official Army Register for1825* (Adjutant and Inspector General's Office, January 1, 1825), BFP 1703.

15. Francis Paul Prucha, *Broadax and Bayonet: The Role of the United States Army in the Development of the Northwest, 1815–1860* (Madison, Wisc., 1953), 29f. and n. 28, 51f.; Prucha, *Sword of the Republic*, 254–55, 258–59; Coffman, *The Old Army*, 45, 49–50, 73f., 100–103; Bauer, *Zachary Taylor*, 9, 39; Edward G. W. Butler to Andrew Jackson, December 17, 1821, Papers of Andrew Jackson, Library of Congress 1967 Film, DLC 31, on microfilm, Tennessee State Library and Archives; Robert Butler to Edward G. W. Butler, January 8, 1822, BFP 34; Edward G. W. Butler to Andrew Jackson, January 22, 1822, BFP 37.

2. EDWARD AND FRANCES

1. Edward G. W. Butler to L. U. Reavis, February 1, 1878, typed copy in author's files; Edward G. W. Butler to Anthony Wayne Butler, July 22, 1822, Folder 63, MSS. 102, Butler Family Papers, Historic New Orleans Collection (hereafter cited as BFP); Cary Nicholas to Edward G. W. Butler, August 19 and September 23, 1822, BFP 936 and 67; Caroline Bell to Edward G. W. Butler, September 22, 1822, BFP 68; Edward G. W. Butler to Anthony Wayne Butler, October 24, 1822, MSS. 600, Twiss Collection of Butler Family Papers, Historic New Orleans Collection (hereafter cited as TCBF Papers); Charles Nourse to Edward G. W. Butler, October 16, 1822, BFP 1069; James Kearney to Edward G. W. Butler, January 23, 1823, BFP 1071; Edward G. W. Butler to Anthony Wayne Butler, May 9, 1823, Edward George Washington Butler Papers, 1821–1888, Duke University Rare Book, Manuscript, and Special Collections Library (hereafter cited as EGWB Papers); William Turnbull to Edward G. W. Butler, May 17, June 7, and June 28, 1823, BFP 94, 98, and 107; James Kearney to Edward G. W. Butler, June 15, 1823, BFP 101; Pauline Wilcox Burke, *Emily Donelson of Tennessee*, 2 vols. (Richmond, Va., 1941), 1:35 n.16, 52, 57–58; "Military Career of William Selby Harney," http://freepages.genealogy.rootsweb.ancestry.com (accessed January 10, 2015); "William S. Harney," http://en.wikipedia.org/wiki/William_S._Harney (accessed September 22, 2007); George Rollie Adams, *General William S. Harney, Prince of Dragoons* (Lincoln, Nebr., 2001), 277, 279.

2. *Official Register of the Officers and Cadets of the United States Military Academy, West Point, N.Y. 1819*, http://digital-library.usma.edu (accessed January 4, 2015); Morgan Lewis Livingston to Edward G. W. Butler, June 12, 1821, and February 26, 1823, BFP 23, 79; Henry A. Thompson to Edward G. W. Butler, May 7, 1823, BFP 92; Edward G. W. Butler to Anthony Wayne Butler, December 29, 1822, EGWB Papers; William Turnbull to Edward G. W. Butler, July 25, 1823, BFP 110. See also Sam Houston to Edward G. W. Butler, July 2, 1823, BFP 107; Mortimer Livingston to Edward G. W. Butler, June 16, 1830, BFP 530. Information about General Morgan Lewis and other members of the Lewis and Livingston families who befriended Butler is at "Lewis, Morgan [1754–1844]—American Statesman," http://freepages.history.rootsweb.com/~dav4is/people/LVNG210.htm (accessed January 11, 2008), and at "Frederick Philipse Family Tree," http://worldconnect.rootsweb.com/cgi-bin/igm.cgi?op=GET&db=mila2&id=I11257 (accessed January 16, 2008). Turnbull's references to "flatbacks" and "coached backs" are evidently to female appearances, or dress styles.

3. Edward G. W. Butler to Anthony Wayne Butler, December 29, 1822, EGWB Papers; Edward G. W. Butler to Anthony Wayne Butler, February 10, 1823, TCBF Papers; Morgan L. Livingston to Edward G. W., Butler, February 26, 1823, BFP 79; Anthony Wayne Butler to Edward G. W. Butler, February 26, 1823, BFP 80; Edward G. W. Butler to Anthony Wayne Butler, March 11, 1823, BFP 81; Henry A. Thompson to Edward G. W. Butler, May 7, 1823, BFP 92.

4. *Official Army Register for1824* (Adjutant and Inspector General's Office, January 1, 1824), BFP 1702; Orders by Edmund P. Gaines, December 8 and 9, 1823, BFP 1072 and 1073; appointment by President James Monroe, January 1, 1824, BFP 1074; *Handbook of Texas Online*, http://www.tshaonline.org/handbook/online/articles/GG/fga3.html (accessed August 24, 2007); James W. Silver, *Edmund Pendleton Gaines, Frontier General* (Baton Rouge, La., 1949), 1f., 109, 110f.; Raphael P. Thian, comp., *Notes Illustrating the Military Geography of the United States* (Washington, D.C., 1881), 63, 106–7.

5. William Turnbull to Edward G. W. Butler, January 24, 1824, BFP 127; Edward G. W. Butler to Anthony Wayne Butler, April 1, 1824, BFP 146; Rawlins Lowndes to Edward G. W. Butler, June

13, 1824, BFP 160; Edmund P. Gaines to Edward G. W. Butler, June 24, August 27, and October 22, 1824, BFP 162, 179, and 193. The military career of Rawlins Lowndes is outlined in Francis B. Heitman, *Historical Register and Dictionary of the United States Army, from Its Organization, September 29, 1789, to March 2, 1903*, 2 vols. (Washington, D.C., 1903; reprint, Urbana, Ill., 1965), 1:645.

6. James F. Hopkins, ed., *The Papers of Henry Clay*, vol. 4, *Secretary of State, 1825* (Lexington, Ky., 1972), 309; Charles Francis Adams, ed., *Memoirs of John Quincy Adams, Comprising Portions of His Diary from 1795 to 1848* (Philadelphia, 1875), 6:538 and 7:58, 67, 505. Butler was listed on January 1, 1825, as still with the 4th Regiment of Artillery, which also included First Lieutenants Thompson and Turnbull. *Official Army Register for 1825* (Adjutant and Inspector General's Office, January 1, 1825), BFP 1703.

7. Edward G. W. Butler to Frances Parke Lewis, May 18, 1825, BFP 230.

8. Michael D. Green, *The Politics of Indian Removal: Creek Government in Crisis* (Lincoln, Nebr., 1982), especially chapters 4 and 5; Edward G. W. Butler to Frances Parke Lewis, July 1, July 11, and August 31, 1825, BFP 235, 239, and 251; Edward G. W. Butler to Frances Parke Lewis, October 21, 1825, TCBF Papers; Edward G. W. Butler to Andrew Jackson, July 14, 1826, Series 6, Reel 72, Andrew Jackson Papers, MSS. 27532, Library of Congress.

9. Anthony Wayne Butler to Thomas Butler, February 16 and August 25, 1824, BFP 132 and 177; Morgan L. Livingston to Edward G. W. Butler, October 13, 1824, BFP 191; William Connell to Edward G. W. Butler, October 20, 1825, BFP 192; Thomas Butler to Edward G. W. Butler, November 20, 1824, BFP 197; Eleanor Parke Lewis to Edward G. W. Butler, n.d., BFP 210; Alexander Duncan Jr. to Edward G. W. Butler, March 14, 1827, and March 5 and April 25, 1868, BFP 353, 673, 674; Kip Sperry, "Alexander Duncan (1805–1889) of Scotland, Connecticut, Rhode Island, New York, and England," in *New England Historical and Genealogical Register* 140 (July 1986): 211–18.

10. David L. Ribblett, *Nelly Custis,Child of Mount Vernon* (Mount Vernon, Va., 1993), 42–58; "Ten Facts about the Distillery: George Washington's Mount Vernon," www.mountvernon.org (accessed January 5, 2015).

11. Edward G. W. Butler to Anthony Wayne Butler, March 11, 1823, BFP 81; Patricia Brady, ed., *George Washington's Beautiful Nelly: The Letters of Eleanor Parke Custis Lewis to Elizabeth Bordley Gibson, 1794–1851* (Columbia, S.C., 1991), 141, 143–44, 151–53; Andrew Jackson to Edward G. W. Butler, April 23, 1824, TCBF Papers; Edward G. W. Butler to Anthony Wayne Butler, May 23, 1824, EGWB Papers.

12. William Turnbull to Edward G. W. Butler, March 14, 1824, BFP 139; Edmund P. Gaines to Edward G. W. Butler, August 7, 1824, BFP 174.

13. Edward G. W. Butler to Eleanor Parke Lewis, September 25, 1824, TCBF Papers; Edward G. W. Butler to Frances Parke Lewis, October 7, 1824, BFP 189.

14. Edward G. W. Butler to Frances Parke Lewis, February 15, 1825, BFP 214; Edward G. W. Butler to Frances Parke Lewis, February 25, 1825, TCBF Papers; Brady, ed., *George Washington's Beautiful Nelly*, 75, 79, 84–85, 164–65; Deed of Sale, April 21, 1826, BFP 1126.

15. Edward G. W. Butler to Frances Parke Lewis, September 4, 1825, TCBF Papers; Margaret Law Callcott, ed. and trans., *Mistress of Riversdale: The Plantation Letters of Rosalie Stier Calvert, 1795–1821* (Baltimore, Md., 1991), 321 and n. 3, 334–35, 345–46; Rawlins Lowndes to Edward G. W. Butler, February 10, 1825, BFP; Brady, ed., *George Washington's Beautiful Nelly*, 68–80, 166; Edward G. W. Butler to Lawrence Lewis, March 30, 1825, Papers of Notable Virginia Families, Accession 2988,

Series III: Lewis Family Papers, Tracy W. McGregor Library, Special Collections, University of Virginia Library, Charlottesville, Virginia; Lucy Leigh Bowie, "Madame Grelaud's French School," *Maryland Historical Magazine* 39 (June 1944), 142–44. See also Elizabeth Fox-Genovese, *Within the Plantation Household: Black and White Women of the Old South* (Chapel Hill, N.C., 1988), 212–13.

16. Brady, ed., *George Washington's Beautiful Nelly*, 169, 175; Morgan Lewis to Edward G. W. Butler, December 16, 1825, BFP 266; Edmund P. Gaines to Edward G. W. Butler, March 18, 1826, BFP 354; Joan E. Cashin, *A Family Venture: Men and Women on the Southern Frontier* (Baltimore, Md., 1994), especially chapter 2.

17. Brady, ed., *George Washington's Beautiful Nelly*, 176–77; Members of Wedding Party of Marriage between Edward G. W. Butler and Frances Parke Lewis, April 4, 1826, BFP 1545; Indenture, April 21, 1821, BFP 1126; Andrew Jackson to Edward G. W. Butler, November 10, 1825, Allyn K. Ford Collection, Minnesota Historical Society, #772 (on microfilm); Andrew Jackson to Edward G. W. Butler, May 8, 1826, TCBF Papers.

3. FROM SOLDIER TO PLANTER

1. Frances Parke Butler to Elizabeth Gibson, May 17, 1826, Papers of Eleanor (Nelly) Parke Custis Lewis, Mount Vernon Ladies' Association Library (hereafter cited as MVLAL); "Andrew Mack," http://en.wikipedia.org/wiki/Andrew_Mack (accessed February 21, 2011); hotel invoices, Folders 1302, 1327, MSS. 102, Butler Family Papers, Historic New Orleans Collection (hereafter cited as BFP).

2. James E. Westheider, "The History of Fort Washington at Cincinnati, Ohio: A Case Study," in *George Rogers Clark: Selected Papers from the 1989 and 1990 George Rogers Clark Trans-Appalachian Frontier History Conferences*, http://npshistory.com/series/symposia/george_rogers_clark/1989-1990/sec4.htm (accessed June 26, 2012); Timothy Flint, *Recollections of the Last Ten Years in the Valley of the Mississippi* (Boston, Mass., 1826; reprint, Carbondale, Ill., 1968), 30–32, 33; W. Bullock, *Bullock's Journey from New Orleans to New York in 1827* (London, 1827; reprint, Carlisle, Mass., 2007), 133–36; Samuel R. Brown, *The Western Gazetteer; or Emigrants' Directory, Containing a Geographical Description of the Western States and Territories* (Auburn, N.Y., 1817; rev. ed. New York, 1971), 276ff.; Edward G. W. Butler to Lawrence Lewis, July 30, 1826, Papers of Notable Virginia Families, Accession 2988, Series III: Lewis Family Papers, Tracy W. McGregor Library, Special Collections, University of Virginia Library, Charlottesville, Virginia (hereafter cited as Papers of Notable Virginia Families, Accession 2988); Caroline Bell to Edward G. W. Butler, June 30, 1826, BFP 299.

3. Hotel and other accounts and lists at BFP 1302, 1305, 1308, 1308, 1311, 1312, 1313, 1327, and 1329; Charles McEvers to Edward G. W. Butler, July 10, 1826, BFP 303; Eleanor Parke Lewis to Edward G. W. Butler, July 16, 1826, BFP 305; Patricia Brady, ed., *George Washington's Beautiful Nelly: The Letters of Eleanor Parke Custis Lewis to Elizabeth Bordley Gibson, 1794–1851* (Columbia, S.C., 1991), 127, 129; Flint, *Recollections of the Last Ten Years*, 179. On Lucinda and slavery in the Northwest, see Edmund P. Gaines to Edward G. W. Butler, March 27, 1826, BFP 287; "List of Negroes, 1835," BFP 1634; Edward G. W. Butler to Charles Gayarré, April 25, 1853, Item 73, Box 11,

Letter Book 401, MSS. 156, Charles Gayarré Collection, LSU Special Collections; Lea VanderVelde, *Mrs. Dred Scott: A Life on Slavery's Frontier* (New York, 2009), 74 and n. 52. See also List of Various Articles Bought by Mrs. Butler in 1827–1828, BFP 1339.

4. Frances Parke Butler to Mary Anna Randolph Custis, October 9, 1826, MSS. 1 L5114 b 68, George Bolling Lee, 1872–1948, Papers, 1732–1870, Sec. 68, Virginia Historical Society; Edward G. W. Butler to Lawrence Lewis, July 30, 1826, and November 19, 1826, Papers of Notable Virginia Families, Accession 2988; Caroline Bell to Edward G. W. Butler, June 30, 1826, BFP 299; Rules for the government of aid de camp acting as Adjutant General, December 14, 1826, BFP 1082. For Nelly Lewis's support for the Jacksons, see Harold D. Moser and David R. Hoth, eds., *The Papers of Andrew Jackson*, vol. 5, *1821–1824* (Knoxville, Tenn., 1996), 341 and nn. 4 and 5; Harold D. Moser and J. Clint Clifft, eds., *The Papers of Andrew Jackson*, vol. 6, *1825–1828* (Knoxville, Tenn., 2002), 259–60.

5. Brady, ed., *George Washington's Beautiful Nelly*, 182–83; Eleanor Custis Lewis to Elizabeth Gibson, December 1, 1826, MVLAL; Names, Birth and Death Dates, BFP 1512; Edward G. W. Butler to Lawrence Lewis, December 13, 1826, Papers of Notable Virginia Families, Accession 2988; hotel charges, December 22, 1826, BFP 1313; "Cold Water for Babies," Own Your Health, http://ownyourhealth.wordpress.com/2008/07/01/cold-water-for-babies/ (accessed May 23, 2014).

6. Names, Birth and Death Dates, BFP 1512; Caroline Bell to Edward G. W. Butler, September 26, 1827, BFP 393; Elizabeth Parke Custis to Edward G. W. Butler, October 10, 1827, BFP 396; Edward G. W. Butler to Lawrence Lewis, October 30, 1827, Papers of Notable Virginia Families, Accession 2988; Order No. 42 by Winfield Scott and Orders Issued by Edward G. W. Butler, November 1, 1827, BFP 1100 and 1101; P. Butler to Edward G. W. Butler, November 14, 1827, BFP 399; E. P. Gaines to Edward G. W. Butler, November 11, 1827, BFP 398; Andrew Jackson to Edward G. W. Butler, May 21, 1827, Papers of Andrew Jackson, 1st Series, Library of Congress 1967 film, #11-0504, on microfilm, Tennessee State Library and Archives; R.E.W. Earl to Edward G. W. Butler, May 22, 1827, BFP 366; Edward G. W. Butler to R.E.W. Earl, June 2, 1827, BFP 371; poems by Edward G. W. Butler on Jackson, January 8, 1828, BFP 1454.

7. Conveyance Book E, Folios 387, 443, and 597, Iberville Parish, La., Records (hereafter cited as COB). The Bells acquired six slaves in Nashville in January 1811, evidence that they had not yet migrated. See Mary Sue Smith, ed., *Davidson County Tennessee Deed Book H, 1809–1821* (Bowie, Md., 2000), 14. The old French arpent was a common measure of land in eighteenth- and nineteenth-century Louisiana. It was used both in a linear sense, as "ten arpents wide," and as a measure of area, as "land of 60 arpents." The arpent was 0.84628 of an acre, and in the linear usage it equaled about 192 feet. The French measure has been replaced gradually by the Anglo-American measure, acre, which can be applied both in area or linear usage. Land along the Mississippi River and other south Louisiana streams was described in legal documents as having "frontage" of so many arpents by a "depth" of so many arpents. Because of the sinuous character of the rivers and bayous, properties fronting on them were for the most part not rectangular in shape but had converging or diverging side lines.

8. Minute Book 1, Deed Book B, and Deed Book F, Robertson County, Tennessee, Archives; Mark R. Cheathem, *Andrew Jackson, Southerner* (Baton Rouge, La., 2013), 15–17; James Parton, *Life of Andrew Jackson*, vol. 1 (New York, 1861), 287–89. On the Bells and McNairys, see, for example, COB G, Fol. 200, Iberville Parish, La., Records; Caroline Bell to Edward G. W. Butler, February 3,

1822; April 19, 1826; January 28, 1827; and September 26, 1827, BFP 42, 293, 347, and 393; Robert Bell to Edward G. W. Butler, February 2, 1829, and March 27, 1830, BFP 447 and 509; Harold D. Moser and Sharon MacPherson, eds., *Papers of Andrew Jackson*, vol. 2, *1804–1813* (Knoxville, Tenn., 1984), 248–49 and n. 3.1.

9. James Pitot, *Observations on the Colony of Louisiana from 1796 to 1802*, trans. Henry C. Pitot (Baton Rouge and London, 1979), 114–16; Amos Stoddard, *Sketches, Historical and Descriptive, of Louisiana* (Philadelphia, 1812; reprint, New York, 1973), 159ff., 165, 331.

10. A subtropical grass, sugar cane in Louisiana is sensitive to severe cold temperatures and is limited geographically to the southern half of the state. See Richard Follett, *The Sugar Masters: Planters and Slaves in Louisiana's Cane World, 1820–1860* (Baton Rouge, La., 2005), 17f.; J. Carlyle Sitterson, *Sugar Country: The Cane Sugar Industry in the South, 1753–1950* (Lexington, Ky., 1953), 10ff., 23–25. For statistical evidence of the expansion of the sugar cane industry during the 1820s, see "Letter from the Secretary of Treasury in reply to a resolution of the House of Representatives of the 25th of January last, upon the subject of cultivation of the sugar cane, and the manufacture and refinement of sugar," January 21, 1831, 21st Congress, 2d Session, Doc. No. 62, 18.

11. Moser and MacPherson, eds., *Papers of Andrew Jackson*, 2:77f., 100f.; John Spencer Bassett, ed. *Correspondence of Andrew Jackson*, vol. 1 (Washington, D.C., 1926), 122; John Spencer Bassett, ed. *Correspondence of Andrew Jackson*, vol. 6 (Washington., D.C., 1933), 426; Alice Pemble White, "The Plantation Experience of Joseph and Lavinia Erwin, 1807–1836" (Master's thesis, Louisiana State University and Agricultural and Mechanical College, 1933), 8–13, 21–22, 26; COB C, Fol. 1, Iberville Parish, La., Records. For Butler's version of the controversial duel, see Edward G. W. Butler to Jefferson Davis, September 20, 1885, in Dunbar Rowland, coll. and ed., *Jefferson Davis, Constitutionalist: His Letters, Papers and Speeches*, vol. 9 (Jackson, Miss., 1923), 393. See also Cheathem, *Andrew Jackson, Southerner*, 42–45.

12. Caroline Bell to Edward G. W. Butler, March 20, 1822, BFP 50; Robert Bell to Anthony Wayne Butler, March 15, 1823, MSS. 805, Edward George Washington Butler Papers, 1821–1888, Duke University Rare Book, Manuscript, and Special Collections Library (hereafter cited as EGWB Papers); COB G, Fol. 608, Iberville Parish, La., Records; Ethel Elizabeth Kramer, "Slavery Legislation in Ante-Bellum Louisiana, 1803–1860" (Master's thesis, Louisiana State University and Agricultural and Mechanical College, 1944), 109–14; Herman Freudenberger and Jonathan Pritchett, "The Domestic United States Slave Trade: New Evidence," *Journal of Interdisciplinary History* 21, no. 3 (winter 1991): 463; Joe Gray Taylor, *Negro Slavery in Louisiana* (Baton Rouge, La., 1963), 35f.; slave sale receipts, December 9 and 20, 1817, Box 1, folders 3 and 4, and Lavinia Erwin to Jane Craighead, April 10, 1818, Box 1, folder 5, MSS. 1295, Gay (Edward J. and Family) Papers, Louisiana State University Special Collections (hereafter cited as Gay Papers). For an illustration in antebellum Virginia of the size of the loss of slave population to forced migration and a consequent growth of the slave trading profession, see Brenda E. Stevenson, *Life in Black and White: Family and Community in the Slave South* (New York, 1996), 175f. and n. 35.

13. Deed Book 46, pp. 119, 120, 124, Frederick County, Va., Records; Caroline Bell to Edward G. W. Butler, March 20, 1822, September 28, 1822, and January 18, 1824, BFP 50, 68, and 126; COB K, Fol. 196, Iberville Parish, La., Records; Caroline Bell to Edward G. W. Butler, March 16, 1823, BFP 83; Bruce Levine, *The Fall of the House of Dixie: The Civil War and the Social Revolution That Transformed the South* (New York, 2013), 28.

14. The arrangements regarding the Llewellyn and Audley farms in the Shenandoah Valley of Virginia are in Deed Book 41, 73; Deed Book 49, 373; and Deed Book 52, 143, Frederick County, Va., Records.

15. Transfer of Land and Notes from Edward G. W. Butler to Frances Parke Butler, COB 10, Fol. 338, Iberville Parish, La., Records. The formal gift was delayed until June 14, 1828. See Caroline Bell to Edward G. W. Butler, January 28, 1827, BFP 347; COB M, Fol. 465, Iberville Parish, La., Records.

16. William Cornelius Reichel, *A History of the Rise, Progress, and Present Condition of the Moravian Seminary for Young Ladies, at Bethlehem, Pa. with a Catalogue of Its Pupils, 1785–1858*, 2nd ed. (Philadelphia, 1870), 346–47; Edward G. W. Butler to Joseph A. Murray, February 23, 1883, Joseph A. Murray Papers, Cumberland County Historical Society and the Hamilton Library Association, Carlisle, Pa.; Caroline Bell to Edward G. W. Butler, January 25, 1825, May 13, 1825, November 26, 1825, January 28, 1827, May 25, 1827, and August 3, 1827, BFP 208, 234, 260, 347, 367, and 380; Robert Bell to Edward G. W. Butler, August 6, 1826, BFP 309.

17. Caroline Bell to Edward G. W. Butler, July 2, 1828, BFP 419; Edward G. W. Butler to Lawrence Lewis, December 14, 1827, Papers of Notable Virginia Families, Accession 2988; Frances Parke Butler to Lawrence Lewis, August 12, 1827, Papers of Notable Virginia Families, Accession 2988.

18. Edward G. W. Butler to Lawrence Lewis, November 19, 1826, Papers of Notable Virginia Families, Accession 2988; Robert Bell to Edward G. W. Butler, August 30, 1827, BFP 384; Edward G. W. Butler to Major Lawrence Lewis, January 31, 1828, BFP 406; Brady, ed., *George Washington's Beautiful Nelly*, 192–93. On public health issues, see Brady, ed., *George Washington's Beautiful Nelly*, 132, 198; Lawrence Lewis to Edward G. W. Butler, March 21, 1837, EGWB Papers; Jo Ann Carrigan, *The Saffron Scourge: A History of Yellow Fever in Louisiana, 1796–1905* (Lafayette, La., 1994), 44, 49, 51. On status, wealth, and southern honor, see Edward M. Coffman, *The Old Army: A Portrait of the American Army in Peacetime, 1784–1898* (New York, 1986), 84–87; Cheathem, *Andrew Jackson, Southerner,*14–15, 16–18; and the indispensable Bertram Wyatt-Brown, *Southern Honor: Ethics and Behavior in the Old South* (New York, 2007), 66, 69, 198. The urge for "status" began no later than with the conquistadors' arrival in the Americas. See Charles C. Mann, *1491: New Revelations of the Americas before Columbus* (New York, 2011), 92 n.

19. Special Order No. 60, July 11, 1828, BFP 1107; S. Cooper to Edward G. W. Butler, December 26, 1828, BFP 1108; Rawlins Lowndes to Edward G. W. Butler, July 9, 1829, BFP 464; Edmund P. Gaines to Edward G. W. Butler, June 6 and September 18, 1829, BFP 461 and 472; Names, Birth, and Death Dates, BFP 1512; Brady, ed., *George Washington's Beautiful Nelly*, 195, 197; bill and itemized list, 1829, BFP 1345; Frances Parke Butler to Edward G. W. Butler, November 21, 1829, BFP 476.

20. Edmund P. Gaines to Edward G. W. Butler, January 5, 1830, BFP 483; John Donelson Jr. to Edward G. W. Butler, February 2, 1830, BFP 487; W. M. Foote to Edward G. W. Butler, March 25, 1830, BFP 507; Roger Jones to Edward G. W. Butler, June 16, 1830, BFP 531; Alexander Duncan to Edward G. W. Butler, July 21, 1830, BFP 536.

21. Caroline Bell to Edward G. W. Butler, November 26, 1825, BFP 260; Edward G. W. Butler to Major Lawrence Lewis, January 31, 1828, BFP 406; Robert Bell to Edward G. W. Butler, April 16 and June 5, 1828, BFP 411, 418; Caroline Bell to Edward G. W. Butler, July 2, 1828, BFP 419; White, "The Plantation Experience," 24; Robert Bell to Edward G. W. Butler, June 21, 1827, and July 22, 1828, BFP 375 and 421.

22. COB K, Fol. 600, Iberville Parish, La., Records; Caroline Bell to Edward G. W. Butler, April 19, 1826, BFP 293.

23. Caroline Bell to Edward G. W. Butler, September 26, 1827, BFP 393; Succession #365, Probate Court, Iberville Parish, La., Records.

24. COB L, Folios 463 and 666, Iberville Parish, La., Records; Robert Bell to Edward G. W. Butler, May 17, 1829, BFP 462; Eliza Wilson to Col. Andrew Hynes, January 29, 1829, Box 3, Folder 19, Gay Papers; Caroline Bell to Edward G. W. Butler, April 6, 1829, BFP 459; William B. Robertson to Col. Andrew Hynes, April 14, 1829, Box 3, Folder 19, Gay Papers.

25. COB M, Fol. 465, Iberville Parish, La., Records; Caroline Bell to Edward G. W. Butler, April 6, 1829, BFP 459; Robert Bell to Edward G. W. Butler, August 4, 1829, and January 7, 1830, BFP 471 and 484; Edward G. W. Butler to Lawrence Lewis, December 14, 1827, and August 27, 1829, Papers of Notable Virginia Families, Accession 2988; U.S. Census, 1830, Iberville Parish, La., Microfilm roll #43, Nicholls State University Library.

26. Robert Bell to Edward G. W. Butler, January 7, 1830, BFP 484; Caroline Bell to Edward G. W. Butler, February 23 and April 28, 1830, BFP 488 and 516; Robert Bell to Edward G. W. Butler, March 14 and March 21, 1830, BFP 496 and 504.

27. Anthony Wayne Butler to Edward G. W. Butler, n.d., BFP 69; Caroline Bell to Edward G. W. Butler, April 6, 1829, BFP 459; Caroline Bell to Edward G. W. Butler, April 28, 1830, BFP 516; Caroline Bell to Edward G. W. Butler, February 20, 1822, March 16, 1823, November 28, 1824, and September 27, 1826, BFP 46, 83, 199, and 319; Daniel Berry to Caroline Bell, November 11, 1827, BFP 401; Daniel Berry to Edward G. W. Butler, January 2, 1829, BFP 443; receipt for board and tuition for Susan Vinson, September 29, 1827, BFP 1292. See also R. J. Bell to Edward G. W. Butler, March 9, 1830, BFP 509; Serene E. Dwight to Edward G. W. Butler, October 16, 1830, BFP 538.

28. Robert Bell to Edward G. W. Butler, June 22, 1830, BFP 534; Caroline Bell to Edward G. W. Butler, September 17,1830, BFP 537; J. D. Hays to Edward G. W. Butler, December 4, 1830, BFP 540.

29. Edward G. W. Butler to Frances Parke Butler, January 3, 1831, EGWB Papers; COB M, Fol. 397, Iberville Parish, La., Records.

30. COB M, Fol. 397, Iberville Parish, La., Records. Edward G. W. Butler to Frances Parke Butler, February 14, 1831, MSS. 600, Twiss Collection of Butler Family Papers, Historic New Orleans Collection (hereafter cited as TCBF Papers).

31. Edward G. W. Butler to Frances Parke Butler, February 14, 1831, TCBF Papers; COB M, Fol. 466 and Fol. 662, Iberville Parish, La., Records; "Letter from the Secretary of the Treasury . . . , January 21, 1831," 28.

32. Andrew Hynes to the President and Directors of the Bank of Louisiana, April 10, 1831, Box 3, folder 21, Gay Papers.

33. COB M, Fol. 465, Iberville Parish, La., Records. Thomas Barrett was a partner in John Hagan and Co. of New Orleans, which became the initial financing and banking institution for Edward G. W. Butler in Louisiana and which acquired the Erwin note that Frances Butler received as a gift from Major Lewis.

34. Edward G. W. Butler to Frances Parke Butler, March 4, 1831, BFP 543; N. & J. Dick & Co. to Col. Andrew Hynes, June 11, 1831, Box 3, Folder 22, Gay Papers; COB M, Fol. 517, Fols. 540 and 541, Iberville Parish, La., Records; promissory note of Lavinia Erwin, March 25, 1831, Box 3, Folder

21, Gay Papers; J. B. Craighead to Col. Andrew Hynes, May 24, 1831, Box 3, Folder 22, Gay Papers; COB M, Fol. 517, Iberville Parish, La., Records; White, "The Plantation Experience," 26.

35. Roger Jones to Edward G. W. Butler, June 16, 1830, BFP 531; Edmund P. Gaines to Edward G. W. Butler, April 2, 1831, EGWB Papers; biographical sketch of Edward G. W. Butler, BFP 1510.

36. Caroline Bell to Frances Parke Butler, July 10, 1831, BFP 545; Jn. G. Chapman to Edward G. W. Butler, n.d. [1831], BFP 163; Eleanor Parke Lewis to Mrs. E.G.W. Butler, May 6, 1832., BFP 556; Caroline Bell to Edward G. W. Butler, April 6, 1829, BFP 459. The Chapman portrait hangs again at Woodlawn.

37. Rawlins Lowndes to Edward G. W. Butler, March 12 and 20, 1826, May 9 and 23, 1830, and June 6, 1831, BFP 282, 286, 518, 523, 544; "The Genealogy of the Lowndes Family of South Carolina," http://www.hillmanc.fsnet.co.uk?lowndes.htm (accessed January 16, 2008); Thomas H. S. Hammersley, ed., *Complete Regular Army Register of the United States, for One Hundred Years (1779 to 1879)*, 3rd ed. (Washington, D.C., 1881), 590. For Butler's friend and co-topographical engineer Henry Thompson, see Hammersley, ed., *Complete Regular Army Register of the United States,* 806; "Death of Gen. [Henry Anthony] Thompson," n.d., BFP 1770; H. A. Thompson to Edward G. W. Butler, May 6, 1872, BFP 695.

4. A SUGAR PLANTATION FAMILY OF IBERVILLE PARISH

1. For family connections, see Patricia Brady, ed., *George Washington's Beautiful Nelly: The Letters of Eleanor Parke Custis Lewis to Elizabeth Bordley Gibson, 1794–1851* (Columbia, S.C., 1991); Pauline Wilcox Burke, *Emily Donelson of Tennessee,* 2 vols. (Richmond, Va., 1941).

2. Edward G. W. Butler to Lawrence Lewis, October 30, 1827, Papers of Notable Virginia Families, Accession 2988, Series III: Lewis Family Papers, Tracy W. McGregor Library, Special Collections, University of Virginia Library, Charlottesville, Virginia (hereafter cited as Papers of Notable Virginia Families, Accession 2988); Frances Parke Butler to Lawrence Lewis, August 12, 1829, Papers of Notable Virginia Families, Accession 2988.

3. Edward G. W. Butler to Lawrence Lewis, December 18, 1831, Papers of Notable Virginia Families, Accession 2988; Folder 1634, Record Book of Edward G. W. Butler, MSS. 102, Butler Family Papers, Historic New Orleans Collection (hereafter cited as BFP); Timothy Flint, *Recollections of the Last Ten Years in the Valley of the Mississippi* (Boston, Mass., 1826; reprint, Carbondale, Ill., 1968), 65, 80–81,175, 188ff.; John Francis McDermott, *The Western Journals of Washington Irving* (Norman, Okla., 1944, 1966), 69–70, 71, 165; Richard O. Campanella, *Lincoln in New Orleans: The 1828–1831 Flatboat Voyages and Their Place in History* (Lafayette, La., 2010), 75, 249–50, 260–61, 270; Asbury C. Jacquess, ed., "The Journals of Davy Crockett, commencing December 20th 1834," *Indiana Magazine of History* 102 (March 2006), 8–24; J. Carlyle Sitterson, *Sugar Country: The Cane Sugar Industry in the South, 1753–1950* (Lexington, Ky., 1953), 138. It is unlikely that Butler was able to comply with the obligation to supply Henry with a new sugar mill before August 1, 1831. Henry probably dismantled the mill and transported it to use elsewhere. The Butler cane was processed by Bell.

4. Edward G. W. Butler to Lawrence Lewis, March 7, 1832, and August 29, 1832, Papers of Notable Virginia Families, Accession 2988; Brady, ed., *George Washington's Beautiful Nelly,* 198–99.

Isabella received a baptism at the St. Gabriel Roman Catholic Church on June 4, 1832, in the presence of her Butler parents and her sponsors, Robert and Caroline Bell. See *Diocese of Baton Rouge, Catholic Church Records*, vol. 5, *(1830–1839)* (Baton Rouge, La., 1984), 129.

5. Frances Parke Butler to Elizabeth Gibson, May 17, 1826, Mount Vernon Ladies' Association Library (hereafter cited as MVLAL); Caroline Bell to Frances Parke Butler, March 3, 1827, BFP 352; Edward G. W. Butler to Lawrence Lewis, December 14, 1827, Papers of Notable Virginia Families, Accession 2988; Frances Parke Butler to Lawrence Lewis, May 29, 1832, Papers of Notable Virginia Families, Accession 2988.

6. Edward G. W. Butler to Lawrence Lewis, March 7, 1832, Papers of Notable Virginia Families, Accession 2988.

7. Edward G. W. Butler to Lawrence Lewis, August 29, 1832, Papers of Notable Virginia Families, Accession 2988; Howard Bodenhorn, *A History of Banking in Antebellum America: Financial Markets and Economic Development in an Era of Nation-Building* (Cambridge, U.K., 2000), 42–44, 121, and chapter 6; George D. Green, *Finance and Economic Development in the Old South: Louisiana Banking, 1804–1861* (Stanford, Calif., 1972), 109f.; William D. Reeves, *From Tally-Ho to Forest Home: The History of Two Louisiana Plantations* (Bayou Goula, La., 2005), 22, 26, 27.

8. Eleanor Parke Lewis to Francis Parke Butler, May 20, 1832, Papers of Notable Virginia Families, Accession 2988. By "digital," Nelly meant common foxglove leaves which when dried make a diuretic and cardiac stimulant, or digitalis.

9. Edward G. W. Butler to Lawrence Lewis, January 28, 1833, Papers of Notable Virginia Families, Accession 2988; Joanne Ryan, interview by David D. Plater, Coastal Environments, Inc., Baton Rouge, September 4, 2014; Joanne Ryan, Thurston H. G. Hahn III, Michael Carpenter, Maegan Smith, and Sid Gray, *Terrestrial Phase I Cultural Resource Investigations for the Proposed Shintech Louisiana, LLC. Chemical Plant Expansion Project, Iberville Parish, Louisiana*, Draft Report (Baton Rouge, La., 2014), 3-55–3-56, 3-58, Figure 3-18; Louisiana: Office Board of State Engineers, Dunboyne Levee, Drawing No. 1231-2, 1872, Department of Public Works Files, Levee District 4, Roll 27, Louisiana Department of Transportation and Development, Baton Rouge.

10. Edward G. W. Butler to Lawrence Lewis, January 28 and February 18, 1833, Papers of Notable Virginia Families, Accession 2988; Caroline Bell to Frances Parke Butler, July 10, 1831, BFP 545; Bills of B. F. Owen, May 7, 1832, and May 24, 1832, BFP 1392, 1393.

11. Edward G. W. Butler to Lawrence Lewis, January 28, 1833, and February 18, 1833, Papers of Notable Virginia Families, Accession 2988. On the Kanawha gift, see Brady, ed., *George Washington's Beautiful Nelly*, 164–65.

12. Edward G. W. Butler to Lawrence Lewis, March 15, 1833, Papers of Notable Virginia Families, Accession 2988.

13. Edward G. W. Butler to Lawrence Lewis, April 10 and May 6, 1833, Papers of Notable Virginia Families, Accession 2988; Conveyance Book N, Fol. 444 (March 29, 1833), Iberville Parish, La., Records (hereafter cited as COB). Regarding the record of Butler's debts to Frances Parke Butler, see Transfer of Land and Notes from Edward G. W. Butler to Frances Parke Butler, May 20, 1871, COB 10, Fol. 338, Iberville, La., Records. Barrett is listed in various New Orleans city directories and commercial registers though 1841. See S. E. Percy and Co., *New Orleans Directory, 1832* (New Orleans: Printed for the authors, 1832), and subsequent directories or registers. They are on microfiche at the Historic New Orleans Collection.

14. Edward G. W. Butler to Lawrence Lewis, May 6, June 11, June 17, July 4, and July 25, 1833, Papers of Notable Virginia Families, Accession 2988; Lawrence Lewis to Edward G. W. Butler, June 14, 1833, BFP 563; Adam Rothman, *Slave Country: American Expansion and the Origins of the Deep South* (Cambridge, Mass., 2005), 198–200. On the sale of the Kanawha River property, see Lawrence Lewis to Edward G. W. Butler, November 26, 1836, #905, Allyn K. Ford Collection, Minnesota Historical Society (on microfilm).

15. Edward G. W. Butler to Lawrence Lewis, June 11, June 17, and July 25, 1833, Papers of Notable Virginia Families, Accession 2988; receipts, July 5, 1833, BFP 1398 and 1399; account receipt of Lancaster, Denby and Company, June 22, 1833, BFP 1395. See also Declaration of Purchase of Slaves, July 26, 1833, COB N, Folio 605, Iberville Parish, La., Records. "Nottoway Plantation" may refer to Nottoway County, Virginia, southwest of Richmond. Aside from corn, only occasional references have been found to Dunboyne's slave diets. From what can be gleaned from plantation and later census records, the plantation grew many food crops. Little remains of the reactions of Dunboyne slaves to their fares. For a useful, recent survey of nineteenth-century American slave diets, see Herbert C. Covey and Dwight Eisnach, *What the Slaves Ate: Recollections of African American Foods and Foodways from the Slave Narratives* (Santa Barbara, Calif., 2009).

16. See Herman Freudenberger and Jonathan B. Pritchett, "The Domestic United States Slave Trade: New Evidence," *Journal of Interdisciplinary History* 21, no. 3 (winter 1991): 457, 474–75; Jonathan B. Pritchett, "The Interregional Slave Trade and the Selection of Slaves for the New Orleans Market," *Journal of Interdisciplinary History* 28, no. 1 (summer 1997): 63–64.

17. Edward G. W. Butler to Lawrence Lewis, June 11, June 17, and July 25, 1833, Papers of Notable Virginia Families, Accession 2988; Alice Pemble White, "The Plantation Experience of Joseph and Lavinia Erwin, 1807–1836" (Master's thesis, Louisiana State University and Agricultural and Mechanical College, 1933), 88–89; Joe Gray Taylor, *Negro Slavery in Louisiana* (Baton Rouge, La., 1963), 119–21. The fired overseer may have been a holdover from the Bell property. Butler commenced his own hires in 1834, according to the Crop Record Book for Dunboyne Plantation, BFP 1635.

18. Edward G. W. Butler Jr. to Edward G. W. Butler, November 21, 1853, BFP 638; Margaret Law Callcott, ed. and trans., *Mistress of Riversdale: The Plantation Letters of Rosalie Stier Calvert, 1795–1821* (Baltimore, Md., 1991), 351. See also Elizabeth Fox-Genovese, *Within the Plantation Household: Black and White Women of the Old South* (Chapel Hill, N.C., 1988), 47–48, 110, 116–17; Brenda E. Stevenson, *Life in Black and White: Family and Community in the Slave South* (New York, 1996), 70–71, 76–78.

19. Frances Parke Butler to Lawrence Lewis, August 11, 1833, Papers of Notable Virginia Families, Accession 2988; Sitterson, *Sugar Country*, 137f.

20. COB N, Fol. 443 and Fol. 472, Iberville Parish, La., Records; Edward G. W. Butler to Lawrence Lewis, October 30, 1827, MSS. 2988, Papers of Notable Virginia Families, Accession 2988; Green, *Finance and Economic Development*, 41–42. See also Bertram Wyatt-Brown, *Southern Honor: Ethics and Behavior in the Old South* (New York, 2007), 345–46.

21. Brady, ed., *George Washington's Beautiful Nelly*, 202–3.

22. Eleanor Parke Lewis to Elizabeth Gibson, August 9, 1833, MVLAL.

23. Brady, ed., *George Washington's Beautiful Nelly*, 210–16.

24. Ibid., 215. See also Dr. Henry P. Daingerfield to Lawrence Lewis, January 14, 1834, Papers of Notable Virginia Families, Accession 2988.

25. Crop Record Book for Dunboyne Plantation, BFP 1635; Brady, ed., *George Washington's Beautiful Nelly*, 211. The Crop Record Book entries for 1833 do not show sales figures prior to January 3, 1834. See Sitterson, *Sugar Country*, 18–19, 134.

26. William F. Krumbhaar to Lawrence Lewis, May 23, 1834, Papers of Notable Virginia Families, Accession 2988.

27. Edward G. W. Butler to Lawrence Lewis, August 23, 1834, Papers of Notable Virginia Families, Accession 2988; Reeves, *Tally-Ho*, 53–53; Lawrence Lewis to Edward G. W. Butler, August 30, 1834, MVLAL; Brady, ed., *George Washington's Beautiful Nelly*, 220–23, 233.

28. Edward G. W. Butler to Lawrence Lewis, August 23, November 8, and December 30, 1834, and January 26, 1835, Papers of Notable Virginia Families, Accession 2988; Eleanor Parke Lewis to Elizabeth Gibson, October 26, 1834, MVLAL; Brady, ed., *George Washington's Beautiful Nelly*, 220. The term "rolling time" derived from the three fluted metal cylinders, or "rollers," through which cane stalks passed and were crushed and squeezed, extracting the juice. See Sitterson, *Sugar Country*, 137f.

29. Edward G. W. Butler to Lawrence Lewis, January 26, February 1, February 25, 1835, Papers of Notable Virginia Families, Accession 2988; Brady, ed., *George Washington's Beautiful Nelly*, 222.

30. Crop Record Book for Dunboyne Plantation, BFP 1635; Sitterson, *Sugar Country*, 143–44; Campanella, *Lincoln in New Orleans*, 336; Jacquess, "Journals of Davy Crockett," 15–17, 21–23. For use of whiskey by slaves, see Covey and Eisnach, *What the Slaves Ate*, 190–92.

31. *Alexandria (La.) Gazette*, May 6, 1841 (from *New Orleans Picayune*, April 23, 1841).

32. Crop Book for Dunboyne Plantation, BFP 1635.

33. Lawrence Lewis to Edward G. W. Butler, February 16, 1835, Twiss Collection of Butler Family Papers, Historic New Orleans Collection (hereafter cited as TCBF Papers); Edward G. W. Butler to Lawrence Lewis, February 25, 1835, Papers of Notable Virginia Families, Accession 2988.

34. Edward G. W. Butler to Charles Gayarré, April 25, 1853, MSS. 156, Charles Gayarré Papers, LSU Special Collections Library; "Negroes on Dunboyne Plantation," in Plantation Record Book, BFP 1634; COB P, Fol. 353, Iberville Parish, La., Records; Transfer of Land and Notes from Edward G. W. Butler to Frances Parke Butler, May 20, 1871, COB 10, Fol. 338, Iberville Parish, La., Records.

35. Brady, ed., *George Washington's Beautiful Nelly*, 213–14, n. 27, 223, 224–26, 228; Eleanor Parke Lewis to Elizabeth Gibson, September 24, 1835, MVLAL.

36. Joan E. Cashin, *A Family Venture: Men and Women on the Southern Frontier* (Baltimore, Md., 1994), 44ff.; Reeves, *Tally-Ho*, 38, 60–62.

37. COB R, Fol. 43, Fol. 44, and Fol. 426, Iberville Parish, La., Records; COB V, Fol. 215, Iberville Parish, La., Records; George W. Stribling to Lawrence Lewis, February 1, 1837, copy sent to author by Colette Endrizzi, October 6, 2012; Abstract of W. Absalom Remington sale to Edward G. W. Butler, November 3, 1836, United States National Slavery Museum Inventory, Doc 19, Item B7, page 5 of 24 (http://cdn.blogs.fredericksburg.com/newsdesk/files/2012/07/slaverydoc1.pdf [accessed May 20, 2012, and January 11, 2015]).

38. Edward G. W. Butler to Thomas Butler, September 27, 1837, Reel 15, Frame 456, MSS. 1026, Butler Family Papers, LSU Special Collections (hereafter cited as Butler Papers 1026); John M. Sacher, *A Perfect War of Politics: Parties, Politicians, and Democracy in Louisiana, 1824–1861* (Baton Rouge, La., 2003), xii, 2, 61, 86–87. Judge Butler, a former gubernatorial candidate, favored the

rechartering of the National Bank. See also Henry O. Robertson, *"In the Habit of Acting Together": The Emergence of the Whig Party in Louisiana, 1828–1840* (Lafayette, La., 2007), 48ff.

39. Lawrence Lewis to Edward G. W. Butler, October 9, 1836, and August 27, 1837, TCBF Papers; Lawrence Lewis to Edward G. W. Butler, January 10, 1837, and March 14, 1838, BFB 568 and 573; COB R, Fol. 258, Iberville Parish, La., Records; Edward G. W. Butler to Lorenzo Lewis, April 21, 1841, MVLAL. See also Brady, ed., *George Washington's Beautiful Nelly,* 14; COB 10, Fol. 338, Iberville Parish, La., Records. Woodlawn is now owned by the National Trust for Historic Preservation.

40. Lawrence Lewis to Edward G. W. Butler, April 10, 1837, MVLAL; Edward G. W. Butler to Thomas Butler, September 27, 1837, Reel 15, Frame 456, Butler Papers 1026; Frances Parke Butler to Lawrence Lewis, March 29, 1838, MVLAL; Eleanor Parke Lewis to Elizabeth Gibson, December 25, 1838, MVLAL; Matthew J. Schott, ed., *Norman's New Orleans and Environs* (1845; reprint, Baton Rouge, La., 1976), 195–96.

41. Edward G. W. Butler to Thomas Butler, September 27, 1837, Reel 15, Frame 456, Butler Papers 1026; Frances Parke Butler to Lawrence Lewis, March 29, 1838, MVLAL; Patricia Brady Schmidt, ed., *Nelly Custis Lewis's Housekeeping Book* (New Orleans, La., 1982), 18–21. Brady, ed., *George Washington's Beautiful Nelly,* 15, and David L. Ribblett, *Nelly Custis, Child of Mount Vernon* (Mount Vernon, Va., 1993), 87, both conclude that Nelly set up residence in Louisiana, leaving Major Lewis alone at Woodlawn or Audley, except for her occasional visits to Virginia. That is not the impression this author has from the letters and other records.

42. Crop Record Book for Dunboyne Plantation, BFP 1635; Eleanor Parke Lewis to Elizabeth Gibson, December 25, 1838, MVLAL.

43. Edward G. W. Butler to Thomas Butler, February 20, 1837, and March 14, 1838, Reel 15, Frames 415 and 507, Butler Papers 1026; Eleanor Parke Lewis to Elizabeth Gibson, December 25, 1838, MVLAL; Lawrence Lewis to Edward G. W. Butler, February 6, 1835, TCBF Papers; Lawrence Lewis to Edward G. W. Butler, April 27, 1839, MVLAL; Phineas Janney to Edward G. W. Butler, August 10, 1839, # 779, Allyn K. Ford Collection, Minnesota Historical Society (on microfilm); Brady, ed., *George Washington's Beautiful Nelly,* 229–30.

44. Names, Birth, and Death Dates, BFP 1512; Edward G. W. Butler to Thomas Butler, December 22, 1839, Reel 15, Frame 625, Butler Papers 1026; Caroline Bell to Andrew Jackson, January 17, 1840, Roll 34, Frame 1179, Papers of Andrew Jackson, Library of Congress Microfilm Supplement 1986. The visit of Jackson to New Orleans and ensuing celebrations are described in Sacher, *A Perfect War,* 99, as the beginning of the 1840 "political campaign season in Louisiana."

45. Lorenzo Lewis to Charles Conrad, April 6, 1840, MVLAL. Brady, ed., *George Washington's Beautiful Nelly,* 15, and Ribblett, *Nelly Custis,* 87, conclude that Nelly Lewis set up residence in Louisiana.

5. A TASTE OF SUCCESS

1. Patricia Brady, ed., *George Washington's Beautiful Nelly: The Letters of Eleanor Parke Custis to Elizabeth Bordley Gibson, 1794–1851* (Columbia, S.C., 1991), 232–35. See also Brenda E. Stevenson, *Life in Black and White, Family and Community in the Slave South* (New York, 1996), 148ff., for a discussion of behavior that might prompt spousal divorce.

2. See, for example, Brady, ed., *George Washington's Beautiful Nelly,* 15, and David L. Ribblett, *Nelly Custis, Child of Mount Vernon* (Mount Vernon, Va., 1993), 93–95.

3. For a rare expression of the feelings of Frances Butler toward her husband, see Frances Parke Butler to Edward G. W. Butler, January 1, 1848, Folder 610, MSS. 102, Butler Family Papers, Historic New Orleans Collection (hereafter cited as BFP). See also Bertram Wyatt-Brown, *Southern Honor: Ethics and Behavior in the Old South* (New York, 2007), chapter 8.

4. Frances Parke Butler to Lawrence Lewis, March 12, 1837, Mount Vernon Ladies' Association Library (hereafter cited as MVLAL); Alexander Duncan to Edward G. W. Butler, May 5, 1841, BFP 577; Record Book of Dunboyne Plantation, BFP 1634; *Cohen's Orleans and Lafayette Directory for 1849,* Historic New Orleans Collection.

5. Edward G. W. Butler to Lorenzo Lewis, April 21, 1841, MVLAL; Charles Conrad to Edward G. W. Butler, June 3, 1839, BFP 575.

6. Map of Butler and Neighbors, n.d., BFP 1246; U.S. Census, 1840, Iberville Parish, La., microfilm roll 129, Nicholls State University Library.

7. Crop Record Book for Dunboyne Plantation, BFP 1635; Brady, ed., *George Washington's Beautiful Nelly,* 296–97.

8. Crop Record Book for Dunboyne Plantation, BFP 1635.

9. Record Book, BFP 1634; William Kaufman Scarborough, *The Overseer, Plantation Management in the Old South* (Baton Rouge, La., 1966), 29; Conveyance Book 3, Fol. 72, and COB U, Fol. 411, Iberville Parish, La., Records (hereafter cited as COB).

10. Biographical Sketch, BFP 1510; J. H. Eaton to Edward G. W. Butler, December 28, 1828, BFP 441; Caroline Bell to Frances Parke Butler, July 10, 1831, BFP 545; Mark R. Cheathem, *Old Hickory's Nephew: The Political and Private Struggles of Andrew Jackson Donelson* (Baton Rouge, La., 2007), 65–73, 80–87; Pauline Wilcox Burke, *Emily Donelson of Tennessee,* 2 vols. (Richmond, Va., 1941), 2:136; John M. Sacher, *A Perfect War of Politics: Parties, Politicians, and Democracy in Louisiana, 1841–1861* (Baton Rouge, La., 2003), 107–8; Glenn R. Conrad, ed., *A Dictionary of Louisiana Biography,* 2 vols. (Lafayette, La., 1988), 1:194, 2:602. Another prominent first cousin from Kentucky, William O. Butler, ran for vice president with Lewis Cass in 1848 after commanding U.S. forces in the war with Mexico. Nicholas, although a Democrat, supported the Whig candidate, Zachary Taylor. Sacher, *A Perfect War,* 145–49, 155. See also P. A. Champomier, *Statement of the Sugar Crop Made in Louisiana in 1855–56* (New Orleans, La., 1856), 28; "Robert Carter Nicholas," *New Orleans Evening Picayune* [from the *Houma (La.) Ceres*], December 29, 1856.

11. Edward Delony [or Delany] to Edward G. W. Butler, June 11, 1842, BFP 580; Edmund P. Gaines to Edward Delony, March 17, 1846, MSS. 805, Edward George Washington Butler Papers, 1821–1888, Duke University Rare Book, Manuscript, and Special Collections Library (hereafter cited as EGWB Papers); Edward G. W. Butler to Charles Conrad, May 18, 1843, BFP 583; Edward G. W. Butler to Thomas Butler, March 8 and June 5, 1844, Reel 16, Frames 146 and 172, MSS. 1026, Butler Family Papers, LSU Special Collections (hereafter referred to as Butler Papers 1026); Sacher, *A Perfect War,* 108–9; William D. Reeves, *From Tally-Ho to Forest Home: The History of Two Louisiana Plantations* (Bayou Goula, La., 2005), 40–41; COB W, Fol. 181 and Fol. 192, Iberville Parish. La., Records; militia appointment, BFP 1115.

12. Joanne Ryan, *Greenfield-Allemania Plantation Sugarhouse (16IV119): Phase II and III Archaeo-*

logical Investigations Iberville Parish, Louisiana (Baton Rouge, La., 2009), 44–47, 52, 63–64, 70–71, 72f., 81f., 95f., 374–75; Edward G. W. Butler to Thomas Butler, March 8, 1844, Reel 16, Frame 146, Butler Papers 1026; J. Carlyle Sitterson, *Sugar Country: The Cane Sugar Industry in the South, 1753–1950* (Lexington, Ky., 1953), 149.

13. Record Book, BFP 1634; Edward G. W. Butler to Thomas Butler, September 17, 1839, and May 24, 1841, Reel 15, Frames 619 and 765, Butler Papers 1026; Eleanor Parke Lewis to Elizabeth Gibson, August 27, 1843, MVLAL; Stevenson, *Life in Black and White*, 112–13, and 137–38 quoting Olmstead; Wyatt-Brown, *Southern Honor*, 134–35, 194–95; Reeves, *Tally-Ho*, 145; Jean E. Friedman, *The Enclosed Garden: Women and Community in the Evangelical South, 1830–1900* (Chapel Hill, N.C., 1985), 99–100.

14. Eleanor Parke Lewis to Elizabeth Gibson, December 19, 1843, MVLAL; Reeves, *Tally-Ho*, 111; Edward G. W. Butler to Thomas Butler, March 8, 1844, Reel 16, Frame 146, Butler Papers 1026; Brady, ed., *George Washington's Beautiful Nelly*, 241 and notes 6 and 7, 244; Father Ennemond Dupuy to Bishop Anthony Blanc, June 22, 1844, University of Notre Dame Archives, Calendar 1844, http://archives.nd.edu:80/calendar/c184406.htm (accessed January 6, 2015). Although Judge Thomas Butler of St. Francisville helped to establish St. Mary's, there is no indication that Edward Butler gave financial assistance in its early existence. No edifice was built until 1850. See *Journals* of the Sixth, Seventh, Eighth, Ninth, Tenth, and Twelfth Annual Conventions of the Protestant Episcopal Church of the Diocese of Louisiana (1844–1848, 1850); Herman C. Duncan, *Convention Journals of Louisiana, 1835–1857* (New Orleans, n.d.).

15. COB T, Fol. 156, COB U, Fol. 403, COB V, Fol. 524, and the 4th Judicial District Court, Suit No. 1683, Iberville Parish, La., Records; Andrew Jackson to Caroline Bell, January 5, 1843, Microfilm 35-1090, Papers of Andrew Jackson, 1st ser., Tennessee State Library and Archives; Caroline Bell to Andrew Jackson, November 27, 1843, Papers of Andrew Jackson, 1st. Series, Library of Congress 1967 Film, Roll 56, Tennessee State Library and Archives; Caroline Bell to Anna Butler, February 1842 (from "Plantation six miles below Donaldsonville"), Reel 15, Frame 815, Butler Papers 1026; P. A. Champomier, *The Annual Statement of Sugar Made in Louisiana in 1844* (New Orleans, La., 1845), 6; "Robert Carter Nicholas" and "Susan Adelaide Vinson," ID: I064960 and ID: I064964, http://rootsweb.ancestry.com (accessed January 6, 2015); COB V, fol. 524, and COB W, Fol. 71, Iberville Parish, La., Records; Andrew Jackson to Edward G. W. Butler, October 4, 1843, MSS. 600, Twiss Collection of Butler Family Papers, Historic New Orleans Collection (hereafter cited as TCBF Papers); Andrew Jackson to Edward G. W. Butler, February 9, 1844, Roll 36, Frame 0241, Microfilm Supplement 1986, Papers of Andrew Jackson, Library of Congress; Affidavit, BFP 1127; Edward G. W. Butler to General Samuel Houston, May 12, 1845, EGWB Papers; "Reminiscences of Gen. E.G.W. Butler," in "A Ward of Old Hickory," *New York Times*, August 10, 1883.

16. Edward G. W. Butler to Andrew Jackson, March 15, 1843, Series 1, Reel 55, MSS. 27532, Andrew Jackson Papers, Library of Congress; Edward G. W. Butler to Andrew Jackson (Jr.), June 27, 1845, Series 1, Reel 58, MSS. 27532, Andrew Jackson Papers, Library of Congress.

17. COB W, Fol. 191, Iberville Parish, La., Records.

18. Memorandum, BFP 1566. See also Frances Parke Butler to Edward G. W. Butler, September 1, 1847, BFP 597.

19. COB W, Fol. 413 and Fol. 414, Iberville Parish, La., Records.

20. See COB X, Fol. 147, Iberville Parish, La., Records. The mortgage was actually a "reinscription" of an earlier one recorded at COB R, Fol. 426. Iberville Parish, La., Records. Mortgagees often were not especially careful in the inventories of land and slaves.

21. P. A. Champomier, *Statement of the Sugar Crop Made in Louisiana in 1845–6* (New Orleans, La., 1846), 32; Crop Record for Dunboyne Plantation, BFP 1635.

22. Frances Parke Butler to Lorenzo Lewis, June 25, 1843, MVLAL; Frances Parke Butler to Mary Custis Lee, June 5, 1847, MSS. 1 L5144 a 710-815, Mary C. Lee 1835–1918 Papers, Virginia Historical Society Library; Stevenson, *Life in Black and White*, 126. See also Joan E. Cashin, *A Family Venture: Men and Women on the Southern Frontier* (Baltimore, Md., 1994), 93ff., 100ff.

23. Eleanor Parke Lewis to Charles Conrad, August 8, 1846, MVLAL; Eleanor Parke Lewis to Elizabeth Gibson, August 29, 1846, MVLAL; William C. Beston to Edward G. W. Butler, April 8, 1847, BFP 586.

24. Edward G. W. Butler to General Samuel Houston, May 12, 1845, EGWB Papers; Eleanor Parke Lewis to Elizabeth Gibson, December 19, 1846, MVLAL; Brady, ed., *George Washington's Beautiful Nelly*, 247–48.

25. Frances Parke Butler to Edward G. W. Butler, June 18, 1847, BFP 588; Commission, BFP 1116. On the McCall family, see Brady, ed., *George Washington's Beautiful Nelly*, 214 and n. 29.

6. WITH THE 3RD DRAGOONS

1. Irving W. Levinson, *Wars within War: Mexican Guerrillas, Domestic Elites, and the United States of America, 1846–1848* (Canada, 2005), xv–xviii, 7, 82–83; Paul Foos, *A Short, Offhand, Killing Affair: Soldiers and Social Conflict during the Mexican-American War* (Chapel Hill, N.C., 2002), 125–26, 139; Joseph E. Chance, ed., *Mexico under Fire, Being the Diary of Samuel Ryan Curtis 3rd Ohio Volunteer Regiment During the Military Occupation of Northern Mexico 1846–1847* (Fort Worth, Tex., 1994), 171ff.; Richard Bruce Winders, *Mr. Polk's Army: The American Military Experience in the Mexican War* (College Station, Tex., 1997), chapter 5; "Army General Order," *Maryland Sun*, March 14, 1847; James W. Oberly, *Sixty Million Acres: American Veterans and the Public Lands before the Civil War* (Kent, Ohio, 1990), 10–12, 161. In lieu of land, bounty applicants could opt for $100 payments in U.S. Treasury script.

2. Francis B. Heitman, *Historical Register and Dictionary of the United States Army from Its Organization, September 29, 1789, to March 2, 1903*, 2 vols. (Washington, D.C., 1903; reprint, Urbana, Ill., 1965), 1:269; William David Butler, John Cromwell Butler, and Joseph Marion Butler, *The Butler Family in America* (St. Louis, Mo., n.d.), 281, 289–90; Orders by Edmund P. Gaines, December 8, 1823, Folder 1072, MSS. 102, Butler Family Papers, Historic New Orleans Collection (hereafter cited as BFP); Frances Parke Butler to Lawrence Lewis, August 12, 1827, Papers of Notable Virginia Families, Accession 2988, Series III: Lewis Family Papers, Tracy W. McGregor Library, Special Collections, University of Virginia Library, Charlottesville, Virginia (hereafter cited as Papers of Notable Virginia Families, Accession 2988); William Carey Crane, *Life and Select Literary Remains of Sam Houston of Texas* (Dallas, Tex., 1884), 250–52; Appointment by Governor Isaac Johnson, November 4, 1846, BFP 1115; P. M. Butler to Edward G. W. Butler, January 20, 1847, BFP 585. See

also a clipping from *New York Tribune,* November 27, 1880, BFP 1752. On reasons that men volunteered to fight in Mexico see, for example, Julius P. Garesché to Mary Blackford, February 29, 1848, Blackford Family Papers, # 01912, Southern Historical Collection, University of North Carolina (hereafter cited as Blackford Family Papers); Foos, *A Short, Offhand, Killing Affair,* 58–59.

3. Benjamin Franklin Scribner, *Camp Life of a Volunteer: A Campaign in Mexico, or a Glimpse of Life in Camp* (New Albany, Ind., 1875; reprint, Austin, Tex., 1975), 13; Brian M. McGowan, "The Second Battle of New Orleans: The Crescent City and the Anglo 'Invasion' of 1846," *Louisiana History* 51 (winter 2010), 30f.; Heitman, *Historical Register,* 1:80, 289, 723. Despite the makeup of the new regiments basically from recruited volunteers, they served under U.S. Army rules.

4. Heitman, *Historical Register,* 1:582; Adjutant General's Office (AGO) to Edward G. W. Butler, March 26,1847, National Archives Records Administration (hereafter cited as NARA), M565, #15, 360; Roger Jones to E.G.W. Butler, April 16, 1847, NARA, M565, #15, 425; Memorandum of companies of the ten Regiments en route for the Army in Mexico, via Point Isabel, April 20, 1847, NARA, RG 94, Box 10, Folder 1, Records of the Adjutant General's Office, 1780s–1917, Letters Received; E.G.W. Butler to Roger Jones, April 30, 1847, NARA, M567, Roll 333 (1847), Letters Received by the Office of the Adjutant General, Main Series; Edward H. Moseley and Paul C. Clark Jr., *Historical Dictionary of the United States-Mexican War* (Lanham, Md., 1997), 139, 209. Some of the captains' first names and places of origin differ between the AGO message to Butler and the officer lists in Heitman, *Historical Register,* vol. 1.

5. Winders, *Mr. Polk's Army,* 20f.; Order No. 2, April 23, 1847, Orders 1847–1848, BFP 1636; Order No. 15, October 13, 1847, Orders 1847–1848, BFP 1638; Order No. 3, January 20, 1848, Orders 1847–1848, BFP 1636; Order No. 3, March 16, 1848, Orders 1847–1848, BFP 1636; Heitman, *Historical Register,* 1:512, 681. On Radziminski, see Heitman, *Historical Register,* 1:812; Francis C. Kajencki, "Charles Radziminski and the United States-Mexican Boundary Survey," *New Mexico Historical Review* 63, no. 3 (July 1988): 210–40, "Obituary of Charles Radziminski," n.p., n.d., BFP 1787.

6. E. B. Gaither to E.G.W. Butler, May 7, 1847, NARA, M567, Roll 333 (1847), Letters Received; J. V. S. Haviland to E.G.W. Butler, May 7, 1847, NARA, M567, Roll 333 (1847), Letters Received; Adjutant General Roger Jones to E.G.W. Butler, May 11, 1847, NARA, M565, Roll 15, 500; E.G.W. Butler to Brig. Gen. R. Jones, May 20, 1847, NARA, M567, Roll 333 (1847), Letters Received; E.G.W. Butler to Maj. Gen. Z. Taylor, May 20, 1847, NARA, RG94, Box 10, Folder 5, Letters Received Mexican War, Army of Occupation; E.G.W. Butler to Brig. Gen. R. Jones, June 3, 1847, and July 3, 1847, NARA, M567, Roll 333 (1847), Letters Received; Zachary Taylor to Edward G. W. Butler, July 6, 1847, Folder 29, Twiss Collection of Butler Family Papers, Historic New Orleans Collection (hereafter cited as TCBF Papers); Justin H. Smith, *The War with Mexico,* 2 vols. (Gloucester, Mass., 1963), 2:364, 432; K. Jack Bauer, *The Mexican War, 1846–1848* (New York, 1974), 221–22.

7. *Plaquemine (La.) Southern Sentinel,* May 16, 1849.

8. Scribner, *Camp Life,* 38; E.G.W. Butler to Maj. W.W.S. Bliss, June 12, 1847, NARA, RG 94, Box 10, Folder 8, Letters Received, Mexican War, Army of Occupation; Order No. 3, June 14, 1847, Orders 1847–1848, BFP 1636; William Davenport to Major W.W.S. Bliss, June 27, 1849, NARA, RG 94, Box 10, Folder 9, Letters Received; Frances Parke Butler to Edward G. W. Butler, July 8, 1847, and December 9, 1847, BFP 589 and 606; Order No. 7, February 14, 1848, Orders 1847–1848, BFP 1636; Heitman, *Historical Register,* 1:355; Moseley and Clark, *Historical Dictionary,* 168. On servants

to handle chores, see Winders, *Mr. Polk's Army,* 126. Dennis and William are named in the plantation slave lists, "Negroes on Dunboyne Plantation," and "Negroes Jan 1, 1835," BFP 1634.

9. Winders, *Mr. Polk's Army,* 144f.; James M. McCaffrey, *Army of Manifest Destiny: The American Soldier in the Mexican War, 1846–1848* (New York, 1992), chapter 4; E.G.W. Butler to Brig. Gen. R. Jones, July 10, 1847, NARA, M567, Roll 333, Letters Received, Main Series, 1822–1860; Frances Parke Butler to Edward G. W. Butler, August 1 and August 19, 1847, BFP 592, 596. See BFP 1801, "Cavalry Tactics—First Part, School of the Trooper" (War Department, 1841), which served as Butler's cavalry guide.

10. William Davenport to Major W.W.S. Bliss, July 13, 1848, NARA, RG 94, Entry 130, Letters Sent 1845–1848; E.G.W. Butler to Major W.W.S. Bliss, July 18, 1847, and August 1, 1847, NARA, RG 94, Box 11, Letters Received, Mexican War, Army of Occupation; E.G.W. Butler to Brig. Gen. R. Jones, August 13, 1847, NARA, M567, Roll 334 (1847), Letters Received by the Office of the Adjutant General, 1822–1860; Edward G. W. Butler to William Davenport, August 16, 1847, Letterbook 1847–1848, BFP 1636.

11. Heitman, *Historical Register,* 1:207, 542; Winders, *Mr. Polk's Army,* 41; Bauer, *The Mexican War,* 223; Chance, ed., *Mexico under Fire,* 151; map showing the movement of the U.S. Army engaged in the conquest of Mexico, 1846, BFP 1114; plat of Dragoon Camp at Mier, n.d., BFP 625; John Butler to Col. E.G.W. Butler, August 9, 1847, NARA, RG 94, Box 11, Letters Received, Mexican War, Army of Occupation; E. D. Hopping to Major W.W.S. Bliss, July 28, 1847, and August 4, 1847, NARA, RG 94, Box 11, Letters Received, Mexican War, Army of Occupation; "Consolidated Morning Reports Troops Stationed at Camp near Mier, Mexico, Commanded by Brigadier General E. D. Hopping," July 6, 1847–August 22, 1847, BFP 1638; W. G. Belknap to Major W.W.S. Bliss, September 1, 1847, NARA, RG 94, Box 11, Letters Received, Mexican War, Army of Occupation; E.G.W. Butler to Gen. R. Jones, September 3, 1847, NARA, M567, Roll 334, Letters Received by the Office of the Adjutant General, Main Series, 1822–1860. On John Butler, see *History of the First Troop Philadelphia City Cavalry, 1774–November 17, 1874* (Philadelphia, 1875). On Mier, see "Journal of a March from Monterrey to Camargo and back between November 8th 1847; and the 21st of the same month," Box 28, Folder 9, SC 1536, John Ellis Wool Papers, New York State Library Archives (hereafter cited as Wool Papers); Francis Parke Butler to Edward G. W. Butler, August 19, 1847, BFP 596. In late August 1847, the makeup of the camp changed. The 10th Infantry Regiment was reassigned to towns along the Rio Grande, the 13th Regiment departed for central Mexico, and the 16th Regiment left for garrison duty at Monterrey. See Chance, ed., *Mexico under Fire,* 283 n. 65.

12. Edward G. W. Butler to Col. Wm. Davenport, September 6, 1847, and William Davenport to Major W.W.S. Bliss, September 8, 1847, NARA, RG 94, Box 11, Letters Received, Mexican War, Army of Occupation; C. Colon to Edward G. W. Butler, September 11, 1847, Letterbook 1847–1848, BFP 1638; Order No. 11, October 18, 1847, Orders 1847–1848, BFP 1636.

13. Chance, ed., *Mexico under Fire,* 153; W.W.S. Bliss to Colonel E.G.W. Butler, October 5, 1847, NARA, RG 94, Entry 130A, 195, Letters Sent, 1845–1848; W.W.S. Bliss to Col. Webb, October 7, 1847, and to Col. E.G.W. Butler, October 17, 1847, NARA, RG 94, Entry 130A, 201, 202; E.G.W. Butler to Major W.W.S. Bliss, September 21, 1847, NARA, RG 94, Box 11, Letters Received; Lewis Cass Jr. to Col. E.G.W. Butler, October 17, 1847, NARA, RG 94, Box 11, Letters Received; Special Order No. 4, July 4, 1847, Orders 1847–1848, BFP 1636; Edward G. W. Butler to Major W.W.S. Bliss,

October 22, 1847, Letterbook 1847–1848, BFP 1638; Edward G. W. Butler to Captain John Butler, October 20, 1847, Letterbook 1847–1848, BFP 1638; Edward G. W. Butler to Capt. R. T. Merrick, November 1, 1847, Letterbook 1847–1848, BFP 1638; Foos, *A Short, Offhand, Killing Affair,* 89–94; Frances Parke Butler to Edward G. W. Butler, September 30, 1847, BFP 602; Moseley and Clark, *Historical Dictionary,* 68–69. On Bliss, who became Taylor's son-in-law, see Heitman, *Historical Register,* 1:225; Moseley and Clark, *Historical Dictionary,* 54–55. On the "veterinarian" Palmer, see Lewis Cass Jr. to Lieut. [Charles] Radziminski, Asst. Adj. Gen., October 26, 1847, NARA, RG 94, Box 11, Letters Received.

14. J. Harris Maddox to E.G.W. Butler, February 20, 1848, NARA, RG 94, Box 11, Letters Received.

15. Edward G. W. Butler to Capt. Irvin McDowell, February 24, 1848, Letters 1847–1848, BFP 1638; Order No. 8, February 26, 1848, Orders 1847–1848, BFP 1638; "Old Army Officers," newspaper clipping, *St. Louis Globe-Democrat,* December 26, 1886, BFP 1792; Heitman, *Historical Register,* 1:683.

16. W.W.S. Bliss to E.G.W. Butler, October 26, 1847, NARA, RG 94, Entry 130A, 206, Letters Sent, 1845–1848; Heitman, *Historical Register,* 1:664; Order No. 11, December 17, 1847, Box 28, Folder 3, SC 15361, Wool Papers; G. W. Caldwell to Col. E.G.W. Butler, December 18, 1847, NARA, RG 94, Box 11, Letters Received; Smith, *War with Mexico,* 2:169–71; Chance, ed., *Mexico under Fire,* 119–20. Levinson, *Wars within War,* 68–69, 85ff. For descriptions of Reynosa and Agua Leguas in 1847, see Chance, ed., *Mexico under Fire,* 119, 152–53.

17. Heitman, *Historical Register,* 1:269, 705, 723, 890; E.G.W. Butler to Brig. Gen. R. Jones, December 20, 1847, NARA, M567, Roll 335, Letters Received by the Office of the Adjutant General, Main Series, 1822–1860; Edward G. W. Butler to Brig. Genl. R. Jones, December 24, 1847, Letterbook 1847–1848, BFP 1638; obituary of Capt. John Butler, n.p., n.d., BFP 1736; Order 25, December 26, 1847, Orders 1847–1848, BFP 1638.

18. Malcolm Bell Jr., *Major Butler's Legacy: Five Generations of a Slaveholding Family* (Athens, Ga., 1987), 303, 488–89; Pierce Butler to E.G.W. Butler, January 14, 1848, and January 22, 1848, BFP 612 and 614; Michael Moore to Edward G. W. Butler, February 24, 1848, BFP 619; Edward G. W. Butler to Captain Irvin McDowell, January 2, 1848, and January 10, 1848, Letterbook 1847–1848, BFP 1638. According to Bell, *Major Butler's Legacy,* 488–89, John and Pierce Mease changed their names to Butler in order to facilitate the inheritance of the estate of their maternal grandfather, Major Pierce Butler, who died in 1822 in South Carolina. See also *New Orleans Daily Picayune,* January 8, 1849, citing the *Hartford Times* (n.d.) on Pierce Butler, husband of Frances Kemble.

19. George Winston Smith and Charles Burnet Judah, eds., *Chronicles of the Gringos: The U.S. Army in the Mexican War, 1846–1848; Accounts of Eyewitnesses and Combatants* (Albuquerque, N.Mex., 1968), 347–48 and n. 78. For a summary of disease-related deaths versus those caused by battle in the war with Mexico, see Winders, *Mr. Polk's Army,* 144f., which relied upon the War Department's report to Congress shortly after the war ended: U.S. Congress, House, *Military Forces Employed in the Mexican War: Letter from the Secretary of War Transmitting, Information in answer to a resolution of the House, July 31, 1848, relative to the military forces employed in the late war with Mexico,* 31st Cong., 1st Sess., Executive Document No. 24.

20. Isabella Butler to Edward G. W. Butler, September 25, 1847, BFP 601; "Acknowledgment of

standard presented to the 3rd Dragoons by the Colonel's 'Good Lady,'" n.d., BFP 966; Frances Parke Butler to Edward G. W. Butler, June 18, July 8, August 9, 1847, September 30, 1847, and April 6, 1848, BFP 588, 589, 593, 602, 623; Frances Parke Butler to Mary Custis Lee, January 10, 1847, "Lee, Mary Custis 1835–1918 Papers," 1694–1917, Sec. 11, Virginia Historical Society (hereafter cited as "Lee, Mary Custis 1835–1918 Papers").

21. Frances Parke Butler to Edward G. W. Butler, January 1, 1848, BFP 610. See also Frances Parke Butler to Edward G. W. Butler, October 21 and December 27, 1847, and January 3 and 20, 1848, BFP 603, 608, 611, 613.

22. Frances Parke Butler to Edward G. W. Butler, January 20, 1848, and January 27, 1848, BFP 613, 615; Frances Parke Butler to Mary Custis Lee, June 5, 1847, "Lee, Mary Custis 1835–1918 Papers."

23. Frances Parke Butler to Edward G. W. Butler, February 15 and 21, 1848, BFP 617, 618.

24. Frances Parke Butler to Edward G. W. Butler, April 10, 1848, BFP 624. See Wyatt-Brown, *Southern Honor: Ethics and Behavior in the Old South* (New York, 2007), especially chapter 14.

25. For example, Frances Parke Butler to Edward G. W. Butler, January 27, 1848, and June 15, 1848, BFP 615, 628.

26. Glenn R. Conrad, ed., *A Dictionary of Louisiana Biography*, 2 vols. (Lafayette, La., 1988), 1:437; Patricia Brady, ed., *George Washington's Beautiful Nelly: The Letters of Frances Parke Custis Lewis to Elzabeth Bordeley Gibson* (Columbia, S.C., 1991), 116–17; Henry Johnson to Edward G. W. Butler, August 10, 1847, BFP 594. In 1829, Johnson married a cousin of Francis Scott Key, Elizabeth Rousby Key, and several members of her family came to reside in Louisiana. See "Henry Johnson (Louisiana)," http://en.wikipedia.org/wiki/Henry_Johnson_(Louisiana) (accessed January 6, 2015); http://sparksfamilytree.net/ghtout/gp4050.htm (accessed January 6, 2015).

27. Jesse Hart to Frances Parke Butler, August 15, 1847, BFP 595; Frances Parke Butler to Edward G. W. Butler, September 30, 1847, BFP 602; Henry Johnson to Edward G. W. Butler, December 27, 1847, BFP 609; Frances Parke Butler to Edward G. W. Butler, January 27, 1848, and February 15, 1848, BFP 615 and 619; Moseley and Clark, *Historical Dictionary*, 50; Irwin McDowell to Edward G. W. Butler, February 20, 1848, Allyn K. Ford Collection, #956, Minnesota Historical Society.

28. Antonio Canales to Colonel Jose Maria Carrasco, January 17, 1848, Box 23, Folder 2; Antonio Canales to General J. E. Wool, January 30, 1848, Box 12, Folder 15; John E. Wool to General Antonio Canales, February 3, 1848, Box 5, Folder 4; and John E. Wool to Edward G. W. Butler, March 5, 1848, Box 57—all in Wool Papers; Julius P. Garesché to Mary Blackford, February 29, 1848, Blackford Family Papers; Bauer, *The Mexican War*, 225.

29. Frances Parke Butler to Edward G. W. Butler, February 21, 1848, BFP 618. The letter did not reach Butler until mid- to late March at the earliest.

30. Edward G. W. Butler to Brig. Gen. Antonio Canales, February 29, 1848, Letterbook 1847–1848, BFP 1638; John E. Wool to Edward G. W. Butler, March 7, 1848, Box 57, Wool Papers; Edward G. W. Butler to Capt. Irvin McDowell, March 8, 1848, Letterbook 1847–1848, BFP 1638; John E. Wool to Edward G. W. Butler, March 12, 1848, and March 13, 1848, Box 5, Folder 4; and John E. Wool to Edward G. W. Butler, March 17, 1848, Box 57—all in Wool Papers; Edward G. W. Butler to Brig. Gen. John E. Wool, March 22, 1848, Letterbook 1847–1848, BFP 1638; John E. Wool to Colonel Edward G. W. Butler, March 21, 1848, BFP 620; Joseph Daniels to Edward G. W. Butler,

March 21, 1848, BFP 621; Headquarters of Army of Occupation to Edward G. W. Butler, April 24, 1848, BFP 625.

31. Edward G. W. Butler to G. W. Woods, February 14, 1848, Letterbook 1847–1848, BFP 1638; Edward G. W. Butler to Lieutenant H. P. Bee, February 6, 1848, Letterbook 1847–1848, BFP 1638; Edward G. W. Butler to Lt. Colonel H. P. Webb, March 11, 1848, Letterbook 1847–1848, BFP 1638; Edward G. W. Butler to Capt. I. McDowell, March 18, 1848, and April 12, 1848, Letterbook 1847–1848, BFP 1638; Heitman, *Historical Register,* 1:683. On Texas and Arkansas volunteers, see Levinson, *Wars within War,* 22–25, 31; Foos, *A Short, Offhand, Killing Affair,* 120–21, 124.

32. Frances Parke Butler to Edward G. W. Butler, May 1, 1848, BFP 626; Zachary Taylor to General Wool, April 19, 1848, Box 12, Folder 11, Wool Papers; Order No. 150, June 11, 1848, Box 64, Wool Papers; Jno. Wool to Edward G. W. Butler, June 14, 1848, BFP 627; Chas. Radziminski to Major E. S. Sibley, June 14, 1848, Letterbook 1847–1848, BFP 1638; Edward G. W. Butler to John E. Wool, June 17, 1848, and June 26, 1848, Box 12, Folder 15, Wool Papers; Edward G. W. Butler to Maj. Genl. J. E. Wool, June 20, 1848, Letterbook 1847–1848, BFP 1638; Order No. 3, June 14, 1848, Orders 1847–1848, BFP 1836; Order No. 164, June 23, 1848, Box 64, Wool Papers; Frances Parke Butler to Edward G. W. Butler, June 15, 1848, BFP 628; Order No. 14, June 30, 1848, Orders 1847–1848, BFP 1636. On Hunt, see Heitman, *Historical Register,* 1:369, 2:56. As he was preparing to leave Mexico, Butler offered to wait for Wool and invited him to visit Dunboyne; the fellowship does not appear to have continued following the war. See Edward G. W. Butler to John E. Wool, June 26, 1848, Box 12, Folder 15, Wool Papers. See BFP 1145 for a description of the sword collection.

33. R. Jones to Edward G. W. Butler, August 28, 1848, NARA, M565, Roll 16, 331 (March 16, 1848–December 31, 1849).

34. William Louis Schley to Edward G. W. Butler, March 29, 1881, MSS. 805, Edward George Washington Butler Papers, 1821–1888, Duke University Rare Book, Manuscript, and Special Collections Library (hereafter cited as EGWB Papers).

35. Frances Parke Butler to Edward G. W. Butler, June 19, 1848, EGWB Papers.

7. "A PROPER SENSE OF ONE'S OBLIGATIONS"

1. Richard Follett, "Documenting Louisiana Sugar, 1845–1917," www.sussex.ac.uk/louisiana sugar (accessed July 10 and July 14, 2008); map of landholdings, n.d., Folder 1246, MSS. 102, Butler Family Papers, Historic New Orleans Collection (hereafter cited as BFP); plat showing elevations of Butler Plantation, n.d., BFP 1247; Warrant No. 992, State of Louisiana to Edward G. W. Butler, February 1, 1854, BFP 1239; A. A. Humphreys and H. L. Abbot, 1851 map, *Mississippi River from Red River Landing to Carrollton (New Orleans),* Record Group 77, MD1-30, U.S. National Archives and Records Administration, Washington, D.C.; Louisiana Board of Public Works, 1866 map, *Mississippi River Levees from Thomas Point to Carrolton (New Orleans),* Chart 11-U, Map LD 5 2001 (20 sheets), Louisiana and Lower Mississippi Valley Collections, LSU Special Collections; Joanne Ryan, Thurston H. G. Hahn III, Michael Carpenter, Maegan Smith, and Sid Gray, *Terrestrial Phase I Cultural Resource Investigations for the Proposed Shintech Louisiana, LLC. Chemical Plant Expansion Project, Iberville Parish, Louisiana,* Draft Report (Baton Rouge, La., 2014), passim; Joanne Ryan and Thur-

ston H. G. Hahn, interviews and email with David D. Plater, September 4, 10, 16, and 30, 2014; P. A. Champomier, *Statement of the Sugar Crop Made in Louisiana in 1849–50* (New Orleans, La., 1850), 14, 15; P. A. Champomier, *Statement of the Sugar Crop Made in Louisiana in 1856–57* (New Orleans, La., 1857), 9, 10; M. Adrien Persac, *Plantations of the Mississippi River from Natchez to New Orleans* (Norman's Chart), 1857, LSU Special Collections; Judy Riffel, ed., *Iberville Parish Records*, vol. 2 (Baton Rouge, La., 1982), 83, 145; John B. Rehder, *Delta Sugar: Louisiana's Vanishing Plantation Landscape* (Baltimore, Md., 1999), 90–100, 103–6, 117–18, 146; Jessie Poesch and Barbara Sorelle Bacot, eds., *Louisiana Buildings, 1720–1940: The Historic American Buildings Survey* (Baton Rouge, La., 1997), 116, 157f.; John Michael Vlatch, *Back of the Big House: The Architecture of Plantation Slavery* (Chapel Hill, N.C., 1993), 191–92; Judy Riffel, ed., *Iberville Parish Records*, vol. 1 (Baton Rouge, La., 1981), 135–37. For slave diets, especially reliance upon pea varieties, corn, potatoes, and various meats, see Herbert C. Covey and Dwight Eisnach, *What the Slaves Ate: Recollections of African American Foods and Foodways from the Slave Narratives* (Santa Barbara, Calif., 2009), 80ff., 84, 86, 96f.

2. Statement concerning Dunboyne Plantation, BFP 1564; Mrs. Eugene Bowman to David Plater, August 3, 2009, author's files; Patricia Brady, ed., *George Washington's Beautiful Nelly: The Letters of Eleanor Parke Custis to Elizabeth Bordley Gibson, 1794–1851* (Columbia, S.C., 1991), 211; Poesch and Bacot, eds., *Louisiana Buildings*, 104, 113, 114, 116; Rehder, *Delta Sugar*, 88–89; Caroline Bell to Frances Parke Butler, July 10, 1831, BFP 545; U.S. Census, 1850, Iberville Parish, La., microfilm roll 231, Nicholls State University; Riffel, ed., *Iberville Parish Records*, 1:135, 136, 137; L. Bouchereau, *Statement of the Sugar and Rice Crops Made in Louisiana in 1868–69* (New Orleans, La., 1869), 5.

3. Itemized Accounts of Dunboyne Plantation Workers, 1833–1870, BFP 1634; Conveyance Book 3, Fol. 72 (February 17, 1853), Iberville Parish, La., Records (hereafter cited as COB); William D. Reeves, *From Tally-Ho to Forest Home: The History of Two Louisiana Plantations* (Bayou Goula, La., 2005); Riffel, ed., *Iberville Parish Records*, 2:69; William Kauffman Scarborough, *The Overseer: Plantation Management in the Old South* (Baton Rouge, La., 1966), 156.

4. Itemized Accounts, BFP 1634; COB 3, Fol. 320 (February 17, 1853), Iberville Parish, La., Records. In 1853, when notified of Lucinda's death, Edward Butler Jr., then at Harvard, wrote about his sorrow for the loss of his "Mammy" and praised Lucinda as "a precious gift" to Johnson, "his *guardian angel*. . . ." Edward G. W. Butler Jr. to Edward G. W. Butler, November 21, 1853, BFP 638.

5. J. Carlyle Sitterson, *Sugar Country: The Cane Sugar Industry in the South, 1753–1950* (Lexington, Ky., 1953), 167ff., 173f.; Richard Follett, *The Sugar Masters: Planters and Slaves in Louisiana's Cane World, 1820–1860* (Baton Rouge, La., 2005), 24–25; Edward G. W. Butler to Daniel Turnbull, November 5 and 13, 1858, Folder 5a, Box 25b, MSS. 1372, 1382, James P. Bowman and Family Papers, 1806–1837, LSU Special Collections (hereafter cited as JPB Papers). See also *Plaquemine (La.) Gazette and Sentinel*, March 24, 1860, for advertisement of the firm of Carson and Kearney.

6. Champomier, *Statement of the Sugar Crop Made in Louisiana in 1849–50*, 14, 15; P. A. Champomier, *Statement of the Sugar Crop Made in Louisiana in 1850–51* (New Orleans, La., 1851), 10, 11; P. A. Champomier, *Statement of the Sugar Crop Made in Louisiana in 1851–52* (New Orleans, La., 1852), 10, 11; P. A. Champomier, *Statement of the Sugar Crop Made in Louisiana in 1852–53* (New Orleans, La., 1853), 10, 11; P. A. Champomier, *Statement of the Sugar Crop Made in Louisiana in 1853–54* (New Orleans, La., 1854), 10, 11; P. A. Champomier, *Statement of the Sugar Crop Made in Louisiana in 1854–55* (New Orleans, La., 1855), 10, 11; P. A. Champomier, *Statement of the Sugar Crop Made in*

Louisiana in 1855–56 (New Orleans, La., 1856), 9, 10, 11; Champomier, *Statement of the Sugar Crop Made in Louisiana in 1856–57*, 9, 10; P. A. Champomier, *Statement of the Sugar Crop of Louisiana of 1857–58* (New Orleans, La., 1858), 9, 10; P. A. Champomier, *Statement of the Sugar Crop of Louisiana of 1858–59* (New Orleans, La., 1859), 9, 10; P. A. Champomier, *Statement of the Sugar Crop Made in Louisiana in 1859–60* (New Orleans, La., 1860), 9, 10; P. A. Champomier, *Statement of the Sugar Crop Made in Louisiana in 1861–62* (New Orleans, La., 1862), vii–viii, 9, 10. See also Joseph Karl Menn, *The Large Slaveholders of Louisiana—1860* (New Orleans, La., 1964), 242f.

7. *Plaquemine (La.) Southern Sentinel*, November 28, 1849; Iberville Parish, La., Police Jury Minutes, August 9, 1858 (Works Progress Administration, on microfilm, Louisiana State University), 182–83.

8. Frances Parke Butler to Edward G. W. Butler, September 30, 1847, BFP 602; Brady, ed., *George Washington's Beautiful Nelly*, 251, 254, 255, 262, 263.

9. Eleanor Parke Lewis to Elizabeth Bordley Gibson, October 23, 1851, Mount Vernon Ladies' Association Library (hereafter cited as MVLAL).

10. Alexander Duncan to Edward G. W. Butler, December 8, 1851, Edward George Washington Butler Papers, 1821–1888, Duke University Rare Book, Manuscript, and Special Collections Library (hereafter cited as EGWB Papers); Kip Sperry, "Alexander Duncan (1805–1889) of Scotland, Connecticut, Rhode Island, New York, and England," *New England Historical and Genealogical Register* 140 (July 1986), 212–14, 215.

11. "A Noted Architect. Death of Henry Howard," *New Orleans Daily Picayune*, November 26, 1884; *Journal of the Thirteenth Annual Convention of the Protestant Episcopal Church in the Diocese of Louisiana* (New Orleans, La., 1851) 9; *Journal of the Fourteenth Annual Convention of the Protestant Episcopal Church in the Diocese of Louisiana* (New Orleans, La., 1852), 55. Records of the Protestant Episcopal Diocese of Louisiana were viewed at the diocesan offices, New Orleans, Louisiana.

12. *Journal of the Fifteenth Annual Convention of the Protestant Episcopal Church in the Diocese of Louisiana* (New Orleans, La., 1853), 13, 21, 46; *Journal of the Seventeenth Annual Convention of the Protestant Episcopal Church in the Diocese of Louisiana* (New Orleans, La., 1855), 47; *Journal of the Eighteenth Annual Convention of the Protestant Episcopal Church in the Diocese of Louisiana* (New Orleans, La., 1856), 60; *Journal of the Nineteenth Annual Convention of the Protestant Episcopal Church in the Diocese of Louisiana* (New Orleans, La., 1857), 26, 27, 67; *Journal of the Twentieth Annual Convention of the Protestant Episcopal Church in the Diocese of Louisiana* (New Orleans, La., 1858), 17, 55; Christian Williamson, "Sacred Trust: The Voluntary Removal and Reburial of Human Remains from a Historic Cemetery in Louisiana" (Master's thesis, Louisiana State University, 2005), 40–42.

13. Brady, *George Washington's Beautiful Nelly*, 255; copy of will of Eleanor Eliza Donelson, November 22, 1848, recorded December 18, 1851, BFP 1152; E. B. Donelson to Edward G. W. Butler, July 7, 1851, BFP 650; Edward G. W. Butler to Daniel Turnbull, June 12, 1857, Folder 23e, Box 4b, JPB Family Papers. The location of Eliza Donelson's monument is unknown. She is listed as buried in the tomb of the McNairy family, Old City Cemetery, Nashville.

14. William Lingan Gaither to Edward G. W. Butler, January 9, 1853, BFP 637; memorandum of Edward G. W. Butler, "Swords," March 12, 1888, BFP 1145. In 1855, Butler lent the sword collection and the cap of his British grenadier grandfather, Captain George Fowler, which Caroline Bell had given him, to the New Orleans factor Goodrich and Hyde, to be put on display. See *New Orleans Delta*, February 2, 1855.

15. Elizabeth Fox-Genovese, *Within the Plantation Household: Black and White Women of the Old South* (Chapel Hill, N.C., 1988), 272–73.

16. "Obituary" of Caroline Butler Turnbull, attributed to Charles Gayarré, BFP 1515; *New Orleans Daily Picayune,* February 14, 1849.

17. *New Orleans Daily Picayune,* February 14, 1849; Robert C. Reinders, *End of an Era: New Orleans, 1850–1860* (New Orleans, La., 1964), 9–15, 41–42, 201; Craig A. Bauer, *A Leader among Peers: The Life and Times of Duncan Farrar Kenner* (Lafayette, La., 1993), 87ff.

18. William Barrow Floyd, *The Barrow Family of Louisiana* (Lexington, Ky., 1963), 12, plate 35; Charles Conrad to Frances Parke Butler, May 10, 1853, EGWB Papers; *New Orleans Daily Picayune,* May 13, 1853; receipt, April 25, 1855, and receipt for clothes, May 1855, Box 4a, MSS. 4026, Turnbull-Bowman-Lyons Family Papers, LSU Special Collections (hereafter cited as TBL Papers); Appointment of Administrator, 1858, Succession of William B. Turnbull, West Feliciana Parish Court Records; Jimmie Jean Bowman to David D. Plater, May 28, 2009, author's files. Rosedown is now a house museum under the Office of State Parks of the Louisiana Department of Culture, Recreation, and Tourism.

19. Statement of J. J. Seiders, June 5, 1856, Box 4a, Folder 22e, JPB Family Papers; succession of William B. Turnbull, Proces Verbal and Inventory, 1858, West Feliciana Parish, La., Records; succession of William B. Turnbull, Opposition of Caroline B; Turnbull to Inventory, 1858, West Feliciana Parish, La., Records; copy of will of Eliza B. Donelson, November 22, 1848, recorded December 18, 1851, BFP 1152; John F. Cushman, *Reports of Cases Argued and Determined in the High Court of Errors and Appeals for the State of Mississippi,* vol. 26 (Boston, Mass., 1855), 178–80; abstract of petition for Robert Carter Nicholas, 1856, St. James Parish, La., https://library.uncg.edu/slavery/details.aspx?pid=8797 (accessed May 3, 2012). The other two-thirds of the ninety-five slaves belonging to Eliza Donelson were left to Isabel Butler and to the minor daughter of Butler's half-sister Susan Vinson Nicholas, named Mary Isabella Nicholas. See the copy of the will of Eliza Donelson in BFP 1152.

20. Glenn R. Conrad, ed., *A Dictionary of Louisiana Biography,* 2 vols. (Lafayette, La., 1988), 2:852; note on Edward G. W. Butler and Frances Parke Butler and descendants, BFP 1513; handwritten list of Edward G. W. Butler descendants with emphasis on Eleanor Eliza Butler, BFP 1495; Thomas T. Williamson to Edward G. W. Butler, August 13, 1853, Twiss Collection of Butler Family Papers, MSS. 600, Historic New Orleans Collection (hereafter cited as TCBFP).

21. "Marriages . . . ," *New Orleans Daily Picayune,* May 12, 1854; Kay Thompson Brown, "Thomas Taylor Williamson" biography, http://files.usgwarchives.org/la/caddo/bios/williatt.txt (accessed April 14, 2011); Edward G. W. Butler to Lawrence Lewis Butler, March 24, 1855, BFP 643; note on Edward G. W. Butler and Frances Parke Butler and descendants, BFP 1513.

22. Rawlins Lowndes to Edward G. W. Butler, April 17, 1849, EGWB Papers; Edward G. W. Butler Jr. to Edward G. W. Butler, November 21, 1853, BFP 638; Bertram Wyatt-Brown, *Southern Honor: Ethics and Behavior in the Old South* (New York, 2007), 393; Linda Lasswell Crist and Mary Seaton Dix, eds., *The Papers of Jefferson Davis,* vol. 5, *1853–1855* (Baton Rouge, La., 1985), 405–6; Thomas H. S. Hammersley, ed., *Complete Regular Army Register of the United States, for One Hundred Years, (1779 to 1879),* 3rd ed. (Washington, D.C., 1881), 707; Edward G. W. Butler to Lawrence Lewis Butler, March 24, 1855, BFP 643; "Appointments by the President, By and with the Advice and Consent of the Senate," *New York Times,* January 28, 1856.

23. Matthias Hare to Edward G. W. Butler, December 21, 1850, BFP 633.

24. G. Miltenberger to Edward G. W. Butler, October 1, 1853, BFP 636; James S. Amory to Edward G. W. Butler, September 20, 1854, EGWB Papers; James S. Amory to Edward G. W. Butler, October 4, 1854, BFP 640; James S. Amory to Edward G. W. Butler, November 25, 1854, EGWB Papers.

25. James S. Amory to Edward G. W. Butler, February 16, 1855, BFP 641; Edward G. W. Butler to Lawrence Lewis Butler, March 24, 1855, BFP 643; James S. Amory to Edward G. W. Butler, May 22, 1855, EGWB Papers; Certificate of Proficiency in the Class of Political Economy at the University of Virginia, June 29, 1857, BFP 1128; Edward G. W. Butler to Daniel Turnbull, July 7, 1857, Box 4b, Folder 23e, JPB Family Papers.

26. Caro B. Turnbull to Daniel Turnbull, January 8, 1857, Box 4b, Folder 23a, JPB Family Papers; C. Turnbull Slave Sale to Mrs. Jennie H. Donelson, July 7, 1857, Notarial Record Book M, Folio 352, West Feliciana Parish, La., Records; Edward G. W. Butler to Daniel Turnbull, June 12, 1857, June 26, 1857, and July 7, 1857, Box 4b, Folder 23e, JPB Family Papers.

27. Edward G. W. Butler to Daniel Turnbull, October 2, 16, and 25, 1857, Box 4b, Folder 23e, JPB Family Papers; Edward G. W. Butler to Daniel Turnbull, February 24, 1858, Box 5a, Folder 4b, JPB Family Papers.

28. Succession of William B. Turnbull, Appointment of Administrator, 1858, West Feliciana Parish, La., Records; Edward G. W. Butler to Daniel Turnbull, November 15, 1858, Box 5a, Folder 256, JPB Family Papers; succession of William B. Turnbull, petition of Caroline B. Turnbull in answer to petition of Towles praying for sale, 1858, West Feliciana Parish, La., Records; inventory of William B. Turnbull property, January 29, 1859, Range C:96, Box 1.1, MSS. 4972, Turnbull (Daniel and Family) Papers, LSU Special Collections (hereafter cited as Turnbull [Daniel and Family] Papers).

29. Succession of William B. Turnbull, Family Meeting Advice, January 1859, West Feliciana Parish, La., Records; succession of William B. Turnbull, Sale to Daniel Turnbull, February 19, 1859 (recorded September 6, 1859), Notarial Record Book N, Folio 130, West Feliciana Parish, La., Records.

30. Caro Turnbull to Martha B. Turnbull, January 28, 1859, Box 5a, Folder 26b, JPB Family Papers; Edward G. W. Butler to Daniel Turnbull, January 29, 1860, Box 5b, Folder 28a, JPB Family Papers; Caro B. Turnbull to Martha H. Turnbull, February 10, 1860, Box 5b, Folder 28b, JPB Family Papers. After Daniel Turnbull's death in 1861, his widow gave additional slaves valued at $12,400 to Caro Turnbull, along with William Turnbull's personal furniture, holding Caro accountable to her sons and to William Turnbull's estate "if anything happens to the . . . Negroes." See "An Understanding of Caro B. Turnbull and Martha B. Turnbull and Martha B. Turnbull," n.d., Range C:115, Box 4c, TBL Papers.

31. Isabel B. Williamson to Edward G. W. Butler, September 9, 1855, EGWB Papers; Isabel B. Williamson to Edward G. W. Butler, September 22, 1858, BFP 653; Caro B. Turnbull to Martha B. Turnbull, January 17, 1859, Box 5a, Folder 26b, JPB Family Papers; Frances Parke Butler to Edward G. W. Butler, February 28, 1859, EGWB Papers.

32. Edward G. W. Butler to Charles Gayarré, November 20, 1858, and January 25, 1858, Box 11, Letter Book 401, Items 123 and 124, MSS. 156, Charles Gayarré Collection, LSU Special Collections (hereafter cited as Gayarré Collection).

33. Alexander Duncan to Edward G. W. Butler, n.d., EGWB Papers; Legation of the United States of America at London for Lawrence Lewis Butler, July 18, 1859, BFP 1130; Lawrence Lewis Butler to Edward G. W. Butler and Frances Parke Butler, August 16, 1859, EGWB Papers.

34. George Peter Alexander Healy to Edward G. W. Butler, October 20, 1860, Microfilm Reel 2814, Frames 1274–1276, George Alexander Healy Letters, 1860–1861, Archives of American Art, Smithsonian Institution, Washington, D.C.

8. "I AM NO SUBMISSIONIST"

1. John M. Sacher, *A Perfect War of Politics: Parties, Politicians, and Democracy in Louisiana, 1824–1861* (Baton Rouge, La., 2003), 50–52, 97ff., 150f.; *Plaquemine (La.) Southern Sentinel*, August 17, 1848, and September 17, 1848.

2. Zachary Taylor to Eleanor Parke Lewis, n.d. (from Baton Rouge), and April 12, 1849 (from Washington, D.C.), Mount Vernon Ladies' Association Library (hereafter cited as MVLAL); Zachary Taylor to Edward G. W. Butler, January 22, 1849, "Extracts from Genl. Taylor Letters," Folder 897, MSS. 102, Butler Family Papers, Historic New Orleans Collection (hereafter cited as BFP).

3. Rawlins Lowndes to Edward G. W. Butler, April 17, 1849, MSS. 805, Edward G. W. Butler Papers, 1821–1888, Duke University Rare Book, Manuscript, and Special Collections Library (hereafter cited as EGWB Papers). For a valuable review of the abolition movement in the nineteenth century, see David Brion Davis, *The Problem of Slavery in the Age of Emancipation* (New York, 2014).

4. Charles Radziminski to Edward G. W. Butler, July 4, 1850, and October 3, 1850, BFP 631 and 632; James S. Amory to Edward G. W. Butler, May 22, 1855, EGWB Papers.

5. Edward G. W. Butler to Charles Gayarré, January 17, 1849; January 30, 1849; June 5, 1853; and November 10, 1853—all in Box 11, Letter Book 401, Folders 61–81, MSS. 156, Charles Gayarré Collection, LSU Special Collections (hereafter cited as Gayarré Collection). See also Caroline Bell to Edward G. W. Butler, May 13, 1825, BFP 234.

6. Edward G. W. Butler to Charles Gayarré, April 25, 1853, Box 11, Letter Book 401, Item 73; and July 16, 1853, Box 11, Letter Book 401, Item 75—all in Gayarré Collection. For the emancipation movement in Britain, of which the Butlers were well cognizant, see Davis, *The Problem of Slavery in the Age of Emancipation*, chapters 10 and 11.

7. Lea VanderVelde, *Mrs. Dred Scott: A Life on Slavery's Frontier* (New York, 2009), 291.

8. Mark R. Cheathem, *Old Hickory's Nephew: The Political and Private Struggles of Andrew Jackson Donelson* (Baton Rouge, La., 2007), 260–61, 288; Edward G. W. Butler to J.D.B. DeBow, March 13, 1857, Box 11, Letter Book 401, Item 121, Gayarré Collection; Sacher, *A Perfect War*, 266.

9. Mark R. Cheathem, *Andrew Jackson, Southerner* (Baton Rouge, La., 2013), 141; Edward G. W. Butler to Martin Van Buren, September 20, 1855, Series 2, Box 59, Reel 33, MSS 43828, Martin Van Buren Papers, Library of Congress; A. L. Diket, *Senator John Slidell and the Community He Represented in Washington, 1853–1861* (Washington, D.C., 1982), 10–11, 68–69, 99; John Slidell to Edward G. W. Butler, January 27, 1854, EGWB Papers; list of land assessed in Iberville Parish, 1856, Record Group 12, John Slidell Papers, Louisiana Historical Center, Louisiana State Museum; Edward G. W. Butler to John Slidell, May 18, 1857 (copy), BFP 648; Sacher, *A Perfect War*, 221f.,

253–54; clipping, "Letter from the Interior," by Hampden, October 7, 1856, *New Orleans Daily Picayune*, BFP 1737.

10. James Buchanan to Edward G. W. Butler, September 15, 1856, and August 7, 1857, EGWB Papers; Diket, *Senator John Slidell.*, 99, 220–21, 224; Sacher, *A Perfect War*, 268f., 284–87; John Slidell to Edward G. W. Butler, August 25, 1860, and November 1, 1860, EGWB Papers.

11. *Plaquemine (La.) Gazette and Sentinel*, November 10, 1860 (on microfilm, LSU Special Collections).

12. Ibid.

13. John Slidell quoted in Diket, *Senator John Slidell*, 229–30; Charles P. Roland, *Louisiana Sugar Plantations during the Civil War* (Baton Rouge, La., 1997), 33–36; *Plaquemine (La.) Gazette and Sentinel*, December 1, 8, and 29, 1860.

14. Sacher, *A Perfect War*, 390; Christopher G. Peña, *Scarred by War: Civil War in Southeast Louisiana* (Bloomington, Ind., 2004), 30–31.

15. *Plaquemine (La.) Gazette and Sentinel*, December 22, 1860; Ralph Wooster, "The Louisiana Secession Convention," *Louisiana Historical Quarterly* 34 (April 1951): 129; Judy Riffel and Arthur Perkins, eds., *Iberville Parish History* (Baton Rouge, La., 1985), 25, 34, 35, 85, 142. Bradburn became editor and publisher of the *Plaquemine (La.) Southern Sentinel* in 1847. The *Southern Sentinel* merged with Iberville Parish's oldest newspaper, the *Iberville (La.) Gazette*, in 1858, with Bradburn in partnership first with Joseph H. Balch, who was succeeded by the *Gazette*'s former publisher, Peter Elmore Jennings. In 1860, Bradburn was forty-four years old and married to a twenty-seven-year-old native of Ireland, with three boys and two girls and an Irish-born eleven-year-old apprentice in his household. See Riffel and Perkins, eds., *Iberville Parish History*, 124; 1860 U.S. Census, Town of Plaquemine, Iberville Parish, La., http://bradburnhistory.com:8082/BH_WS_Archives/1860-0040.jpg (accessed November 24, 2010).

16. Sacher, *A Perfect War*, 291–93; Peña, *Scarred by War*, 30; Charles B. Dew, "Who Won the Secession Election in Louisiana?" *Journal of Southern History* 36 (February 1970): 21.

17. "Letter from Col. Butler," *Plaquemine (La.) Gazette and Sentinel*, December 27, 1860, BFP 1740.

18. *Plaquemine (La.) Gazette and Sentinel*, January 5, 1861.

19. Charles B. Dew, "The Long Lost Returns: The Candidates and Their Totals in Louisiana's Secession Election," *Louisiana History* 10 (1969): 358, 362; Dew, "Who Won the Secession Election in Louisiana?" 30–32. The runner-up, Schlatre (1822–83), owned "Homestead Plantation" on Bayou Jacob and was elected captain of Iberville's first military company, organized on November 18, 1860. Riffel and Perkins, eds., *Iberville Parish History*, 73, 85. Talbot's opponent, Breaux, born in Bayou Goula in 1838, later became a distinguished educator and an associate justice, then chief justice of the Louisiana Supreme Court. Glenn R. Conrad, ed., *A Dictionary of Louisiana Biography*, 2 vols. (Lafayette, La., 1988), 1:186.

20. *Plaquemine (La.) Gazette and Sentinel*, January 12, 1861.

21. James L. Roark, *Masters without Slaves: Southern Planters in the Civil War and Reconstruction* (New York, 1977), 2–25; Sean Wilentz, "Why Did Southerners Secede?," in *In the Cause of Liberty: How the Civil War Redefined American Ideals*, ed. William J. Cooper Jr. and John M. McCardell Jr. (Baton Rouge, La., 2009), 28, 30, 33; "Journal of State Convention" (in facsimile); or "Official Journal

of the Proceedings of the Convention of the State of Louisiana" (New Orleans, La., 1861), in *Louisiana History* 2 (winter 1961): 14, 15, 18, 36, 64, 75–76; Charles P. Roland, "Louisiana and Secession," *Louisiana History* 19 (1978): 396; Roland, *Louisiana Sugar Plantations,* 21–22; Ralph A. Wooster, *The Secession Conventions of the South* (Princeton, N.J., 1962), 104f.; "A Ward of Old Hickory, Reminiscences of Gen. E.G.W. Butler. Something about His Family," *New York Times,* August 10, 1883, from *St. Louis Republican,* August 7, 1883. There is no mention of an offer from Davis in Lynda Lasswell Crist and Mary Seaton Dix, eds., *The Papers of Jefferson Davis, 1861,* vol. 7, *1861* (Baton Rouge, La., 1992), nor in Dunbar Rowland, coll. and ed., *Jefferson Davis, Constitutionalist: His Letters, Papers and Speeches,* vols. 1–10 (Jackson, Miss., 1923).

22. U.S. War Department, *The War of the Rebellion: A Compilation of the Official Records of the Union and Confederate Armies,* 70 vols. in 4 series (Washington, D.C., 1880–1901; republished, Harrisburg, Pa.: National Historical Society, 1971; reprint, Historical Times, 1985), series 1, vol. 1, 497.

23. Roland, *Louisiana Sugar Plantations,* 24–25 (citing "Historical Records Survey, Transcriptions of Parish Records of Louisiana," Number 24, Iberville Parish [Plaquemine], Series I, Police Jury Minutes [Baton Rouge, April, 1940–March, 1942], April 9, 1861); Iberville Parish Police Jury Records, June 4, 1861, 273–74, Reel 232, MSS. 2984, W.P.A. Collection Historical Records Survey Transcriptions of Louisiana Police Jury Records, LSU Special Collections; Roark, *Masters without Slaves,* 74–75.

24. Charles P. Roland, with John David Smith, ed., *History Teaches Us to Hope: Reflections on the Civil War and Southern History* (Lexington, Ky., 2007), 104ff., 108–10, 112–15; Roland, "Louisiana and Secession," 391–92.

9. "SOIL & LIBERTIES HAVE BEEN INVADED"

1. Lynda Lasswell Crist and Mary Seaton Dix, eds., *The Papers of Jefferson Davis,* vol. 7, *1861* (Baton Rouge, La., 1992), 195; Charles P. Roland, *Louisiana Sugar Plantations during the Civil War* (Baton Rouge, La., 1997), 24; P. A. Champomier, *Statement of the Sugar Crop Made in Louisiana in 1861–62* (New Orleans, La., 1862), vi–vii; "Mustered Out," *St. Louis Post-Dispatch,* September 6, 1888, cutout, Folder 1758, MSS. 102, Butler Family Papers, Historic New Orleans Collection (hereafter cited as BFP); John Slidell to Edward G. W. Butler, May 30, 1861, MSS. 805, Edward George Washington Butler Papers, 1821–1888, Duke University Rare Book, Manuscript, and Special Collections Library (hereafter cited as EGWB Papers); James Philson to Edward G. W. Butler, July 19, 1861, #1112, Allyn K. Ford Collection, Minnesota Historical Society (on microfilm); Michael Moore to Isabel B. Williamson, November 3, 1861, and Isabel B. Williamson to Lawrence Lewis Butler, November 7, 1861, both in EGWB Papers.

2. John Slidell to Edward G. W. Butler, June 15, 1861, EGWB Papers; Arthur W. Bergeron Jr., *Guide to Louisiana Confederate Military Units, 1861–1865* (Baton Rouge, La., 1989), 98–99; Confederate States of America Appointment, July 19, 1861, BFP 1132; Extract from Special Orders 140, September 1, 1861, BFP 1134; Military Appointment, Lawrence Lewis Butler, October 28, 1861, BFP 1135. See, however, Andrew B. Booth, comp., *Records of Louisiana Confederate Soldiers and Louisiana Confederate Commands,* 3 vols. (New Orleans, La., 1920), 2:204.

3. Edward G. W. Butler Jr. to Frances Parke Butler, September 27, 1861, BFP 662; M. A. Knox to Edward G. W. Butler, October 28, 1861, BFP 665. Slaves belonging to Susan Nicholas may have been at hire on Albemarle, facing Bayou Lafourche. In 1861, the plantation was owned by Robert C. Martin. M. A. Knox to Edward G. W. Butler, October 28, 1861, BFP 665. For a criticism of Polk's occupation of Kentucky, see Bryan S. Bush, "Confederate General Leonidas Polk and the Collapse of the Confederate Command Structure in the Western Theater," www.bryansbush.com (accessed January 7, 2015).

4. U.S. War Department, *The War of the Rebellion: A Compilation of the Official Records of the Union and Confederate Armies,* 70 vols. in 4 series (Washington, D.C., 1880–1901; republished, Harrisburg, Pa.: National Historical Society, 1971; reprint, Historical Times, 1985), series 1, vol. 3, 306–8, 353–55 (hereafter cited as *OR*).

5. John H. Brinton, *Personal Memoirs of John H. Brinton, Civil War Surgeon, 1861–1865* (New York, 1914; reprint, Carbondale, Ill., 1996), 80–81.

6. Leonidas Polk to Edward G. W. Butler, November 9, 1861 (copy), BFP 901; Mrs. Eugene McLean, "A Northern Woman in the Confederacy," *Harper's Magazine* (February 1914), 450–51, copy at BFP 1709; Lawrence Lewis Butler to Mrs. Moore & Other Ladies, n.d., BFP 909. Polk was unaware of Dr. Brinton's assistance to Major Butler. See also R. E. Lee to Edward G. W. Butler, November 7, 1862 (extract), BFP 901; William David Butler, John Cromwell Butler, and Joseph Marion Butler, *The Butler Family in America* (St. Louis, Mo., n.d.), 294.

7. *OR,* ser. I, vol. 3, 306–10; Clarissa to Edward G. W. Butler, November 21, 1861, BFP 668. On coffee substitutes during wartime, see Herbert C. Covey and Dwight Eisnach, *What the Slaves Ate: Recollections of African American Foods and Foodways from the Slave Narratives* (Santa Barbara, Calif., 2009), 182. Clarissa, a rare example of a literate Butler slave, is evidence that the Butlers taught some of their servants to read and write.

8. Isabel B. Williamson to Lawrence Lewis Butler, November 7, 1861, and Frances Parke Butler to Lawrence Lewis Butler, December 19, 1861, EGWB Papers.

9. Report of Col. Robert H. Barrow to Col. R. M. Russell, April 30, 1862, *OR,* ser. 1, vol. 10, part 1, 420–22; Leonidas Polk to Hon. L. R. Walker, *OR,* ser. 1, vol. 3, 618; Booth, comp., *Records of Louisiana Confederate Soldiers,* 3:1112; Isabel B. Williamson to Lawrence Lewis Butler, November 7, 1861, EGWB Papers; J. P. Benjamin to Leonidas Polk, March 31, 1862, *OR,* ser. 1, vol. 10, part 1, 416–18; S. B. Maxey to Major Lawrence Lewis Butler, April 23, 1862, *OR,* ser. 1, vol. 10, part 2, 434–35; Lawrence Lewis Butler to Major General Cheatham and Major General Withers, December 26, 1862, *OR,* ser. 1, vol. 20, part 2, 462; Polk's Report, *OR,* ser. 1, vol. 20, part 1, 692; Order of Lieutenant General E. Kirby Smith, April 30, 1863, and December 10, 1863, *OR,* ser. 1, vol. 22, part 2, 833 and 1094; A. G. Dickinson to E. P. Turner, October 12, 1863, *OR,* ser. 1, vol. 53, Supplement, 899; S. S. Anderson to George Williamson, February 28, 1864, *OR,* ser. 2, vol. 6, 997; George Williamson to S. B. Maxey, April 28, 1864, General Orders No. 1, *OR,* ser. 1, vol. 34, part 1, 845; General Orders No. 43, June 13, 1864, *OR,* ser. 1, vol. 34, part 4, 668–69.

10. Report of Brigadier-General Gideon Pillow, October 8, 1863, *OR,* ser. 4, vol. 2, 859–63; Robert L. Kerby, *Kirby Smith's Confederacy: The Trans-Mississippi South, 1863–1865* (New York, 1972), 264–66, 390–91.

11. Roland, *Louisiana Sugar Plantations,* 43–47, 75–78; James L. Roark, *Masters without Slaves:*

Southern Planters in the Civil War and Reconstruction (New York, 1977), 36–37; Elise Bragg to Braxton Bragg, April 20, 1862, Box 3H81, Braxton Bragg Papers, Dolph Briscoe Center for American History, University of Texas at Austin (hereafter cited as Braxton Bragg Papers); Frances Parke Butler to Lawrence Lewis Butler, December 17, 1861, EGWB Papers; Edward G. W. Butler to Edward J. Gay, June 6, 1864, Box 46, Folder 450, MSS. 1295, Gay (Edward J. and Family) Papers, LSU Special Collections (hereafter cited as Gay Papers). On John Augustine Washington III and Anna Fitzhugh, see Charles Moore, *The Family Life of George Washington* (Boston, Mass., 1926), 180, 204; John W. Wayland, *The Washingtons and Their Homes* (1944; facsimile reprint, Berryville, Va., 1973), 299, 303. For a discussion of mourning practices in the Civil War South, see Drew Gilpin Faust, *Mothers of Invention: Women of the Slaveholding South in the American Civil War* (Chapel Hill, N.C., 1996), 188–89.

12. Donald S. Frazier, *Fire in the Cane Field: The Federal Invasion of Louisiana and Texas, January 1861–January 1863* (Buffalo Gap, Tex., 2009), 50ff., 55ff., 60.

13. Ibid., 67; Elise Bragg to Braxton Bragg, May 9, 1862, Box 3H81, Braxton Bragg Papers.

14. Frazier, *Fire in the Cane Field*, 76–77, 139ff.; Christopher G. Peña, *Scarred by War: Civil War in Southeast Louisiana* (Bloomington, Ind., 2004), 114–15.

15. Peña, *Scarred by War*, 168–88, 191, 192–93.

16. Roland, *Louisiana Sugar Plantations*, 92–94; Robert F. Pace, "'It Was Bedlam Let Loose': The Louisiana Sugar Country and the Civil War," *Louisiana History* 39 (fall 1998): 397; Frazier, *Fire in the Cane Field*, 181–83.

17. Frazier, *Fire in the Cane Field*, 222–23; G. Weitzel to Edward G. W. Butler, December 5, 1862, BFP 671.

18. On the problems that citizens along Bayou Lafourche and along the Mississippi River encountered upon invasion by Union forces between 1862 and 1864, see John William DeForest, *A Volunteer's Adventures: A Union Captain's Record of the Civil War* (New Haven, 1946), 73ff.; Kathleen Langdon-Haven McInerney, *Dear Nell: The True Story of the Haven Sisters* (N.p., 2009), 64–65, 76–77; and Henry T. Johns, *Life with the Forty-Ninth Massachusetts Volunteers* (Pittsfield, Mass., 1864), 335. On the evolving Union Army policies in 1862 and 1863 and during the entire war, see Mark Grimsley, *The Hard Hand of War: Union Military Policy toward Southern Civilians, 1861–1865* (Cambridge, U.K., 1995), 92, passim.

19. Peña, *Scarred by War*, 196–97; Roland, *Louisiana Sugar Plantations*, 50ff., 61ff., 66–69; Frank M. Flinn, *Campaigning with Banks in Louisiana in '63 and '64, and with Sheridan in the Shenandoah Valley in '64 and '65* (Lynn, Mass., 1887), 15. On wartime Confederate policies outside the Union lines in Louisiana, see Kerby, *Kirby Smith's Confederacy*, 23–24.

20. *OR*, ser. 1, vol. 15, 191f.; Peña, *Scarred by War*, 396f.; Stephen S. Michot, "'War Is Still Raging in This Part of the Country': Oath-Taking, Conscription, and Guerrilla War in Louisiana's Lafourche Region," *Louisiana History* 38 (spring 1997): 157–58, 164–69; Frazier, *Fire in the Cane Field*, 305ff., 308–9.

21. *OR*, ser. I, vol. 26, part 1, 217; Kerby, *Kirby Smith's Confederacy*, 106–7, 112–13, 118–20.

22. *OR*, ser. 1, vol. 34, part 2, 277, 331–32, 368–69; Richard C. Shaw to Geo. W. Capt., A.A.A.G., May 5, 1864, and June 29, 1864, Entry 1033, Letters Sent, National Archives Records Administration Record Group 393 (hereafter cited as NARA Record Group 393): Records of the United States Army

Continental Commands, Part IV, Military Installations, 1821–1881, Entry 1033, Vol. 318, Letters Sent, February 1864–June 1865, Plaquemine, Louisiana, 38, 42; J. H. Sypher to Major George B., A. A. General, August 29, 1864, Entry 1033, NARA Record Group 393, Vol. 318, Letters Sent February 1864–June 1865, Plaquemine, Louisiana, 66–67.

23. Roland, *Louisiana Sugar Plantations*, 82–83.

24. Peña, *Scarred by War*, 409–18, passim; Michot, "'War Is Still Raging,'" 173–74.

25. Alexander Duncan to Edward G. W. Butler, December 22, 1863, EGWB Papers. On the problems of irregular mail communication, see Elise Bragg to Braxton Bragg, April 20, 1862, Box 3H81, Braxton Bragg Papers; Faust, *Mothers of Invention*, 116–17.

26. Ellen M. Pugh to Alex. F. Pugh, January 25, February 2, and February 18, 1863, Alexander Franklin Pugh Papers, Box 2F354, Pugh Family Papers, 1807–1907, Briscoe Center for American History, University of Texas at Austin.

27. Grimsley, *Hard Hand of War*, 75, 78, 139–40; Frazier, *Fire in the Cane Field*, 228–29; Pace, "'It Was Bedlam,'" 399; Roland, *Louisiana Sugar Plantations*, 104–6; John C. Rodrigue, *Reconstruction in the Cane Fields: From Slavery to Free Labor in Louisiana's Sugar Parishes, 1862–1880* (Baton Rouge, La., 2001), 35, 37–38, 40–42; Moon-Ho Jung, *Coolies and Cane: Race, Labor, and Sugar in the Age of Emancipation* (Baltimore, Md., 2006), 57f.

28. U.S. Sequestration Commission Order, February 5, 1863, Box 45, Folder 433, Gay Papers; Peña, *Scarred by War*, 401; Roland, *Louisiana Sugar Plantations*, 113ff., 118; Rodrigue, *Reconstruction in the Cane Fields*, 44–45, 48ff.; John C. Rodrigue, "The Freedmen's Bureau and Wage Labor in the Louisiana Sugar Region," in *The Freedmen's Bureau and Reconstruction: Reconsiderations*, ed. Paul A. Cimbala and Randall M. Miller (New York, 1999), 196–98; *De Bow's Review*, September 1867, N.S., 239–40. For the effects on morale and on the institution of slavery in the Confederacy in Louisiana following the conscription of whites and then of slaves, see Kerby, *Kirby Smith's Confederacy*, 256–58, 433–34.

29. Rodrigue, *Reconstruction in the Cane Fields*, 60; accounts of workers on Dunboyne, 1865, BFP1640. For Confederate trade across the lines of combatants, see Kerby, *Kerby Smith's Confederacy*, 378ff.; Pace, "'It Was Bedlam,'" 401–2.

30. Itemized Accounts, 1833–1870, BFP 1634.

31. Peña, *Scarred by War*, 416–17.

32. Michot, "'War Is Still Raging,'" 169–71; Peña, *Scarred by War*, 431; *OR*, ser. 1, vol. 41, 219; W. O. Fiske to R. C. Shaw, August 19, 1864, NARA Record Group 393, Entry 1038, Letters Received 1864–1865, Plaquemine, La.

33. Kerby, *Kirby Smith's Confederacy*, 401–2; Michot, "'War Is Still Raging,'" 176f.; Peña, *Scarred by War*, 444–46, 452–53; *OR*, ser. 1, vol. 48, part 1, 62, 602, 619, 626–27; Charles H. Parkhurst, *Personal Narratives of the Battles of the Rebellion No. 7: Incidents of Cavalry Service in Louisiana* (Providence, R.I., 1879), 18–19.

34. Peña, *Scarred by War*, 454f.

35. Mary Susan Gay (Butler) Diary, 1863–1864, Subgroup 1, Gay Family (1814–1979), Series V, Box 10, Folder 5, MSS. 4872, Gay-Butler-Plater Family Papers, LSU Special Collections (reference has been made to a typed and annotated copy of the Mary Susan Gay Diary by Ormonde Plater [n.d.]); from Gay Papers: Declaration of Domicile, Box 38, Folder 340; M. Martin to Edward J. Gay,

December 16, 1860, Box 40, Folder 373; and William T. Gay to Edward J. Gay, January 12, 1861, Box 40, Folder 377; Document of Cooperation and Order of N. P. Banks, August 20 and September 20, 1864, Box 47, Folder 462. See also Roland, *Louisiana Sugar Plantations*, 135 (citing Frank H. Mason, *The Forty-Second Ohio Infantry: A History of the Organization and Service of That Regiment in the War of the Rebellion* [Cleveland, Ohio, 1876], 247, which described the entertainment of patriotic music provided to the Union troops in Plaquemine; girls wept when his unit left town.)

36. McInerney, *Dear Nell*, 68–69; Edward G. W. Butler to Edward J. Gay, June 6, 1864, Box 46, Folder 450, Gay Papers; anonymous to Comdg. Officer at Donaldsonville, La., December 2, 1864, NARA Record Group 393, Entry 1033, Vol. 318, Letters Sent February 1864–June 1865, Plaquemine, La., 87; Col. J. H. Sypher to Mr. J. A., Local Special Agent, March 13, 1865, NARA Record Group 393, Entry 1033, Vol. 318, Letters Sent February 1864–June 1865, Plaquemine, La., 139. For the fate of noncombatants' property from treatment by William T. Sherman and similar commanders late in the Civil War, see Grimsley, *Hard Hand of War*, 116.

37. *OR*, ser. 1, vol. 48, part 1, 151, 194, 240–41. See also Faust, *Mothers of Invention*, 60.

38. Alexander Duncan to Edward G. W. Butler, December 18, 1851, March 7, (1858?), and March 27, ___, all at EGWB Papers; A. Miltenberger to Lawrence Lewis Butler, September 4, 1869, BFP 679; Alexander Duncan to Edward G. W. Butler, March 21, 1864, May 4, 1865, undated (but apparently May–June 1865), and June 19, 1865, all at EGWB Papers.

10. HARDSHIPS AND SORROWS

1. U.S. War Department, *The War of the Rebellion: A Compilation of the Official Records of the Union and Confederate Armies*, 70 vols. in 4 series (Washington, D.C., 1880–1901; republished, Harrisburg, Pa.: National Historical Society, 1971; reprint, Historical Times, 1985), ser. 1, vol. 3, 348–49 (hereafter cited as *OR*); *OR*, ser. 1, vol. 49, part 2, 641–42.

2. J. T. Haskell to Agent of Bureau of R. F. and A. L., June 9, 1866, Unregistered Letters Received January 1865–June 1868, "Records of the Assistant Subassistant Commissioner in Iberville and West Baton Rouge Parishes and Predecessor," in *Records of the Freedmen's Hospital and the New Orleans Area Field Offices of the Bureau of Refugees, Freemen, and Abandoned Lands 1865–1869*, Record Group 105, National Archives (on microfilm), Roll 8, the Historic New Orleans Collection and the National Archives (hereafter cited as Iberville Freedmen's Bureau); F. A. Osbourn to W. H. Stirling, April 10, 1867, Letters Sent April 11, 1867–July 13, 1867, #425, Iberville Freedmen's Bureau; "Circular Letter," Police Jury of Iberville Parish, April 16, 1867, Iberville Freedmen's Bureau; F. A. Osbourn to W. H. Stirling, April 29, 1867, Iberville Freedmen's Bureau; Geo. O. Forest to F. A. Osbourn, May 11, 1867, Unregistered Letters Received January 1865–June 1868, Iberville Freedmen's Bureau; L. D. Parker to F. A. Osbourn, June 14, 1867, #243, Iberville Freedmen's Bureau; Lucius H. Warren to C. E. Merrill, March 7, 1868, #273, Iberville Freedmen's Bureau.

3. Kathleen Langdon-Haven McInerney, *Dear Nell: The True Story of the Haven Sisters* (N.p., 2009), 101; *DeBow's Review*, N.S., 4 (September 1867), 237–38; Robert F. Pace, "'It Was Bedlam Let Loose': The Louisiana Sugar Country and the Civil War," *Louisiana History* 39 (fall 1998): 391–403; John C. Rodrigue, *Reconstruction in the Cane Fields: From Slavery to Free Labor in Louisiana's Sugar Parishes, 1862–1880* (Baton Rouge, La., 2001), 59–60.

4. For a still important study of the overall challenges to the relationships between white planters and their ex-slaves, see James L. Roark, *Masters without Slaves: Southern Planters in the Civil War and Reconstruction* (New York, 1977), particularly 95–96, 100–101, 106–7, 141–42, 190–92, 199–201. There are several recent, useful studies of the Civil War and Reconstruction in the Sugar Belt: John C. Rodrigue: "The Freedmen's Bureau and Wage Labor in the Louisiana Sugar Region," in *The Freemen's Bureau and Reconstruction: Reconsiderations*, ed. Paul A. Cimbala and Randall M. Miller (New York, 1999), 195–218; John C. Rodrigue, "Labor Militancy and Black Grassroots: Political Mobilization in the Louisiana Sugar Region, 1865–1868," in *The Louisiana Purchase Bicentennial Series in Louisiana History*, vol. 6, *Reconstructing Louisiana*, ed. Lawrence N. Powell (Lafayette, La., 2001), 481–502; John C. Rodrigue, *Reconstruction in the Cane Field*, notably 52–54, 69ff., 72–73, 75–77, 83–85, 88f.; and Matthew Pratt Guterl, *American Mediterranean: Southern Slaveholders in the Age of Emancipation* (Cambridge, Mass., 2008), 128–30. See also the unpublished undergraduate senior thesis by Princeton University student Sarah Labouisse, "Regaining Ground: Edward J. Gay's Experiences as a Sugar Planter from 1865 to 1875" (Senior thesis, Princeton University, 1985).

5. Civil Suit 1798 (1879), 5th Judicial District Court, Iberville Parish, La., Records.

6. Joanne Ryan, *Greenfield-Allemania Sugarhouse (16IV119): Phase II and III Archaeological Investigations Iberville Parish, Louisiana* (Baton Rouge, La., 2009), 116, 120–23; L. Bouchereau, *Statement of the Sugar and Rice Crops Made in Louisiana in 1868–69* (New Orleans, La., 1869), 5, passim.

7. Itemized Accounts, Dunboyne Plantation Workers, Folder 1634, MSS. 102, Butler Family Papers, Historic New Orleans Collection (hereafter cited as BFP); Account Book for Former Slaves on Dunboyne Plantation, BFP 1640; Record Book of Edward G. W. Butler, 1868–1871, BFP 1641. On the Ricard family, see Judy Riffel and Arthur Perkins, eds., *Iberville Parish History* (Baton Rouge, Louisiana, 1985), 67; Victor Patin, "Cyprian Ricard and Creole-African Lineage in Louisiana," http://boards.ancestry.com (accessed November 3, 2012, and January 7, 2015).

8. Account Book for Former Slaves on Dunboyne Plantation, BFP 1640.

9. Monthly Report, April 30, 1866, April 30, 1867, and October 31, 1868, Monthly Inspection Reports, May 1866–December 1868, Roll 9, RG 105, Iberville Freedmen's Bureau; Saturday, November 14th 1868, Journals of Business August 1867–December 1868, #431, Iberville Freedmen's Bureau. See also: J. Carlyle Sitterson, *Sugar Country: The Cane Sugar Industry in the South, 1753–1950* (Lexington, Ky., 1953), 243–45.

10. Nelson Kenyon to T. W. Conway, August 29, 1865, Unregistered Letters Received, January 1865–June 1868, Iberville Freedmen's Bureau, Roll 8, R.G. 105; Circular No. 24, October 30, 1865, Registered Letters Received, July–December 1868, Iberville Freedmen's Bureau, Roll 8, R.G. 105.

11. F. A. Osbourn to W. H. Stirling, January 25, 1867, Unregistered Letters Received January 1865–June 1868, Iberville Freedmen's Bureau, Roll 8, R.G. 105; Special Orders No. 66, F. A. Osbourn, April 4, 1867, Special Orders Received April 1866–April 1867, Iberville Freedmen's Bureau, Roll 8, R.G. 105; F. A. Osbourn to W. H. Stirling, April 10, 1867, Letters Sent April 1, 1867–July 13, 1867, #425, Iberville Freedmen's Bureau, Roll 8, R.G. 105.

12. Circular Letter, F. A. Osbourn, May 30, 1867, Letters Sent #425, Iberville Freedmen's Bureau, Roll 8, R.G. 105.

13. F. A. Osbourn to J. M. Lee, December 22, 1867, Letters Sent #427, "Iberville Freedmen's Bureau," Roll 8, R.G. 105.

14. F. A. Osbourn to W. H. Webster, October 26, 1867, Letters Sent #426, Iberville Freedmen's

Bureau, Roll 8, R.G. 105; Charles E. Merrill to J. M. Lee, January 20, 1868, Letters Sent # 427, Iberville Freedmen's Bureau, Roll 8, R.G. 105; Charles E. Merrill to Lucius H. Warren, February 20, 1868, Iberville Freedmen's Bureau, Roll 8, R.G. 105.

15. E.G.W. Butler, August 28, 1867, and December 23, 1867, Registers of Letters Received, July 1867–April 1868 and July 1868–December 1868, #116–117, Iberville Freedmen's Bureau, Roll 8, R.G. 105; "Saturday, December 28th 1867," Journals of Business, August 1867–December 1868, # 54, Iberville Freedmen's Bureau, Roll 9, R.G. 105; F. A. Osbourn to Edward G. W. Butler, December 28, 1867, Letters Sent, #427, Iberville Freedmen's Bureau, Roll 8, R.G. 105; General Winfield Scott Hancock to Edward G. W. Butler, December 30, 1867, #678, Allyn K. Ford Collection, Minnesota Historical Society, on microfilm.

16. Edward G. W. Butler, January 5, 1868, and January 31, 1868, Registers of Letters Received, July 1867–April 1868 and December 1868, # 118–121, Iberville Freedmen's Bureau, Roll 8, R.G. 105; Charles E. Merrill to G. Hebert Justice of the Peace, January 23, 1868, Letters Sent December 24, 1867–June 30, 1868, #427, Iberville Freedmen's Bureau, Roll 8, R.G. 105. See also Lucius H. Warren to C. E. Merrill, February 10, 1868, Unregistered Letters Received January 1865–June 1868, #201, Iberville Freedmen's Bureau, Roll 8, R.G. 105.

17. Rodrigue, "Labor Militancy and Black Grassroots," 486–87, 491ff.; Alexander Duncan to Edward G. W. Butler, n.d., MSS. 805, Edward George Washington Butler Papers, 1821–1888, Duke University Rare Book, Manuscript, and Special Collections Library (hereafter cited as EGWB Papers); Mark R. Cheathem, *Old Hickory's Nephew: The Political and Private Struggles of Andrew Jackson Donelson* (Baton Rouge, La., 2007), 327; McInerney, *Dear Nell,* 93; Elizabeth Fox-Genovese, *Within the Plantation Household: Black and White Women of the Old South* (Chapel Hill, N.C., 1988), 396. The broad geographic nature of the postwar labor problems, and the search for labor alternatives, are thoroughly treated in Guterl, *American Mediterranean.*

18. James Buchanan to Edward G. W. Butler, April 29, 1867; John Slidell to Edward G. W. Butler, December 21, 1867; and Robert E. Lee to Edward G. W. Butler, January 25, 1867—all in EGWB Papers; Robert E. Lee to Edward G. W. Butler, October 11, 1867, MSS. GLC 05275, Gilder Lehman Institute of American History.

19. Note on Edward G. W. Butler and Frances Parke Butler and Descendants, c. 1881, BFP 1513; Isabel B. Williamson to Frances Parke Butler, October 29, 1865, BFP 672; obituary of Eleanor Isabel Butler, June 11, 1866, BFP 1767. See also Drew Gilpin Faust, *Mothers of Invention: Women of the Slaveholding South in the American Civil War* (Chapel Hill, N.C., 1996), 77–78; McInerney, *Dear Nell,* 104–5, 107.

20. Sue G. Butler to John H. Gay Jr., October 23, 1870, Box 65, Folder 697, MSS. 1295, Gay (Edward J. and Family) Papers, LSU Special Collections (hereafter cited as Gay Papers); Lawrence L. Butler to Edward J. Gay. July 8, 1875, Box 90, Folder 1038, Gay Papers.

21. M. D. Winter to Martha B. Turnbull, 187_, Box 1 MSS. 4026, Turnbull-Bowman-Lyons Family Papers, LSU Special Collections (hereafter cited as TBL Family Papers).

22. Petition of Caroline B. Turnbull, May 24, 1866, May 24, 1866, Box 4c, TBL Family Papers; Daniel Turnbull Succession, No. 132, 5th Judicial District Court, Iberville Parish, La., Records. For the record of Charles M. Conrad in the Congress of the Confederate States of America, see, for example, F. D. Conrad to Edward Sparrow, C. M. Conrad, and D. F. Kenner, October 3, 1863, *OR,*

ser. 4, vol. 2, 854. For the CSA military record of Conrad's sons, Charles A. and Lewis Conrad, see Andrew B. Booth, comp., *Records of Louisiana Confederate Soldiers and Louisiana Confederate Commands,* 3 vols. (New Orleans, La., 1920), 2:417, 418; Janet B. Hewitt, ed., *Supplement to the Official Records of the Union and Confederate Armies* (Wilmington, N.C., 1996), part 2, ser. 35, 566, 568–69, and part 2, ser. 36, 221.

23. Martha B. Turnbull to "John," September 6, 1868, and Martha B. Turnbull to "Madame," January 21, 1870, Box 1, Folder 1, MSS. 4973, Turnbull (Daniel and Family) Papers 1803–1913, LSU Special Collections (hereafter cited as Turnbull [Daniel and Family] Papers); W. B. Turnbull to Martha B. Turnbull, June 27, 1870, Turnbull (Daniel and Family) Papers.

24. Daniel Turnbull Succession, No. 132, 5th Judicial District Court, Iberville Parish, La., Records; Succession of Daniel Turnbull Sale to Mrs. C. B. Turnbull & S. T. Bowman, December 14, 1871, recorded December 20, 1871, Notarial Record Q, Folio 213, West Feliciana Parish, La., Records; Lawrence L. Butler to Edward J. Gay, July 8 and 29, 1875, Box 90, Folders 1038 and 1044, Gay Papers.

25. Faust, *Mothers of Invention,* 7, 251–52, 254; Rodrigue, *Reconstruction in the Cane Fields,* 104.

26. Alexander Duncan to Edward G. W. Butler, March 5, 1868, BFP 673; April 25, 1868, BFP 674; May 15, 1868, BFP 675; and June 2, 1868, BFP 676; Alexander Duncan to Edward G. W. Butler, April 16, 1869, EGWB Papers.

27. *Journal of the Twenty-Fifth Annual Convention of the Protestant Episcopal Church in the Diocese of Louisiana* (New Orleans, La., 1866), 62–63; *Journal of the Twenty-Sixth Annual Convention of the Protestant Episcopal Church in the Diocese of Louisiana* (New Orleans, La., 1867), 74. (The *Journals* are located at the offices of the Episcopal Diocese of Louisiana, New Orleans).

28. See Gay Papers, specifically: Safeguard, Box 45, Folder 444, HQ Dept. of the Gulf, N. O., December 11, 1863; Statement of Allegiance, Box 46, Folder 447; Arms Permit, April 27, 1864, Box 46, Folder 453; Order for Laborers (one of several similar orders), Box 46, Folder 455; and Presidential Pardon, December 24, 1866, Y:1, Box 49, Folder 498.

29. A. Miltenberger to Major Lawrence Lewis Butler, September 4, 1869, BFP 678; Lavinia Hynes Gay to Anna M. Gay, October 27, 1869, Box 2, MSS. 637, Gay, Price, and Butler Family Papers, Historic New Orleans Collection (hereafter cited as Gay, Price, and Butler Family Papers); Sue Gay Butler to Anna M. Gay, October 30, 1869, and December 5, 1869, Box 2, Gay, Price, and Butler Family Papers.

30. Bouchereau, *Statement of Sugar and Rice Crops,* 5; Record Book, 1868–1871, BFP 1641; Ryan, *Greenfield-Allemania Plantation Sugarhouse,* 118f., 123; Rodrigue, *Reconstruction in the Cane Field,* 124–25, 140; Moon-Ho Jung, *Coolies and Cane: Race, Labor, and Sugar in the Age of Emancipation* (Baltimore, Md., 2006), 158–63, 190–95; Lawrence L. Butler to Edward J. Gay, October 15, 1870, Box 65, Folder 695, Gay Papers; Lawrence L. Butler to Messrs. Johnson and Peterson, October 19, 1870, Box 65, Folder 696, Gay Papers; receipt from Johnson and Peterson, October 19, 1870, Gay Papers; Lawrence L. Butler to Edward J. Gay, October 19, 1870, Box 65, Folder 696, Gay Papers; William J. Gay to Edward J. Gay, October 7, 1870, Box 65, Folder 694, Gay Papers; *Edward J. Gay vs. Yook Chow et al.,* April 27, 1871, Box 68, Folder 731, Gay Papers; A. Miltenberger to Lawrence Lewis Butler, September 4, 1868, BFP 678; Alexander Duncan to Edward G. W. Butler, February 6 and 15, 1871, and March 18, 1871, EGWB Papers; Conveyance Book 10, Fol. 107, April 21, 1870, Iberville

Parish, La., Records (hereafter cited as COB). Actual production and wage figures on Dunboyne are difficult to determine. See Richard Follett, "Documenting Louisiana Sugar 1845–1917," www.sussex.ac.uk/louisianasugar (accessed July 10, 2008).

31. Lavinia H. Gay to Anna M. Gay, February 17, 1870, and April 22, 1870, Box 2, Gay, Price, and Butler Family Papers; Lavinia H. Gay to John H. Gay Jr., February 14, 1870, Box 62, Folder 669, Gay Papers; Sue G. Butler to John H. Gay Jr., December 4, 1870, Box 65, Folder 697, Gay Papers; Lawrence Lewis Butler to Anna M. Gay, May 1, 1870, Gay, Price, and Butler Family Papers; Robert E. Lee to Edward G. W. Butler, February 10, 1870, #901, Allyn K. Ford Collection, on microfilm.

32. COB 10, Fol. 280, March 4, 1871, Iberville Parish, La., Records; "John Henderson Gay," *The United States Biographical Dictionary and Portrait Gallery of Eminent and Self-Made Men—Missouri Volume* (New York, 1878) (copy from Missouri Historical Society vertical files); "My Genealogy Home Page: Information about William Henry Glasgow, Jr.," http://familytreemaker.genealogy.com (accessed January 8, 2015).

11. THE PASS

1. Lavinia H. Gay to Anna M. Gay, March 11, 1871, Box 2, MSS. 637, Gay, Price, and Butler Family Papers, Historic New Orleans Collection (hereafter cited as Gay, Price, and Butler Family Papers); Sue G. Butler to John H. Gay, April 4, 1871, Box 68, Folder 726, MSS. 1295, Gay (Edward J. and Family) Papers, LSU Special Collections (hereafter cited as Gay Papers); Charlton Jones, "The Butler-McCutchon House History" (Pass Christian, Miss., 1992), in author's personal files.

2. Sue G. Butler to Anna M. Gay, April 3, 1871, Box 2, Gay, Price, and Butler Family Papers; Lavinia H. Gay to Anna M. Gay, April 6, 1871, Gay, Price, and Butler Family Papers.

3. COB 10, Fol. 338, May 20, 1871, Iberville Parish, La., Records. The assignment did not include the Glasgow debt.

4. See Edward G. W. Butler to Lawrence L. Butler, May 10, 1871, Folder 681, MSS. 102, Butler Family Papers, Historic New Orleans Collection (hereafter cited as BFP).

5. Caro B. Turnbull to Lawrence L. Butler, May 22, 1872, BFP 696; "For Sale" (advertisement for Pass Christian house, 1868), MSS. U-158, McCutchon (Samuel) Papers, LSU Special Collections; Frances Parke Butler to "Dainger," July 8, 1871, BFP 682; Jones, "Butler-McCutchon House." The term "cabinet" refers to an enclosure or small room normally at an end of a rear gallery.

6. Frances P. Butler to Lawrence L. Butler, August 4, 1871, BFP 683; August 22, 1871, BFP 684; October 15, 1871, BFP 687; and December 23, 1871, BFP 689; Samuel Cranwill to Edward J. Gay, May 23, 1872, Box 73, Folder 806, Gay Papers. One may wonder where Frances Butler planned to acquire funds for such financial assistance to Lawrence Butler.

7. Will of Frances Parke Butler, BFP 1149. The will, which required official recognition first in Mississippi, was not probated before the Chancery Clerk of Harrison County until March 31, 1876, nine months following the death of Frances Butler. Her handwriting was attested to by Daniel Turnbull and Percival McCutchon.

8. See Thomas D. Schoonover, *The United States in Central America, 1860–1911: Episodes of Imperialism and Imperial Rivalry in the World System* (Durham, N.C., 1991), 48–49; Glenn R. Conrad, ed., *A Dictionary of Louisiana Biography*, 2 vols. (Lafayette, La., 1988), 2:852.

9. Mary E. Butler to Edward G. W. Butler, September 25, 1871, Folder 31, MSS. 600, Twiss Collection of Butler Family Papers, Historic New Orleans Collection (hereafter cited as TCBF Papers); Francis A. Meason to Edward G. W. Butler, January 8, 1872, BFP 691; F. A. Meason to Edward G. W. Butler, March 15, 1872, Folder 32, TCBF Papers; H. A. Thompson to Edward G. W. Butler, May 6, 1872, BFP 695.

10. Lavinia H. Gay to Anna M. Gay, May 21, 1871, Box 2, Gay, Price, and Butler Family Papers; William H. Glasgow Jr. to Edward J. Gay, May 3, 1871, Box 68, Folder 733; May 13, 1871, Box 68, Folder 735; June 6, 1871, Box 69, Folder 740; June 20, 1871, Box 69, Folder 742; and July 25, 1871, Box 69, Folder 747—all in Gay Papers; agreement between Fales and Glasgow, draft, June 20, 1871, by Edward J. Gay, Box 69, Folder 742, Gay Papers; Henry D. Fales to Edward J. Gay, July 26, 1871, Box 69, Folder 747, Gay Papers.

11. Lavinia H. Gay to Anna M. Gay, November 17, 1872, Box 4, Gay, Price, and Butler Family Papers; Lavinia H. Gay to Anna M. Gay, January 12, 1873, Box 5, Gay, Price, and Butler Family Papers; William H. Glasgow to Lawrence L. Butler, July 20, 1873, BFP 699.

12. Frances Parke Butler to Lawrence L. Butler, January 7, 1874, MSS. 805, Edward George Washington Butler Papers, 1821–1888, Duke University Special Collections (hereafter cited as EGWB Papers); Lawrence L. Butler to Edward J. Gay, August 18, 1872, Box 74, Folder 821; agreement of co-partnership, September 26, 1872, Box 75, Folder 827; and Dunboyne payroll for June 1875, Box 90, Folder 1037—all in Gay Papers. Hubbard's father died in 1874 and is buried in the Episcopal Church of the Nativity churchyard in Rosedale, Louisiana. See http://en.wikipedia.org/wiki/David_Hubbard (accessed March 13, 2012).

13. On the illness and death of Frances Butler, see Charles A. Conrad to Edward J. Gay Jr., June 23, 1875, and Sue G. Butler to Anna M. Gay, July 5, 1875, Box 1, MSS. 4872, Gay-Butler-Plater Family Papers, LSU Special Collections (hereafter cited as Gay-Butler-Plater Papers). Many details of the Butlers' financial difficulties at the time are found in the official Iberville Parish, La., Records, notably in the succession of Frances Parke Butler and in Civil Suit 1647, *Lawrence Lewis Butler vs. Henry D. Fales*, December 27, 1875. In addition, see documents in the Gay Papers, including Lawrence L. Butler to Edward J. Gay, July 2, 1875, July 8, 1875, Box 90, Folder 1038; Sue Gay Butler to Edward J. Gay, July 30, 1875, Box 90, Folder 1044; and Lawrence L. Butler to Edward J. Gay, August 9, 1875, and August 17, 1875, Box 90, Folder 1047. See also Lawrence L. Butler to Edward J. Gay, July 2, 1875, Box 1, Gay-Butler-Plater Papers.

14. Lawrence L. Butler to Edward J. Gay, July 2, 1875, Box 90, Folder 1037; July 8, 1875, Box 90, Folder 1038; and July 29, 1875, Box 90, Folder 1044—all in Gay Papers; Caro B. Turnbull to Edward J. Gay, July 31, 1875, Box 90, Folder 1044; and August 10, 1875, Box 90, Folder 1047, Gay Papers. On the Turnbull sons, see Lawrence L. Butler to Edward J. Gay, August 11, 1875, Box 90, Folder 1047, Gay Papers.

15. Lawrence L. Butler to Edward J. Gay, July 19, 1875, Box 90, Folder 1041; and August 23, 1875, Box 90, Folder 1049—all in Gay Papers.

16. Civil Suit 1647, COB 13, Folio 13, July 5, 1876, Iberville Parish, La., Records.

17. See Edward G. W. Butler to L. U. Reavis, May 20, 1878 (typed copy), Box 5, Gay, Price, and Butler Family Papers; Edward Spencer to Col. E.G.W. Butler, July 9, 1875, and July 15, 1875, EGWB Papers; obituary of Mrs. Frances Parke Butler (N.p., n.d.) (in the author's personal papers); Edward G. W. Butler to Edward J. Gay, March 14, 1876, Box 95, Folder 1102, Gay Papers.

12. "ARE YOU AFRAID TO DIE?"

1. Charles M. Conrad to Edward G. W. Butler, January 23, 1872, MSS. 805, Edward George Washington Butler Papers, 1800–1888, Duke University Rare Book, Manuscript, and Special Collections Library (hereafter cited as EGWB Papers); Caroline B. Turnbull lease to L. Moyer, March 8, 1872, Notarial Records Q, Fol. 288, West Feliciana Parish, La., Records.

2. Nannie Randolph to Anna M. Gay, August 28, 1869, Box 2, MSS. 637, Gay, Price, and Butler Family Papers, Historic New Orleans Collection (hereafter cited as Gay, Price, and Butler Family Papers); Sue Gay Butler to Anna M. Gay, July 4, 1871, Box 2, Gay, Price, and Butler Family Papers; Sue Gay Butler to Anna M. Gay, February 16, 1873, Box 5, Gay, Price, and Butler Family Papers.

3. William Barrow Floyd, *The Barrow Family of Louisiana* (Lexington, Ky., 1963), 63–65, 97, 103, 132–33; University of the South Librarian Mary O'Neil to David D. Plater, November 1, 2012, and Vaughn Stanley, Washington and Lee University Special Collections, to David D. Plater, September 9, 2012, author's personal records; Hamilton Fish to Edward G. W. Butler, March 11, 1873, Folder 697, MSS. 102, Butler Family Papers, Historic New Orleans Collection (hereafter cited as BFP); Anna Butler to Lawrence L. Butler, February 22, 1876, Box 1, Folder 11, MSS. 4872, Gay-Butler-Plater Family Papers, LSU Special Collections (hereafter cited as Gay-Butler-Plater Papers); William B. Turnbull and Sarah L. Barrow marriage license, January 1, 1876, Marriages C, 1873–1879, West Feliciana Parish, La., Records. In 1877 Sarah Barrow Turnbull remarried, to another cousin, Herman Groesbeck Barrow (b. 1848), and they had one daughter. See Floyd, *The Barrow Family*, 132–33.

4. Alexander Duncan to Edward G. W. Butler, February 8, 1876, EGWB Papers.

5. Caro B. Turnbull to Lawrence L. Butler, September 4, 1875, Box 1, Gay-Butler-Plater Papers.

6. Lawrence L. Butler to Edward J. Gay, March 10, 1876, Box 94, Folder 1100; Edward G. W. Butler to Edward J. Gay, March 16, 1876, Box 94, Folder 1101; and Lawrence L. Butler to Major D. C. Hubbard, March 20, 1876, Box 94, Folder 1101—all in MSS. 1295, Gay (Edward J. and Family) Papers, LSU Special Collections (hereafter cited as Gay Papers).

7. Edward G. W. Butler to Edward J. Gay, March 14, 1876, Box 94, Folder 1102, Gay Papers; Wm. G. Harrison to Lawrence L. Butler, April 13, 1876, BFP 713; Rep. R. L. Gibson to Edward G. W. Butler, March 29, 1876, BFP 712. The Cervantes books were retrieved and survived, and over 125 years later a descendant of the Butlers, Colonel Edward Twiss, sold them to the Mount Vernon Ladies' Association. The volumes are in safekeeping in the Mount Vernon Library.

8. Lawrence L. Butler to Edward J. Gay, March 25, 1876, and March 27, 1876, Box 94, Folder 1102; and April 6, 1876, April 7, 1876, and April 12, 1876, Box 94, Folder 1105—all in Gay Papers.

9. Edward J. Gay Jr. to Lawrence L. Butler, April 14, 1876, Box 1, Gay-Butler-Plater Papers.

10. Edward G. W. Butler to Lawrence L. Butler, May 21, 1876, BFP 715.

11. Lawrence L. Butler to Edward J. Gay, April 21, 1876, and April 28, 1876, Box 94, Folder 1108, Gay Papers. On Dennis, born in 1819 and listed in the Dunboyne group of slaves in the mid- and late 1830s as a "Present from Lawrence Lewis," see "Negroes on Dunboyne Plantation," BFP 1634; Edward G. W. Butler to Anna Margaret Gay Price, November 14, 1887, Gay-Price-Butler Family Papers. After the Civil War he acquired the last name Parker.

12. Edward G. W. Butler to Lawrence L. Butler, May 21, 1776, BFP 715; Succession 181, Adine D. Hubbard and Duncan C. Hubbard, Parish Court, Iberville Parish, La., Records.

13. Samuel Cranwill to Edward J. Gay, September 13, 1876, Box 97, Folder 1133, Gay Papers; death certificate, succession of Caroline Butler Turnbull, No. 69776, Civil District Court, Orleans Parish (transferred from 2nd District Court, Orleans Parish, No. 38984); obituary of Caroline Swanwick Butler Turnbull, BFP 1515; Samuel Wilson, *New Orleans Architecture: The University Section* (New Orleans, La., 2000), 31ff.

14. See "Marie Isabella Nicholas," ID: I064967, and "George Joseph Frederick Burthe," ID: I064969, http://wc.rootsweb.ancestry.com (accessed April 18, 2012, and January 8, 2015); Images of New Orleans Wards 1870, Wikipedia, http://en.wikimedia.org/wiki/file:NOLA_Wards_1880.jpg (accessed May 25, 2012, and January 8, 2015). Susan Vinson Nicholas died in New Orleans on August 31, 1870, evidently also then living with a daughter, probably Marie. See "Susan Adelaide Vinson," ID: I064964, http://wc.rootsweb.ancestry.com (accessed April 18, 2012, and January 8, 2015).

15. Andrew H. Gay to Anna M. Gay, September 15, 1876, Gay, Price, and Butler Family Papers; Lavinia H. Gay to Anna M. Gay, September 17, 1876, Box 1, Gay-Butler-Plater Papers; succession of Caroline Butler Turnbull, No. 69776, Civil District Court, Parish of Orleans; Judgment of Possession, October 4, 1876, recorded March 9, 1877, Notarial Records R, Fol. 434, West Feliciana Parish, La., Records; W. B. Turnbull and D. P. Turnbull sale, March 29, 1878, Notarial Records R, Fol. 614, West Feliciana Parish, La., Records; Lawrence L. Butler to Edward J. Gay, May 5, 1878, Box 109, Folder 1258; May 20, 1878, Box 109, Folder 1261; and June 27, 1878, Box 109, Folder 1266—all in Gay Papers.

16. Edward G. W. Butler to Lawrence L. Butler, May 21, 1876, BFP 715; Edward G. W. Butler to Edward J. Gay, June 6, 1876, Box 97, Folder 1133, Gay Papers; A. Hamilton to Edward G. W. Butler, December 11, 1876, EGWB Papers; Thos. J. Bloodgood to Edward G. W. Butler, July 9, 1879, BFP 741. Butler's friend Alexander Hamilton was a grandson of the nation's first secretary of the treasury, Alexander Hamilton.

17. Edward G. W. Butler to Lawrence L. Butler, January 1, 1877, BFP 720; Edward G. W. Butler to Edward J. Gay, March 14, 1877, Box 100, Folder 1172; and April 23, 1877, Box 106, Folder 1180—both in Gay Papers; Edward G. W. Butler to Anna M. Gay, August 1, 1877, BFP 724. George Williamson Jr., born in 1857, achieved distinction as the chairman of the biology department at Louisiana State Normal School, the future Northwestern State University in Natchitoches, Louisiana, and as a geologist and archaeologist. A museum named for him is located on the university campus. http://library.nsula.edu/assets/CGHRC_Finding/williamsong.htm (accessed May 16, 2012). Butler seems to have misidentified as his grandson a Pierce Williamson, as no one of that name was born to Isabel Butler Williamson.

18. Edward G. W. Butler to Lawrence L. Butler, September 22, 1877, BFP 726; "Obituary of Rawlins Lowndes," *Charleston (S.C.[?]) Journal*, 1877 [clipping], BFP 1749.

19. Sale of Dunboyne Plantation, COB 13, Fol. 13, Iberville Parish, La., Records; Lawrence L. Butler to Edward J. Gay, February 23, 1877, Box 100, Folder 1169, Gay Papers. Commenting on the "promising crop" of cane in May 1876, which had been helped by "fine rains," Colonel Butler also could not resist a poke at "Maj. Hubbard's notion of *buying*, instead of making, corn." Edward G. W. Butler to Lawrence L. Butler, May 21, 1876, BFP 715.

20. Voter registration for D. C. Hubbard, September 6, 1870, Box 97, Folder 1133, Gay Papers; sale from Charles F. Lefeaux to Joseph A. Erwin and Duncan C. Hubbard, COB 10, Fol. 197, Iberville Parish, La., Records; Succession No. 181, Adine E. Hubbard and Duncan C. Hubbard, Parish Court, Iberville Parish, La., Records.

21. Wm. H. Ely to John H. Gay Jr., October 6 and 8, 1878, Box 110, Folder 1274; and William Bloomfield to John D. Slack, October 25 and 29, 1878, Box 110, Folder 1275—all in Gay Papers; Succession No. 181, Adine E. Hubbard and Duncan C. Hubbard, Parish Court, Iberville Parish, La., Records. Among the bills for the Hubbard succession to pay was one for $200 from "Dr. Snell," who irritated Gay with a several months' delay in providing a death certificate required by the Phoenix Mutual Life Insurance Company. See William Bloomfield to John D. Slack, October 29, 1878, Box 110, Folder 1275; November 8, 1878, Box 110, Folder 1276; and December 2, 1878, Box 111, Folder 1279; Edward J. Gay to John D. Slack, November 23, 1878, Box 110, Folder 1278—all in Gay Papers.

22. Edward J. Gay to John D. Slack, December 2, 1878, Box 121, Folder 1279; and January 1, 1879, Box 111, Folder 1295—both in Gay Papers.

23. Succession No. 181, Adine E. Hubbard and Duncan C. Hubbard, Parish Court, Iberville Parish, La., Records; *Lawrence L. Butler vs. Succession D. C. Hubbard and Adine Edmundson wife*, 23rd Judicial District Court, COB 14, Fol. 292, May 12, 1880, Iberville Parish, La., Records.

24. Succession No. 132 of Frances P. Butler, Parish Court, Iberville Parish, La., Records.

25. Sale by Lawrence l. Butler to Amedée Hebert, Recorded July 23, 1881, COB 15, Fol. 221, Iberville Parish, La., Records.

26. Sue G. Butler to Anna M. Gay, April 7, 1878, Box 1, Gay-Butler-Plater Papers.

27. Edward G. W. Butler to L. U. Reavis, February 1, 1878 (typed copy), Box 5, Gay, Price, and Butler Family Papers; Sue G. Butler to Anna M. Gay, April 7, 1878, Box 1, Gay-Butler-Plater Papers; Edward G. W. Butler to L. U. Reavis, May 20, 1878, typed copy in author's files. In *The Life and Military Services of Gen. William Selby Harney* (St. Louis, 1878), Reavis quoted from Butler's correspondence with him. See also a more recent biography of Harney, George Rollie Adams, *General William S. Harney, Prince of Dragoons* (Lincoln, Nebr., 2001), 5, 14, 16, 17. Butler commonly received the title "Col." in family letters, as for instance in the note that Sue Butler wrote her sister Nannie in April 1878.

28. "History—Lucas Place," Campbell House Museum, http://campbellhousemuseum.org/history/lucas-place/ (accessed May 28, 2012 and January 8, 2015); Michael R. Allen, "St. Louis and the 1880 Census," http://preservationresearch.com/2011/02/st-louis-and-the-1880-census/ (accessed May 17, 2012); Sue G. Butler to Lavinia H. Gay, June 12, 1879, Box 5, Gay, Price, and Butler Family Papers. Butler often received mail to the care of E. J. Gay & Co., St. Louis, where it would be delivered to his son. See BFP.

29. Sue G. Butler to Anna M. Gay, January 23, 1879, Box 1, Folder 12; Sue G. Butler to "Fannie," July 10, 1881, Box 1, Folder 13; and Sue G. Butler to Lavinia H. Gay, January 23, 1881, Box 1, Folder 13—all in Gay-Butler-Plater Papers.

30. Edward G. W. Butler to L. U. Reavis, May 20, 1878 (typed copy), Box 5, Gay, Price, and Butler Family Papers; Sue G. Butler to Anna M. Gay, May 23, 1879, Box 1, Folder 12, Gay-Butler-Plater Papers; Edward G. W. Butler to Anna M. Gay Price, February 11, 1881, BFP 761; Dunbar Rowland, coll. and ed., *Jefferson Davis, Constitutionalist: His Letters, Papers and Speeches*, vol. 9 (Jackson, Miss.,

1923), 145; Alexander Duncan to Edward G. W. Butler, May 4, 1880, EGWB Papers; Adams, *General William S. Harney*, 276ff.

31. Rev. J. A. Murray, D.D., "The Butlers of the Cumberland Valley," *Historical Register: Notes and Queries, Historical and Genealogical, Relative to Interior Pennsylvania, for the Year 1883* (Harrisburg, Pa., 1883), 1:1–17; Edward G. W, Butler to Joseph A. Murray, February 9, 1883, and March 8, 1883, Joseph A. Murray Papers, Cumberland County Historical Society and The Hamilton Library Association, Carlisle, Pennsylvania (hereafter cited as Joseph A. Murray Papers).

32. "DIED. Mary Susan Butler," *St. Louis Post-Dispatch*, March 28, 1882, page 5; Missouri Death Records, 1834–1910, http://interactive.ancestry.com (accessed January 9, 2015); Lawrence L. Butler to Anna M. G. Price, April 18, 1882, and November 26, 1882, Box 1, Folder 14, Gay-Butler-Plater Papers; Edward G. W. Butler to Anna M. G. Price, March 1, 1883, Gay, Price, and Butler Family Papers.

33. Edward G. W. Butler to Joseph A. Murray, September 22, 1883, Joseph A. Murray Papers; Montgomery Blair to Edward G. W. Butler, March 9, 1875, BFP 707; Montgomery Blair to Edward G. W. Butler, October 17, 1875, BFP 747; Montgomery Blair, "Views on Negro Suffrage," from *North American Review* (reprint), BFP 1728; "Mr. Lincoln's White House: Montgomery Blair (1813–1883)," http://www.mrlincolnswhitehouse.org/content_inside.asp?ID=84&subjectID=2 (accessed May 29, 2012).

34. Edward G. W. Butler to Joseph A. Murray, September 22, 1883, Joseph A. Murray Papers.

35. Edward G. W. Butler to Jefferson Davis, April 11 and July 11, 1883, in Rowland, coll. and ed., *Jefferson Davis*, 9:207, 215.

36. Edward G. W. Butler to Jefferson Davis, October 12, 1883, in Rowland, coll. and ed., *Jefferson Davis*, 9:262; Edward G. W. Butler to Anna Gay Butler, December 22, 1883, Gay, Price, and Butler Family Papers.

37. Jefferson Davis to Edward G. W. Butler, May 13, 1884, #438, Allyn Ford Collection, Minnesota Historical Society (on microfilm); Edward G. W. Butler to Anna G. Butler, December 22, 1883, Gay, Price, and Butler Family Papers; Edward G. W. Butler to Edward Gay Butler, January 10, 1884, BFP 782; Edward G. W. Butler to Jefferson Davis, July 29, 1884, in Rowland, coll. and ed., *Jefferson Davis*, 9:289.

38. Edward G. W. Butler to Jefferson Davis, January 8, 1884, in Rowland, coll. and ed., *Jefferson Davis*, 9:274; Edward G. W. Butler to Jefferson Davis, July 29, 1884, in Rowland, coll. and ed., *Jefferson Davis*, 9:289; Edward G. W. Butler to Jefferson Davis, October 8, 1884, in Rowland, coll. and ed., *Jefferson Davis*, 9:297; Edward G. W. Butler to Jefferson Davis, October 19, 1884, in Rowland, coll. and ed., *Jefferson Davis*, 9:299; Edward G. W. Butler to Jefferson Davis, November 10, 1884, in Rowland, coll. and ed., *Jefferson Davis*, 9:304. On William Pitt Kellogg, the native Vermonter and post–Civil War Louisiana politician, see "William Pitt Kellogg," Wikipedia, http://en.wikipedia.org/wiki/William_Pitt_Kellogg (accessed May 18, 2012).

39. Edward G. W. Butler to Joseph R. Murray, March 8, 1833, Joseph A. Murray Papers; Joseph A. Murray to Edward G. W. Butler, October 14, 1884, BFP 788. The "photograph" of Butler sent to Murray probably was his daguerreotype taken while he was with the 3rd Dragoons, which is preserved at the Amon Carter Museum in Fort Worth, Texas. See Martha A. Sandweiss, Rick Stewart, and Ben Huseman, *Eyewitness to War: Prints and Daguerreotypes of the Mexican War, 1846–1848* (Fort Worth, Tex., and Washington, D.C., 1989), 218–19. He also may have sent Murray a photo of his portrait painted around 1848, in his dress uniform. There are at least three such portraits of

him documented in the Butler Family Papers, MSS. 102, at the Historic New Orleans Collection, where a large oil portrait of Butler now hangs. Another is in a private home of a relative of Isabel Williamson, in Shreveport, Louisiana. A small oil portrait of Butler from the 1830s is at the Lewis home, Woodlawn. Other photographs as life images of Butler so far have not surfaced, although a set of family photos was sent to Lord Dunboyne in Ireland in 1871. See BFP 688.

40. Lawrence L. Butler to Mrs. Andrew Price, December 26, 1884, Box 1, Folder 16, Gay-Butler-Plater Papers.

41. Lawrence L. Butler to Anna M. Price, January 14, 1885, Box 1 Folder 16, Gay-Butler-Plater Papers; Edward G. W. Butler to Jefferson Davis, March 7, 1885, in Rowland, coll. and ed., *Jefferson Davis,* 9:350; Edward G. W. Butler to Jefferson Davis, September 20, 1885, in Rowland, coll. and ed., *Jefferson Davis,* 9:393. Susan Mastin's nephew Frank O'Fallon was married into the Glasgow family, the relations and business partners of Edward J. Gay. See "John Julius O'Fallon," "Frank Mastin O'Fallon," "Caroline Levert Mastin," and "Susan Ann Pope Mastin," http://familytreemaker.genealogy.com (accessed May 12, 2012, and January 9, 2015).

42. Congressman J. R. Tucker to Hon. Edward J. Gay, January 8, 1886, BFP 800; Congressman J. R. Tucker to Edward G. W. Butler, March 4, 1886, BFP 802; Act to remove the Disabilities of Edward G. W. Butler, of Missouri, Approved March 2, 1886, *United States Statutes at Large,* vol. 24 (U.S. Government Printing Office, 1886), 682; Adams, *General William S. Harney,* 280; Edward G. W. Butler to Anna Gay Price, January 2, 1886, Gay, Price, and Butler Family Papers; Joseph A. Murray to Edward G. W. Butler, February 27, 1887, BFP 807.

43. J. E. Johnston to Edward G. W. Butler, July 27, 1887, MSS. 600, Twiss Collection of Butler Family Papers, Historic New Orleans Collection; "A Ward of Old Hickory: Reminiscences of Gen. E.G.W. Butler—Something about His Family," and "Jackson's Letters. Interesting Communications to Gen. E.G.W. Butler, His Ward," *New York Times,* August 10 and August 11, 1886, www.nytimes.com (accessed May 22, 2012, and January 9, 2015); *St. Louis Republican,* August 7, 1883, reprinted in the *New York Times,* August 10, 1883, www.nytimes.com; "Old Army Officers. Two Venerable Soldiers Who Reside in St. Louis," clipping from the *St. Louis Globe-Democrat,* December 26, 1886, BFP 1792.

44. "Topics of the Day: The Oldest Surviving Graduate of West Point," *Washington (D.C.) Critic-Record,* October 6, 1885; "Entertainment," *Eighteenth Annual Reunion of the Association of the Graduates of the United States Military Academy, at West Point, New York, June 9th, 1887* (East Saginaw, Mich., 1887), 8.

45. Mary Pugh to Edward Pugh, November 4 and November 25, 1887, MSS. 897/1055, Pugh (Mrs. Mary W.) Papers, 1864–1925, I, LSU Special Collections; Anna M. Gay Price to Lavinia Gay, November 25 and 29, 1887, G:43, Box 1, Folder 17, Gay-Butler-Plater Papers; Edward G. W. Butler to Anna Gay Price, November 14, 1887, Gay, Price, and Butler Family Papers; Edward G. W. Butler to Anna Gay Price, January 25, 1888, BFP 821. Following accounts by earlier historians, there have been recent reexaminations of the "Thibodaux Massacre" that place it into a context both of post–Civil War labor history and of the pressures during the 1880s and 1890s to reestablish political and social white supremacy. See, for example, William Ivy Hair, *Bourbonism and Agrarian Protest: Louisiana Politics 1877–1900* (Baton Rouge, La., 1969), 177–86, passim; Jeffrey Gould, "The Strike of 1887:

Louisiana Sugar War," *Southern Exposure* (November–December 1984): 45–55, passim; Rebecca J. Scott, "Fault Lines, Color Lines, and Party Lines: Race, Labor, and Collective Action in Louisiana and Cuba," in *Beyond Slavery: Explorations of Race, Labor, and Citizenship in Postemancipation Societies*, ed. Frederick Cooper, Thomas C. Holt, and Rebecca J. Scott (Chapel Hill, N.C., 2000), 65–83, passim; Rebecca J. Scott, *Degrees of Freedom: Louisiana and Cuba after Slavery* (Cambridge, Mass., 2005), 77–88, passim. On Theophile T. Allain, whose connection to Butler's servant Dennis is otherwise undocumented, see "Theo Allain, Business and Elected Official in Louisiana," African American Registry, http://www.aaregistry.org/historic_events/view/theo-allain-businessman-and-elected-official-louisiana (accessed January 9, 2015). See also Conrad, ed., *Dictionary of Louisiana Biography*, 1:8.

46. "Swords," BFP 1145; Edward G. W. Butler to Andrew Price, June 12, 1888, Gay, Price, and Butler Family Papers; "Mustered Out," clipping from *St. Louis Post Dispatch*, September 6, 1888, BFP 1758. Butler's sword collection does not include the swords of his father, Capt. Edward Butler, lent or given by his mother, Isabella Butler, after her husband's death to the father of Confederate general James Patton Anderson and never retrieved. See Edward G. W. Butler to Genl. P. Anderson, February 10, 1872, MSS 247, James Patton Anderson Papers, George A. Smathers Libraries Special and Area Studies Collections, University of Florida. The letter is digitized at http://ufdc.ufl.edu/UF00085719/00002 (accessed May 22, 2012).

47. On McCall, see "Biographies of Ascension Parish," *Genealogy Trails*, http://genealogytrails.com/lou/ascension/bios.html (accessed May 25, 2012).

48. "Deaths," *St. Louis Post-Dispatch*, September 7, 1888; Lawrence L. Butler to Anna M. Price, September 19, 1888, Box 1, Folder 18, Gay-Butler-Plater Papers. Based only on the written description of E.G.W. Butler's death by Lawrence Butler, the author's "medical opinion" was confirmed by internal medicine and neurology specialist Dr. Louis L. Caplan of Boston, Massachusetts, on June 2, 2012.

EPILOGUE

1. David Brion Davis, *The Problem of Slavery in the Age of Revolution, 1770–1823* (New York, 1999), 41.

2. Differences of opinion exist about Washington's attitudes toward slavery, although there is agreement that his testamentary order to free his slaves after Martha Washington's death was a courageous action. See, for example, Davis, *The Problem of Slavery in the Age of Revolution*, 170–71; Ron Chernow, *Washington: A Life* (New York, 2010), 708–10, 758f., 799f.

3. Alexis de Toqueville, *Democracy in America* (New York, 1957), 1:397.

4. James S. Amory to Edward G. W. Butler, July 4 and October 31, 1850, MSS. 102, Butler Family Papers, Historic New Orleans Collection; Rawlins Lowndes to Edward G. W. Butler, April 17, 1849, MSS. 805, Edward George Washington Butler Papers, 1821–1888, Duke University Rare Book, Manuscript, and Special Collections Library. Expressing the typical dilemma for whites, Lowndes acknowledged his doubts about the capacity of emancipated slaves to function in a "freer society."

5. David Brion Davis, *The Problem of Slavery in the Age of Emancipation* (New York, 2014), 145.

6. Edward G. W. Butler to Anna Gay Price, November 14, 1887, MSS. 637, Gay-Price-Butler Papers, Historic New Orleans Collection; Davis, *The Problem of Slavery in the Age of Emancipation,* 166; Toqueville, *Democracy in America,* 1:373.

7. Davis, *The Problem of Slavery in the Age of Revolution,* 18.

BIBLIOGRAPHY

MANUSCRIPT COLLECTIONS

Cumberland County Historical Society and the Hamilton Library Association, Carlisle, Pennsylvania
    Joseph A. Murray Papers

Duke University Rare Book, Manuscript, and Special Collections Library, Durham, North Carolina
    MSS. 805, Edward George Washington Butler Papers, 1821–1888

Gilder Lehman Institute of American History, New York, New York
    MSS. GLC 05275

Historic New Orleans Collection, Williams Research Center, New Orleans, Louisiana
    MSS. 102, Butler Family Papers
    MSS. 637, Gay, Price, and Butler Family Papers
    MSS. 600, Twiss Collection of Butler Family Papers

Louisiana Historical Center, Louisiana State Museum, New Orleans, Louisiana
    RG 12, John Slidell Papers

Louisiana State University, Hill Memorial Library, Special Collections Division, Baton Rouge, Louisiana
    Louisiana Board of Public Works, 1866 map, *Mississippi River Levees from Thomas Point to Carrollton (New Orleans)*, Chart 11-U, Map LD 5 2001 (20 sheets), Louisiana and Lower Mississippi Valley Collections
    Louisiana Board of Public Works, 1866 Humphreys/Abbot map, Louisiana and Lower Mississippi Valley Collections

MSS. 1372 and 1382, James P. Bowman and Family Papers 1806–1937
MSS. 4872, Gay-Butler-Plater Family Papers
MSS. 1295, Gay (Edward J. and Family) Papers
MSS. 156, Charles Gayarré Collection
MSS. U-158, McCutchon (Samuel) Papers
MSS. 897/1055, Pugh (Mrs. Mary W.) Papers, 1864–1925, I
MSS. 4026, Turnbull-Bowman-Lyons Family Papers
MSS. 4973, Turnbull (Daniel and Family) Papers 1803–1913
MSS. 2984, W. P. A. Collection Historical Record Survey Transcriptions of Louisiana Police Jury Records
Persac, M. Adrien, *Plantations of the Mississippi River from Natchez to New Orleans* (Norman's Chart), 1857

Minnesota Historical Society, St. Paul, Minnesota
Allyn K. Ford Collection

Mount Vernon Ladies' Association Library, Mount Vernon, Virginia
The Papers of Eleanor (Nelly) Parke Custis Lewis

New York State Library Archives, Albany, New York
SC 15361, John Ellis Wool Papers

Smithsonian Institution, Archives of American Art, Washington, D.C.
George Peter Alexander Healy Letters, 1860–1861

Tennessee State Library and Archives, Nashville, Tennessee
MF 1099, Jackson, Andrew, 1767–1845, Papers at the Hermitage
The Papers of Andrew Jackson: 1st Series (microfilm)
Library of Congress 1967 film
Microfilm Supplement 1983
Microfilm Supplement 1986

United States Military Academy Library Special Collections, West Point, New York
MSS. 257, George Douglas Ramsay "Recollections."

University of Florida, George A. Smathers Libraries, Special Collections and Area Studies Collections, Gainesville, Florida
MSS 247, James Patton Anderson Papers

University of North Carolina, Southern Historical Collection, Chapel Hill, North Carolina
F01912, Blackford Family Papers

University of North Carolina–Greensboro, Greensboro, North Carolina
Digital Library on American Slavery, library.uncg.edu/slavery/psearch.aspx

University of Notre Dame, Notre Dame, Indiana
University of Notre Dame Archives, http://archives.nd.edu

University of Texas, Dolph Briscoe Center for American History, Austin, Texas
Braxton Bragg Papers
Alexander Franklin Pugh Papers
Pugh Family Papers, 1807–1907

University of Virginia, Tracy W. McGregor Library, Special Collections, University of Virginia Library, Charlottesville, Virginia
Papers of Notable Virginia Families, Accession 2988, Series III: Lewis Family Papers,

Virginia Historical Society, Richmond, Virginia
MSS. 1 L5114 b 68, George Bolling Lee, 1872–1948, Papers, 1732–1870, Sec. 68
MSS. 1 L5144 a 710-815, "Lee, Mary Custis 1835–1918 Papers," 1694–1917, Sec. 11
MSS. 1 L5144 a 1320-1322, Sec. 23, Mary Randolph Custis Lee Correspondence, 1844–1847

NEWSPAPERS

Alexandria (La.) Gazette
Liberty (Mo.) Weekly Tribune
Maryland Sun
New Orleans Bee
New Orleans Daily Picayune
New Orleans Delta
New Orleans Evening Picayune
New York Times
Philadelphia North American
Plaquemine (La.) Gazette and Sentinel

Plaquemine (La.) Southern Sentinel
St. Louis Globe-Democrat
St. Louis Post-Dispatch
Washington (D.C.) Critic-Record

GOVERNMENT DOCUMENTS

State/County/Parish

Louisiana

Louisiana: Office Board of State Engineers. Dunboyne Levee, Drawing No. 1231-2, 1872, Department of Public Works files, Levee District 4, Roll 27. Louisiana Department of Transportation and Development, Baton Rouge

Louisiana: Office Board of State Engineers. Dunboyne and Carroll Levees, Iberville Parish R. B. 1879–80. Drawing No. 1284-2, Department of Public Works files, Levee District 4, Roll 27. Louisiana Department of Transportation and Development, Baton Rouge

United States Engineers. Location of Dunboyne Levee, Iberville Parish, La., 1891. Drawing No. 1023-1, Department of Public Works Files, Levee District 4, Roll 27. Louisiana Department of Transportation and Development, Baton Rouge

Iberville Parish Conveyance Records

Iberville Parish Court Records
- Parish Court Records
- Succession Records, Parish Court
- Succession Records, 5th Judicial District Court
- Suits, 5th Judicial District Court
- Suits, 6th Judicial District Court
- Suits, 23rd Judicial District Court

Iberville Parish Police Jury Minutes

Orleans Parish Court Records
- Civil District Court Records
- Succession Records

West Feliciana Parish Records
- Marriage Records
- Notarial Records
- Succession Records

Missouri

Death Records, 1834–1910

Tennessee
Davidson County Deeds
Robertson County Deeds
Robertson County Minutes
Robertson County Wills

Virginia
Frederick County Deeds

United States

Library of Congress
MSS 27532, Andrew Jackson Papers
  Series 1, Reels 16, 18, 22, 23, 34, 40, 53, 54, 55, 57, 58
  Series 6, Reel 72
MSS 43828, Martin Van Buren Papers
  Series 2, Box 59, Reel 33

National Archives Records Administration, Washington, D.C.
Record Group 64
Record Group 77, MD1-30, A. A. Humphreys and H. L. Abbot, 1851 map, *Mississippi River from Red River Landing to Carrollton (New Orleans)*
Record Group 94, Records of the Adjutant General's Office, 1780s–1917
M565, Letters Received by the Office of the Adjutant General, Main Series, 1800–1890, vol. 25–26
M567, Letters Received by the Office of the Adjutant General, Main Series, 1822–1860
Record Group 393, Records of the United States Army Continental Commands, Part IV, Military Installations, 1821–1881
Record Group 105, Records of the Freedmen's Hospital and New Orleans Area Field Offices of the Bureau of Refugees, Freedmen, and Abandoned Lands 1865–1869, Rolls 8 and 9 (microfilm)

U.S. Printing Office, Washington, D.C.
"Letter from the Secretary of the Treasury in reply to a resolution of the House of Representatives . . . , January 21, 1831," Document No. 62, 1831, 31st U.S. Cong., 1st Sess., Executive Document No. 24
Official Army Register for 1821
Official Army Register for 1822
Official Army Register for 1823

Official Army Register for 1824
U.S. Census. 1830 (microfilm)
U.S. Census. 1850 (microfilm)
U.S. Census. 1860 (microfilm)
U.S. Military Academy Library Archives and Special Collections, West Point, New York
Annual Report of the Board of Visitors to the United States Military Academy Made to Congress and the Secretary of War, for the Year 1819. http://digital-library.usma.edu. Accessed January 4, 2015.
Edward Butler and E.G.W. Butler Military References file (digital access)
Official Register of the Officers and Cadets of the U.S. Military Academy, West Point, N.Y., 1818
Official Register of the Officers and Cadets of the U.S. Military Academy, West Point, N.Y., 1819
Official Register of the Officers and Cadets of the U.S. Military Academy, West Point, N.Y., 1820
U.S. Statutes at Large. Vol. 24 (1886)
U.S. War Department. *The War of the Rebellion: A Compilation of the Official Records of the Union and Confederate Armies*. 70 volumes in 4 series. Washington, D.C.: Government Printing Office, 1880–1901. Republication, Harrisburg, Pa.: National Historical Society, 1971. Reprint, Historical Times, 1985.

PUBLISHED CORRESPONDENCE, MEMOIRS, DIARIES, PRIMARY SOURCE BOOKS, AND GOVERNMENT DOCUMENTS

Adams, Charles Francis, ed. *Memoirs of John Quincy Adams, Comprising Portions of His Diary from 1795 to 1848*. Vols. 6 and 7. Philadelphia: Lippincott, 1875.

Bassett, John Spencer, ed. *Correspondence of Andrew Jackson*. Vols. 1, 3, and 6. Washington, D.C.: Carnegie Institution of Washington, D.C., 1926, 1928, 1933.

Bouchereau, L. *Statement of the Sugar and Rice Crops Made in Louisiana in 1868–69*. New Orleans: Young, Bright, 1869.

Brady, Patricia, ed. *George Washington's Beautiful Nelly: The Letters of Eleanor Parke Custis Lewis to Elizabeth Bordley Gibson, 1794–1851*. Columbia: Univ. of South Carolina Press, 1991.

Brinton, John H. *Personal Memoirs of John H. Brinton, Civil War Surgeon, 1861–1865*. New York: Neal Publishing Co., 1914. Reprint, Carbondale, Ill.: Southern Illinois Univ. Press, 1996.

Brown, Samuel R. *The Western Gazetteer; or Emigrants' Directory, Containing a Geographi-*

cal Description of the Western States and Territories. Auburn, N.Y.: H. C. Southwick, Printer, 1817. Revised ed., New York: Arno Press, 1971.

Bullock, W. *Bullock's Journey from New Orleans to New York in 1827.* London, 1827. Reprint, Carlisle, Mass.: Applewood Books, 2007.

Callcott, Margaret Law, ed. and trans. *Mistress of Riversdale: The Plantation Letters of Rosalie Stier Calvert, 1795–1821.* Baltimore: Johns Hopkins Univ. Press, 1991.

Champomier, P. A. *The Annual Statement of the Sugar Crop Made in Louisiana in 1844.* New Orleans: Cook, Young, 1845.

———. *Statement of the Sugar Crop Made in Louisiana in 1845–46.* New Orleans: Cook, Young, 1846.

———. *Statement of the Sugar Crop Made in Louisiana in 1849–50.* New Orleans: Cook, Young, 1850.

———. *Statement of the Sugar Crop Made in Louisiana in 1850–51.* New Orleans: Cook, Young, 1851.

———. *Statement of the Sugar Crop Made in Louisiana in 1851–52.* New Orleans: Cook, Young, 1852.

———. *Statement of the Sugar Crop Made in Louisiana in 1852–53.* New Orleans: Cook, Young, 1853.

———. *Statement of the Sugar Crop Made in Louisiana in 1853–54.* New Orleans: Cook, Young, 1854.

———. *Statement of the Sugar Crop Made in Louisiana in 1854–55.* New Orleans: Cook, Young, 1855.

———. *Statement of the Sugar Crop Made in Louisiana in 1855–56.* New Orleans: Cook, Young, 1856.

———. *Statement of the Sugar Crop Made in Louisiana in 1856–57.* New Orleans: Cook, Young, 1857.

———. *Statement of the Sugar Crop of Louisiana of 1857–58.* New Orleans: Cook, Young, 1858.

———. *Statement of the Sugar Crop of Louisiana of 1858–59.* New Orleans: Cook, Young, 1859.

———. *Statement of the Sugar Crop Made in Louisiana in 1859–60.* New Orleans: Cook, Young, 1860.

———. *Statement of the Sugar Crop Made in Louisiana in 1860–61.* New Orleans: Cook, Young, 1861.

———. *Statement of the Sugar Crop Made in Louisiana in 1861–62.* New Orleans: Cook, Young, 1862.

Chance, Joseph E., ed. *Mexico under Fire, Being the Diary of Samuel Ryan Curtis 3rd Ohio Volunteer Regiment During the Military Occupation of Northern Mexico 1846–1847.* Fort Worth: Texas Christian Univ. Press, 1994.

Crist, Lynda Lasswell, and Mary Seaton Dix, eds. *The Papers of Jefferson Davis.* Vol. 5, *1853–1855*. Baton Rouge: Louisiana State Univ. Press, 1985.

———. *The Papers of Jefferson Davis.* Vol. 7, *1861*. Baton Rouge: Louisiana State Univ. Press, 1992.

Cushman, John F. *Reports of Cases Argued and Determined in the High Court of Errors and Appeals for the State of Mississippi.* Vol. 26. Boston: Little, Brown, 1855.

Davis, Varina. *Jefferson Davis, Ex President of the Confederate States of America, A Memoir by His Wife.* New York: Belford, 1890.

DeForest, John William. *A Volunteer's Adventures: A Union Captain's Record of the Civil War.* New Haven: Yale Univ. Press, 1946.

Duncan, Herman C. *Convention Journals of Louisiana, 1835–1857.* New Orleans, n.d.

Evans, Estwick. "A Pedestrious Tour of Four Thousand Miles, through the Western Territories, during the Winter and Spring of 1818." In Reuben Gold Thwaites, *Early Western Travels, 1748–1846*. Concord, N.H.: Joseph C. Spear, 1819. Reprint, Cleveland, Ohio: A. H. Clark, 1904.

Flinn, Frank M. *Campaigning with Banks in Louisiana in '63 and '64, and with Sheridan in the Shenandoah Valley in '64 and '65*. Lynn, Mass.: Thos. O. Nichols, 1887.

Flint, Timothy. *Recollections of the Last Ten Years in the Valley of the Mississippi.* Boston: Cummings, Hilliard, 1826. Reprint, Carbondale: Southern Illinois Univ. Press, 1968.

Follett, Richard. "Documenting Louisiana Sugar, 1845–1917." www.sussex.ac.uk/louisianasugar/. Accessed July 10 and 14, 2008.

Hemphill, W. Edwin, ed. *The Papers of John C. Calhoun.* Vol. 5, *1820–1821*. Columbia: Univ. of South Carolina Press, 1971.

Hewett, Janet B., ed. *Supplement to the Official Records of the Union and Confederate Armies.* Parts 1 and 2. Wilmington, N.C.: Broadfoot, 1996.

Hopkins, James F., ed. *The Papers of Henry Clay.* Vol. 4, *Secretary of State, 1825*. Lexington: Univ. of Kentucky Press, 1972.

Jacquess, Asbury C., ed. "The Journals of Davy Crockett, commencing December 20th 1831." *Indiana Magazine of History* 102 (March 2006), 8–24.

Johns, Henry T. *Life with the Forty-Ninth Massachusetts Volunteers.* Pittsfield, Mass.: Author's publication, 1864.

Journal of the Fourteenth Annual Convention of the Protestant Episcopal Church in the Diocese of Louisiana. New Orleans, La., 1852.

Journal of the Fifteenth Annual Convention of the Protestant Episcopal Church in the Diocese of Louisiana. New Orleans, La., 1853.

Journal of the Seventeenth Annual Convention of the Protestant Episcopal Church in the Diocese of Louisiana. New Orleans, La., 1855.

Journal of the Eighteenth Annual Convention of the Protestant Episcopal Church in the Diocese of Louisiana. New Orleans, La., 1856.

Journal of the Nineteenth Annual Convention of the Protestant Episcopal Church in the Diocese of Louisiana. New Orleans, La., 1857.

Journal of the Twentieth Annual Convention of the Protestant Episcopal Church in the Diocese of Louisiana. New Orleans, La., 1858.

Journal of the Twenty-Fifth Annual Convention of the Protestant Episcopal Church in the Diocese of Louisiana. New Orleans, La., 1866.

Journal of the Twenty-Sixth Annual Convention of the Protestant Episcopal Church in the Diocese of Louisiana. New Orleans, La., 1867.

"Official Journal of the Proceedings of the Convention of the State of Louisiana." (Journal of State Convention, in facsimile). New Orleans, La., 1861. In *Louisiana History* 2 (winter 1961): 7–105.

Latrobe, John H. B. "West Point Reminiscences." In *Eighteenth Annual Reunion of the Association of the Graduates of the United States Military Academy, at West Point, New York, June 9th, 1887.* East Saginaw, Mich.: Evening News Printing and Binding House, 1887.

McDermott, John Francis. *The Western Journals of Washington Irving.* Norman: Univ. of Oklahoma Press, 1944, 1966.

Moser, Harold D., and J. Clint Clifft, eds. *The Papers of Andrew Jackson.* Vol. 6, *1825–1828.* Knoxville: Univ. of Tennessee Press, 2002.

Moser, Harold D., and David R. Hoth, eds. *The Papers of Andrew Jackson.* Vol. 5, *1821–1824.* Knoxville: Univ. of Tennessee Press, 1996.

Moser, Harold D., and Sharon Macpherson, eds. *The Papers of Andrew Jackson.* Vol. 2, *1804–1813.* Knoxville: Univ. of Tennessee Press, 1984.

Nolte, Vincent. *Fifty Years in Both Hemispheres; or, Reminiscences of the Life of a Former Merchant.* New York: Redfield, 1854.

Parkhurst, Charles H. *Personal Narratives of the Battles of the Rebellion No. 7: Incidents of Cavalry Service in Louisiana.* Providence, R.I.: Sidney S. Rider, 1879.

Pitot, James. *Observations on the Colony of Louisiana from 1796 to 1802.* Trans. Henry C. Pitot. Baton Rouge: Louisiana State Univ. Press, 1979.

Rowland, Dunbar, coll. and ed. *Jefferson Davis, Constitutionalist: His Letters, Papers and Speeches.* Vol. 9. Jackson: Mississippi Department of Archives and History, 1923.

Scribner, Benjamin Franklin. *Camp Life of a Volunteer: A Campaign in Mexico, or a Glimpse of Life in Camp.* New Albany, Ind.: Grigg, Elliot, and Co. 1875. Reprint, Austin, Tex.: Jenkins, 1975.

Smith, Mary Sue, ed. *Davidson County Tennessee Deed Book H, 1809–1821.* Bowie, Md.: Heritage, 2000.

Smith, Sam B., and Harriet Chappel Owsley, eds. *The Papers of Andrew Jackson.* Vol. 1, *1770–1803.* Knoxville: Univ. of Tennessee Press, 1980.

Stoddard, Amos. *Sketches, Historical and Descriptive, of Louisiana*. Philadelphia: Carey, 1812. Reprint, New York: AMS Press, 1973.

Thian, Raphael P., comp. *Notes Illustrating the Military Geography of the United States*. Washington, D.C.: Government Printing Office, 1881.

Toqueville, Alexis de. *Democracy in America*, vol. 1. New York: Vintage Books, 1957.

Whitley, Edythe Rucker, comp. *Marriages of Davidson County, Tennessee 1789–1847*. Baltimore: Genealogical Publishing, 1981.

UNPUBLISHED CORRESPONDENCE/INTERVIEWS

Jimmy Jean Bowman, interviews and correspondence with David D. Plater, various dates.

Mary O'Neil, correspondence with David D. Plater, November 1, 2012.

Joanne Ryan and Thurston H. G. Hahn, interviews with David D. Plater at Coastal Environments, Inc., Baton Rouge, September 4, 10, 16, and 30, 2014.

Joanne Ryan, e-mail correspondence with David D. Plater, September 10, 16, and 30, 2014.

Vaughn Stanley, correspondence with David D. Plater, September 9, 2012.

Jean Meaney Wheatley, correspondence with David D. Plater, various dates.

PRIVATE COLLECTIONS

Jimmy Jean Bowman, Shreveport, Louisiana

Colette Endrizzi, Tucson, Arizona

David D. Plater, Thibodaux, Louisiana

Ann Weller, St. Francisville, Louisiana

Jean Meaney Wheatley, Lawton, Oklahoma

SECONDARY SOURCES: BOOKS

Adams, George Rollie. *General William S. Harney, Prince of Dragoons*. Lincoln: Univ. of Nebraska Press, 2001.

Ambrose, Stephen E. *Duty, Honor, Country: A History of West Point*. Baltimore, Md.: Johns Hopkins Univ. Press, 1999.

Banker, Luke Henry. *Fort Southwest Point, Kingston, Tennessee: The Development of a Frontier Post, 1792–1807*. Kingston, Tenn.: Roane County Heritage Commission, 1984.

Bauer, Craig A. *A Leader among Peers: The Life and Times of Duncan Farrar Kenner*. Lafayette, La.: Center for Louisiana Studies, 1993.

Bauer, K. Jack. *The Mexican War, 1846–1848.* New York: Macmillan, 1974.

———. *Zachary Taylor: Soldier, Planter, Statesman of the Southwest.* Baton Rouge: Louisiana State Univ. Press, 1985.

Bell, Malcolm, Jr. *Major Butler's Legacy: Five Generations of a Slaveholding Family.* Athens, Ga.: Univ. of Georgia Press, 1987.

Bleser, Carol, ed. *In Joy and Sorrow: Women, Family, and Marriage in the Victorian South, 1830–1900.* New York: Oxford Univ. Press, 1991.

Bodenhorn, Howard. *A History of Banking in Antebellum America: Financial Markets and Economic Development in an Era of Nation-Building.* Cambridge, U.K.: Cambridge Univ. Press, 2000.

Brady, Patricia. *A Being So Gentle: The Frontier Love Story of Rachel and Andrew Jackson.* New York: Palgrave Macmillan, 2011.

Brasseaux, Carl A., and Keith P. Fontenot. *Steamboats on Louisiana's Bayous.* Baton Rouge: Louisiana State Univ. Press, 2004.

Burke, Pauline Wilcox. *Emily Donelson of Tennessee.* 2 vols. Richmond, Va.: Garrett and Massie, 1941.

Butler, William David, John Cromwell Butler, and Joseph Marion Butler. *The Butler Family in America.* St. Louis, Mo.: Shallcross Printing Co., n.d.

Campanella, Richard O. *Lincoln in New Orleans: The 1828–1831 Flatboat Voyages and Their Place in History.* Lafayette: University of Louisiana at Lafayette Press, 2010.

Carrigan, Jo Ann. *The Saffron Scourge: A History of Yellow Fever in Louisiana, 1796–1905.* Lafayette, La.: Center for Louisiana Studies, 1994.

Cashin, Joan E. *A Family Venture: Men and Women on the Southern Frontier.* Baltimore: Johns Hopkins Univ. Press, 1994.

Cheathem, Mark R. *Andrew Jackson, Southerner.* Baton Rouge: Louisiana State Univ. Press, 2013.

———. *Old Hickory's Nephew: The Political and Private Struggles of Andrew Jackson Donelson.* Baton Rouge: Louisiana State Univ. Press, 2007.

Chernow, Ron. *Washington: A Life.* New York: Penguin Press, 2010.

Clement, W. E. *Plantation Life on the Mississippi.* New Orleans: Pelican Publishing Company, 1952.

Coffman, Edward M. *The Old Army: A Portrait of the American Army in Peacetime, 1784–1898.* New York: Oxford Univ. Press, 1986.

Covey, Herbert C., and Dwight Eisnach. *What the Slaves Ate: Recollections of African American Foods and Foodways from the Slave Narratives.* Santa Barbara, Calif.: Greenwood Press, 2009.

Crane, William Carey. *Life and Select Literary Remains of Sam Houston of Texas.* Dallas, Tex.: William G. Scarff, 1884.

Davis, David Brion. *The Problem of Slavery in the Age of Emancipation.* New York: Knopf, 2014.

———. *The Problem of Slavery in the Age of Revolution, 1770–1823*. New York: Oxford Univ. Press, 1999.

Diket, A. L. *Senator John Slidell and the Community He Represented in Washington, 1853–1861*. Washington, D.C.: Univ. Press of America, 1982.

Faust, Drew Gilpin. *Mothers of Invention: Women of the Slaveholding South in the American Civil War*. Chapel Hill: Univ. of North Carolina Press, 1996.

———. *This Republic of Suffering: Death and the American Civil War*. New York: Vintage, 2008.

Floyd, William Barrow. *The Barrow Family of Louisiana*. Lexington, Ky.: Author's publication, 1963.

Follett, Richard. *The Sugar Masters: Planters and Slaves in Louisiana's Cane World, 1820–1860*. Baton Rouge: Louisiana State Univ. Press, 2005.

Foos, Paul. *A Short, Offhand, Killing Affair: Soldiers and Social Conflict during the Mexican-American War*. Chapel Hill: Univ. of North Carolina Press, 2002.

Fox-Genovese, Elizabeth. *Within the Plantation Household: Black and White Women of the Old South*. Chapel Hill: Univ. of North Carolina Press, 1988.

Frazier, Donald S. *Fire in the Cane Field: The Federal Invasion of Louisiana and Texas, January 1861–January 1863*. Buffalo Gap, Tex.: State House Press, 2009.

Friedman, Jean E. *The Enclosed Garden: Women and Community in the Evangelical South, 1830–1900*. Chapel Hill: Univ. of North Carolina Press, 1985.

Green, George D. *Finance and Economic Development in the Old South: Louisiana Banking, 1804–1861*. Stanford, Calif.: Stanford Univ. Press, 1972.

Green, Michael D. The *Politics of Indian Removal: Creek Government in Crisis*. Lincoln: Univ. of Nebraska Press, 1982.

Green, Thomas Marshall. *Historic Families of Kentucky*. Cincinnati: R. Clarke & Company, 1889. Reprint, Baltimore: Regional Publishing Co., 1966.

Greve, Charles Theodore. *Centennial History of Cincinnati and Representative Citizens*, vol. 1. Chicago, Ill.: Biographical Publishing Company, 1904.

Grimsley, Mark. *The Hard Hand of War: Union Military Policy toward Southern Civilians, 1861–1865*. Cambridge, U.K.: Cambridge Univ. Press, 1995.

Gunn, John C. *Gunn's Domestic Medicine*. Knoxville: Published by the author, 1830. Facsimile of first edition, Knoxville, Tennessee: Univ. of Tennessee Press, 1986.

Guterl, Matthew Pratt. *American Mediterranean: Southern Slaveholders in the Age of Emancipation*. Cambridge, Mass.: Harvard Univ. Press, 2008.

Hair, William Ivy. *Bourbonism and Agrarian Protest: Louisiana Politics 1877–1900*. Baton Rouge: Louisiana State Univ. Press, 1969.

History of the First Troop, Philadelphia City Cavalry 1774–November 17, 1874. Philadelphia: Hallowell, 1874.

Hunter, Louis C., and Beatrice Jones Hunter. *Steamboats on the Western Rivers: An Economic and Technological History*. Cambridge, Mass.: Harvard Univ. Press, 1949.

James, Marquis. *Andrew Jackson: Portrait of a President*. Indianapolis: Bobbs-Merrill, 1940.

Jung, Moon-Ho. *Coolies and Cane: Race, Labor, and Sugar in the Age of Emancipation.* Baltimore: Johns Hopkins Univ. Press, 2006.

Karcher, Carolyn L. *The First Woman in the Republic: A Cultural Biography of Lydia Maria Child.* Durham: Duke Univ. Press, 1994.

Kerby, Robert L. *Kirby Smith's Confederacy: The Trans-Mississippi South, 1863–1865.* New York: Columbia Univ. Press, 1972.

Levine, Bruce. *The Fall of the House of Dixie: The Civil War and the Social Revolution That Transformed the South.* New York: Random House, 2013.

Levinson, Irving W. *Wars within War: Mexican Guerrillas, Domestic Elites, and the United States of America, 1846–1848.* Canada: Irving W. Levinson, 2005.

Mann, Charles C. *1491: New Revelations of the Americas before Columbus.* New York: Vintage, 2011.

McCaffrey, James M. *Army of Manifest Destiny: The American Soldier in the Mexican War, 1846–1848.* New York: New York Univ. Press, 1992.

McInerney, Kathleen Langdon-Haven. *Dear Nell: The True Story of the Haven Sisters.* N.p.: Kathleen McInerney, 2009.

Menn, Joseph Karl. *The Large Slaveholders of Louisiana—1860.* New Orleans: Pelican Publishing Company, 1964.

Moore, Charles. *The Family Life of George Washington.* Boston: Houghton Mifflin, 1926.

Oberly, James W. *Sixty Million Acres: American Veterans before the Civil War.* Kent, Ohio: Kent State Univ. Press, 1990.

Owsley, Frank Lawrence, Jr. *Struggle for the Gulf Borderlands: The Creek War and the Battle of New Orleans.* Gainesville: Univ. Presses of Florida, 1981.

Parton, James. *Life of Andrew Jackson.* Vol. 1. New York: Mason Brothers, 1861.

Peña, Christopher G. *Scarred by War: Civil War in Southeast Louisiana.* Bloomington, Ind.: AuthorHouse, 2004.

Poesch, Jessie, and Barbara Sorelle Bacot, eds. *Louisiana Buildings, 1720–1940: The Historic American Buildings Survey.* Baton Rouge: Louisiana State Univ. Press, 1997.

Prucha, Francis Paul. *Broadax and Bayonet: The Role of the United States Army in the Development of the Northwest, 1815–1860.* Madison: State Historical Society of Wisconsin, 1953.

———. *The Sword of the Republic: The United States Army on the Frontier, 1783–1846.* Toronto: Macmillan, 1969.

Reeves, William D. *From Tally-Ho to Forest Home: The History of Two Louisiana Plantations.* Bayou Goula, La.: D. Denis Murrell and David R. Denis, 2005.

Rehder, John B. *Delta Sugar: Louisiana's Vanishing Plantation Landscape.* Baltimore: John's Hopkins Univ. Press, 1999.

Reichel, William Cornelius. *A History of the Rise, Progress, and Present Condition of the Moravian Seminary for Young Ladies, at Bethlehem, Pa. with a Catalogue of Its Pupils, 1785–1858,* 2nd ed. Philadelphia: Lippincott, 1870.

Reinders, Robert C. *End of an Era: New Orleans, 1850–1860.* New Orleans, La.: Pelican Publishing Company, 1964.

Remini, Robert V. *Andrew Jackson and His Indian Wars.* New York: Viking Penguin, 2001.

———. *Andrew Jackson and the Course of American Empire, 1767–1821*, vol. 1. New York: Harper and Row, 1977.

———. *The Battle of New Orleans: Andrew Jackson and America's First Military Victory.* New York: Viking Penguin, 1999.

Ribblett, David L. *Nelly Custis, Child of Mount Vernon.* Mount Vernon, Va.: Mount Vernon Ladies' Association, 1993.

Roark, James L. *Masters without Slaves: Southern Planters in the Civil War and Reconstruction.* New York: Norton, 1977.

Robertson, Henry O. *"In the Habit of Acting Together": The Emergence of the Whig Party in Louisiana, 1828–1840.* Lafayette, La.: Center for Louisiana Studies, 2007.

Rodrigue, John C. *Reconstruction in the Cane Fields: From Slavery to Free Labor in Louisiana's Sugar Parishes, 1862–1880.* Baton Rouge: Louisiana State Univ. Press, 2001.

Roland, Charles P., with John David Smith, ed. *History Teaches Us to Hope: Reflections on the Civil War and Southern History.* Lexington, Ky.: Univ. Press of Kentucky, 2007.

———. *Louisiana Sugar Plantations during the Civil War.* Baton Rouge: Louisiana State Univ. Press, 1997.

Rothman, Adam. *Slave Country: American Expansion and the Origins of the Deep South.* Cambridge, Mass.: Harvard Univ. Press, 2005.

Ryan, Joanne. *Greenfield-Allemania Plantation Sugarhouse (16IV119): Phase II and III Archaeological Investigations Iberville Parish, Louisiana.* Baton Rouge, La.: Coastal Environments, 2009.

Ryan, Joanne, with Thurston H. G. Hahn III, Michael Carpenter, Maegan Smith, and Sid Gray. *Terrestrial Phase I Cultural Resource Investigations for the Proposed Shintech Louisiana, LLC. Chemical Plant Expansion Project, Iberville Parish, Louisiana.* Draft Report. Baton Rouge: Coastal Environments, 2014.

Sacher, John M. *A Perfect War of Politics: Parties, Politicians, and Democracy in Louisiana, 1824–1861.* Baton Rouge: Louisiana State Univ. Press, 2003.

Sandweiss, Martha A., Rick Stewart, and Ben Huseman. *Eyewitnesses to War: Prints and Daguerreotypes of the Mexican War, 1846–1848.* Fort Worth, Tex., and Washington, D.C.: Amon Carter Museum and Smithsonian Institution Press, 1989.

Scarborough, William Kauffman. *The Overseer: Plantation Management in the Old South.* Baton Rouge: Louisiana State Univ. Press, 1966.

Schmidt, Patricia Brady, ed. *Nelly Custis Lewis's Housekeeping Book.* New Orleans, La.: Historic New Orleans Collection, 1982.

Schoonover, Thomas D. *The United States in Central America, 1860–1911: Episodes of Social Imperialism and Imperial Rivalry in the World System.* Durham: Duke Univ. Press, 1991.

Scott, Rebecca J. *Degrees of Freedom: Louisiana and Cuba after Slavery.* Cambridge, Mass.: Belknap Press of Harvard Univ. Press, 2005.

Silver, James W. *Edmund Pendleton Gaines, Frontier General.* Baton Rouge: Louisiana State Univ. Press, 1949.

Sitterson, J. Carlyle. *Sugar Country: The Cane Sugar Industry in the South, 1753–1950.* Lexington: Univ. of Kentucky Press, 1953.

Smith, George Winston, and Charles Burnet Judah, eds. *Chronicles of the Gringos: The U.S. Army in the Mexican War, 1846–1848; Accounts of Eyewitnesses and Combatants.* Albuquerque: Univ. of New Mexico Press, 1968.

Smith, Justin H. *The War with Mexico.* 2 vols. Revision of 1919 edition. Gloucester, Mass.: Peter Smith, 1963.

Stevenson, Brenda E. *Life in Black and White: Family and Community in the Slave South.* New York: Oxford Univ. Press, 1996.

Taylor, Joe Gray. *Negro Slavery in Louisiana.* Baton Rouge: Louisiana Historical Association, 1963.

VanderVelde, Lea. *Mrs. Dred Scott: A Life on Slavery's Frontier.* New York: Oxford Univ. Press, 2009.

Vlatch, John Michael. *Back of the Big House: The Architecture of Plantation Slavery.* Chapel Hill: Univ. of North Carolina Press, 1993.

Wayland, John W. *The Washingtons and Their Homes.* 1944. Facsimile reprint, Berryville, Va.: Virginia Book Company, 1973.

Wesley, Edgar Bruce. *Guarding the Frontier: A Study of Frontier Defense from 1815 to 1825.* Minneapolis: Univ. of Minnesota Press, 1935.

Wilson, Samuel. *New Orleans Architecture: The University Section.* New Orleans: Pelican Publishing Company, 2000.

Winders, Richard Bruce. *Mr. Polk's Army: The American Military Experience in the Mexican War.* College Station, Tex.: Texas A&M Univ. Press, 1997.

Wooster, Ralph A. *The Secession Conventions of the South.* Princeton: Princeton Univ. Press, 1962.

Wyatt-Brown, Bertram. *Southern Honor: Ethics and Behavior in the Old South.* New York: Oxford Univ. Press, 2007.

SECONDARY SOURCES: ARTICLES

Allen, Michael R. "St. Louis and the 1880 Census." http://preservationresearch.com/2011/02/st-louis-and-the-1880-census/. Accessed May 17, 2012.

Beers, Henry P. "A History of the U.S. Topographical Engineers, 1818–1863." http://www.topogs.org/History2.htm. Accessed August 24, 2009.

Begnaud, Allen. "The Louisiana Sugar Cane Industry: An Overview." In *Green Fields:*

Two Hundred Years of Louisiana Sugar. Lafayette, Louisiana: Center for Louisiana Studies, 1980.

Bush, Bryan S. "Confederate General Leonidas Polk and the Collapse of the Confederate Command Structure in the Western Theater." www.bryansbush.com. Accessed January 7, 2015.

Bowie, Lucy Leigh. "Madam Grelaud's French School." *Maryland Historical Magazine* 39 (June 1944), 141–48.

Brown, Kay Thompson. "Thomas Taylor Williamson." http://files.usgwarchives.net/la/caddo/bios/williatt.txt. Accessed April 14, 2011.

"George Joseph Frederick Burthe," ID: I064969, http://wc.rootsweb.ancestry.com. Accessed January 8, 2015.

Campbell House Museum. "History—Lucas Place." http://campbellhousemuseum.org/history/lucas-place/. Accessed May 28, 2012 and January 8, 2015.

"Capt. Samuel McCutchon—Rebecca Butler." General Forum. http://genforum.genealogy.com. Accessed January 10, 2015.

Clinton, Catherine. "'Southern Dishonor': Flesh, Blood, Race, and Bondage." In *In Joy and Sorrow: Women, Family, and Marriage in the Victorian South, 1830–1900.* Edited by Carol Bleser, 52–68. New York: Oxford Univ. Press, 1991.

Crabb, Alfred Leland. "James Priestly, Pioneer Schoolmaster." *Tennessee Historical Quarterly* 12 (1953): 129–43.

DeBow's Review, N.S., 4 (September 1867).

Dew, Charles B. "The Long Lost Returns: The Candidates and Their Totals in Louisiana's Secession Election." *Louisiana History* 10 (1969): 353–69.

———. "Who Won the Secession Election in Louisiana?" *Journal of Southern History* 36 (February 1970): 18–32.

"DIED. Mary Susan Butler," *St. Louis Post-Dispatch,* March 28, 1882, page 5.

"Entertainment." *Eighteenth Annual Reunion of the Association of the Graduates of United States Military Academy, at West Point, June 9th, 1887.* Saginaw, Mich.: Evening News Printing and Binding House, 1887.

Eustace, Nicole. "Oh Say Can You See . . . ? How the War of 1812 Gave Us Something Worth Fighting For." *American History* 48, no. 2 (June 2013): 33–39.

Farrell, Mary D. "Henderson, Frances Cox (1820–1897)." *Handbook of Texas Online.* Texas State Historical Association. http://www.tshaonline.org/handbook/online/articles/fhe59. Accessed 2010.

Fox-Genovese, Elizabeth. "Family and Female Identity in the Antebellum South: Sarah Gayle and Her Family." In *In Joy and Sorrow: Women, Family, and Marriage in the Victorian South, 1830–1900,* edited by Carol Bleser, 15–31. New York: Oxford Univ. Press, 1991.

Freudenberger, Herman, and Jonathan B. Pritchett. "The Domestic United States Slave

Trade: New Evidence." *Journal of Interdisciplinary History* 21, no. 3 (winter 1991): 447–77.

"The Genealogy of the Lowndes Family of South Carolina." http://www.hillmanc.fsnet.co.uk/lowndes.htm. Accessed 2013.

Gould, Jeffrey. "The Strike of 1887: Louisiana Sugar War." *Southern Exposure* (November–December 1984): 45–55.

Grubb, Alan. "House and Home in the Victorian South: The Cookbook as Guide." In *In Joy and Sorrow: Women, Family, and Marriage in the Victorian South, 1830–1900*, edited by Carol Bleser, 154–75. New York: Oxford Univ. Press, 1991.

"William S. Harney." Wikipedia. http://en.wikipedia.org/wiki/William_S._Harney. Accessed January 10, 2015.

Hickey, Donald R. "Andrew Jackson and the Army Haircut: Individual Rights vs. Military Discipline." *Tennessee Historical Quarterly* 35 (winter 1976): 365–75.

"Inventory of Randolph and Yates Family Papers, MSS. Dept. UNC . . . ." http://www.lib.unc.edu/mss/inv/r/Randolph_and_Yates_Family.html. Accessed August 31, 2009.

"The Issaquena Genealogy and History Project: The Wade Hampton Family." http://www.rootsweb.ancestry.com/~msissaq2/hampton.html. Accessed August 18, 2009.

Jones, Charlton. "The Butler-McCutchon House History." Pass Christian, Miss.: n.p., 1992.

Kajencki, Francis C. "Charles Radziminski and the United States-Mexican Boundary Survey." *New Mexico Historical Review* 63, no. 3 (July 1988): 210–40.

"Marie Isabella Nicholas." *ID*:I064967, http://wc.rootsweb.ancestry.com. Accessed April 18, 2012, and January 1, 2015.

McGowan, Brian M. "The Second Battle of New Orleans: The Crescent City and the Anglo 'Invasion' of 1846." *Louisiana History* 51 (winter 2010): 27–40.

McLean, Mrs. Eugene. "A Northern Woman in the Confederacy." *Harper's Magazine* (February 1914): 440–51.

Michot, Stephen S. "'War Is Still Raging in This Part of the Country': Oath-Taking, Conscription, and Guerrilla War in Louisiana's Lafourche Region." *Louisiana History* 38 (spring 1977): 157–84.

"Military Career of William Selby Harney." http://freepages.genealogy.rootsweb.ancestry.com. Accessed January 10, 2015.

"Mr. Lincoln's White House: Montgomery Blair (1813–1883)." http://www.mrlincolnswhitehouse.org/content_inside.asp?ID=84&subjectID=2. Accessed May 29, 2012.

Murray, Rev. J. A., D.D. "The Butlers of Cumberland Valley." *Historical Register: Notes and Queries, Historical and Genealogical, Relative to Interior Pennsylvania, for the Year 1883*, vol. 1 (Harrisburg, Pennsylvania, January 1883), 1–17.

Pace, Robert F. "'It Was Bedlam Let Loose': The Louisiana Sugar Country and the Civil War." *Louisiana History* 39 (fall 1998): 389–409.

Patin, Victor. "Cyprian Ricard and Creole-African Lineage in Louisiana." http://boards.ancestry.com. Accessed November 3, 2012, and January 8, 2015.

Pritchett, Jonathan B. "The Interregional Slave Trade and the Selection of Slaves for the New Orleans Market." *Journal of Interdisciplinary History* 28, no.1 (summer 1997): 57–85.

"Robert Carter Nicholas." *ID*:I064960, http://wc.rootsweb.ancestry.com. Accessed January 6, 2015.

Rodrigue, John C. "The Freedman's Bureau and Wage Labor in the Louisiana Sugar Region." In *The Freedman's Bureau and Reconstruction: Reconsiderations,* edited by Paul A. Cimbale and Randall M. Miller, 195–218. New York: Fordham Univ. Press, 1999.

———. "Labor Militancy and Black Grassroots: Political Mobilization in the Louisiana Sugar Region, 1865–1868." In *The Louisiana Purchase Bicentennial Series in Louisiana History,* vol. 6, *Reconstructing Louisiana,* edited by Lawrence N. Powell, 481–502. Lafayette, La.: Center for Louisiana Studies, 2001.

Roland, Charles P. "Louisiana and Secession." *Louisiana History* 19 (1978): 389–99.

Roth, Mitchell. "Role of the Media: War Correspondents." From *The United States and Mexico at War.* http://www.pbs.org/kera/usmexicanwar/war/war_correspondents.html. Accessed January 10, 2015.

Russell, Sarah. "Intermarriage and Intermingling: Constructing the Planter Class in Louisiana's Sugar Parishes, 1803–1850." *Louisiana History* 46 (fall 2005): 407–34.

Scott, Rebecca J. "Fault Lines, Color Lines, and Party Lines: Race, Labor, and Collective Action in Louisiana and Cuba." In *Beyond Slavery: Explorations of Race, Labor, and Citizenship in Postemancipation Societies,* edited by Frederick Cooper, Thomas C. Holt, and Rebecca J. Scott, 65–83. Chapel Hill: Univ. of North Carolina Press, 2000.

Sperry, Kip. "Alexander Duncan (1805–1889) of Scotland, Connecticut, Rhode Island, New York, and England." *New England Historical and Genealogical Register* 140 (July 1986): 211–18.

Steimle, Douglas. "Women of Hampton-Preston: Mary Cantey Preston." http://www.examiner.com/article/women-of-hampton-preston-mary-cantey-hampton. Accessed January 10, 2015.

"Susan Adelaide Vinson." *ID*:I064964. http://wc.rootsweb.ancestry.com. Accessed April 18, 2012, and January 8, 2015.

"Ten Facts about the Distillery: George Washington's Mount Vernon." www.mountvernon.org. Accessed January 5, 2015.

Thweatt, John H. "James Priestly: Classical Scholar of the Old South." *Tennessee Historical Quarterly* 39 (winter 1980): 423–39.

Westheider, James E. "The History of Fort Washington at Cincinnati, Ohio: A Case Study," in *George Rogers Clark: Selected Papers from the 1989 and 1990 George Rogers Clark Trans-Appalachian Frontier History Conferences.* http://npshistory.com/series/symposia/george_rogers_clark/1989-1990/sec4.htm. Accessed June 26, 2012.

Whitten, David O. "Slave Buying in 1835 Virginia as Revealed by Letters of a Louisiana Negro Sugar Planter." *Louisiana History* 11, no. 3 (summer 1970): 231–44.

Wilentz, Sean. "Why Did Southerners Secede?" In *In the Cause of Liberty: How the Civil War Redefined American Ideals,* edited by William J. Cooper Jr. and John M. McCardell Jr., 25–39. Baton Rouge: Louisiana State Univ. Press, 2009.

Wooster, Ralph. "The Louisiana Secession Convention." *Louisiana Historical Quarterly* 34 (April 1951): 103–33.

Wyatt-Brown, Bertram. "Andrew Jackson's Honor." *Journal of the Early American Republic* 17 (spring 1997): 1–36.

THESES AND DISSERTATIONS

Kramer, Ethel Elizabeth. "Slavery Legislation in Ante-Bellum Louisiana, 1803–1860." Master's thesis, Louisiana State University and Agricultural and Mechanical College, 1944.

Labouisse, Sarah. "Regaining Ground: Edward J. Gay's Experience as a Sugar Planter from 1865 to 1875." Senior thesis, Princeton University, 1985.

White, Alice Pemble: "The Plantation Experience of Joseph and Lavinia Erwin, 1807–1836." Master's thesis, Louisiana State University and Agricultural and Mechanical College, 1933.

Williamson, Christian. "Sacred Trust: The Voluntary Removal and Reburial of Human Remains from a Historic Cemetery in Louisiana." Master's thesis, Louisiana State University, 2005.

REFERENCE WORKS AND SOURCES

Aaregistry.org.

Adams, Paxton John. *New Orleans Directory and Register.* New Orleans: Printed for the author, 1830. Microfiche, Historic New Orleans Collection.

Ancestry.com.

Answers.com.

Bergeron, Arthur W., Jr. *Guide to Louisiana Confederate Military Units, 1861–1865.* Baton Rouge: Louisiana State Univ. Press, 1989.

Booth, Andrew B., comp. *Records of Louisiana Confederate Soldiers and Louisiana Confederate Commands.* 3 vols. New Orleans, La.: N.p., 1920. Microfiche, Historic New Orleans Collection.

Bradburnhistory.com

Cohen's Orleans and Lafayette Directory for 1849. New Orleans: N.p., 1849. Historic New Orleans Collection.

"Cold Water for Babies." *Own Your Health*. http://ownyourhealth.wordpress.com/2008/07/01/cold-water-for-babies/. Accessed May 23, 2014.

Conrad, Glenn R., ed. *A Dictionary of Louisiana Biography*. 2 vols. Lafayette, La.: Center for Louisiana Studies, 1988.

Diocese of Baton Rouge, Catholic Church Records. Vol. 5, *(1830–1839)*. Baton Rouge: Catholic Diocese of Baton Rouge, Department of Archives, 1984.

Familytreemaker.genealogy.com

Garnett, James Mercer. *Biographical Sketch of Hon. James Mercer Garnett of Elmwood, Essex County, Virginia, with Mercer-Garner and Mercer Genealogies*. Richmond, Va.: Whittet and Shepperson, Printers, 1910.

Gendisasters.com.

Genealogy.com.

Genealogytrails.com.

Gibson, John. *Gibson's Guide and Directory of the State of Louisiana and the Cities of New Orleans and Lafayette*. New Orleans: J. Gibson, 1838.

Gunstonhall.org

Hammersley, Thomas H. S., ed. *Complete Regular Army Register of the United States, for One Hundred Years (1779 to 1879)*, 3rd edition. Washington, D.C.: T.H.S. Hammersley, 1881.

Heitman, Francis B. *Historical Register and Dictionary of the United States Army, from Its Organization, September 29, 1789, to March 2, 1903*. 2 vols. Washington, D.C.: Government Printing Office, 1903. Reprint, Urbana: Univ. of Illinois Press, 1965.

Johnson, Robert Winder, comp. *The Ancestry of Rosalie Morris Johnson: Daughter of George Calvert Morris and Elizabeth Kuhn, His Wife*. Philadelphia: Ferris and Leach, Printers, 1905.

Library.nsula.edu. Northwestern State University, Natchitoches.

Library.unc.edu. University of North Carolina, Chapel Hill.

Library.uncg.edu. University of North Carolina, Greensborough.

Library.yale.edu. Yale University.

Louisville.edu. University of Louisville.

Menn, Joseph Karl. *The Large Slaveholders of Louisiana—1860*. New Orleans, La.: Pelican Publishing Company, 1964.

Michel and Co., *New Orleans Directory for 1841*. New Orleans: Michel and Co., 1841.

Moseley, Edward H., and Paul C. Clark Jr. *Historical Dictionary of the United States-Mexican War*. Lanham, Md.: Scarecrow Press, 1997.

Mygenealogy.com.

New Orleans Annual and Commercial Register for 1846. New Orleans: E. H. Michel and Co., 1847.

New York City Marriage Notices 1843–1856, vol. 2. New York: N.p., n.d.. New York Society Library. http://www.nysoclib.org/king/king2.html. Accessed January 11, 2015.

Riffel, Judy, and Arthur Perkins, eds., *Iberville Parish History*. Baton Rouge, La.: Curtis Media Corporation, 1985.

———, ed. *Iberville Parish Records*. Vol. 1. N. p.: Judy Riffel, 1981.

———, ed. *Iberville Parish Records*. Vol. 2. Baton Rouge: VAAPR, 1982.

Rootsweb.com.

Rootsweb.ancestry.com.

Schott, Matthew J., ed. *Norman's New Orleans and Environs*. Facsimile reproduction of 1845 edition published by author Benjamin Moore Norman. Baton Rouge: Louisiana State Univ. Press, 1976.

Search.ancestry.com.

S. E. Percy and Co. *New-Orleans Directory, 1832*. New Orleans: Printed for the authors, 1832.

Spiller, Roger J., ed. *Dictionary of American Military Biography*. 3 vols. Westport, Conn.: Greenwood, 1984.

Tudorplace.org

The United States Biographical Dictionary and Portrait Gallery of Eminent and Self-Made Men—Missouri Volume. New York: Biographical Publishing Company, 1878.

United States National Slavery Museum Inventory. Document 19, item B7. http://cdn.blogs.fredericksburg.com/newsdesk/files/2012/07/slaverydoc1.pdf. Accessed May 20, 2012, and January 11, 2015.

Usgwarchives.net

Wikipedia.org.

Yale University. "Obituary Record of Graduates of Yale University Deceased during the Academical Year Ending in June, 1896." N. P.: n.p., 1896.

INDEX

The use of [brackets] indicates misspellings found in original documents.
The use of {braces} indicates names not found in source documents.